**SEVENTH EDITION**

# Discovering the American Past

## A Look at the Evidence

### VOLUME II: SINCE 1865

**William Bruce Wheeler**
*University of Tennessee*

**Susan D. Becker**
*University of Tennessee, Emerita*

**Lorri Glover**
*St. Louis University*

WADSWORTH
CENGAGE Learning™

Australia • Brazil • Japan • Korea • Mexico • Singapore • Spain • United Kingdom • United States

**WADSWORTH**
CENGAGE Learning™

**Discovering the American Past: A Look at the Evidence, Volume II: Since 1865, Seventh Edition**
William Bruce Wheeler, Susan D. Becker, and Lorri Glover

Senior Publisher: Suzanne Jeans

Senior Sponsoring Editor: Ann West

Development Editor: Kirsten Guidero

Assistant Editor: Megan Chrisman

Senior Marketing Manager: Katherine Bates

Marketing Coordinator: Lorreen Pelletier

Executive Marketing Communications Manager: Talia Wise

Associate Content Project Manager: Anne Finley

Senior Art Director: Cate Rickard Barr

Senior Print Buyer: Judy Inouye

Senior Rights Acquisition Specialist, Text: Katie Huha

Senior Image Rights Acquisition Specialist: Jennifer Meyer Dare

Production Service: MPS Limited, A Macmillan Company

Cover Designer: Walter Kopec, Boston

Cover Image: Steve Skjold/Alamy Images

Compositor: MPS Limited, A Macmillan Company

For product information and technology assistance, contact us at **Cengage Learning Customer & Sales Support, 1-800-354-9706**
For permission to use material from this text or product, submit all requests online at **www.cengage.com/permissions**.
Further permissions questions can be emailed to **permissionrequest@cengage.com**.

Library of Congress Control Number: 2010929054

ISBN-13: 978-0-495-91501-0

ISBN-10: 0-495-91501-7

**Wadsworth**
20 Channel Center Street
Boston, MA 02210
USA

Cengage Learning is a leading provider of customized learning solutions with office locations around the globe, including Singapore, the United Kingdom, Australia, Mexico, Brazil, and Japan. Locate your local office at **international.cengage.com/region**

Cengage Learning products are represented in Canada by Nelson Education, Ltd.

For your course and learning solutions, visit **www.cengage.com**

Purchase any of our products at your local college store or at our preferred online store **www.cengagebrain.com**.

Printed in the United States of America
1 2 3 4 5 6 7 14 13 12 11 10

# Contents

Preface     x

◆

CHAPTER **1**

**Reconstructing Reconstruction: The Political
Cartoonist and Public Opinion**     1

The Problem     1
Background     2
The Method     9
The Evidence     11
     *Cartoons of Thomas Nast*
Questions to Consider     25
Epilogue     26

◆

CHAPTER **2**

**The Road to True Freedom: African American
Alternatives in the New South**     29

The Problem     29
Background     31
The Method     35
The Evidence     39
     *Excerpt from Ida B. Wells's* United States Atrocities *(1892)*
     *Booker T. Washington's Atlanta Exposition Address (1895)*
     *Excerpt from Henry McNeal Turner's "The American Negro and His
       Fatherland" (1895)*
     *Excerpts from W. E. B. DuBois's "The Talented Tenth" (1903) and Niagara
       Address (1906)*
     *Excerpt from E. W. Harper's "Enlightened Motherhood" (1892)*
     *Table showing migration of Negro population by U.S. region, 1870–1920*
Questions to Consider     55
Epilogue     57

CHAPTER **3**

## Selling Consumption, 1890–1930     61

The Problem     61
Background     62
The Method     68
The Evidence     69
    *Excerpts from essays on the business of advertising*
    *Advertisements from leading department stores, 1876–1926*
    *Department store architecture*
Questions to Consider     99
Epilogue     100

CHAPTER **4**

## Child Labor Reform and the Redefinition of Childhood, 1880–1920     102

The Problem     102
Background     103
The Method     107
The Evidence     108
    *Photographs of impoverished working children*
    *Excerpts from Jacob Riis,* How the Other Half Lives
    *Florence Kelley describes child labor and sweatshops*
    *Letters to the Children's Bureau*
    *Experts' advice to parents*
    *Changes in child labor laws*
Questions to Consider     130
Epilogue     132

CHAPTER **5**

## Homogenizing a Pluralistic Nation: Propaganda During World War I     133

The Problem                                                         133
Background                                                          135
The Method                                                          139
The Evidence                                                        141
  *War songs and poetry*
  *Advertisements and posters*
  *Editorial cartoons*
  *Speeches*
  *Motion picture stills and ads*
Questions to Consider                                               162
Epilogue                                                            164

CHAPTER **6**

## The "New" Woman: Debating Women's Roles in the 1920s 169

The Problem                                                         169
Background                                                          170
The Method                                                          175
The Evidence                                                        176
  *Experts' advice for women*
  *Social science literature on working women*
  *Marital advice literature*
  *Photographs and newspaper reports about "flappers"*
Questions to Consider                                               203
Epilogue                                                            204

CHAPTER **7**

## Understanding Rural Poverty During the Great Depression 206

The Problem                                                         206
Background                                                          207
The Method                                                          211
The Evidence                                                        213
  *Children's letters to Eleanor Roosevelt*
  *Documentary photographs from the Farm Security
    Administration*
Questions to Consider                                               232
Epilogue                                                            233

CHAPTER **8**

## The American Judicial System and Japanese American Internment During World War II: *Korematsu v. United States* (323 U.S. 214)    236

The Problem    236
Background    238
The Method    245
The Evidence    247
     *United States Supreme Court opinion and dissenting opinions in Korematsu v. U.S. (323 U.S. 214)*
Questions to Consider    256
Epilogue    257

CHAPTER **9**

## The 1960 Student Campaign for Civil Rights    260

The Problem    260
Background    262
The Method    267
The Evidence    269
     *Jim Crow laws*
     *Sample literacy test*
     *Excerpts from interviews with student sit-in leaders*
     *Sit-in literature and songs*
     *National news coverage of the student sit-ins*
     *Excerpt of 1961 speech by the Rev. Martin Luther King, Jr.*
     *Photographs of sit-in participants*
Questions to Consider    308
Epilogue    309

CHAPTER **10**

## A Generation in War and Turmoil: The Agony of Vietnam    313

The Problem    313
Background    314

The Method    320

The Evidence    324

*Sample release forms for oral history interviews*

*Interviews and photographs with a sampling of the Vietnam Generation*

Questions to Consider    346

Epilogue    347

CHAPTER **11**

## Who Owns History? The Texas Textbook Controversy

Who Owns History? The Texas Textbook Controversy    349

The Problem    349

Background    351

The Method    356

The Evidence    357

*Texas state educational code*

*Proceedings of the Texas Educational Agency*

*Texans debate their history standards*

*National media coverage of the Texas textbook debate*

Questions to Consider    382

Epilogue    383

# Preface

In his 1990 State of the Union Address, President George Herbert Walker Bush set forth a set of National Education Goals, one of which was the objective that by the year 2000 "American students will leave grades four, eight, and twelve having demonstrated competency in ... English, mathematics, science, history, and geography."[1]

Almost immediately large committees were established in each of the above disciplines, including the National Council for History Standards, composed of history professors, pre-college teachers, members of numerous organizations, educators, and parents. For two years the Council worked to draft a voluntary set of National History Standards that would provide teachers, parents, and American history textbook publishers with guidelines regarding what students ought to know about the United States' past.

Yet before the Standards even were released to the general public, a storm of controversy arose, in which the Council was accused of a "great hatred of traditional history," of giving in to "political correctness," and of jettisoning the Founding Fathers, the Constitution, and people and events that have made the nation great in favor of individuals and events that portrayed the United States in a less complimentary light. Finally, in January 1995, the U.S. Senate, by a vote of 99-1, approved a "sense-of-the-Senate" resolution condemning the standards developed by the National Council for History Standards and urging that any future guidelines for history should not be based on them.[2]

This was not the first time that American history standards and textbooks had been the sources of bitter controversy. In the late nineteenth century, northern and southern whites had radically different ideas about the Civil War and Reconstruction and demanded that public school textbooks reflect those notions. As a result, publishers created separate chapters on these periods for northern and southern schools. At the same time, Roman Catholic

---

1. Transcript, State of the Union Address, January 31, 1990, in C-SPAN.org/Transcripts/SOTU-1990.aspx. See also U.S. Department of Education, *National Goals for Education* (Washington: Dept. of Education, 1990), p. 1.
2. The Senate proceedings are summarized in Gary B. Nash, Charlotte Crabtree, and Ross E. Dunn, *History on Trial: Culture Wars and the Teaching of the Past* (New York: Alfred A. Knopf, 1997), pp. 231–235. The lone Senator who voted against the resolution was Bennett Johnston of Louisiana.

leaders in the United States complained about the Protestant control of public education and of the history textbooks, resulting in Catholics writing their own textbooks for their parochial schools.[3]

Then, in the 1940s, the popular American history textbooks of Professor Harold Rugg of Columbia University were assaulted as being too radical, mainly because Rugg had discussed subjects such as economic classes, inequality, and what he called the apparent failure of laissez-faire economics. By 1944, sales of his public school textbooks had dropped 90 percent, and by 1951 they had totally disappeared from American classrooms. The Cold War and the fear of communism extended this controversy and led to the removal from most textbooks of the sensitive subjects that had gotten Rugg into so much trouble.[4]

By the 1960s, scholars in many American colleges and universities had begun to view the nation's past in decidedly different ways, due in part to the gradual inclusion of African Americans, women, Native Americans, laborers, immigrants, and the "common folk" in the story of America's past. As these individuals took their places alongside the nation's founders, presidents, generals, corporate leaders, and intellectuals (almost all male and white), the texture and shape of American history began to change. At the same time, the Vietnam War prompted some scholars to look at the United States' overseas record in new, less laudable ways.[5]

By the 1980s, this "new history" began to be included in pre-college American history textbooks. Since the nineteenth century, America's public schools have relied heavily on textbooks, in part as "substitutes for well-trained teachers." But as the quality of teachers improved, most of them continued to rely on textbooks that were dramatically larger, more inclusive, and generally more interesting to students. At the same time, however, both teachers and students came to realize that any American history textbook inevitably reflects the views of the author(s) and is not a completely objective, unbiased view of the past. Indeed, many understood what George Orwell meant when he wrote (in *1984*), "He who controls the past controls the

3. Joseph Moreau, *Schoolbook Nation: Conflicts over American History Textbooks from the Civil War to the Present* (Ann Arbor: University of Michigan Press, 2003), pp. 15–20.

4. *Ibid.*, pp. 219–221; Frances Fitzgerald, *America Revised: History Schoolbooks in the Twentieth Century* (Boston: Atlantic Monthly Press, 1979), pp. 36–37. For one attack on textbooks, see E. Merrill Root, *Brainwashing in the High Schools: An Examination of Eleven American History Textbooks* (New York: The Devin-Adair Co., 1958).

5. On the "inclusion" movements of the 1960s and 1970s, see Joyce Appleby, Lynn Hunt, and Margaret Jacob, *Telling the Truth About History* (New York: W.W. Norton, 1994), pp. 147–198.

future." Hence, conflicts over textbooks (see Chapter 11 in Volume 2) are not only warm but inevitable.[6]

How can students hope to come to *their own* understanding of America's past? One way to do this is to go directly to the sources themselves, the "raw material" of history. In *Discovering the American Past*, we have included an engaging and at the same time challenging mixture of types of evidence, ranging from more traditional sources such as letters, newspapers, public documents, speeches, and oral reminiscences to more innovative evidence such as photographs, art, statistics, cartoons, films, interviews, and so forth. In each chapter students will use these as evidence to solve the problem or answer the central question that each chapter poses. Soon they will understand that the historian operates in much the same way as a detective in novels, films, or television programs does when solving a crime.[7]

As much as possible, we have tried to "let the evidence speak for itself" and have avoided (we hope) leading students toward one particular interpretation or another. *Discovering the American Past,* then, is a sort of historical sampler that we believe will help students learn the methods and skills all educated people must be able to master, as well as help them learn the historical content. In the words of an old West African saying, "However far the stream flows, it never forgets its source." Nor, we trust, will you.[8]

◆

## Format of the Book

Each chapter is divided into six parts: The Problem, Background, The Method, The Evidence, Questions to Consider, and Epilogue. Each part builds upon the others, creating a uniquely integrated chapter structure that helps guide the reader through the analytical process. The Problem section begins with a brief discussion of the central issues of the chapter and then states the questions students will explore. A Background section follows, designed to help students understand the historical context of the problem. The Method section gives students suggestions for studying and analyzing the evidence. The Evidence section is the heart of the chapter, providing a variety of primary source material

6. On the heavy reliance on textbooks, see Fitzgerald, *America Revised*, p. 19. Subjectivity was understood early by college professors. See Charles A. Beard, "Written History as an Act of Faith," in *American Historical Review*, vol. 39 (1933), pp. 219–231; Robert Allen Skotheim, ed., *The Historian and the Climate of Opinion* (Reading, MA: Addison-Wesley, 1969).
7. See the exciting Robin W. Winks, ed., *The Historian as Detective: Essays on Evidence* (New York: Harper & Row, 1968), esp. pp. xiii–xxiv.
8. For the saying, see Nash, *History on Trial*, p. 8.

on the particular historical event or issue described in the chapter's Problem section. Questions to Consider, the section that follows, focuses students' attention on specific evidence and on linkages among different evidence material. The Epilogue section gives the aftermath or the historical outcome of the evidence—what happened to the people involved, who won an election, how a debate ended, and so on.

## Changes in the Seventh Edition

Each chapter in this edition has had to pass three important screening groups: (1) the authors (and some of our graduate students) who used the chapters to teach our students, (2) student evaluators who used *Discovering the American Past* in class, and (3) instructors who either used the book or read and assessed the new and revised chapters. With advice from our screeners, we have made the following alterations that we believe will make this edition of *Discovering the American Past* even more useful and contemporary.

Volume I contains six entirely new chapters: Chapter 1, "A History Mystery: What Happened at Roanoke?"; Chapter 3, "Colonies, Commerce, and Empire: The British Plantation System in the Chesapeake and Caribbean"; Chapter 5, "The Evolution of American Citizenship: The Louisiana Purchase, 1803–1812"; Chapter 6, "Church, State, and Democracy: The Sunday Mail Controversy, 1827–1831"; Chapter 8, "Women's Equality"; and Chapter 10, "Civil Liberties in Time of War: The Case of Clement Vallandigham." In addition, Chapter 4 includes more evidence from the 1770 trial of Captain Thomas Preston. Chapter 7 has incorporated more Native American voices. Chapter 9 has added more reminiscences of former slaves. Finally, Chapter 11, "Reconstructing Reconstruction," appeared in earlier editions of *Discovering the American Past*, and has been brought back by student and instructor requests.

Volume II offers four completely new chapters: Chapter 3, "Selling Consumption, 1890–1930" (on department stores); Chapter 8, "The American Judicial System and Japanese American Internment During World War II"; Chapter 9, "The 1960 Student Campaign for Civil Rights"; and Chapter 11, "Who Owns History? The Texas Textbook Controversy." More evidence has been added to Chapters 5 and 6, and Chapter 7 contains some dramatically different evidence that makes it virtually a new chapter.

In all, we have paid close attention to students, fellow instructors, and reviewers in our efforts to keep *Discovering the American Past* fresh, challenging, and relevant. Earlier editions have shown clearly students' positive responses to the challenge of being, as Robin Winks put it, "historical detectives" who use historical evidence to reach their own conclusions.

◆

## Instructor's Resource Manual

Because we value the teaching of American history and yet fully understand how difficult it is to do well, we have written our own Instructor's Resource Manual to accompany *Discovering the American Past*. In this manual, we explain our specific content and skills objectives for each chapter. In addition, we include an expanded discussion of the Method and Evidence sections. We also answer some of our students' frequently asked questions about the material in each problem. Our suggestions for teaching and evaluating student learning draw not only upon our own experiences but also upon the experiences of those of you who have shared your classroom ideas with us. Finally, we wrote updated bibliographic essays for each problem.

◆

## Acknowledgments

We would like to thank all the students and instructors who have helped us in developing and refining our ideas for this edition. Also, Bruce and Susan would like to welcome to our team Dr. Lorri Glover, Professor of History at Saint Louis University. She has brought fresh ideas and new insights to this edition. All three of us extend deep thanks to those reviewers who evaluated the sixth edition and gave us candid feedback for preparing this new edition to be even more comprehensive and impactful: Carl Guarneri, Saint Mary's College of California; Juan Garcia, The University of Arizona; Molly Ladd-Taylor, York University; Earl Mulderink, Southern Utah University; Sean Taylor, Minnesota State University—Moorhead; Michael Sherfy, Western Illinois University; Zachery Williams, University of Akron; and Allan Winkler, Miami University.

All three of us would also like to thank the members of the publishing team who worked together to make this edition a reality. We thank Suzanne Jeans and Ann West for handling the big-picture details of the project; Kirsten Guidero and Megan Chrisman for shepherding the book through development;

Anne Finley and Lauren MacLachlan for managing all the little details and pulling things together; Cate Rickard Barr for handling the art; Katie Huha and Jennifer Meyer Dare for running the complex permissions processes for art and print; Judy Inouye and Marcia Locke for their production work; and Katherine Bates and Talia Wise for their excellent marketing management.

# 1

# Reconstructing Reconstruction: The Political Cartoonist and Public Opinion

◆

## The Problem

The cable that arrived at the U.S. State Department from Guayaquil, Ecuador, on the afternoon of December 7, 1902, was brief: "Nast died today, yellow fever."[1]

Impoverished and nearly forgotten, political cartoonist Thomas Nast had accepted a position as a consular official in out-of-the-way Ecuador as a political favor from President Theodore Roosevelt. The fairly undemanding job paid $4,000, a very nice salary in 1902 but nowhere near his total income in 1879 of $25,000 as America's most well-known and influential political cartoonist, for *Harper's Weekly* in New York City.[2] In that year, Thomas Nast had been at the peak of his career, had been influential in the overthrow of the nation's most powerful political boss (William Marcy Tweed), and had played a major role in every

presidential election since 1864. But by the 1880s, the public had grown tired of his anger, his outrage, and his crusading zeal. And so the cartoonist who had given Americans the first modern depiction of Santa Claus (January 3, 1863), the Democratic donkey (January 15, 1870), the Republican elephant (November 7, 1874),[3] and countless cartoons for *Harper's Weekly* from 1862 to 1886, faded gradually but not quietly from the scene, and in 1902 swallowed his considerable pride and accepted a political favor. Four months later he was dead.

The end of the War of the Rebellion[4] in 1865 left the United States with a

1. Albert Bigelow Paine, *Th. Nast: His Period and His Pictures* (New York: Macmillan Co., 1904), p. 574.
2. Nast's salary as a customs officer would be comparable to $103,000 in 2009 dollars. His 1879 total income would be $555,000 in 2009 dollars. See http://eh.net.

3. All the dates refer to issues of *Harper's Weekly*.
4. Many northerners used the term War of the Rebellion during and immediately after the war. The official records of the conflict, published by the U.S. Government Printing Office from 1880 to 1901 were titled *The Official Records of the War of the Rebellion*. President Lincoln and others, however, preferred the term "Civil War," that was ultimately adopted. During the war, many southerners referred to the War for Southern Independence, and later to the War Between the States.

♦ CHAPTER 1

Reconstructing
Reconstruction:
The Political
Cartoonist and
Public Opinion

host of difficult questions. What should happen to the defeated South? Should the states of the former Confederacy be permitted to take their pre-war places in the Union as quickly and smoothly as possible, with minimum concessions to their northern conquerors? Or should the United States insist on a more drastic reconstruction of the South? Tied to these questions was the thorny constitutional issue of whether the southern states actually had left the Union at all in 1861. But perhaps the most difficult questions the Union's victory raised concerned the status of the former slaves. To be sure, they were no longer in bondage, but should they possess the same rights as whites? Should they be allowed to vote?[5] Should they be assisted in becoming landowners? If not, how would they earn a living? Indeed, while the war settled a number of questions, its conclusion left all Americans with other dilemmas.

In all these questions, public opinion in the victorious North was a critical factor in shaping or altering the federal government's policies designed to reconstruct the South. Earlier democratic

reforms (such as universal white male suffrage, rotation in office, the evolution of political campaigns, and so forth) made it unlikely that either the president or Congress could defy public opinion successfully. Yet public opinion can shift with remarkable speed, and political figures forever must be sensitive to its sometimes fickle winds.

Although public opinion is a crucial factor in a democratic republic such as the United States, that same public opinion often can be shaped or manipulated by political figures, interest groups, or the press. In this chapter, you will be examining and analyzing how Thomas Nast, through his cartoons, attempted to influence and shape public opinion in the North. Although Nast certainly was not the only person who sought to do so, many of his contemporaries, friends and foes alike, admitted that his political cartoons ranked among the most powerful opinion shapers during the era of Reconstruction.

What were Nast's views on the controversial issues of the Reconstruction era? How did his cartoons attempt to influence public opinion?

♦

## Background

By early 1865, it seemed evident to most northerners and southerners that the Civil War was nearly over. While Grant was hammering at Lee's

5. Until the ratification of the Fifteenth Amendment in 1870, some northern states, most prominently New York, did not grant African Americans the right to vote.

depleted forces in Virginia, Union general William Tecumseh Sherman broke the back of the Confederacy with his devastating march through Georgia and then northward into the Carolinas. Atlanta fell to Sherman's troops in September 1864, Savannah in December, and Charleston and Columbia, South Carolina, in February 1865. Two-thirds of Columbia lay in ashes. Meanwhile, General Philip Sheridan had driven the Confederates out of the Shenandoah Valley of Virginia, thus blocking any escape attempts by Lee and further cutting southern supply routes.

In the South, all but the extreme diehards recognized that defeat was inevitable. One Georgian probably spoke for a majority of southerners when he wrote, "The people are soul-sick and heartily tired of the hateful, hopeless strife. . . . We have had enough of want and woe, of cruelty and carnage, enough of crippling and corpses."[6] As the Confederate government made secret plans to evacuate Richmond, most southerners knew that the end was very near.

The triumph of Union arms had established that the United States was "one nation indivisible," from which no state could secede.[7] And yet, even with victory almost in hand, many northerners had given little thought to what should happen after the war. Would southerners accept the changes that defeat would force on them (especially the end of slavery)? What demands should the victors make on the vanquished? Should the North assist the South in rebuilding after the devastation of war? If so, should the North dictate how that rebuilding, or reconstruction, would take place? What efforts should the North make to ensure that the former slaves were able to exercise the rights of free men and women? During the war, few northerners had seriously considered these questions. Now that victory lay within their grasp, they could not avoid them.

One person who had been wrestling with these questions was Abraham Lincoln. In December 1863, the president announced his own plan for reconstructing the South, a plan that reflected the hope later expressed in his second inaugural address, for "malice toward none; with charity for all; . . . Let us . . . bind up the nation's wounds."[8] In Lincoln's plan, a southern state could resume its normal activities in the Union as soon as 10 percent of the voters of 1860 had taken an oath of loyalty to the United States. High-ranking Confederate leaders would be excluded, and some blacks might gain the right to vote. No mention was made of protecting the civil rights of former slaves; it was presumed that this matter would be left to the slaves' former masters and mistresses.

To many northerners, later known as Radical Republicans, Lincoln's plan seemed much too lenient. In the opinion of these people, a number of whom had been abolitionists, the

6. The letter probably was written by Georgian Herschel V. Walker. See Allan Nevins, *The Organized War to Victory, 1864–1865*, Vol. IV of *The War for the Union* (New York: Charles Scribner's Sons, 1971), p. 221.

7. In response to President Benjamin Harrison's 1892 appeal for schoolchildren to mark Columbus's discovery with patriotic exercises, Bostonian Francis Bellamy (brother of the novelist Edward Bellamy) composed the pledge of allegiance to the American flag, from which the phrase "one nation indivisible" comes. In 1942, Congress made it the official pledge to the flag, and in 1954 added the words "under God" in the middle of Bellamy's phrase.

8. The full text of Lincoln's second inaugural address, delivered on March 4, 1865, can be found in Roy P. Basler, ed., *The Collected Works of Abraham Lincoln*, Vol. VIII (New Brunswick, N. J.: Rutgers University Press, 1953), pp. 332–333.

◆ CHAPTER 1

Reconstructing
Reconstruction:
The Political
Cartoonist and
Public Opinion

South, when conquered, should not be allowed to return to its former ways. Not only should slavery be eradicated, they claimed, but freed blacks should be assisted in their efforts to attain economic, social, and political equity. Most of the Radical Republicans favored education for African Americans, and some advocated carving the South's plantations into small parcels to be given to the freedmen. To implement these reforms, Radical Republicans wanted detachments of the United States Army to remain in the South and favored the appointment of provisional governors to oversee the transitional governments in the southern states. Lincoln approved plans for the Army to stay and supported the idea of provisional governors. But he opposed the more far-reaching reform notions of the Radical Republicans, and as president he was able to block them.

In addition to having diametrically opposed views of Reconstruction, Lincoln and the Radical Republicans differed over the constitutional question of which branch of the federal government would be responsible for the reconstruction of the South. The Constitution made no mention of secession, reunion, or reconstruction. But Radical Republicans, citing passages in the Constitution giving Congress the power to guarantee each state a republican government, insisted that the reconstruction of the South should be carried out by Congress.[9] For his part,

however, Lincoln maintained that as chief enforcer of the law and as commander in chief, the president was the appropriate person to be in charge of Reconstruction. Clearly, a stalemate was in the making, with Radical Republicans calling for a more reform-minded Reconstruction policy and Lincoln continuing to block them.

President Lincoln's death on April 15, 1865 (one week after Lee's surrender at Appomattox Court House),[10] brought Vice President Andrew Johnson to the nation's highest office. At first, Radical Republicans had reason to hope that the new president would follow policies more to their liking. A Tennessean, Johnson had risen to political prominence from humble circumstances, had become a spokesperson for the common white men and women of the South, and had opposed the planter aristocracy. Upon becoming president, he excluded from amnesty all former Confederate political and military leaders as well as all southerners who owned taxable property worth more than $20,000 (an obvious slap at his old planter-aristocrat foes). Moreover, Johnson issued a proclamation setting up provisional military governments in the conquered South and told his cabinet he favored black suffrage, although as a states' rightist he insisted that states adopt the measure voluntarily. At the outset, then, Johnson appeared to be all the Radical Republicans wanted, preferable to the more moderate Lincoln.

9. See Article IV, Section 4, of the Constitution. Later Radical Republicans also justified their position using the Thirteenth Amendment, adopted in 1865, which gave Congress the power to enforce the amendment ending slavery in the South.

10. The last Confederate army to give up, commanded by General Joseph Johnston, surrendered to Sherman at Durham Station, North Carolina, on April 18, 1865.

Yet it did not take Radical Republicans long to realize that President Johnson was not one of them. Although he spoke harshly, he pardoned hundreds of former rebels, who quickly captured control of southern state governments and congressional delegations. Many northerners were shocked to see former Confederate generals and officials, and even former vice president Alexander Stephens, returned to Washington. The new southern state legislatures passed a series of laws, known collectively as black codes, that so severely restricted the rights of freedmen that they were all but slaves again. Moreover, Johnson privately told southerners that he opposed the Fourteenth Amendment to the Constitution, which was intended to confer full civil rights on the newly freed slaves. He also used his veto power to block Radical Republican Reconstruction measures in Congress and seemed to do little to combat the general defiance of the former Confederacy (exhibited in many forms, including insults thrown at U.S. occupation soldiers, the desecration of the United States flag, and the formation of organized resistance groups such as the Ku Klux Klan).

To an increasing number of northerners, the unrepentant spirit of the South and Johnson's acquiescence to it were appalling. Had the Civil War been fought for nothing? Had more than 364,000 federal soldiers died in vain? White southerners were openly defiant, African Americans were being subjugated by white southerners and virtually ignored by President Johnson, and former Confederates were returning to positions of power and prominence. Radical Republicans had

sufficient power in Congress to pass harsher measures, but Johnson kept vetoing them, and the Radicals lacked the votes to override his vetoes.[11] Indeed, the impasse that had existed before Lincoln's death continued.

In such an atmosphere, the congressional elections of 1866 were bitterly fought campaigns, especially in the northern states. President Johnson traveled throughout the North, defending his moderate plan of Reconstruction and viciously attacking his political enemies. However, the Radical Republicans were even more effective. Stirring up the hostilities of wartime, they "waved the bloody shirt" and excited northern voters by charging that the South had never accepted its defeat and that the 364,000 Union dead and 275,000 wounded would be for nothing if the South was permitted to continue its arrogant and stubborn behavior. Increasingly, Johnson was greeted by hostile audiences as the North underwent a major shift in public opinion.

The Radical Republicans won a stunning victory in the congressional elections of 1866 and thus broke the stalemate between Congress and the president. Armed with enough votes to override Johnson's vetoes almost at will, the new Congress proceeded rapidly to implement the Radical Republican vision of Reconstruction. The South was divided into five military districts to be ruled by martial law. Southern states had to ratify the Fourteenth Amendment and institute black suffrage before being allowed to take

11. Congress was able to override Johnson's vetoes of the Civil Rights Act and a revised Freedmen's Bureau bill.

✦ CHAPTER 1

Reconstructing
Reconstruction:
The Political
Cartoonist and
Public Opinion

their formal places in the Union. The Freedmen's Bureau, founded earlier, was given additional federal support to set up schools for African Americans, negotiate labor contracts, and, with the military, help monitor elections. Only the proposal to give land to blacks was rejected, being seen as too extreme even by some Radical Republicans. Congressional Reconstruction had begun.

President Johnson, however, had not been left completely powerless. Determined to undercut the Radical Republicans' Reconstruction policies, he issued orders increasing the powers of civil governments in the South and removed military officers who were enforcing Congress's will, replacing them with commanders less determined to protect black voting rights and more willing to turn the other way when disqualified white southerners voted. Opposed most vigorously by his own secretary of war, Edwin Stanton, Johnson tried to discharge Stanton. To an increasing number of Radicals, it became clear that the president would have to be removed from office.

In 1868, the House of Representatives voted to impeach Andrew Johnson. Charged with violating the Tenure of Office Act and the Command of the Army Act (both of which had been passed over Johnson's vetoes), the president was tried in the Senate, where two-thirds of the senators would have to vote against Johnson for him to be removed.[12] The vast majority of senators disagreed with the president's Reconstruction policies, but they feared that impeachment had become a political tool that, if successful,

threatened to destroy the balance of power between the branches of the federal government. The vote on removal fell one short of the necessary two-thirds, and Johnson was spared the indignity of removal. Nevertheless, the Republican nomination of General Ulysses Grant and his subsequent landslide victory (running as a military hero, Grant carried twenty-six out of thirty-four states) gave Radical Republicans a malleable president, one who, although not a Radical himself, could ensure the continuation of their version of Reconstruction.[13]

The Democratic party, however, was not dead, even though the Republican party dominated national politics in the immediate aftermath of the Civil War. In addition to white farmers and planters in the South and border states, the Democratic party attracted many northerners who favored conservative ("sound money") policies, voters who opposed Radical Reconstruction, and first- and second-generation Irish immigrants who had settled in urban areas and had established powerful political machines such as Tammany Hall in New York City.

By 1872, a renewed Democratic party believed it had a chance to oust Grant and the Republicans. The Grant administration had been rocked by a series of scandals, some involving men quite close to the president. Although honest himself, Grant had lost a good deal of popularity by defending the

12. See Article I, Sections 2 and 3, of the Constitution.

13. In 1868, southern states, where the Democratic party had been strong, either were not in the Union or were under the control of Radical Reconstruction governments. Grant's victory, therefore, was not as sweeping as it may first appear.

culprits and naively aiding in a cover-up of the corruption. These actions, along with some of his other policies, triggered a revolt within the Republican party, in which a group calling themselves Liberal Republicans bolted the party ranks and nominated well-known editor and reformer Horace Greeley to oppose Grant for the presidency. Hoping for a coalition to defeat Grant, the Democrats also nominated the controversial Greeley.

Greeley's platform was designed to attract as many different groups of voters as possible to the Liberal Republican-Democratic fold. He favored civil service reform, the return to a "hard money" fiscal policy, and the reservation of western lands for settlers rather than for large land companies. He vowed an end to corruption in government. But the most dramatic part of Greeley's message was his call for an end to the bitterness of the Civil War, a thinly veiled promise to bring an end to Radical Reconstruction in the South. "Let us," he said, "clasp hands over the bloody chasm."

For their part, Radical Republicans attacked Greeley as the tool of diehard southerners and labeled him as the candidate of white southern bigots and northern Irish immigrants manipulated by political machines. By contrast, Grant was labeled as a great war hero and a friend of blacks and whites alike. The incumbent Grant won easily, capturing 55 percent of the popular vote. Greeley died soon after the exhausting campaign.

Gradually, however, the zeal of Radical Republicanism began to fade. An increasing number of northerners grew tired of the issue. Their commitment to full civil rights for African Americans had never been strong, and they had voted for Radical Republicans more out of anger at southern intransigence than out of any lofty notions of black equality. Thus northerners did not protest when, one by one, southern Democrats returned to power in the states of the former Confederacy.[14] As an indication of how little their own attitudes had changed, white southerners labeled these native Democrats "Redeemers," who were swept back into power by anti-northern rhetoric and violence.

Although much that was fruitful and beneficial was accomplished in the South during the Reconstruction period (most notably black suffrage and public education), some of this was to be temporary, and many opportunities for progress were lost. By the presidential election of 1876, both candidates (Rutherford B. Hayes and Samuel Tilden) promised an end to Reconstruction, and the Radical Republican experiment, for all intents and purposes, was over.

It is clear that northern public opinion from 1865 to 1876 was far from static but was almost constantly shifting. This public opinion was influenced by a number of factors, among them speeches, newspapers, and word of mouth. Especially influential were editorial cartoons, which captured the issues visually, often simplifying them so that virtually everyone could understand them. Perhaps the

14. Southerners regained control of the state governments in Tennessee and Virginia in 1869, North Carolina in 1870, Georgia in 1871, Arkansas and Alabama in 1874, and Mississippi in early 1876. By the presidential election of 1876, only South Carolina, Louisiana, and Florida were still controlled by Reconstruction governments.

◆ CHAPTER 1

Reconstructing
Reconstruction:
The Political
Cartoonist and
Public Opinion

master of this style was Thomas Nast, a political cartoonist whose career, principally with *Harper's Weekly,* spanned the tumultuous years of the Civil War and Reconstruction. Throughout his career, Nast produced more than three thousand cartoons, illustrations for books, and paintings. Congratulating themselves for having hired Nast, the editors of *Harper's Weekly* once exclaimed that each of Nast's drawings was at once "a poem and a speech."

Apparently, Thomas Nast developed his talents early in life. Born in the German Palatinate (one of the German states) in 1840, Nast was the son of a musician in the Ninth Regiment Bavarian Band. The family moved to New York City in 1846, at which time young Thomas was enrolled in school. It seems that art was his only interest. One teacher admonished him, "Go finish your picture. You will never learn to read or figure." After unsuccessfully trying to interest their son in music, his parents eventually encouraged the development of his artistic talent. By the age of fifteen, Thomas Nast was drawing illustrations for *Frank Leslie's Illustrated Newspaper.* He joined *Harper's Weekly* in 1862 (at the age of twenty-two), where he developed the cartoon style that was to win him a national reputation, as well as enemies.[15] He received praise from Abraham Lincoln, Ulysses Grant, and Samuel Clemens (also known as Mark Twain, who in 1872 asked Nast to do

the illustrations for one of his books so that "then I will have good pictures"). In contrast, one of Nast's favorite targets, political boss William Marcy Tweed of New York's Tammany Hall, once shouted, "Let's stop these damn pictures. I don't care so much what the papers say about me—my constituents can't read; but damn it, they can see pictures!"

It is obvious from his work that Nast was a man of strong feelings and emotions. In his eyes, those people whom he admired possessed no flaws. Conversely, those whom he opposed were, to him, capable of every conceivable villainy. As a result, his characterizations often were terribly unfair, gross distortions of reality and more than occasionally libelous. In his view, however, his central purpose was not to entertain but to move his audience, to make them scream out in outrage or anger, to prod them to action. The selection of Nast's cartoons in this chapter is typical of the body of his work for *Harper's Weekly*: artistically inventive and polished, blatantly slanted, and brimming with indignation and emotion.

The evidence in this chapter consists of fourteen cartoons by Thomas Nast that were published in *Harper's Weekly* between August 5, 1865, and December 9, 1876. Your tasks in this chapter are to determine Nast's views on the controversial issues of the Reconstruction era, and how his cartoons attempted to sway public opinion on those issues.

15. Nast began to make the transition from artistry to caricature in 1867. Note the differences between Sources 1 and 2 and Sources 3 through 14. As you can see, the transition was more gradual than immediate.

# The Method

Although Thomas Nast developed the political cartoon into a true art form, cartoons and caricatures had a long tradition in both Europe and America before Nast. English artists helped bring forth the cartoon style that eventually made *Punch* (founded in 1841) one of the liveliest illustrated periodicals on both sides of the Atlantic. In America, Benjamin Franklin is traditionally credited with publishing the first newspaper cartoon in 1754—the multidivided snake (each part of the snake representing one colony) with the ominous warning "Join or Die." By the time Andrew Jackson sought the presidency, the political cartoon had become a regular and popular feature of American political life. Crude by modern standards, these cartoons influenced some people far more than did the printed word.

As we noted, the political cartoon, like the newspaper editorial, is intended to do more than objectively report events. It is meant to express an opinion, a point of view, approval or disapproval. Political cartoonists want to move people, to make them laugh, to anger them, or to move them to action. In short, political cartoons do not depict exactly what is happening; rather, they portray popular reaction to what is happening and try to persuade people to react in a particular way.

How do you analyze political cartoons? First, using your text and the Problem and Background sections of this chapter, make a list of the most important issues and events (including elections) of the period between 1865 and 1876. As you examine the cartoons in this chapter, try to determine what event or issue is being portrayed. Often a cartoon's caption, dialogue, or date will help you discover its focus.

Next, look closely at each cartoon for clues that will help you understand the message that Nast was trying to convey. People who saw these cartoons more than one hundred years ago did not have to study them so carefully, of course. The individuals and events shown in each cartoon were immediately familiar to them, and the message was obvious. But you are historians, using these cartoons as evidence to help you understand how people were reacting to important events many years ago.

As you can see, Nast was a talented artist. Like many political cartoonists, he often explored the differences between what he believed was the ideal (justice, fairness) and the reality (his view of what was actually happening). To "read" Nast's cartoons, you should identify the issue or event on which the cartoon is based. Then look at the *imagery* Nast used: the situation, the setting, the clothes people are wearing, and the objects in the picture. It is especially important to note how people are portrayed: Do they look handsome and noble, or do they look like animals? Are they happy or sad? Intelligent or stupid?

Political cartoonists often use *symbolism* to make their point, sometimes in the form of an *allegory*. In an

◆ CHAPTER 1

Reconstructing
Reconstruction:
The Political
Cartoonist and
Public Opinion

allegory, familiar figures are shown in a situation or setting that everyone knows—for example, a setting from the Bible, a fairy tale, or another well-known source. For instance, a cartoon showing a tiny president of the United States holding a slingshot, dressed in sandals and rags, and fighting a giant, muscular man labeled "Congress" would remind viewers of the story of David and Goliath. In that story, the small man won. The message of the cartoon is that the president will win in his struggle with Congress.

Other, less complicated symbolism is often used in political cartoons. In Nast's time, as today, the American flag was an important symbol of the ideals of our democratic country, and an olive branch or dove represented the desire for peace. Some symbols have changed, however. Today, the tall, skinny figure we call Uncle Sam represents the United States. In Nast's time, Columbia, a tall woman wearing a long classical dress, represented the United States. Also in Nast's time, an hourglass, rather than a clock, symbolized that time was running out. And military uniforms, regardless of the fact that the Civil War had ended in 1865, were used to indicate whether a person had supported the Union (and, by implication, was a Republican) or the Confederacy (by implication, a Democrat).

As you can see, a political cartoon must be analyzed in detail to get the full meaning the cartoonist was trying to convey. From that analysis, one can discover the message of the cartoon, along with the cartoonist's views on the subject and the ways in which the cartoonist was trying to influence public opinion. Now you are ready to begin your analysis of the Reconstruction era through the cartoons of Thomas Nast.

# The Evidence

Sources 1 through 14 from *Harper's Weekly. A Journal of Civilization*, August 5, 1865; June 30, 1866; March 30, 1867; September 5, October 3, 1868; April 13, August 3, September 21, 1872; March 14, September 26, December 5, 1874; September 2, December 9, November 4, 1876.

## 1. Columbia—"Shall I Trust These Men, And Not This Man?," August 5, 1865.

◆ CHAPTER 1

Reconstructing
Reconstruction:
The Political
Cartoonist and
Public Opinion

## 4. "This Is a White Man's Government," September 5, 1868.

## 5. "The Modern Samson," October 3, 1868.

THE MODERN SAMSON.

✦ CHAPTER 1

Reconstructing
Reconstruction:
The Political
Cartoonist and
Public Opinion

## 6. "The Republic Is Not Ungrateful," April 13, 1872.

THE REPUBLIC IS NOT UNGRATEFUL.

"It is not what is *charged* but what is *proved* that damages the party defendant. Any one may be accused of the most heinous offenses ; the Saviour of mankind was not only arraigned but convicted ; but what of it? Facts alone are decisive."—*New York Tribune, March 13, 1872.*

© 1999 HARPWEEK®

## 7. "Baltimore 1861–1872," August 3, 1872.

♦ CHAPTER 1

Reconstructing
Reconstruction:
The Political
Cartoonist and
Public Opinion

8. "Let Us Clasp Hands over the Bloody Chasm" (Horace Greeley)
   September 21, 1872.

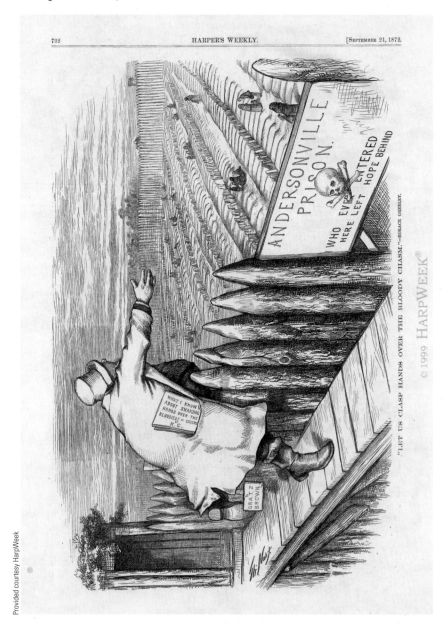

Provided courtesy HarpWeek

**9. "Colored Rule in Reconstructed (?) State," March 14, 1874.**

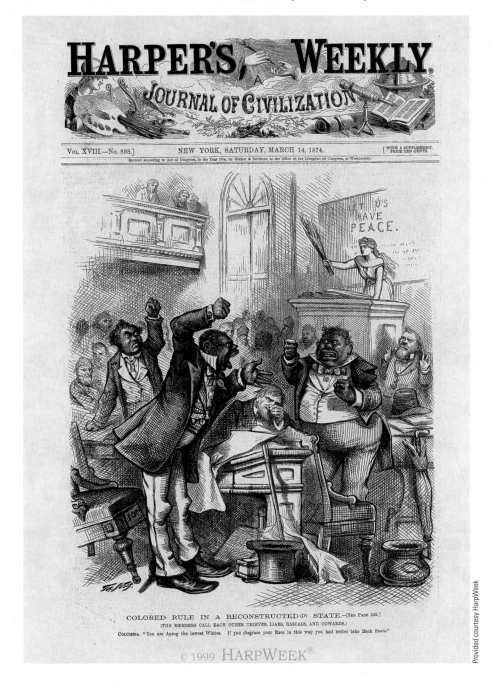

COLORED RULE IN A RECONSTRUCTED (?) STATE.—[See Page 242.]
(THE MEMBERS CALL EACH OTHER THIEVES, LIARS, RASCALS, AND COWARDS.)

COLUMBIA. "You are Aping the lowest Whites. If you disgrace your Race in this way you had better take Back Seats."

◆ CHAPTER 1

Reconstructing
Reconstruction:
The Political
Cartoonist and
Public Opinion

## 10. "The Commandments in South Carolina," September 26, 1874.

**11. "Now Gnaw Away!," December 5, 1874.**

NOW GNAW AWAY!

✦ CHAPTER 1

Reconstructing
Reconstruction:
The Political
Cartoonist and
Public Opinion

**12.** **"Is This a Republican Form of Government? Is This Protecting Life, Liberty, or Property? Is This the Equal Protection of the Laws?," September 2, 1876.**

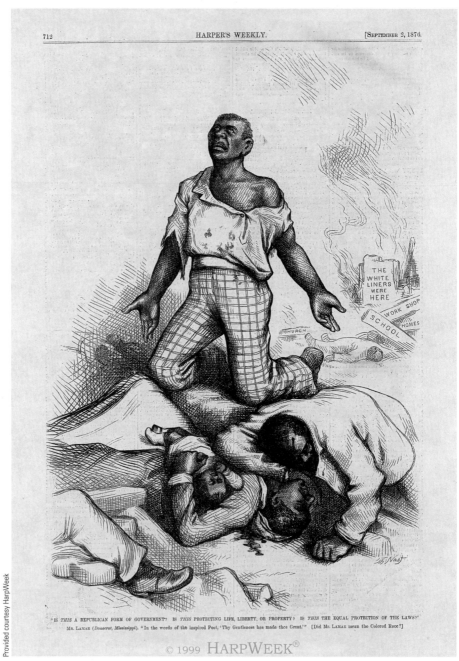

**13. "The Ignorant Vote—Honors Are Easy," December 9, 1876.**

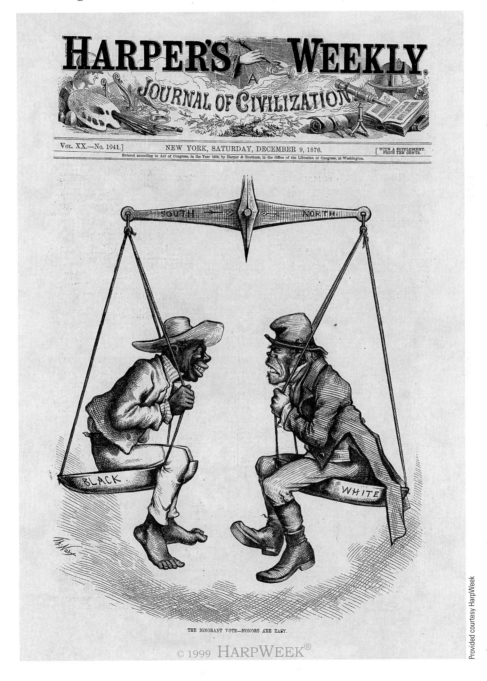

♦ CHAPTER 1

Reconstructing
Reconstruction:
The Political
Cartoonist and
Public Opinion

14. "The Solid South Against the Union," November 4, 1876.

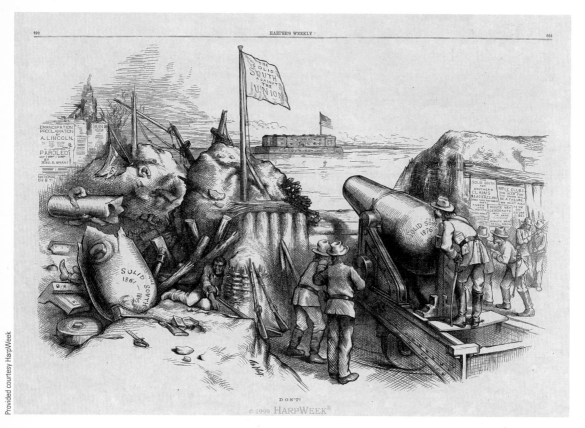

# Questions to Consider

Begin by reviewing your list of the important issues and events of the Reconstruction era. Then systematically examine the cartoons, answering the following questions for each one:

1. What issues or event is represented by this cartoon?
2. Who are the principal figures, and how are they portrayed?
3. What *imagery* is used?
4. Is this cartoon an *allegory*? If so, what is the basis of the allegory?
5. What *symbols* are used?
6. How was Nast trying to influence public opinion through this cartoon?

You may find that making a chart is the easiest way to do this.

Sources 1 through 3 represent Nast's view of Presidential Reconstruction under Andrew Johnson. Who is the woman in Source 1? Who are the men kneeling before her in the left frame? What do they seek? Who does the African American in the right frame represent? Can you formulate one sentence that summarizes Nast's "message" in Source 1?

Source 2 is more complex: two drawings within two other drawings. If you do not already know what purpose Andersonville and Fortress Monroe served, consult a text on this time period, an encyclopedia, or a good Civil War history book. Then look at the upper left and upper right outside drawings. Contrast the appearance of the man entering with the man leaving. Now examine the lower left and lower right outside drawings the same way. What was Nast trying to tell? The larger inside drawings explain the contrast. What were the conditions like at Andersonville? At Fortress Monroe? What did the cartoonist think were the physical and psychological results?

On July 30, 1866, several blacks attending a Radical Republican convention in New Orleans were shot and killed by white policemen. Who is the emperor in Source 3, and how is he portrayed? What kind of setting is used in this cartoon? Who is the person in the lower left intended to represent? What did Nast think caused this event? What was his own reaction to it?

Each of the three people standing in Source 4 represents part of the Democratic party coalition, and each has something to contribute to the party. Can you identify the groups that the man on the right and the man in the center represent? What do they offer the party? Notice the facial features of the man on the left as well as his dress, particularly the hatband from Five Points (a notorious slum section of New York City). Who is this man supposed to represent, and what does he give the party (see the club in his left hand)? Notice the knife and the belt buckle of the man in the middle. Who does he represent? The man on the right probably is meant to represent Horatio Seymour, the Democratic party's nominee for president to oppose Republican nominee Ulysses Grant. What is the African American U.S. Army veteran reaching for? What is Nast's "message" in Source 4? How does Source 4 relate

◆ CHAPTER 1

Reconstructing
Reconstruction:
The Political
Cartoonist and
Public Opinion

to Source 5? What is the *allegory* Nast was using? Who are the men on the left of the cartoon? Who does the statue on the right represent? What is Nast's "message" here?

Sources 6 through 8 dealt with the presidential election of 1872, which pitted the incumbent President Grant against the Democratic challenger editor Horace Greeley.[16] Grant is depicted in Source 6, protected by Miss Liberty. What does the bust behind Grant represent? What is Nast's message here? Hoping to finally put an end to what he considered a fruitless Reconstruction, Greeley called for northerners and southerners to "clasp hands over the bloody chasm." How did Nast use (or misuse) Greeley's statement? How would you assess Nast's cartoons in Sources 7 and 8?

Sources 9 through 13 reflect Nast's thinking in the later years of Reconstruction. Sources 9 and 10 portray his opinion of Reconstruction in South Carolina, presided over by Radical Republican governor Franklin J. Moses (caricatured in Source 10). How are African Americans portrayed in Sources 9, 10, and 13 (compared to portrayals in Sources 1, 4, 5, and 7)? What is the meaning of Source 13? Of Source 11? Source 12?

The last cartoon (Source 14) is Nast's reaction to a bill in Congress to grant amnesty to hundreds of unpardoned former Confederates. What is the *allegory* Nast was using here? What does the fort represent? What is the significance of the African American hiding on the left side of the panel? Who are the men preparing to fire on the fort? What do the two cannons represent? What is Nast's troubling "message" here? Now return to the central questions asked earlier. What significant events took place during Reconstruction? How did Nast try to influence public opinion on the important issues of the era? How did Nast's own views change between 1865 and 1876? Why did Reconstruction finally end?

◆

## Epilogue

Undoubtedly, Thomas Nast's work had an important impact on northern opinion of Reconstruction, the Democratic Party, Andrew Johnson, Ulysses Grant, Horace Greeley, Irish-Americans, and a host of other individuals and issues.

16. Angered at the corruption of Grant's administration, several Liberal Republicans bolted their party and supported Greeley.

Yet gradually, northern ardor began to decline as other issues and concerns eased Reconstruction out of the limelight and as it appeared that the crusade to reconstruct the South would be an endless one. Gradually southern Democrats regained control of their state governments, partly through intimidation of black voters and partly through appeals to whites to return the

South to the hands of white southerners.[17] Fearing northern outrage and a potential return to Radical Reconstruction, however, on the surface most southern political leaders claimed to accept emancipation and decried against widespread lynchings and terror against former slaves.

Meanwhile in the North, those Radical Republicans who had insisted on equality for the freedmen either were dying or retiring from politics, replaced by conservative Republicans who spoke for economic expansion, industrialism and commerce, and prosperous farmers. For their part, northern Democrats envisaged a political reunion of northern and southern Democrats that could win control of the federal government. Like their Republican counterparts but for different reasons, northern Democrats had no stomach for assuring freedom and rights to former slaves.

Finally, in the late 1880s, when white southerners realized that the Reconstruction spirit had waned in the North, southern state legislatures began instituting rigid segregation of schools, public transportation and accommodations, parks, restaurants and theaters, elevators, drinking fountains, and so on. Not until the 1950s did those chains begin to be broken.

As the reform spirit waned in the later years of Reconstruction, Nast's popularity suffered. The public appeared to tire of his anger, his self-righteousness, and his relentless crusades. Meanwhile newspaper and magazine technology was changing, and Nast had great difficulty adjusting to the new methodology.[18] Finally, the new publisher of *Harper's Weekly* sought to make the publication less political, and in such an atmosphere there was no place for Thomas Nast. His last cartoon for *Harper's Weekly* appeared on Christmas Day of 1886. He continued to drift from job to job, in 1893 briefly owned his own paper, *Nast's Weekly*, which turned out to be a financial disaster, and by 1901 was deeply in debt. It was then that President Roosevelt came to his aid with a minor consular post in Ecuador, where he died four months after his arrival. He was buried in a quiet ceremony in Woodlawn Cemetery in The Bronx, New York.

Although Nast was only sixty-two years old when he died, most of the famous subjects of his cartoons had long predeceased him. William Marcy Tweed, the political boss of New York's Tammany Hall who Nast had helped to bring down, was sentenced to twelve years in prison in late 1873. But "Boss" Tweed escaped in 1875 and fled to Cuba, where he was apprehended by authorities who identified him with the assistance of a Nast cartoon. He died in prison in 1878.

17. Conservative Democrats regained control of southern state governments in Tennessee and Virginia (1869); Georgia (1872); Alabama, Arkansas, and Texas (1874); Mississippi (1876); North Carolina, South Carolina, Louisiana, and Florida (1877).

18. Nast began drawing his cartoons in soft pencil on wooden blocks that were then prepared by engravers. Around 1880 photomechanical reproduction of ink drawings replaced the older and slower method. J. Chal Vinson, *Thomas Nast, Political Cartoonist* (Athens: University of Georgia Press, 1967), p. 35; and Morton Keller, *The Art and Politics of Thomas Nast* (London: Oxford University Press, 1968), p. 327.

✦ CHAPTER 1

Reconstructing
Reconstruction:
The Political
Cartoonist and
Public Opinion

Nast's hero, Ulysses S. Grant, left the White House in 1877 after an administration marked by corruption and scandal. Not a wealthy man, Grant hurried to finish his memoirs (to provide for his wife Julia) before the throat cancer he had been diagnosed with killed him. He died on July 23, 1885, and was interred in Central Park in New York City, not far from Nast's modest grave. In 1897, a magnificent tomb was dedicated to Grant and his remains were relocated there. When Julia died in 1902, she was laid to rest in what grammatically should be called Grants' Tomb.

Thomas Nast was a pioneer of a tradition and a political art form that remains extremely popular today. As Joel Pett, cartoonist for the Lexington (KY) *Herald-Leader* put it, "If [newspaper publishers] . . . sign on to the quaint but true notion that journalism ought to comfort the afflicted and afflict the comfortable, there's no better way to afflict the comfortable than with editorial cartoons."[19] Nast couldn't have said it better himself.

19. Chris Lamb, *Drawn to Extremes: The Use and Abuse of Editorial Cartoons* (New York: Columbia University Press, 2004), p. 238.

# 2

# The Road to True Freedom: African American Alternatives in the New South

## The Problem

By 1895, when the venerable Frederick Douglass died, African Americans in the South had been free for thirty years. Yet in many ways, their situation had barely improved from that of servitude, and in some ways, it had actually deteriorated. Economically, very few had been able to acquire land of their own, and the vast majority continued to work for white landowners under various forms of labor arrangements and sometimes under outright peonage.[1] Political and civil rights supposedly had been guaranteed under the 14th and 15th Amendments to the Constitution (ratified in 1868 and 1870, respectively), but those rights often were violated, federal

courts offered little protection, and, beginning in the early 1890s, southern states began a successful campaign to disfranchise black voters and to institute legal segregation through legislation that collectively became known as Jim Crow laws.[2] In some ways more threatening, violence against African Americans was increasing and in most cases going unpunished. Between 1889 and 1900, 1,357 lynchings of African Americans were recorded in the United States, the vast majority in the states of the former Confederacy. In 1898, in New Bern, North Carolina, one white orator proposed "choking the Cape Fear River with the bodies of Negroes." In truth,

1. Whatever names were given to these labor arrangements (tenancy, sharecropping, and so on), in most of the arrangements a white landowner or merchant furnished farm workers with foodstuffs and fertilizer on credit, taking a percentage of the crops grown in return. For a fascinating description of how the system worked, see Theodore Rosengarten, *All God's Dangers: The Life of Nate Shaw* (New York: Alfred A. Knopf, 1974).

2. The term *Jim Crow*, generally used to refer to issues relating to African Americans, originated in the late 1820s with white minstrel singer Thomas "Daddy" Rice, who performed the song "Jump Jim Crow" in blackface makeup. By the 1840s, the term was used to refer to racially segregated facilities in the North.

✦ CHAPTER 2

The Road to
True Freedom:
African American
Alternatives in the
New South

by the 1890s it had become evident for all who cared to see that Lincoln's emancipation of southern slaves had been considerably less than complete.

Economic semiservitude, disfranchisement, assaults on black women, and widespread lynchings combined to undercut the African American male's sense of his own manhood. Alternately portrayed by whites as childlike creatures or as brutish sexual predators, black males tried desperately though not always successfully to assert their manhood. At the beginning of the Spanish-American War in 1898, many African American men rushed to enlist in the armed services, and one unit actually rescued Theodore Roosevelt's Rough Riders from a difficult situation in their soon-to-be-famous "charge up San Juan Hill."

Many whites, however, refused to allow African American men to express their masculinity. Indeed, more than a few white men actually believed that *they themselves* displayed their own masculinity by keeping blacks in their "place." During the racially charged North Carolina state elections in 1898, one newspaper published a poem that specifically expressed that sentiment:

> Rise, ye sons of Carolina!
> Proud Caucasians, one and all;
> Be not deaf to Love's appealing—
> Hear your wives and daughters call,
> See their blanched and anxious faces,
> Note their frail, but lovely forms
> Rise, defend their spotless virtue
> With your strong and manly arms.[3]

Thus, in the eyes of many African Americans, their lot appeared not to be rising but rather descending. A number of spokespersons offered significantly different strategies for improving the situation of African Americans in the South. For this chapter's Evidence section, we have chosen five such spokespersons, all of them well known to blacks in the New South. Ida B. Wells (1862–1931) was a journalist, lecturer, and crusader who was highly regarded in both the United States and Europe. Booker T. Washington (1856–1915) was a celebrated educator, author, and political figure who many believed should have inherited the mantle of Frederick Douglass as the principal spokesperson for African Americans. Henry McNeal Turner (1834–1915) was a bishop of the African Methodist Episcopal Church and a controversial speaker and writer. W. E. B. DuBois (pronounced *Du Boys'*, 1868–1963) was an academician and editor and one of the founders of the National Association for the Advancement of Colored People (NAACP). Finally, Frances Ellen Watkins Harper (1825–1911) was a popular poet and writer who gave numerous speeches in support of both African American and women's rights. Each of these spokespersons offered a contrasting alternative for African Americans in the New South.

In this chapter, you will be analyzing the situation that southern blacks faced in the years after Reconstruction and identifying the principal alternatives

3. *Wilmington (NC) Messenger,* November 8, 1898, quoted in Glenda Elizabeth Gilmore, *Gender and Jim Crow: Women and the Politics of White Supremacy in North Carolina,* *1896–1920* (Chapel Hill: University of North Carolina Press, 1996), p. 91. Gilmore's study is highly recommended for anyone who wishes to delve more deeply into this topic.

open to them. What different strategies did Wells, Washington, Turner, DuBois, and Harper offer African Americans? Were there other options they did not address? Based on your examination of the different alternatives advocated by these five African American spokes-persons, what do you think were the strengths and weaknesses of each approach? Finally, keep in mind that the five spokepersons advocated taking different paths to the *same* ultimate goal: full equality for African Americans.

---

## Background

The gradual end of Reconstruction by the federal government left the South in the hands of political and economic leaders who chose to call themselves "Redeemers." Many of these men came from the same planter elite that had led the South prior to the Civil War, thus giving the post-Reconstruction South a high degree of continuity with earlier eras. Also important, however, was a comparatively new group of southerners, men who called for a "New South" that would be highlighted by increased industrialization, urbanization, and diversified agriculture.

In many ways, the New South movement was an undisguised attempt to imitate the industrialization that was sweeping through the North in the mid to late nineteenth century. Indeed, the North's industrial prowess had been one reason for its ultimate military victory. As Reconstruction collapsed in the southern states, many southern bankers, business leaders, and newspaper editors became convinced that the South should not return to its previous, narrow economic base of plantations and one-crop agriculture but instead should follow the North's lead toward modernization through industry. Prior to the Civil War, many of these people had called for economic diversification, but they had been overwhelmed by the plantation aristocracy that dominated southern state politics and had used that control to further its own interests. By the end of Reconstruction, however, the planter elite had lost a good deal of its authority, thus creating a power vacuum into which advocates of a New South could move.

Nearly every city, town, and hamlet of the former Confederacy had its New South boosters. Getting together in industrial societies or chambers of commerce, the boosters called for the erection of mills and factories. Why, they asked, should southerners export their valuable raw materials elsewhere, only to see them return from northern and European factories as costly finished products? Why couldn't southerners set up their own manufacturing establishments and become prosperous within a self-contained economy? And if the southerners were short of capital, why not encourage rich northern investors to put up money in return for promises of great profits? In fact, the South had all the ingredients

✦ CHAPTER 2

The Road to
True Freedom:
African American
Alternatives in the
New South

required of an industrial system: raw materials, a rebuilt transportation system, labor, potential consumers, and the possibility of obtaining capital. As they fed each other's dreams, the New South advocates pictured a resurgent South, a prosperous South, a triumphant South, a South of steam and power rather than plantations and cotton.

Undoubtedly, the leading spokesman of the New South movement was Henry Grady, editor of the *Atlanta Constitution* and one of the most influential figures in the southern states. Born in Athens, Georgia, in 1850, Grady was orphaned in his early teens when his father was killed in the Civil War. Graduating from his hometown college, the University of Georgia, Grady began a long and not particularly profitable career as a journalist. In 1879, aided by northern industrialist Cyrus Field, he purchased a quarter interest in the *Atlanta Constitution* and became that newspaper's editor. From that position, he became the chief advocate of the New South movement.

Whether speaking to southern or northern audiences, Grady had no peer. Addressing a group of potential investors in New South industries in New York in 1886, he delighted his audience by saying that he was glad the Confederacy had lost the Civil War, for that defeat had broken the power of the plantation aristocracy and provided the opportunity for the South to move into the modern industrial age. Northerners, Grady continued, were welcome: "We have sown towns and cities in the place of theories, and put business above politics . . . and have . . . wiped

out the place where Mason and Dixon's line used to be."[4]

To those southerners who envisioned a New South, the central goal was a harmonious, interdependent society in which each person and thing had a clearly defined place. Most New South boosters stressed industry and the growth of cities because the South had few factories and mills and almost no cities of substantial size. But agriculture also would have its place, although it would not be the same as the cash-crop agriculture of the pre-Civil War years. Instead, New South spokespersons advocated a diversified agriculture that would still produce cash crops for export but would also make the South more self-sufficient by cultivating food crops and raw materials for the anticipated factories. Small towns would be used for collection and distribution, a rebuilt railroad network would transport goods, and northern capital would finance the entire process. Hence, each part of the economy and, indeed, each person would have a clearly defined place in the New South, and that would ensure everyone a piece of the New South's prosperity.

But even as Grady and his counterparts were fashioning their dreams of a New South and selling that vision to both northerners and southerners, a less beneficial, less prosperous side of the New South was taking shape. In spite of the New South advocates' successes in establishing factories and mills (for example, Knoxville, Tennessee,

4. Grady's speech is in Richard N. Current and John A. Garraty, eds., *Words That Made American History* (Boston: Little, Brown, 1962), Vol. II, pp. 23–31.

witnessed the founding of more than ninety such enterprises in the 1880s alone), the post-Reconstruction South remained primarily agricultural. Furthermore, many of the farms were worked by sharecroppers or tenant farmers who eked out a bare subsistence while the profits went to the landowners or to the banks. This situation was especially prevalent in the lower South, where by 1910 a great proportion of farms were worked by tenants: South Carolina (63.0 percent), Georgia (65.6 percent), Alabama (60.2 percent), Mississippi (66.1 percent), and Louisiana (55.3 percent).[5] Even as factory smokestacks were rising on portions of the southern horizon, the majority of southerners remained in agriculture and in poverty.

Undeniably, African Americans suffered the most. More than four million African American men, women, and children had been freed by the Civil War. During Reconstruction, some advances were made, especially in the areas of public education and voter registration. Yet even these gains were either impermanent or incomplete. By 1880 in Georgia, only 33.7 percent of the black school-age population was enrolled in school, and by 1890 (twenty-five years after emancipation), almost half of all blacks aged ten to fourteen in the Deep South were still illiterate.[6] As for voting rights, the vast majority of African American men chose not

to exercise them, fearing intimidation and violence.

Many blacks and whites at the time recognized that African Americans would never be able to improve their situation economically, socially, or politically without owning land. Yet even many Radical Republicans were reluctant to give land to the former slaves. Such a move would mean seizing land from the white planters, a proposal that clashed with the notion of the sanctity of private property. As a result, most African Americans were forced to take menial, low-paying jobs in southern cities or to work as farmers on land they did not own. By 1880, only 1.6 percent of the landowners in Georgia were African Americans, although blacks constituted 47 percent of the state's population.

As poor urban laborers or tenant farmers, African Americans were dependent on their employers, land-owners, or bankers and prey to vagrancy laws, the convict lease system, peonage, and outright racial discrimination. Moreover, the end of Reconstruction in the southern states was followed by a reimposition of rigid racial segregation, at first through a return to traditional practices and later (in the 1890s) by state laws governing nearly every aspect of southern life. For example, voting by African Americans was discouraged, initially by intimidation and then by more formal means such as poll taxes and literacy tests. African Americans who protested or strayed from their "place" were dealt with harshly. Between 1880 and 1918, more than twenty-four hundred African Americans were lynched by southern white mobs, each action being a grim reminder to

5. Bureau of the Census, *Farm Tenancy in the United States* (Washington: Government Printing Office, 1924), pp. 207–208.
6. Roger L. Ransom and Richard Sutch, *One Kind of Freedom: The Economic Consequences of Emancipation* (Cambridge: Cambridge University Press, 1977), pp. 28, 30.

◆ CHAPTER 2

The Road to
True Freedom:
African American
Alternatives in the
New South

African Americans of what could happen to those who challenged the status quo. For their part, the few southern whites who spoke against such outrages were themselves subjects of intimidation and even violence. Indeed, although most African American men and women undoubtedly would have disagreed, African Americans' relative position in some ways had deteriorated since the end of the Civil War.

To be sure, a black middle class did exist and was growing in the South, principally in cities such as New Orleans, Richmond, Durham, and Atlanta. Most were men and women who served the African American community (editors, teachers, clergy, undertakers, retailers, restauranteurs, realtors, and so forth), people who owned their own homes, saw to it that their sons and daughters received good educations, and maintained a standard of living superior to the majority of whites and blacks in the South.[7] Although some of them spoke out in the interests of fellow African Americans, still more preferred to live out of the spotlight and challenged the region's status quo quietly—when they did so at all.

Many New South advocates openly worried about how potential northern investors and politicians might react to the disturbing erosion of African Americans' position or to the calls of some middle-class blacks for racial justice. Although the dream of the New South rested on the concept of a harmonious,

interdependent society in which each component (industry or agriculture, for example) and each person (white or black) had a clearly defined place, it appeared that African Americans were being kept in their "place" largely by intimidation and violence. Who would want to invest in a region where the status quo of mutual deference and "place" often was maintained by force? To calm northern fears, Grady and his cohorts assured northerners that African Americans' position was improving and that southern society was one of mutual respect between the races. "We have found," Grady stated, "that in the summing up the free Negro counts more than he did as a slave."[8] Most northerners believed Grady because they wanted to, because they had no taste for another bitter Reconstruction, and in many cases because they shared white southerners' prejudice against African Americans. Grady was able to reassure them because they wanted to be reassured.

Thus, for southern African Americans, the New South movement had done little to better their collective lot. Indeed, in some ways their position had deteriorated. Tied economically either to land they did not own or to the lowest-paying jobs in towns and cities, subjects of an increasingly rigid code of racial segregation and loss of political rights, and victims of an upswing in racially directed violence, African Americans in the New South had every reason to question the oratory of Henry Grady

7. On home ownership, in North Carolina in 1870, only 5.6 percent of African Americans owned their own homes. By 1910, that figure had risen to 26 percent. Gilmore, *Gender and Jim Crow*, p. 15.

8. *The New South: Writings and Speeches of Henry Grady* (Savannah: The Beehive Press, 1971), p. 8.

and other New South boosters. Jobs in the New South's mills and factories generally were reserved for whites, so the opportunities that European immigrants in the North had to work their way gradually up the economic ladder were closed to southern blacks.

How did African Americans respond to this deteriorating situation? In the 1890s, numerous African American farmers joined the Colored Alliance, part of the Farmers' Alliance Movement that swept the South and Midwest in the 1880s and 1890s. This movement attempted to reverse the farmers' eroding position through the establishment of farmers' cooperatives (to sell their crops together for higher prices and to purchase manufactured goods wholesale) and by entering politics to elect candidates sympathetic to farmers (who would draft legislation favorable to farmers). Many feared, however, that this increased militancy of farmers—white and black—would produce a political backlash that would leave them even worse off. Such a backlash occurred in

the South in the 1890s with the defeat of the Populist revolt.

Wells, Washington, Turner, DuBois, and Harper offered southern African Americans alternative means of confronting the economic, social, and political difficulties they faced. And, as African American men and women soon discovered, there were other options as well.

Your task in this chapter is to analyze the evidence in order to answer the following central questions:

1. What were the different alternatives offered by Wells, Washington, Turner, DuBois, and Harper?
2. Were there other options those five spokespersons did not mention?
3. What were the strengths and weaknesses of each alternative? Note: Remember that you are evaluating the five alternatives *not* from a present-day perspective but in the context and time in which they were advocated (1892–1906).
4. How would you support your assessment of the strengths and weaknesses of each alternative?

---

## The Method

In this chapter, the evidence is from speeches delivered by five well-known African Americans or from their writings that were also given as speeches. Although all five spokespersons were known to southern African Americans, they were not equally prominent. It is almost impossible to tell which of the five was the best known (or least known) in her or his time, although fragmentary evidence suggests that Washington

and Harper were the most famous figures among African Americans in various socioeconomic groups.

The piece by Ida B. Wells (Source 1) is excerpted from a pamphlet published simultaneously in the United States and England in 1892, but it is almost certain that parts of it were delivered as a speech by wells in that same year. The selections by Booker T. Washington (Source 2), Henry McNeal Turner

◆ CHAPTER 2

The Road to
True Freedom:
African American
Alternatives in the
New South

(Source 3), W. E. B. DuBois (Source 4 and 5), and Frances E. W. Harper (Source 6) are transcriptions, or printed versions, of speeches delivered between 1895 and 1906.

Ida Bell Wells was born a slave in Holly Springs, Mississippi, in 1862. After emancipation, her father and mother, as a carpenter and a cook, respectively, earned enough money to send her to freedmen's school. In 1876, her parents died in a yellow fever epidemic. Only fourteen years old, Wells lied about her age and got a job teaching in a rural school for blacks, eventually moving to Memphis, Tennessee, to teach in the city's school for African Americans. In September 1883, she was forcibly removed from a railroad passenger car for refusing to move to the car reserved for "colored" passengers (she bit the conductor's hand in the scuffle). She won a lawsuit against the Chesapeake and Ohio Railroad, but that lawsuit was overturned by the Tennessee Supreme Court in 1887.[9] About this time Wells began writing articles for many black-owned newspapers (one of which, *Free Speech*, she co-owned), mostly on the subject of unequal educational opportunities for whites and blacks in Memphis. As a result, the Memphis school board discharged her, and she became a full-time journalist and lecturer. Then, in March 1892, three black men, one of them a friend of Wells, were lynched in Memphis. Her angry editorial in *Free Speech* resulted in the

9. Wells was not the first African American woman to challenge Tennessee's racial segregation of railroad passenger cars. See Paula J. Giddings, *Ida, A Sword Among Lions: Ida B. Wells and the Campaign Against Lynching* (New York: Amistad, 2008), pp. 52–59.

newspaper's destruction. The other co-owner was threatened with hanging and castration, the paper's former owner was pistol-whipped, and Wells herself was threatened with lynching if she returned to Memphis (she was in New York when her editorial was published). Relocating to Chicago, in 1895 she married black lawyer-editor Ferdinand Lee Barnett and from that time went by the name Ida Wells-Barnett, a somewhat radical practice in 1895.

Like Wells, Booker T. Washington was born a slave, in Franklin County, Virginia. Largely self-taught before entering Hampton Institute, a school for African Americans, at age seventeen, he worked his way through school, mostly as a janitor. While a student at Hampton Institute, he came to the attention of Gen. Samuel C. Armstrong (1839–1893), one of the school's founders, who recommended Washington for the post as principal of the newly-charted normal school for blacks in Tuskegee, Alabama. Washington spent thirty-four years as the guiding force at Tuskegee Institute, shaping the school into his vision of how African Americans could better their lot. In great demand as a speaker to white and black audiences alike, Washington received an honorary degree from Harvard College in 1891. Four years later, he was chosen as the principal speaker at the opening of the Negro section of the Cotton States and International Exposition in Atlanta, after which he became the most well-known African American in the United States, courted by corporate leaders, philanthropists, and United States presidents. His invitation by President Theodore Roosevelt to have dinner at the White House outraged southern white leaders, including one senator from South Carolina who charged that it was an act so obnoxious that it would require "lynching a thousand niggers in the South before they will learn their place again."[10]

Henry McNeal Turner was born a free black near Abbeville, South Carolina. Mostly self-taught, he joined the Methodist Episcopal Church, South, in 1848 and was licensed to preach in 1853. In 1858, he abandoned that denomination to become a minister in the African Methodist Episcopal (AME) Church, and by 1862 he was the pastor of the large Israel Church in Washington, D.C. During the Civil War he served as chaplain in the Union army, assigned to the 1st U.S. Colored Regiment. After the war, he became an official of the Freedmen's Bureau in Georgia and afterward held a succession of political appointments. One of the founders of the Republican Party in Georgia, Turner was made bishop of the AME Church in Georgia in 1880. In that position, he met and befriended Ida B. Wells, who also was a member of the AME Church.

William Edward Burghardt DuBois was born in Great Barrington, Massachusetts, one of approximately fifty blacks in a town of five thousand people. He was educated with the white children in the town's public school and, in 1885, was enrolled at Fisk University, a college for African Americans in Nashville, Tennessee. It was there, according to his autobiography, that he first encountered overt racial prejudice. Graduated from Fisk in 1888, he entered Harvard as a junior. He received his bachelor's degree in 1890 and his Ph.D. in 1895. His book, *The Philadelphia Negro,* was published in 1899. In this book DuBois asserted that the problems African Americans faced were the results of their history (slavery and racism) and environment, not of some imagined genetic inferiority. By the early twentieth century, he had emerged as Washington's principal rival as the leader of and spokesman for African Americans. In 1909, he was one of the founders of the National Association for the Advancement of Colored People (NAACP), a biracial group of white liberals and northern blacks who sought to overthrow Booker T. Washington, whom they generally considered too accommodating to powerful whites and too conservative in his strategies for African American progress.[11]

Frances Ellen Watkins Harper was born in Maryland in 1825, the only child of free parents. Orphaned at an early age, she was raised by an aunt, who enrolled her in a school for free blacks run by an uncle, who headed the Academy for Negro Youth and was a celebrated African American abolitionist (he was friends with both William Lloyd Garrison and Benjamin Lundy). Ending her formal education at the age of thirteen, Harper worked as a seamstress and needlework teacher. But she yearned to write and, in 1845, published her first book of poetry. It was

---

10. Robert J. Norrell, *Up from History: The Life of Booker T. Washington* (Cambridge: Harvard University Press, 2009), p. 4.

11. For the first decade or so of the NAACP's history, the majority of offices and power were held by whites, principally Mary White Ovington, William English Walling, and Oswald Garrison Villard. Other prominent white members included Jane Addams, John Dewey, Lincoln Steffens, William Dean Howells, Ray Stannard Baker, Stephen Wise, Clarence Darrow, and Franz Boaz.

✦ CHAPTER 2

The Road to
True Freedom:
African American
Alternatives in the
New South

later followed by ten more volumes of poetry (all commercially successful), a short story—the first to be published by a black woman—in 1859, and an immensely popular novel in 1892. She was a founder of the National Association of Colored Women, along with Ida B. Wells, and served as the organization's vice president. In 1860, she married Fenton Harper, who died in 1864. The couple had one child, a daughter, who was in continuous poor health and died in 1909.

This is not the first time that you have had to analyze speeches. Our society is virtually bombarded by speeches delivered by politicians, business figures, educators and others, most of whom are trying to convince us to adopt a set of ideas or actions. As we listen to such speeches, we invariably weigh the options presented to us, often using other available evidence to help us make our decisions. One purpose of this exercise is to help you think more critically and use evidence more thoroughly when assessing different options.

In analyzing the speeches in the Evidence, it would be very helpful to know the backgrounds of the respective speakers, as those backgrounds clearly may have influenced the speakers' ideas and proposals. For example, how would the fact that Washington lived and worked in Alabama and was dependent on white philanthropists and politicians help to shape his thinking? Or that DuBois was born and grew up in a town in western Massachusetts in which African Americans comprised only one percent of the population? Or that Wells and Harper were women? Before you begin analyzing the speeches in the Evidence, study the backgrounds of the speakers.

It is logical to begin by analyzing each of the speeches in turn. As you read each selection, make a rough chart like the one below to help you remember the main points.

Once you have carefully defined the alternatives presented by Wells, Washington, Turner, DuBois, and Harper, return to the Background section of the chapter. As you reread that section, determine the strengths and weaknesses of each alternative offered for African Americans living in the New South in the late nineteenth and early twentieth centuries. What evidence would you use to determine each alternative's strengths and weaknesses?

| African American Alternatives | | | |
|---|---|---|---|
| Speaker | Suggested Alternatives | How Does Speaker Develop Her/His Arguments? | Strengths and Weaknesses (Fill in later) |
| Wells | | | |
| Washington | | | |
| Turner | | | |
| DuBois | | | |
| Harper | | | |

◆

# The Evidence

Source 1 from Ida B. Wells, *United States Atrocities* (London: Lux Newspaper and Publishing Co., 1892), pp. 13–18. In the United States, the pamphlet was titled *Southern Horrors*. See Jacqueline Jones Royster, ed., *Southern Horrors and Other Writings: The Anti-Lynching Campaign of Ida B. Wells, 1892–1900* (Boston: Bedford Books, 1997), pp. 49–72.

## 1. Ida B. Wells's *United States Atrocities,* 1892 (excerpt).

Mr. Henry W. Grady, in his well-remembered speeches in New England and New York, pictured the Afro-American as incapable of self-government. Through him and other leading men the cry of the South to the country has been "Hands off! Leave us to solve our problem." To the Afro-American the South says, "The white man must and will rule." There is little difference between the Ante-bellum South and the New South. Her white citizens are wedded to any method however revolting, any measure however extreme, for the subjugation of the young manhood of the dark race. They have cheated him out of his ballot, deprived him of civil rights or redress in the Civil Courts thereof, robbed him of the fruits of his labour, and are still murdering, burning and lynching him.

The result is a growing disregard of human life. Lynch Law has spread its insiduous influence till men in New York State, Pennsylvania and on the free Western plains feel they can take the law in their own hands with impunity, especially where an Afro-American is concerned. The South is brutalised to a degree not realised by its own inhabitants, and the very foundation of government, law, and order are imperilled.

Public sentiment has had a slight "reaction," though not sufficient to stop the crusade of lawlessness and lynching. The spirit of Christianity of the great M. E. Church was sufficiently aroused by the frequent and revolting crimes against a powerless people, to pass strong condemnatory resolutions at its General Conference in Omaha last May. The spirit of justice of the grand old party[12] asserted itself sufficiently to secure a denunciation of the wrongs, and a feeble declaration of the belief in human rights in the Republican platform at Minneapolis, June 7th. A few of the great "dailies" and "weeklies" have swung into line declaring that Lynch Law must go. The President of the United States issued a proclamation that it be not tolerated in the territories over which he has jurisdiction. . . .

These efforts brought forth apologies and a short halt, but the lynching mania has raged again through the past twelve months with unabated fury. The strong

12. *Grand old party* refers to the Republican party, the GOP.

✦ CHAPTER 2

The Road to
True Freedom:
African American
Alternatives in the
New South

arm of the law must be brought to bear upon lynchers in severe punishment, but this cannot and will not be done unless a healthy public sentiment demands and sustains such action. The men and women in the South who disapprove of lynching and remain silent on the perpetration of such outrages are *particeps criminis*—accomplices, accessories before and after the fact, equally guilty with the actual law-breakers, who would not persist if they did not know that neither the law nor militia would be deployed against them.

In the creation of this healthier public sentiment, the Afro-American can do for himself what no one else can do for him. The world looks on with wonder that we have conceded so much, and remain law-abiding under such great outrage and provocation.

To Northern capital and Afro-American labour the South owes its rehabilitation. If labour is withdrawn capital will not remain. The Afro-American is thus the backbone of the South. A thorough knowledge and judicious exercise of this power in lynching localities could many times effect a bloodless revolution. The white man's dollar is his god, and to stop this will be to stop outrages in many localities.

The Afro-Americans of Memphis denounced the lynching of three of their best citizens, and urged and waited for the authorities to act in the matter, and bring the lynchers to justice. No attempt was made to do so, and the black men left the city by thousands, bringing about great stagnation in every branch of business. Those who remained so injured the business of the street car company by staying off the cars, that the superintendent, manager, and treasurer called personally on the editors of the *Free Speech,* and asked them to urge our people to give them their patronage again. Other business men became alarmed over the situation, and the *Free Speech* was suppressed that the coloured people might be more easily controlled. A meeting of white citizens in June, three months after the lynching, passed resolutions for the first time condemning it. *But they did not punish the lynchers.* Every one of them was known by name because they had been selected to do the dirty work by some of the very citizens who passed these resolutions! Memphis is fast losing her black population, who proclaim as they go that there is no protection for the life and property of any Afro-American citizen in Memphis who will not be a slave. . . .

*[Wells then urged African Americans in Kentucky to boycott railroads in the state, since the legislature had passed a law segregating passenger cars. She claimed that such a boycott would mean a loss to the railroads of $1 million per year.]*

The appeal to the white man's pocket has ever been more effectual than all the appeals ever made to his conscience. Nothing, absolutely nothing, is to be gained by a further sacrifice of manhood and self-respect. By the right exercise of his power as the industrial factor of the South, the Afro-American can demand and secure his rights, the punishment of lynchers, and a fair trial for members of his race accused of outrage.

Of the many inhuman outrages of this present year, the only case where the proposed lynching did *not* occur, was where the men armed themselves in Jacksonville, Florida, and Paducah, Kentucky, and prevented it. The only times an Afro-American who was assaulted got away has been when he had a gun, and used it in self-defence. The lesson this teaches, and which every Afro-American should ponder well, is that a Winchester rifle should have a place of honour in every black home, and it should be used for that protection which the law refuses to give. When the white man, who is always the aggressor, knows he runs a great risk of biting the dust every time his Afro-American victim does, he will have greater respect for Afro-American life. The more the Afro-American yields and cringes and begs, the more he has to do so, the more he is insulted, outraged, and lynched.

Source 2 from Louis R. Harlan, ed., *The Booker T. Washington Papers* (Urbana: University of Illinois Press, 1974), Vol. III, pp. 583–587.

## 2. Booker T. Washington's Atlanta Exposition Address (standard printed version), September 1895.

[Atlanta, Ga., Sept. 18, 1895]

Mr. President and Gentlemen of the Board of Directors and Citizens:

One-third of the population of the South is of the Negro race. No enterprise seeking the material, civil, or moral welfare of this section can disregard this element of our population and reach the highest success. I but convey to you, Mr. President and Directors, the sentiment of the masses of my race when I say that in no way have the value and manhood of the American Negro been more fittingly and generously recognized than by the managers of this magnificent Exposition at every stage of its progress. It is a recognition that will do more to cement the friendship of the two races than any occurrence since the dawn of our freedom.

Not only this, but the opportunity here afforded will awaken among us a new era of industrial progress. Ignorant and inexperienced, it is not strange that in the first years of our new life we began at the top instead of at the bottom; that a seat in Congress or the state legislature was more sought than real estate or industrial skill; that the political convention or stump speaking had more attractions than starting a dairy farm or truck garden.

◆ CHAPTER 2

The Road to
True Freedom:
African American
Alternatives in the
New South

A ship lost at sea for many days suddenly sighted a friendly vessel. From the mast of the unfortunate vessel was seen a signal, "Water, water; we die of thirst!" The answer from the friendly vessel at once came back, "Cast down your bucket where you are." A second time the signal, "Water, water; send us water!" ran up from the distressed vessel, and was answered, "Cast down your bucket where you are." And a third and fourth signal for water was answered, "Cast down your bucket where you are." The captain of the distressed vessel, at last heeding the injunction, cast down his bucket, and it came up full of fresh, sparkling water from the mouth of the Amazon River. To those of my race who depend on bettering their condition in a foreign land or who underestimate the importance of cultivating friendly relations with the Southern white man, who is their next-door neighbour, I would say: "Cast down your bucket where you are"—cast it down in making friends in every manly way of the people of all races by whom we are surrounded.

Cast it down in agriculture, mechanics, in commerce, in domestic service, and in the professions. And in this connection it is well to bear in mind that whatever other sins the South may be called to bear, when it comes to business, pure and simple, it is in the South that the Negro is given a man's chance in the commercial world, and in nothing is this Exposition more eloquent than in emphasizing this chance. Our greatest danger is that in the great leap from slavery to freedom we may overlook the fact that the masses of us are to live by the productions of our hands, and fail to keep in mind that we shall prosper in proportion as we learn to dignify and glorify common labour, and put brains and skill into the common occupations of life; shall prosper in proportion as we learn to draw the line between the superficial and the substantial, the ornamental gewgaws of life and the useful. No race can prosper till it learns that there is as much dignity in tilling a field as in writing a poem. It is at the bottom of life we must begin, and not at the top. Nor should we permit our grievances to overshadow our opportunities.

To those of the white race who look to the incoming of those of foreign birth and strange tongue and habits for the prosperity of the South, were I permitted I would repeat what I say to my own race, "Cast down your bucket where you are." Cast it down among the eight millions of Negroes whose habits you know, whose fidelity and love you have tested in days when to have proved treacherous meant the ruin of your firesides. Cast down your bucket among these people who have, without strikes and labour wars, tilled your fields, cleared your forests, builded your railroads and cities, and brought forth treasures from the bowels of the earth, and helped make possible this magnificent representation of the progress of the South. Casting down your bucket among my people, helping and encouraging them as you are doing on these grounds, and to education of head, hand, and heart, you will find that they will buy your surplus land, make blossom the waste places in your fields, and run your factories. While doing this, you can be sure in the future, as in the past, that you and your families will be surrounded by the most patient, faithful, law-abiding, and unresentful people that the world has seen. As we have proved our loyalty to you in the past, in nursing your children, watching by the sick-bed of your mothers and fathers, and often following them with tear-dimmed eyes to their graves, so in the future, in our humble way, we shall stand by you with a devotion that no foreigner can approach, ready to lay down our lives, if need be, in defense of yours, interlacing our industrial, commercial, civil, and religious life with yours in a way that shall make the interests of both races one. In all things that are purely social we can be as separate as the fingers, yet one as the hand in all things essential to mutual progress.

There is no defense or security for any of us except in the highest intelligence and development of all. If anywhere there are efforts tending to curtail the fullest growth of the Negro, let these efforts be turned into stimulating, encouraging, and making him the most useful and intelligent citizen. Effort or means so invested will pay a thousand per cent interest. These efforts will be twice blessed—"blessing him that gives and him that takes."

There is no escape through law of man or God from the inevitable:—

"The laws of changeless justice bind
    Oppressor with oppressed;
And close as sin and suffering joined
    We march to fate abreast."

Nearly sixteen millions of hands will aid you in pulling the load upward, or they will pull against you the load downward. We shall constitute one-third and more of the ignorance and crime of the South, or one-third [of] its intelligence and progress; we shall contribute one-third to the business and industrial prosperity of the South, or we shall prove a veritable body of death, stagnating, depressing, retarding every effort to advance the body politic.

Gentlemen of the Exposition, as we present to you our humble effort at an exhibition of our progress, you must not expect overmuch. Starting thirty years ago with ownership here and there in a few quilts and pumpkins and chickens (gathered from miscellaneous sources), remember the path that has led from these to the inventions and production of agricultural implements, buggies, steam-engines, newspapers, books, statuary, carving, paintings, the management of drug stores and banks, has not been trodden without contact with thorns and thistles. While we take pride in what we exhibit as a result of our independent efforts, we do not for a moment forget that our part in this exhibition would fall far short of your expectations but for the constant

✦ CHAPTER 2

The Road to
True Freedom:
African American
Alternatives in the
New South

help that has come to our educational life, not only from the Southern states, but especially from Northern philanthropists, who have made their gifts a constant stream of blessing and encouragement.

The wisest among my race understand that the agitation of questions of social equality is the extremest folly, and that progress in the enjoyment of all the privileges that will come to us must be the result of severe and constant struggle rather than of artificial forcing. No race that has anything to contribute to the markets of the world is long in any degree ostracized. It is important and right that all privileges of the law be ours, but it is vastly more important that we be prepared for the exercise of these privileges. The opportunity to earn a dollar in a factory just now is worth infinitely more than the opportunity to spend a dollar in an opera-house.

In conclusion, may I repeat that nothing in thirty years has given us more hope and encouragement, and drawn us so near to you of the white race, as this opportunity offered by the Exposition; and here bending, as it were, over the altar that represents the results of the struggles of your race and mine, both starting practically empty-handed three decades ago, I pledge that in your effort to work out the great and intricate problem which God has laid at the doors of the South, you shall have at all times the patient, sympathetic help of my race; only let this be constantly in mind, that, while from representations in these buildings of the product of field, of forest, of mine, of factory, letters, and art, much good will come, yet far above and beyond material benefits will be that higher good, that, let us pray God, will come, in a blotting out of sectional differences and racial animosities and suspicions in a determination to administer absolute justice, in a willing obedience among all classes to the mandates of law. This, coupled with our material prosperity, will bring into our beloved South a new heaven and a new earth.

Source 3 from Edwin S. Redkey, ed., *Respect Black: The Writings and Speeches of Henry McNeal Turner* (New York: Arno Press, 1971), pp. 167–171. Reprinted by permission.

### 3. Henry McNeal Turner's "The American Negro and His Fatherland," December 1895 (excerpt).

It would be a waste of time to expend much labor, the few moments I have to devote to this subject, upon the present status of the Negroid race in the United States. It is too well-known already. However, I believe that the Negro was brought to this country in the providence of God to a heaven-permitted if not a divine-sanctioned manual laboring school, that he might have direct contact with the mightiest race that ever trod the face of the globe.

The heathen Africans, to my certain knowledge, I care not what others may say, eagerly yearn for that civilization which they believe will elevate them and make them potential for good. The African was not sent and brought to this country by chance, or by the avarice of the white man, single and alone. The white slave-purchaser went to the shores of that continent and bought our ancestors from their African masters. The bulk who were brought to this country were the children of parents who had been in slavery a thousand years. Yet hereditary slavery is not universal among the African slaveholders. So that the argument often advanced, that the white man went to Africa and stole us, is not true. They bought us out of a slavery that still exists over a large portion of that continent. For there are millions and millions of slaves in Africa today. Thus the superior African sent us, and the white man brought us, and we remained in slavery as long as it was necessary to learn that a God, who is a spirit, made the world and controls it, and that that Supreme Being could be sought and found by the exercise of faith in His only begotten Son. Slavery then went down, and the colored man was thrown upon his own responsibility, and here he is today, in the providence of God, cultivating self-reliance and imbibing a knowledge of civil law in contradistinction to the dictum of one man, which was the law of the black man until slavery was overthrown. I believe that the Negroid race has been free long enough now to begin to think for himself and plan for better conditions [than] he can lay claim to in this country or ever will. *There is no manhood future in the United States for the Negro.* He may eke out an existence for generations to come, but he can never be a *man*—full, symmetrical and undwarfed. . . .

*[Here Turner asserted that a "great chasm" continued to exist between the races, that whites would have no social contact with blacks, and (without using Booker T. Washington's name) that any black who claimed that African Americans did not want social equality immediately "is either an ignoramus, or is an advocate of the perpetual servility and degradation of his race. . . . "]*

. . . And as such, I believe that two or three millions of us should return to the land of our ancestors, and establish our own nation, civilization, laws, customs, style of manufacture, and not only give the world, like other race varieties, the benefit of our individuality, but build up social conditions peculiarly our own, and cease to be grumblers, chronic complainers and a menace to the white man's country, or the country he claims and is bound to dominate.

The civil status of the Negro is simply what the white man grants of his own free will and accord. The black man can demand nothing. He is

✦ CHAPTER 2

The Road to
True Freedom:
African American
Alternatives in the
New South

deposed from the jury and tried, convicted and sentenced by men who do not claim to be his peers. On the railroads, where the colored race is found in the largest numbers, he is the victim of proscription, and he must ride in the Jim Crow car or walk. The Supreme Court of the United States decided, October 15th, 1883, that the colored man had no civil rights under the general government,[13] and the several States, from then until now, have been enacting laws which limit, curtail and deprive him of his civil rights, immunities and privileges, until he is now being disfranchised, and where it will end no one can divine. . . .

The discriminating laws, all will concede, are degrading to those against which they operate, and the degrader will be degraded also. "For all acts are reactionary, and will return in curses upon those who curse," said Stephen A. Douglass [*sic*], the great competitor of President Lincoln. Neither does it require a philosopher to inform you that degradation begets degradation. Any people oppressed, proscribed, belied, slandered, burned, flayed and lynched will not only become cowardly and servile, but will transmit that same servility to their posterity, and continue to do so *ad infinitum,* and as such will never make a bold and courageous people. The condition of the Negro in the United States is so repugnant to the instincts of respected manhood that thousands, yea hundreds of thousands, of miscegenated will pass for white, and snub the people with whom they are identified at every opportunity, thus destroying themselves, or at least *unracing* themselves. They do not want to be black because of its ignoble condition, and they cannot be white, thus they become monstrosities. Thousands of young men who are even educated by white teachers never have any respect for people of their own color and spend their days as devotees of white gods. Hundreds, if not thousands, of the terms employed by the white race in the English language are also degrading to the black man. Everything that is satanic, corrupt, base and infamous is denominated *black,* and all that constitutes virtue, purity, innocence, religion, and that which is divine and heavenly, is represented as *white.* Our Sabbath-school children, by the time they reach proper consciousness, are taught to sing to the laudation of white and to the contempt of black. Can any one with

13. On October 15, 1883, the Supreme Court handed down one decision that applied to five separate cases that had been argued before the Court, all of them having to do with racial segregation by private businesses (inns, hotels, theaters, and a railroad). Writing for the majority, Justice Joseph P. Bradley ruled that the Thirteenth, Fourteenth, and Fifteenth amendments did not give the federal government the power to outlaw discriminatory practices by private organizations, but only by states. See 109 U.S. 3, 3 S. Ct., 18, 27, L. Ed. 835 (1883).

an ounce of common sense expect that these children, when they reach maturity, will ever have any respect for their black or colored faces, or the faces of their associates? But, without multiplying words, the terms used in our religious experience, and the hymns we sing in many instances, are degrading, and will be as long as the black man is surrounded by the idea that *white* represents God and black represents the devil. The Negro should, therefore, build up a nation of his own, and create a language in keeping with his color, as the whites have done. Nor will he ever respect himself until he does it. . . .

What the black man needs is a country and surroundings in harmony with his color and with respect for his manhood. Upon this point I would delight to dwell longer if I had time. Thousands of white people in this country are ever and anon advising the colored people to keep out of politics, but they do not advise themselves. If the Negro is a man in keeping with other men, why should he be less concerned about politics than any one else? Strange, too, that a number of would-be colored leaders are ignorant and debased enough to proclaim the same foolish jargon. For the Negro to stay out of politics is to level himself with a horse or a cow, which is no politician, and the Negro who does it proclaims his inability to take part in political affairs. If the Negro is to be a man, full and complete, he must take part in everything that belongs to manhood. If he omits a single duty, responsibility or privilege, to that extent he is limited and incomplete.

Time, however, forbids my continuing the discussion of this subject, roughly and hastily as these thoughts have been thrown together. Not being able to present a dozen or two more phases, which I would cheerfully and gladly do if opportunity permitted, I conclude by saying the argument that it would be impossible to transport the colored people of the United States back to Africa is an advertisement of folly. Two hundred millions of dollars would rid this country of the last member of the Negroid race, if such a thing was desirable, and two hundred and fifty millions would give every man, woman and child excellent fare, and the general government could furnish that amount and never miss it, and that would only be the pitiful sum of a million dollars a year for the time we labored for nothing, and for which somebody or some power is responsible. The emigrant agents at New York, Boston, Philadelphia, St. John, N.B., and Halifax, N.S., with whom I have talked, establish beyond contradiction, that over a million, and from that to twelve hundred thousand persons, come to this country every year, and yet there is no public stir about it. But in the case of African emigration, two or three millions only of self-reliant men and women would be necessary to establish the conditions we are advocating in Africa.

◆ CHAPTER 2

The Road to
True Freedom:
African American
Alternatives in the
New South

Source 4 from Nathan Huggins, comp., *W. E. B. DuBois Writings* (New York: Library of America, 1986), pp. 842, 846–848, 860–861.

### 4. W. E. B. DuBois's "The Talented Tenth," 1903 (excerpt).

The Negro race, like all races, is going to be saved by its exceptional men. The problem of education, then, among Negroes must first of all deal with the Talented Tenth; it is the problem of developing the Best of this race that they may guide the Mass away from the contamination and death of the Worst, in their own and other races. Now the training of men is a difficult and intricate task. Its technique is a matter for educational experts, but its object is for the vision of seers. If we make money the object of man-training, we shall develop money-makers but not necessarily men; if we make technical skill the object of education, we may possess artisans but not, in nature, men. Men we shall have only as we make manhood the object of the work of the schools—intelligence, broad sympathy, knowledge of the world that was and is, and of the relation [of] men to it—this is the curriculum of that Higher Education which must underlie true life. On this foundation we may build bread-winning skill of hand and quickness of brain, with never a fear lest the child and man mistake the means of living for the object of life. . . .

*[Here DuBois argued against those who asserted that African American "leadership should have begun at the plow and not in the Senate" by stating that for 250 years blacks had been at the plow and were still "half-free serfs" without political rights. He then went on to say that many people focused their attention on "death, disease, and crime" among blacks, ignoring those who had achieved education, professions, homes, and the like.]*

Can the masses of the Negro people be in any possible way more quickly raised than by the effort and example of this aristocracy of talent and character? Was there ever a nation on God's fair earth civilized from the bottom upward? Never; it is, ever was and ever will be from the top downward that culture filters. The Talented Tenth rises and pulls all that are worth the saving up to their vantage ground. This is the history of human progress; and the two historic mistakes which have hindered that progress were the thinking first that no more could ever rise save the few already risen; or second, that it would better the unrisen to pull the risen down.

How then shall the leaders of a struggling people be trained and the hands of the risen few strengthened? There can be but one answer: The best and most capable of their youth must be schooled in the colleges and universities of the land. We will not quarrel as to just what the university of the Negro should teach or how it should teach it—I willingly admit that each soul and each race-soul needs its own peculiar curriculum. But this is true: A university is a human invention for the transmission of knowledge and culture from generation to generation, through the training of quick minds and pure hearts, and for this work no other human invention will suffice, not even trade and industrial schools.

All men cannot go to college but some men must; every isolated group or nation must have its yeast, must have for the talented few centers of training where men are not so mystified and befuddled by the hard and necessary toil of earning a living, as to have no aims higher than their bellies, and no God greater than Gold. This is true training, and thus in the beginning were the favored sons of the freedmen trained.

Thus, again, in the manning of trade schools and manual training schools we are thrown back upon the higher training as its source and chief support. There was a time when any aged and wornout carpenter could teach in a trade school. But not so to-day. Indeed the demand for college-bred men by a school like Tuskegee, ought to make Mr. Booker T. Washington the firmest friend of higher training. Here he has as helpers the son of a Negro senator, trained in Greek and the humanities, and graduated at Harvard; the son of a Negro congressman and lawyer, trained in Latin and mathematics, and graduated at Oberlin; he has as his wife, a woman who read Virgil and Homer in the same class room with me; he has as college chaplain, a classical graduate of Atlanta University; as teacher of science, a graduate of Fisk; as teacher of history, a graduate of Smith,— indeed some thirty of his chief teachers are college graduates, and instead of studying French grammars in the midst of weeds, or buying pianos for dirty cabins, they are at Mr. Washington's right hand helping him in a noble work. And yet one of the effects of Mr. Washington's propaganda has been to throw doubt upon the expediency of such training for Negroes, as these persons have had.

Men of America, the problem is plain before you. Here is a race transplanted through the criminal foolishness of your fathers. Whether you like it or not the millions are here, and here they will remain. If you do not lift them up, they will pull you down. Education and work are the levers to uplift a people. Work alone will not do it unless inspired by the right ideals and guided by intelligence. Education must not simply teach work—it must teach Life. The Talented Tenth of the Negro race must be made leaders of thought and missionaries of culture among their people. No others can do this work and Negro colleges must train men for it. The Negro race, like all other races, is going to be saved by its exceptional men.

[ 49 ]

✦ CHAPTER 2

The Road to
True Freedom:
African American
Alternatives in the
New South

Source 5 from Herbert Atheker, ed., *Pamphlets and Leaflets by W. E. B. DuBois* (White Plains, N.Y.: Kraus-Thomson Organization Ltd., 1986), pp. 63–65.

## 5. DuBois's Niagara Address, 1906 (excerpt).[14]

In detail our demands are clear and unequivocal. First, we would vote; with the right to vote goes everything: Freedom, manhood, the honor of your wives, the chastity of your daughters, the right to work, and the chance to rise, and let no man listen to those who deny this.

We want full manhood suffrage, and we want it now, henceforth and forever.

Second. We want discrimination in public accommodation to cease. Separation in railway and street cars, based simply on race and color, is un-American, undemocratic, and silly. We protest against all such discrimination.

Third. We claim the right of freemen to walk, talk, and be with them that wish to be with us. No man has a right to choose another man's friends, and to attempt to do so is an impudent interference with the most fundamental human privilege.

Fourth. We want the laws enforced against rich as well as poor; against Capitalist as well as Laborer; against white as well as black. We are not more lawless than the white race, we are more often arrested, convicted and mobbed. We want justice even for criminals and outlaws. We want the Constitution of the country enforced. We want Congress to take charge of Congressional elections. We want the Fourteenth Amendment carried out to the letter and every State disfranchised in Congress which attempts to disfranchise its rightful voters. We want the Fifteenth Amendment enforced and no State allowed to base its franchise simply on color.

The failure of the Republican Party in Congress at the session just closed to redeem its pledge of 1904 with reference to suffrage conditions [in] the South seems a plain, deliberate, and premeditated breach of promise, and stamps that party as guilty of obtaining votes under false pretense.

Fifth. We want our children educated. The school system in the country districts of the South is a disgrace and in few towns and cities are the Negro schools what they ought to be. We want the national government to step in and wipe out illiteracy in the South. Either the United States will destroy ignorance or ignorance will destroy the United States.

And when we call for education we mean real education. We believe in work. We ourselves are workers, but work is not necessarily education. Education is the development of power and ideal. We want our children trained as intelligent human beings should be, and we will fight for all time against any proposal to

---

14. The Niagara Movement was organized by DuBois in 1905. It called for agitation against all forms of segregation. This is a selection from DuBois's address to the group in 1906.

educate black boys and girls simply as servants and underlings, or simply for the use of other people. They have a right to know, to think, to aspire.

These are some of the chief things which we want. How shall we get them? By voting where we may vote, by persistent, unceasing agitation, by hammering at the truth, by sacrifice and work.

We do not believe in violence, neither in the despised violence of the raid nor the lauded violence of the soldier, nor the barbarous violence of the mob, but we do believe in John Brown, in that incarnate spirit of justice, that hatred of a lie, that willingness to sacrifice money, reputation, and life itself on the altar of right. And here on the scene of John Brown's martyrdom we reconsecrate ourselves, our honor, our property to the final emancipation of the race which John Brown died to make free.

Our enemies, triumphant for the present, are fighting the stars in their courses. Justice and humanity must prevail. We live to tell these dark brothers of ours—scattered in counsel, wavering and weak—that no bribe of money or notoriety, no promise of wealth or fame, is worth the surrender of a people's manhood or the loss of a man's self-respect. We refuse to surrender the leadership of this race to cowards and trucklers. We are men; we will be treated as men. On this rock we have planted our banners. We will never give up, though the trump of doom find us still fighting.

And we shall win. The past promised it, the present foretells it. Thank God for John Brown! Thank God for Garrison and Douglass! Sumner and Phillips, Nat Turner and Robert Gould Shaw,[15] and all the hallowed dead who died for freedom! Thank God for all those today, few though their voices be, who have not forgotten the divine brotherhood of all men, white and black, rich and poor, fortunate and unfortunate.

We appeal to the young men and women of this nation, to those whose nostrils are not yet befouled by greed and snobbery and racial narrowness: Stand up for the right, prove yourselves worthy of your heritage and whether born north or south dare to treat men as men. Cannot the nation that has absorbed ten million foreigners into its political life without catastrophe absorb ten million Negro Americans into that same political life at less cost than their unjust and illegal exclusion will involve?

Courage, brothers! The battle for humanity is not lost or losing. All across the skies sit signs of promise. The Slav is rising in his might, the yellow millions are tasting liberty, the black Africans are writhing toward the light, and everywhere the laborer, with ballot in his hand,

---

15. Robert Gould Shaw was a Massachusetts white man who during the Civil War commanded African American troops. While leading those soldiers into battle, Shaw was killed on July 18, 1863. He was portrayed in the 1989 film *Glory*.

♦ CHAPTER 2

The Road to
True Freedom:
African American
Alternatives in the
New South

is voting open the gates of Opportunity and Peace. The morning breaks over blood-stained hills. We must not falter, we may not shrink. Above are the everlasting stars.

Source 6 from Frances Smith Foster, ed., *A Brighter Coming Day: A Frances Ellen Watkins Harper Reader* (New York: Feminist Press, 1990), pp. 285–292.

### 6. Frances E. W. Harper's "Enlightened Motherhood," an Address to the Brooklyn Literary Society, November 15, 1892 (excerpt).

It is nearly thirty years since an emancipated people stood on the threshold of a new era, facing an uncertain future—a legally unmarried race, to be taught the sacredness of the marriage relation; an ignorant people, to be taught to read the book of the Christian law and to learn to comprehend more fully the claims of the gospel of the Christ of Calvary. A homeless race, to be gathered into homes of peaceful security and to be instructed how to plant around their firesides the strongest batteries against the sins that degrade and the race vices that demoralize. A race unversed in the science of government and unskilled in the just administration of law, to be translated from the old oligarchy of slavery into the new commonwealth of freedom, and to whose men came the right to exchange the fetters on their wrists for the ballots in their right hands—a ballot which, if not vitiated by fraud or restrained by intimidation, counts just as much as that of the most talented and influential man in the land.

While politicians may stumble on the barren mountain of fretful controversy, and men, lacking faith in God and the invisible forces which make for righteousness, may shrink from the unsolved problems of the hour, into the hands of Christian women comes the opportunity of serving the ever blessed Christ, by ministering to His little ones and striving to make their homes the brightest spots on earth and the fairest types of heaven. The school may instruct and the church may teach, but the home is an institution older than the church and antedates school, and that is the place where children should be trained for useful citizenship on earth and a hope of holy companionship in heaven. . . .

The home may be a humble spot, where there are no velvet carpets to hush your tread, no magnificence to surround your way, nor costly creations of painter's art or sculptor's skill to please your conceptions or gratify your tastes; but what are the costliest gifts of fortune when placed in the balance with the confiding love of dear children or the true devotion of a noble and manly husband whose heart can safely trust in his wife? You may place upon the brow of a true wife and mother the greenest laurels; you may crowd her hands with civic honors; but, after all, to her there will be no place like home, and the crown of her motherhood will be more precious than the diadem of a queen. . . .

Marriage between two youthful and loving hearts means the laying [of] the foundation stones of a new home, and the woman who helps erect that home should be careful not to build it above the reeling brain of a drunkard or the weakened fibre of a debauchee. If it be folly for a merchant to send an argosy, laden with the richest treasures, at midnight on a moonless sea, without a rudder, compass, or guide, is it not madness for a woman to trust her future happiness, and the welfare of the dear children who may yet nestle in her arms and make music and sunshine around her fireside, in the unsteady hands of a characterless man, too lacking in self-respect and self-control to hold the helm and rudder of his own life; who drifts where he ought to steer, and only lasts when he ought to live?

The moment the crown of motherhood falls on the brow of a young wife, God gives her a new interest in the welfare of the home and the good of society. If hitherto she had been content to trip through life a lighthearted girl, or to tread amid the halls of wealth and fashion the gayest of the gay, life holds for her now a high and noble service. She must be more than the child of pleasure or the devotee of fashion. Her work is grandly constructive. A helpless and ignorant babe lies smiling in her arms. God has trusted her with a child, and it is her privilege to help that child develop the most precious thing a man or woman can possess on earth, and that is a good character. Moth may devour our finest garments, fire may consume and floods destroy our fairest homes, rust may gather on our silver and tarnish our gold, but there is an asbestos that no fire can destroy, a treasure which shall be richer for its service and better for its use, and that is a good character. . . .

Are there not women, respectable women, who feel that it would wring their hearts with untold anguish, and bring their gray hairs in sorrow to the grave, if their daughters should trail the robes of their womanhood in the dust, yet who would say of their sons, if they were trampling their manhood down and fettering their souls with cords of vice, "O, well, boys will be boys, and young men will sow their wild oats."

I hold that no woman loves social purity as it deserves to be loved and valued, if she cares for the purity of her daughters and not her sons; who would gather her dainty robes from contact with the fallen woman and yet greet with smiling lips and clasp with warm and welcoming hands the author of her wrong and ruin. How many mothers to-day shrink from a double standard for society which can ostracise the woman and condone the offense of the man? How many mothers say within their hearts, "I intend to teach my boy to be as pure in his life, as chaste in his conversation, as the young girl

◆ CHAPTER 2

The Road to
True Freedom:
African American
Alternatives in the
New South

who sits at my side encircled in the warm clasp of loving arms?" How many mothers strive to have their boys shun the gilded saloon as they would the den of a deadly serpent? Not the mother who thoughtlessly sends her child to the saloon for a beverage to make merry with her friends. How many mothers teach their boys to shrink in horror from the fascinations of women, not as God made them, but as sin has degraded them? . . .

I would ask, in conclusion, is there a branch of the human race in the Western Hemisphere which has greater need of the inspiring and uplifting influences that can flow out of the lives and examples of the truly enlightened than ourselves? Mothers who can teach their sons not to love pleasure or fear death; mothers who can teach their children to embrace every opportunity, employ every power, and use every means to build up a future to contrast with the old sad past. Men may boast of the aristocracy of blood; they may glory in the aristocracy of talent, and be proud of the aristocracy of wealth, but there is an aristocracy which must ever outrank them all, and that is the aristocracy of character.

The work of the mothers of our race is grandly constructive. It is for us to build above the wreck and ruin of the past more stately temples of thought and action. Some races have been overthrown, dashed in pieces, and destroyed; but to-day the world is needing, fainting, for something better than the results of arrogance, aggressiveness, and indomitable power. We need mothers who are capable of being character builders, patient, loving, strong, and true, whose homes will be an uplifting power in the race. This is one of the greatest needs of the hour. No race can afford to neglect the enlightenment of its mothers. If you would have a clergy without virtue or morality, a manhood without honor, and a womanhood frivolous, mocking, and ignorant, neglect the education of your daughters. But if, on the other hand, you would have strong men, virtuous women, and good homes, then enlighten your women, so that they may be able to bless their homes by the purity of their lives, the tenderness of their hearts, and the strength of their intellects. From schools and colleges your children may come well versed in ancient lore and modern learning, but it is for us to learn and teach, within the shadow of our own homes, the highest and best of all sciences, the science of a true life. When the last lay of the minstrel shall die upon his ashy lips, and the sweetest numbers of the poet cease to charm his death-dulled ear; when the eye of the astronomer shall be too dim to mark the path of worlds that roll in light and power on high; and when all our earthly knowledge has performed for us its mission, and we are ready to lay aside our environments as garments we have outworn and outgrown: if we have learned the science of a true life, we may rest assured that this acquirement will go with us through the valley and shadow of death, only to grow lighter and brighter through the eternities.

# Questions to Consider

The Background section of this chapter strongly suggests that the prospects for African Americans in the post-Reconstruction South were bleak. Although blacks certainly preferred sharecropping or tenancy to working in gangs as in the days of slavery, neither system offered African Americans much chance to own their own land. Furthermore, the industrial opportunities available to European immigrants, which allowed many of them gradually to climb the economic ladder, were generally closed to southern blacks, in part because the South was never able to match the North in the creation of industrial jobs and in part because what jobs the New South industrialization did create often were closed to blacks. As we have seen, educational opportunities for African Americans in the South were severely limited—so much so that by 1890, more than 75 percent of the adult black population in the Deep South remained illiterate (as opposed to 17.1 percent of the adult white population). In addition, rigid segregation laws and racial violence had increased dramatically. Indeed, the prospects for southern blacks were far from promising.

Begin by analyzing Ida B. Wells's response (Source 1) to the deteriorating condition of African Americans in the South. In her view, how did blacks in Memphis and Kentucky provide a model for others? What was that model? In addition to that model, Wells tells us how blacks in Jacksonville, Florida, and Paducah, Kentucky, were able to prevent lynchings in those towns. What alternative did those blacks present? Was Wells advocating it? Finally, what role did Wells see the African American press playing in preventing lynchings?

The alternative presented by Booker T. Washington (Source 2) differs markedly from those offered by Wells. In his view, what *process* should African Americans follow to enjoy their full rights? How did he support his argument? What did Washington conceive the role of southern whites in African Americans' progress to be? Remember that his *goals* were roughly similar to those of Wells. Also use some inference to imagine how Washington's audiences would have reacted to his speech. How would southern whites have greeted his speech? Southern blacks? What about northern whites? Northern blacks? To whom was Washington speaking?

Now move on to Henry McNeal Turner's alternative (Source 3). At first Bishop Turner seems to be insulting blacks. What was he really trying to say? Why did he think that God ordained blacks to be brought to America in chains? In Turner's view, once blacks were freed, what was their best alternative? Why? Turner's view of whites is at serious odds with that of Washington. How do the two views differ on this point? Why do you think this was so? How did Turner use his view of whites to support his alternative for blacks?

Taken together, the two speeches by W. E. B. DuBois (Sources 4 and 5) present a consistent view, even though their subject matter and emphasis are

♦ CHAPTER 2

The Road to
True Freedom:
African American
Alternatives in the
New South

different. What was the "Talented Tenth"? In DuBois's view, what crucial role must that group play? How is that view at odds with Washington's view? In his Niagara Address of 1906, DuBois states what the goals of the "Talented Tenth" should be. What are those objectives? How does his suggested *process* differ from that of Washington? Furthermore, how does DuBois's view differ from Washington's with respect to timing? Tactics? Tone? Remember, however, that the long-term goals of both men were similar.

Perhaps you have been struck by the fact that both Turner and DuBois pinned their hopes for progress on African American *men*. Turner refers frequently to "manhood" and DuBois to "exceptional men." Why do you think this was so? Why do you think the concept of African American manhood was important to these two thinkers?

For Frances E. W. Harper (Source 6), the hopes of African Americans lay not with black men but with black *women*. Why did she believe this was so? As opposed to education, work, or the political arena, in Harper's view what was the importance of the African American home? Would Harper have agreed or disagreed with Wells? Washington? Turner? DuBois? How might African American men such as Washington, Turner, and DuBois have reacted to her arguments?

The ideas of Wells and Harper differed significantly from those of Washington, Turner, and DuBois. What role do you think gender played in the formation of Wells's and Harper's ideas? Of Washington's? Turner's? DuBois's?

After you have examined each of the alternatives, move on to your assessment of the strengths and weaknesses of each argument. As noted earlier, you will need to review the Background section of this chapter in order to establish the historical context in which the five arguments were made. Then, keeping in mind that context, try to imagine the reactions that these alternatives might have elicited in the following situations:

1. What would have happened if southern African Americans had adopted Wells's alternatives? Where might the process outlined by Wells have led? Were there any risks for African Americans? If so, what were they?
2. What would have happened if southern African Americans had adopted Washington's alternative? How long would it have taken them to realize Washington's goals? Were there any risks involved? If so, what were they?
3. What would have happened if southern African Americans had adopted Turner's alternative? Were there any risks involved? How realistic was Turner's option?
4. What would have happened if southern African Americans had adopted DuBois's alternative? How long would DuBois's process have taken? Were there any risks involved?
5. Was white assistance necessary according to Wells? To Washington? To Turner? To DuBois? How did each spokesperson perceive the roles of the federal government and the federal courts? How did the

government and courts stand on this issue at the time? [*Clue:* What was the Supreme Court decision in *Plessy v. Ferguson* (1896)?]

6. How might blacks and whites have reacted to Harper's arguments? Black women? Black men? As with the ideas of Washington, how long would it have taken African Americans who embraced Harper's ideas to reach the goals of social, economic, and political equality?

To be sure, it is very nearly impossible for us to put ourselves completely in the shoes of these men and women. Although racism still is a strong force in American life today, the intellectual and cultural environment was dramatically different in the time these five spokespersons were offering their ideas to African Americans. Even so, by placing each spokesperson in a historical context, we should be able to evaluate the strengths and weaknesses of each argument.

◆

# Epilogue

For the advocates of the New South, the realization of their dream seemed to be right over the horizon, always just beyond their grasp. Many factories did make a good deal of money, but profits often flowed out of the South to northern investors. And factory owners usually maintained profits by paying workers pitifully low wages, which led to the rise of a poor white urban class that lived in slums and faced enormous problems of malnutrition, poor health, family instability, and crime. To most of those who had left their meager farms to find opportunities in the burgeoning southern cities, life there appeared even worse than it had been in the rural areas. Many whites returned to their rural homesteads disappointed and dispirited by urban life. For African Americans, their collective lot was even worse.

For roughly twenty years after his 1895 Atlanta address, Booker T. Washington remained the nominal leader of

and spokesman for African Americans. On the surface an accommodationist and a gradualist, beneath the surface Washington worked to secure government jobs for blacks; protested discrimination on railroads, in voting, in education, and regarding lynching; and organized and funded court challenges to disfranchisement, all-white juries, and peonage. By 1913, he had openly criticized southern white leaders, stating that "the best white citizenship must take charge of the mob and not have the mob take charge of civilization."[16]

Yet Washington's style, as well as his jealous guarding of his own power, caused serious divisions among black leaders. African American editor William Monroe Trotter accused Washington of being "a miserable toady"

16. Norrell, *Up from History*, pp. 392–293, 408–410.

◆ CHAPTER 2

The Road to
True Freedom:
African American
Alternatives in the
New South

and "the Benedict Arnold of the Negro race." The NAACP was founded by Washington's critics in 1909 with the main objective of wresting power from Washington and being considerably more assertive in demanding equal rights for the nation's black people.[17]

Yet at the May 1909 organizational meeting of the NAACP, Washington's opponents were themselves sharply divided. DuBois purposely removed Wells-Barnett's name from the Committee of Forty (later the "Founding Forty"), causing her to walk out of the meeting (she later returned), perhaps because he feared that she was too strident, or because she opposed so many of the organization's offices being given to whites, or because he feared her popularity and power. It took years for the chasm and the power struggle within the organization to be mended.[18]

Meanwhile, for an increasing number of African Americans, the solution

seemed to be to abandon the South entirely. Beginning around the time of World War I (1917–1918), a growing number of African Americans migrated to the industrial cities of the Northeast, Midwest, and West Coast (Source 7). But there, too, they met racial hostility and racially inspired riots.

In the North, African Americans could vote and thereby influence public policy. By the late 1940s, it had become clear that northern urban African American voters, by their very number, could force politicians to deal with racial discrimination. By the 1950s, it seemed equally evident that the South would have to change its racial policies, if not willingly then by force. It took federal courts, federal marshals, and occasionally federal troops, but the crust of discrimination in the South began to be broken in the 1960s. Attitudes changed slowly, but the white southern politician draped in the Confederate flag and calling for resistance to change became a figure of the past. Although much work still needed to be done, the Civil Rights Movement brought profound change to the South, laying the groundwork for more changes ahead. Indeed, by the 1960s, the industrialization and prosperity (largely through in-migration) of the Sunbelt seemed to show that Grady's dream of a New South might become a reality.

Yet, for all the hopeful indications (black voting and officeholding in the South, for instance), in many ways the picture was a somber one. By the 1970s, several concerned observers, both black and white, feared that the poorest 30 percent of all black families, instead of climbing slowly up the economic

---

17. For Trotter see David L. Lewis, *W. E. B. DuBois: A Biography* (New York: Henry Holt & Co., 2009), pp. 78–79 and *passim*; Norrell, *Up from History*, pp. 6–7. Trotter graduated from Harvard in 1895, the first man of color to be awarded a Phi Beta Kappa key.

18. The story of the DuBois-Wells conflict at the May 1909 meeting has been often told. See Lewis, *W. E. B. DuBois*, p. 259; Patricia A. Schechter, *Ida B. Wells-Barnett and American Reform, 1880–1930* (Chapel Hill: University of North Carolina Press, 2001), pp. 136–137; Linda O. McMurry, *To Keep the Waters Troubled: The Life of Ida B. Wells* (New York: Oxford University Press, 1998), pp. 280–282; and Giddings, *Ida*, pp. 474–479. Mary White Ovington, a white leader in the NAACP, later wrote that Wells-Barnett was "perhaps not fitted to accept the restraint of organization." See Ovington's *The Walls Came Tumbling Down* (New York: Schocken Books, 1947), p. 106.

Source 7 from U.S. Bureau of the Census, *Historical Statistics of the United States, Colonial Times to 1970* (Washington, D.C.: U.S. Government Printing Office, 1975), Vol. I, p. 95.

## 7. Estimated Net Intercensal Migration* of Negro Population by Region, 1870–1920 (in thousands).

| Region | 1870–1880 | 1880–1890 | 1890–1900 | 1900–1910 | 1910–1920 |
|---|---|---|---|---|---|
| New England[1] | 4.5 | 6.6 | 14.2 | 8.0 | 12.0 |
| Middle Atlantic[2] | 19.2 | 39.1 | 90.7 | 87.2 | 170.1 |
| East North Central[3] | 20.8 | 16.4 | 39.4 | 45.6 | 200.4 |
| West North Central[4] | 15.7 | 7.9 | 23.5 | 10.2 | 43.7 |
| South Atlantic[5] | −47.9 | −72.5 | −181.6 | −111.9 | −158.0 |
| East South Central[6] | −56.2 | −60.1 | −43.3 | −109.6 | −246.3 |
| West South Central[7] | 45.1 | 62.9 | 56.9 | 51.0 | −46.2 |

*A net intercensal migration represents the amount of migration that took place between U.S. censuses, which are taken every ten years. The net figure is computed by comparing in-migration to with out-migration from a particular state. A minus figure means that out-migration from a state was greater than in-migration to it.
1. Maine, New Hampshire, Vermont, Massachusetts, Rhode Island, and Connecticut.
2. New York, New Jersey, and Pennsylvania.
3. Ohio, Indiana, Illinois, Michigan, and Wisconsin.
4. Minnesota, Iowa, Missouri, North Dakota, South Dakota, Nebraska, and Kansas.
5. Delaware, Maryland, District of Columbia, Virginia, West Virginia, North Carolina, South Carolina, Georgia, and Florida.
6. Kentucky, Tennessee, Alabama, and Mississippi.
7. Arkansas, Louisiana, Oklahoma, and Texas.

ladder, were in the process of forming a permanent underclass, complete with a social pathology that included crime, drugs, violence, and grinding poverty. Equally disturbing in the 1980s was a new wave of racial intolerance among whites, a phenomenon that even invaded many American colleges and universities. In short, although much progress had been made since the turn of the nineteenth century, in many ways, as in the New South, the dream of equality and tolerance remained over the horizon.

By this time, of course, Wells, Washington, Turner, DuBois, and Harper were dead. Wells continued to write militant articles for the African American press, became deeply involved in the women's suffrage movement, and carried on a successful crusade to prevent the racial segregation of the Chicago city schools. She died in Chicago in 1931. For his part, Washington publicly clung to his notion of self-help while secretly supporting more aggressive efforts to gain political rights for African Americans. He died in Tuskegee, Alabama, in 1915.

✦ CHAPTER 2

The Road to
True Freedom:
African American
Alternatives in the
New South

Turner's dream of thousands of blacks moving to Africa never materialized. In response, he grew more strident and critical of African Americans who opposed his ideas. In 1898, Turner raised a storm of protest when his essay "God Is a Negro" was published. The essay began, "We have as much right . . . to believe that God is a Negro, as you buckra, or white, people have to believe that God is a fine looking, symmetrical and ornamented white man."[19] He died while on a speaking trip to Canada in 1915. As for DuBois, he eventually turned away from his championship of a "Talented Tenth" in favor of more mass protests. As a harbinger of many African Americans of the 1960s and 1970s, he embraced pan-Africanism, combining it with his long-held Marxist ideas. He died in Ghana on the midnight before the historic March on Washington of August 28, 1963. DuBois's death was announced to the 250,000 who attended the event just a few minutes before the Rev. Martin Luther King, Jr. began his "I Have a Dream" speech. To many people, the two events taking place on the same day represented a symbolic passing of the torch of African American leadership from DuBois to King.[20]

Harper was one of the most popular poets of her time. After her husband's death, she became increasingly vocal on feminist issues, was a friend and ally of Susan B. Anthony, and, in 1866, delivered a moving address before the National Women's Rights Convention. She died in Philadelphia, Pennsylvania, from heart disease in 1911. Her home has been preserved as a national historic landmark.

In their time, Wells, Washington, Turner, DuBois, and Harper were important and respected figures. Although often publicly at odds with one another, they shared the same dream of African Americans living with pride and dignity in a world that recognized them as equal men and women. In an era in which few people championed the causes of African Americans in the New South, these five spokespersons stood out as courageous individuals.

19. Redkey, *Respect Black:* pp. 176–177.

20. Lewis, *W. E. B. DuBois*, pp. 1–4.

# 3

# Selling Consumption, 1890–1930

◆

## The Problem

In the fall of 1894, Civil War veteran Benjamin Armstead Rogers left his home in middle Tennessee to start a new chapter of his life in Florence, Alabama, population 6,500. With his two sons, Benjamin Jr. and Thomas, the fifty-eight-year-old retired lawyer established a store on Court Street, in the center of Florence's emerging commercial district. The Rogers family operated that business, on that same site, for over one hundred years.

B. A. Rogers built a successful company and outlasted his competitors by embracing innovative business practices and bringing big-city shopping experiences to this small Alabama town. Rogers announced the opening of his "Surprise Store" in the *Florence Times*; within a year he was buying full-page advertisements with arresting graphics touting the latest fashions. While his competition continued to advertise dry goods as "yours for corn," Rogers abandoned the barter tradition. The "Surprise Store" was the first one-price retailer in Florence, with newspaper advertisements promising customers "a square deal to All Alike." Every visitor to the store was warmly greeted and equally treated, whether or

not they made a purchase. B. A. Rogers bought a broader array of merchandise from more markets more frequently than other merchants in Florence. Seeing the success of Sears Roebuck & Company, he added a mail order department to expand his customer base. In 1901, a full-page advertisement in the *Florence Times* proclaimed the store "Santa Claus Headquarters." The following spring, the store hosted a UDC day, with proceeds from that day's receipts contributing to a Confederate Veteran's Monument. When B. A. passed away in 1902, Thomas took over the business. He successfully pressured the city council to pass an ordinance mandating the removal of dilapidated fences on Court Street. And he paid for the first cement sidewalk in town to front what after 1910 became known as Rogers Department Store. That year, when a fire destroyed the original space, Thomas Rogers oversaw the construction of a three-story, 27,000-square-foot establishment, with mahogany-paneled elevators to carry customers to various departments of the immaculately maintained store. Thomas became the head of the Chamber of Commerce, sat on the board of directors for the city's new hospital, and championed municipal funding of bridges and roads. His son followed in his footsteps, as did his son's son, and for a hundred years, the family business never experienced a losing year.[1]

B. A. Rogers introduced to Florence, Alabama, a new culture of department store shopping, savvy advertising, and conspicuous consumption that was sweeping America at the turn of the twentieth century. Why did this consumer culture emerge in the late nineteenth and early twentieth centuries? What values did modern department stores tap into? What changes did these stores reflect? What can consumer culture tell us about America at the turn of the twentieth century?

✦

## Background

Between the 1890s and the 1920s, the United States was profoundly altered by industrialization. The process of mechanizing the production of goods emerged in Europe in the late eighteenth century and was transplanted into the young American republic. Some American cities adopted factory-based textile production in the early nineteenth century. The steamboat, canals, and particularly the coming of the railroad all influenced the U.S. economy in that era. Some scholars point out that the rise of consumer culture can be traced even further back in time. But none of these changes was as transformative as those that emerged after the American Civil War. Driven in large measure by the rapid growth of railroads in the second half of the nineteenth century, American industries became truly national in scope. Raw materials could be transported from previously remote, inaccessible areas; economical, identical factory-produced goods reached an ever-widening cross-section of Americans. Coal from eastern Kentucky, oil from Texas, meat from Chicago, and textiles from New York City crisscrossed the country. Opportunity fueled innovation—and prodigious profits for a select few. By the turn of the twentieth century, the industrial process was becoming increasingly dominated by one or two gigantic corporations that could basically set prices and control markets. The success of those corporations created a new class of fabulously rich industrialists—captains of industry to their friends, robber barons to their enemies. So sweeping was their power that names like Armour, Westinghouse, Pillsbury, Rockefeller, and Carnegie became household words, as much for the renown of the industrialists as for the goods they created. Many Americans still recognize those names and their products today.

Urbanization went hand in hand with industrialization. One of the defining features of the period between the 1890s and the 1920s was the tremendous

1. Author interview with Thomas McLemore Rogers III, March 1991; *Florence Times*, miscellaneous issues, 1894–1911.

growth of cities. Urban growth occurred on every level, from county seats to major metropolitan centers. In the past, the sizes of cities had been limited by the availability of nearby food, fuel, and employment opportunities. But the expanding network of railroads and the rise of large factories removed those limitations. The number of large cities grew exponentially. In 1860, only nine American cities had populations larger than 100,000. Within two decades, that number more than doubled, to twenty. By 1890, there were thirty-eight cities with more than 100,000 residents. New York City, the largest metropolis then as now, hit the 1,000,000 resident mark in 1880. More and more Americans migrated to cities—large and small—drawn by jobs and dreams of upward mobility. But only half the growth of cities can be attributed to rural-to-urban migration. The other half of these burgeoning city populations were foreign immigrants.[2]

Cities increasingly set much of the tone for the entire nation, and urbanization alongside industrialization altered nearly every facet of American society. Railroads standardized time. Factories linked work to wage earning and separated work from home, with powerful consequences for middle-class women. Even the most intimate parts of peoples' lives were transformed. Family size decreased. As families became dependent on wages, couples consciously limited the number of children they had, sometimes through what today is known as the "rhythm method" and sometimes through new technologies.

The impact of industrialization and urbanization, while thoroughgoing, varied according to class. Factory work attracted foreign immigrants, including significant numbers of poor, unskilled workers who were quickly exploited by profit-driven industrialists. Recent immigrants tended to congregate in large cities—where most of the jobs were—and great numbers suffered in abject poverty. Some working-class Americans rejected the consumer culture fueling industrial expansion. Workers tried to unionize—and were often met by company-led and government-sanctioned violence. Some embraced socialism as an alternative to capitalism. Anarchists such as Emma Goldman represented an even more extreme response to the damaging costs of unchecked industrial growth. Semi-skilled workers and middle-class professionals, meanwhile, benefited from the exploitation of immigrant and unskilled laborers. Members of the middle class saw their earning potential and status rise during the industrial era. And they bought the goods produced in dangerous, oppressive, largely unregulated factories. A growing proportion of Americans—excluding the poorest working classes—could afford to enjoy electric lights, streetcars, telephones, household appliances, and, eventually, Henry Ford's automobile.

As factories produced more and more to buy, advertisers convinced Americans that they needed goods that were by their very nature optional luxuries. Today, Americans are inundated with

2. For a brief overview of urban growth in this era, see Robert G. Barrows, "Urbanizing America," in Charles W. Calhoun, ed., *The Gilded Age: Perspectives on the Origins of Modern America* (Rowman and Littlefield, 2006), pp. 91–110.

advertising. Each new technology, from television to the Internet, offers market researchers novel venues for selling products. Alongside these new methods, older approaches—radio broadcasts, print advertisements, billboards—continue to create consumer desire. Yet advertising is a relatively new phenomenon, developing in the late nineteenth and early twentieth centuries. Even as late as the 1860s and 1870s, most merchants announced the availability of goods through simple newspaper notices, akin to modern "want ads." But those traditional practices faded fast around the turn of the century. Sears Roebuck & Company was founded in 1893, and its "wish book," or catalogue, rapidly became popular reading for millions of people, especially those who lived in rural areas. Almost one thousand pages long, these catalogues offered a dazzling variety of consumer goods and were filled with testimonial letters from satisfied customers.

More and more businessmen realized that sustaining profits on mass-produced consumer goods demanded a national market—and therefore national marketing campaigns. Smaller entrepreneurs such as B. A. Rogers saw that, just like the large corporations, they would thrive by campaigning for customers and creating a brand identity. Advertising expenditures boomed. American companies spent $40 million on advertising in 1880 and $140 million in 1904.

Advertisers had to convince consumers that their products were more than desirable—they were necessary. In the process of selling merchandise, advertising innovations reshaped culture. Advertising not only helped differentiate one brand of product from another,

or one store from its competition; it also helped break down regional disparities and differences between rural and urban lifestyles. Women living on farms in Kansas could order the latest New York fashions from a mail-order catalogue, and families in small midwestern towns or the rural Southwest could acquire the newest furniture and appliances enticingly displayed in mass-circulation magazines. More and more people abandoned traditional approaches to doing things and embraced new ways of life that resulted from the application of modern technology, mass production, and efficient distribution of products. Why undertake the time-consuming, onerous task of making soap if you could buy better-quality "Ivory" in town? Procter & Gamble marketed their soap as pure and inexpensive, and in their first slogan declared "It Floats!"

Perhaps no innovation better illustrates the merging of industrialization, urbanization, advertising, and consumerism than the rise of downtown department stores. Such businesses did not exist before the second half of the nineteenth century. Before then, larger merchants practiced specialization, whereas dry goods dealers maintained a wider, if sporadic, range of goods. Wherever they acquired goods, Americans could expect to haggle over price. Personal relationships often factored into these transactions. The barter system still remained the standard means of acquiring goods. Farmers and laborers swapped eggs or tobacco or services like blacksmithing for finished products. Customers were expected to leave having affected a trade—"shopping" in the modern sense of looking without buying was rare and disdained. Returns were infrequent and unpleasant.

Borrowing a new business model emerging in Europe, American department store innovators changed all of this.[3] John Wanamaker in Philadelphia, Adam Gimbel in Milwaukee, Marshall Field in Chicago, and Rowland Macy in New York City led the way. They diversified goods and constantly updated their inventories. Merchandise was grouped according to type in "departments" and displayed to convey attractiveness and opulence. Visiting was actively encouraged, pressuring sales shunned. Returns were graciously obliged, and every item that proved unsatisfactory merited a full refund. Perhaps most importantly, prices were fixed and prominently displayed. "One price" shopping became a hallmark of every successful department store in America. Buying in bulk, pricing close to the margin, and offering stellar service allowed department store entrepreneurs to enjoy rapid turnover of their inventory—and consistently strong profits.

Marketing infused every level of department store culture. The desire to cater to customers with a vast variety of merchandise pushed physical expansion. Space became its own promotion as retailers put a great deal of time and money into fashioning the most attractive setting for their wages. For example, in 1903, Wanamaker's opened its new flagship department store. It stood twelve stories high, with a 150-foot tall

grand court. The court was anchored at one end with the second largest organ in the world. When Gimbel's opened its new store in 1927, it contained no less than twenty seven escalators. The point was to awe—and therefore attract—shoppers. Wanamaker's organ, like Marshall Field's clock and Macy's windows, became hallmarks of these stores' identities.

Leading entrepreneurs focused on architectural beauty married to technological innovation. Stores moved to more open, light-infused interiors. After 1890, innovations made it possible to cheaply produce large, strong plate glass windows. Glass display cases added to the luster of the shopping experience. Department store magnates were at the forefront of adopting electric lighting, much to the delight of visitors. Electric lights extended shopping hours and cultivated an image of progressive, alluring fashionableness that customers could, literally, buy into. Successful establishments were immaculately maintained, but the emphasis on cleanliness transcended sanitation. Both Macy's and Wanamaker's installed telephone systems in the 1880s in order to avoid the visual clutter and physical agitation of runners. Pneumatic tube systems (like those at today's drive-in banks) also efficiently and subtly conveyed paperwork and cash. Gimbel's introduced cash registers, to the same effect, in the 1880s. In 1913, the already iconic Milwaukee store erected the largest electrical sign in the world. It contained 2,500 lights and reputedly could be seen from thirty miles away. Small-city entrepreneurs adopted these strategies. The second building of Rogers Department Store

3. Aristide Boucicaut originated the idea of a "department store" in Paris in the 1850s.

[ 65 ]

in Florence, Alabama, was fronted by street-level large glass show windows, and mahogany-paneled elevators transported guests from floor to floor.

Visitors to major retailers were treated to innovative spectacles and inspired service. By 1910 and the 1920s, department stores such as Macy's maintained pet shops, restaurants, rooftop gardens, and art exhibits. They hired musicians, put on seasonal entertainments, and hosted community activities. Stores introduced an ever-widening range of services to draw in prospective customers and make it easier for them to linger. The largest retailers offered free nurseries for the young children of browsing mothers, complimentary candy and flowers to shoppers, lending libraries, post offices, and telegraph stations.[4]

Department stores enlivened the downtowns that begat them; they made city centers exciting, inviting places for all classes of men and women to visit. Unlike other venues of entertainment—theatres, zoos, museums— department stores never charged admission. Department stores were aided in invigorating downtowns by transportation innovations. By 1890, five hundred

street railway lines in three hundred U.S. cities, mostly electric streetcars or trolleys, safely and conveniently ferried shoppers from the ever-expanding borders of urban centers. Department store owners promoted the cities that made them rich. They intentionally fostered festive moods in their stores and acted as boosters within their communities. Stores sponsored fairs, civic pride events, and parades—most famously, perhaps, the Macy's Thanksgiving Day Parade, inaugurated in 1924.

Customers learned of all of these innovations through brilliant advertising campaigns. John Wanamaker, the visionary entrepreneur behind Philadelphia's famous "Grand Depot," built his department store empire on this conviction: "The time to advertise is all the time." Department store magnates were not only selling consumer goods—they were selling their name and an identity to their customers. Between the 1870s and the 1920s, print advertising—and, indeed, the newspaper business—was transformed, with department stores at the forefront of marketing trends. Rowland Macy led the shift away from classified-style advertising. He marketed his goods using imaginative layouts, arresting visuals, and compelling copy. John Wanamaker bought the first full-page newspaper advertisement for his store in 1879. The innovations of Wanamaker and Macy spread like wildfire, because they worked. Over 70,000 people came to opening day at Wanamaker's in 1877. Through savvy marketing, Macy's quickly became the leading retailer in New York City; its sales topped $1,000,000 in 1870. Department

4. This chapter's discussion of department stores relies particularly on Susan Porter Benson, *Counter Cultures: Saleswomen, Managers, and Customers in American Department Stores, 1890–1940* (University of Illinois Press, 1987); and William R. Leach, "Transformations in a Culture of Consumption: Women and Department Stores, 1890–1925," *Journal of American History* 71 (September 1984): 319–342. See also William R. Leach, *Land of Desire: Merchants, Power, and the Rise of a New American Culture* (Vintage, 1994); and Jan Whitaker, *Service and Style: How the American Department Store Fashioned the Middle Class* (St. Martin's, 2006).

stores such as Wanamaker's and Macy's profited so handsomely by promoting conspicuous consumption. In 1908, a retailer aptly observed, "fashion imparts to merchandise a value over and above its intrinsic worth." Self-consciously creating an image of fashionableness, retail magnates succeeded in convincing shoppers that style was necessary. Their department stores became the main institutional expression of capitalist consumerism.[5]

The consumer culture embodied by department stores particularly influenced women's lives. Until the post-Civil War era, most middle-class Americans believed that the proper place for women was in the home. Men occupied the public sphere of politics and business while women held dominion over the household and children. The domestic sphere protected women from the perils of the larger world. But department stores drew women into that public world, where they often traveled alone or only in the company of other women. Shopping made them more commercially engaged and the principal arbiters of fashion. Department store advertisements promoted this new image of womanhood—which was very much in their fiscal interest. Among other things, department stores also helped erode class distinctions between women. These businesses carried a wide price-range of goods and marketed themselves to middle-rank women as well as working classes. Fake jewels and furs allowed non-elite women to "dress up"—to erase the stark lines between elites and non-elites.

Women were not only the main consumers of department store culture; they contributed to the supply side as well. Women worked for lower wages than men, which certainly mattered to business leaders. More importantly, they were perceived to truly understand the predominately female customer base. Finally, department store managers believed that women were more ethical than men. This stereotype helped encourage the hiring of female store clerks and buyers. As one retailer explained, "I've been a manager thirteen years, and we never had but four dishonest girls, and we've had over forty boys in the same time. Boys smoke and lose at cards, and do a hundred things that women don't, and they get worse instead of better. I go in for women." For all these reasons, department stores recruited growing numbers of women as both clerks and buyers. In 1880, 8,000 women worked in retail sales. By 1890, that number had swelled to 58,000. John Wanamaker hired so many female clerks that he opened a residential hotel for them.[6] By 1924, over one third of department store buyers were women.

Department stores, conspicuous consumption, and "retail therapy" are such ubiquitous parts of contemporary America that it can be hard to imagine they have a history. And it may seem that the history of retail shopping can tell us relatively little about the American past. But, in fact, the rise of department stores occurred in the context of a number of sweeping economic, business, demographic, and cultural changes. Studying department stores allows us to understand how that often

5. Leach, "Transformations in a Culture of Consumption," 321, 327.

6. Benson, *Counter Cultures*, 23.

complicated set of changes reshaped early twentieth-century America.

In this chapter you will be looking at three kinds of evidence: department store architecture, contemporary analyses of the advertising business, and department store advertisements. Collectively these materials provide a window into the intentions of retailers in the late nineteenth and early twentieth centuries.

Your reading of these sources will go beyond this, however. You will analyze these various kinds of evidence to better understand the consumer culture that emerged in that era. What values were department stores selling? Why did their campaigns resonate with so many Americans, particularly women? What can we learn about early twentieth-century America by studying consumerism?

# The Method

One way to understand the lives of middle-class Americans during the post-Civil War era is to look at the things with which they surrounded themselves: clothing, possessions, and buildings. Advertising and architecture, retrievable evidence of material culture, provide a wealth of evidence that can be used to understand the late nineteenth and early twentieth centuries. Of course advertisements of preceding decades (or today's marketing campaigns, for that matter) do not tell you how people actually lived. Pictures of buildings cannot convey behaviors inside walls. But by carefully studying advertisements and architecture, we can trace Americans' changing habits, interests, and tastes. By analyzing the kinds of emotional appeals used in advertisements and the messages conveyed in architecture, we can begin to understand the aspirations and goals as well as the fears and anxieties of the people who lived in the rapidly changing society of the late nineteenth and early twentieth centuries. Why did certain fashions and designs appeal to this

generation of Americans? What kind of impression were department store entrepreneurs trying to make on customers? What does their success reveal about that era?

As the author of one of the following sources put it, advertising was designed to "create a desire where none existed before." People who worked in the emerging advertising business studied the most effective ways of creating consumer desire, and they employed a variety of tactics. The first selection of sources offers a revealing look at the efforts of advertisers to shape "the trend of the crowd." If you read closely, their writings also disclose their underlying assumptions about consumers, gender, and class. Both what these writers said and what they believed became visible in marketing campaigns.

Advertisements shaped shoppers' perceptions by using both positive and negative messages. Positive advertisements show the benefits—direct or indirect, explicit or implicit—that would come from owning a product. Such advertisements depict an ideal.

Negative advertisements demonstrate the dire consequences of not owning the product. Some of the most effective advertisements combine both negative and positive approaches ("I was a lonely 360-pound man before I discovered Dr. Quack's Appetite Suppressors. Now I am a fit 170 pounds and engaged to be married to a beautiful woman!"). Advertisements also attempt to evoke an emotional response from potential consumers that will encourage the purchase of a particular product or service. In looking at the advertisements in this chapter, first determine whether the approach used in each one is positive, negative, or a combination of both. What were the expected consequences of using (or not using) the product? How did the advertisement try to sell the product or service? What emotional responses were expected?

Now deepen your analysis. What can each advertisement tell you about earlier generations of Americans and the times in which they lived? Examine each advertisement carefully. What does it reveal about the values of the time period? Gender played a particularly significant role in the intentions of advertisers and the copy they produced. What do these materials tell you about the roles of men and women? The attitudes about gender in that era?

Department store advertising campaigns transcended goods. The services offered by stores and the images they projected in advertisements offer us valuable insight. Finally, the edifices and architectural layout of department stores can be "read" by historians. What were department store owners selling through design of physical space? Why did these spaces attract not just visitors, but *customers*? What does the overall marketing strategy of downtown department stores—goods, services, entertainments, and physical spaces—tell you about Americans in this period of history?

◆

## The Evidence

Sources 1–4, excerpts on the new business of advertising, 1898–1927.

### 1. Advertising and Photography.

From "Photographs in Advertising," *Printers' Ink*, August 17, 1898, p. 18.

It may have been noticed that the trend of modern magazine advertising is toward the use of photographs. . . . An advertisement that contains the photograph of a beautiful woman is certain to be attractive, and consequently its success is largely guaranteed. . . . But there are a host of articles on the market that can be advertised to great advantage by the introduction of a lady into the picture, and many advertisers have already seen this. . . .

But though the photographs of pretty women are only supposed to be attractive to the male sex, the picture of a baby or "cute" child will immediately captivate ninety-nine percent of humanity. . . . Whatever he or she is supposed to advertise, we feel kindly toward, even if it is only for introducing us to the baby.

## 2. The Business of Advertising.

From Earnest Elmo Calkins, *The Business of Advertising* (1915; reprint, New York: D. Appleton and Co., 1920), pp. 1, 9.

It is hard to find a satisfactory definition of advertising. A picturesque way of putting it is to call it business imagination, an imagination that sees in a product possibilities which can be realized only by appealing to the public in new ways to create a desire where none existed before. . . .

Advertising modifies the course of the people's daily thoughts, gives them new words, new phrases, new ideas, new fashions, new prejudices and new customs. In the same way it obliterates old sets of words and phrases, fashions and customs. It may be doubted if any other one force, the school, the church and the press excepted, has so great an influence as advertising. To it we largely owe the prevalence of good roads, rubber tires, open plumbing, sanitary underwear, water filters, hygienic waters, vacuum cleaners, automobiles, kitchen cabinets, pure foods. These are only a few of the things which the public has been taught by advertising to use, to believe in, and to demand.

## 3. Gender and Advertising.

From S. Roland Hall, *The Advertising Handbook: A Reference Work Covering the Principles and Practice of Advertising* (New York: McGraw-Hill, 1921), pp. 79–80, 101–103.

In other words, certain thoughts have become fixed in our minds in connection with certain other thoughts, and when we bring up one end of the connection the other is likely to follow. . . .

There is a motive, and a good one, in calling an automobile the "Lincoln," for that suggests sturdy, honest qualities.

No writer would undertake to make a real hero out of a character known as "Percy," for this name suggests "sissiness." . . .

Man is the stronger, as a rule. He is the bread-winner, to a large extent. His job is more in the outside world. He grows up to severer tasks, as a rule. He is more accustomed to rebuffs.

Though woman has progressed a long way in taking her place on an equal plane with that of man in business, politics and the professions, yet she is still to a large extent more sheltered than man. Her affairs are more within the home. Her sex makes her interest in clothes, home-furnishings, and the like keener than man's as a general thing. . . .

Because of her years of comparative non-acquaintance with mechanical matters, woman is generally less apt in understanding mechanical description and directions, and such advertising must use greater care when appealing to women. . . .

On the other hand it is generally admitted that men are more democratic, more gregarious, than women—that women move more within their own circle or "clique."

A man is not likely to care if several other men in his circle have a hat exactly like his own. A woman would hardly care to buy a hat exactly like one worn by several other women in her town or community. A woman ordinarily will think nothing of shopping at several places to look at hats. A man is likely to visit only one shop.

## 4. Class and Advertising.

From Claude C. Hopkins, *My Life in Advertising* (1927), reprinted as Claude C. Hopkins, *My Life in Advertising and Scientific Advertising* (Chicago: Advertising Publications, 1966), pp. 8–9, 119.

I am sure that I could not impress the rich, for I do not know them. I have never tried to sell what they buy. . . . But I do know the common people. I love to talk to laboring-men, to study housewives who must count their pennies, to gain the confidence and learn the ambitions of poor boys and girls. Give me something which they want and I will strike the responsive chord. My words will be simple, my sentences short. Scholars may ridicule my style. The rich and vain may laugh at the factors which I feature. But in millions of humble homes the common people will read and buy. They will feel that the writer knows them. And they, in advertising, form 95 percent of our customers. . . . People are like sheep. They cannot judge values, nor can you and I. We judge things largely by others' impressions, by popular favor. We go with the crowd. So the most effective thing I have ever found in advertising is the trend of the crowd.

Sources 5–13, department store advertisements, 1870s–1920s.

## 5. Christmas at Macy's, 1876.

NEW YORK CITY.—HOLIDAY EXHIBITION OF DOLLS IN A WINDOW AT MACY'S, FOURTEENTH STREET AND SIXTH AVENUE, FOR THE BENEFIT OF INFANT ASYLUMS.—SEE PAGE 271.

## A HOLIDAY SPECTACLE AT "MACY'S."

FOR many years "Macy's" has been one of the foremost institutions of the metropolis, and the Christmas displays of the great *Bon Marché*, on the corner of Sixth Avenue and Fourteenth Street, are one of the sights of the town. From far and near, the rich and the poor, the young and old, representing all classes and conditions in life, throng around the spacious windows and gaze in wonder and delight upon the brilliant and attractive spectacle. At no point in the great city can a more suggestive and instructive view of the many-sided, eager life of the metropolis be obtained, than on "Macy's" corner, during a pleasant afternoon in the height of the Christmas shopping season. This year, the spectacular display in the window is more than usually unique and elaborate, and the throngs of spectators, greater than ever, testify the popular appreciation. Mechanical skill, the costumer's taste, and the poet's fancy, have all combined to produce a panorama of exceeding beauty, variety and brilliancy. Within the great bazaar, the ceaseless current of trade flows steadily from morn till eve. The number of customers in "Macy's" during an ordinary shopping day, probably exceeds that of any similar store in the world—about 60,000—while on special days, just preceding Christmas, the store is, as a lady shopper said, "a sight to behold." Macy & Co. have just issued their Fall Catalogue, a handsome pamphlet of 118 broad pages, finely illustrated, which will be sent, post-paid, to any one applying for it. The catalogue gives a better idea than can be otherwise obtained, of the immense volume and variety of the stock of the house, and is, moreover, with its fine illustrations, an exceedingly interesting and instructive gazette of New York fashions, fabrics, ornaments and styles. The mail order business of Macy & Co. has become very large, and by means of the catalogue and the mail the shopper in the remotest hamlet buys at an equal advantage and from an assortment as large as the purchaser at the counter. The name of the house of Macy & Co.,

6. **Christmas at Macy's, 1884.**

NEW YORK CITY.—A HOLIDAY SPECTACLE—THE SHOW WINDOW OF MACY & CO., CORNER OF SIXTH AVENUE AND FOURTEENTH STREET.
FROM A SKETCH BY A STAFF ARTIST.—SEE PAGE 263.

## 7. Marshall Field Advertisements, 1893.

**In this Retail Store:**
—400,000 sq. ft. of floor space.
—708 ft. of street frontage.
—23 elevators.
—12 separate entrances.
—100 distinct departments.
—3,000 employes.

**An Exposition in itself.**
—Our Retail Store, owing to its enormous size, its perfect arrangement, its wonderful variety of merchandise shown and its great stocks, is one of the most noteworthy sights in Chicago.

**MARSHALL FIELD & CO.**
STATE · WASHINGTON & WABASH.

Just seven weeks ago we invited all Chicago to attend the opening of our new Annex—shown on the right of above cut. In these few weeks we have proved, beyond all peradventure, the wonderful success of this new building.

*The aisles of every floor—the 1st, 2d, 3d, 4th, and Basement—of this beautiful new annex have been continually thronged with visitors and buyers—especially with buyers, as every floor displays special lines of goods at prices heretofore considered out of the question. The annex is a success, from the start. . . . . . The main store has been doing its share. It always does; and with the recently added large store, on the north, this main store is showing a greater, far greater, result than ever before.*

From each of the hundred departments of this store we could for this advertisement select a column of items— *at prices* (this we print in italics) *at prices unquestionably lower than are quoted elsewhere in Chicago or America.* As characteristic items of the many we select a few, as below:

## 8th Semi=Annual Sale of Gloves begins to=day.

This Great Sale, which is of interest to almost every one in Chicago, will be continued 3 weeks. During these sales we always offer great quantities of *new, fresh, stylish* Kid Gloves—for Ladies, Men, Misses, Youths, and Children—including the newest shades and most recent cuts—*at prices greatly under our usual low quotations.* . . . . For the present sale our preparations have been *greater in every way* than ever before. We have been able to purchase a wonderfully fine lot of several thousand dozens. Notwithstanding the unusual excellence of these Gloves we shall hold the prices at the same extremely low point—namely:

## About 30 per cent less than our usual low prices.

Our new Glove Departments—south end of first floor, annex—are the largest in America. We anticipate so great a result from this announcement, however, that we have opened branch glove departments in a dozen or more different parts of the house, in each of which *a complete assortment* will be on sale.

We recommend that these gloves be purchased in half dozen, dozen, or larger assortments.

Many other departments contribute toward making this a great week.

# MARSHALL FIELD & CO.

**The Last Week of "Christmas '93" Buying**--One more week in which to push up our sales to the highest point we have ever reached, and in which to reduce our too large stocks to the proper amount.

**Christmas Articles of Real Merit**--Nowhere in all America can a more excellent assortment of meritorious Christmas Goods be found and, we believe, that nowhere else is displayed assortments of Christmas articles *anywhere near as large, as complete, or as desirable*—certainly not elsewhere in Chicago—nor perhaps in *any two stores combined* is shown an equal variety of *desirable* goods.

**Another point, which we print in heavy type--a point which we are prepared to prove--do prove-- every hour in the week--is this: "Our prices are emphatically the lowest in Chicago"="lower than are charged elsewhere (and we prove it hourly) for inferior goods."**

From our 100 departments we name, below, only a few items. We could, if space permitted, increase the list by many hundreds.

**Handkerchiefs**—Much has been said about Handkerchiefs, but the fact remains the same that our Handkerchief Department is by far the largest in Chicago and its sales are very much in the lead. Every grade, every style, every price, and bargains in every quality.

**Gloves**—For ladies, for misses, for children, for youths, for little or much money. A pair almost always proves acceptable. We are showing several extraordinary bargains in Kid Gloves, in Lined Gloves, and in Knit Gloves and Mittens.

**Men's Neckwear**—Our department long since won a position of supremacy in Men's Neckwear. The finest, the newest, the most stylish shapes are shown here this Christmas season. The 50c section is an important part of this department. We show by far the largest assortment of 50c ties in Chicago.

**Smoking Jackets**—Every quality, every size, every pattern, of every desired material and every price, from the lowest priced desirable Jackets up to the finest. Comparison will prove that our prices are the lowest.

**Silk Umbrellas**—Natural wood handles, stag horn handles, silver handles, etc. Light roll, English or American makes, at prices which have won for our Umbrella department the leading position in this country.

**Toys! Toys**—In the greatest profusion—four entire aisles in the new annex basement devoted to Iron Toys, blocks, games, electrical and mechanical toys skin horses, carts, etc., etc.—all desirable articles at prices lower than ever before.

**Dolls**—From the elaborately costumed doll with her extensive wardrobe we show every grade (in dressed and undressed dolls) down to the smallest size, smallest price doll made. Doll trunks, tea sets, beds, etc., etc. Our Department is unquestionably "Doll Headquarters."

**Leather Goods**—There is probably not the equal of our assortment of these much desired goods shown in any other establishment in the world, and our low prices are not equaled anywhere in this country.—1st floor Annex and Basement Salesroom.

**Cut Glass**—An excellent variety of vases, glasses and goblets, punch bowls, pepper and salts, sugar sifters, etc., etc., *at prices very much less than usually asked for equal qualities.*

**Dress Patterns**—From any of the departments selling Dress fabrics the customer can select a dress pattern that embodies latest styles and only best materials at prices which are satisfactory, because they are the lowest.

**Slippers**—Heretofore always in the lead with Holiday Slippers, the much increased stock this season has placed our Shoe Dept. far beyond the reach of comparison, either in beauty and size of assortments or in lowness of prices.

**Banquet Lamps**—And Piano or Library Lamps, we are displaying a most splendidly assorted stock—one section of our spacious third floor Annex is devoted to Lamps. The enormous sales' record is proof that the prices *are right.*

**Emb. Linens**—In Fine Art, Piece Em'y. Linens our Linen Dept. has no rival. The best and choicest pieces from Europe and from our own Art Linen workrooms are now displayed for Christmas buyers. Visit the Art Linen Room, 3d floor, Annex.

**Clocks**—The tall wall-sweep, the dauntiest boudoir clock, and hundreds of all sizes and all prices are shown. The enlarging of this Dept. was made imperative by its increasing business—this fact alone recommends it to careful buyers.

**Opera Glasses**—Our Opera Glasses form one of the strongest branches of our Optical Dept. We display only the reliable makes of glasses in the most fashionable, desirable patterns. These rank among the most acceptable presents for ladies.

**Cuff Buttons**—For either lady or gentleman a pair of cuff buttons well selected is a much admired present. Our Jewelry Department can furnish every grade, in all the latest patterns, at prices which are indeed remarkably low.

**Piece Silverware**—With two enormous Depts. displaying Silverware—one with all the newest things in silver toilet pieces and office fittings—the other with all the newest novelties in Silver, we supply every want at prices that others positively cannot meet.

**Furs**—Since the "Gigantic Fur Sale" of Nov. 21 our Dept. has replaced the closed lines with December designs in Cloaks, Capes, etc., which are in demand for presents. The prices are equal to the November sale prices. This is *the Fur opportunity* of the holiday season.

**Rugs**—Rugs need not be looked upon as "the higher order of expensive presents." In fact, they are inexpensive, serviceable, and becoming more and more desirable each year for Christmas tokens.

**Antique Furniture**—To those whose tastes are in this direction we show more exquisite valuable pieces than all other houses in Chicago combined. The lately added pieces make the collection complete in every feature.

**Pictures**—Too much care can hardly be exercised in selecting a picture to be given as a present. To make sure of only the newest, best pieces we recommend holiday buyers to our 3d Floor Annex. The collection is absolutely good and the prices the lowest in this city.

**Our Great Basement Salesroom is filled to overflowing with enormous assortments of the less expensive Christmas Goods. The prices quoted in Basement Salesroom are always "The Lowest."**

## 8. Wanamaker's Advertisements, 1880s–1890s.

**THE OVER-LARGENESS SALE!**

Everything in our various stocks is moving at a steady and even rapid selling pace. We are satisfied to have you know just what we are about.

Ladies' Silk Seal Cloth Coats.

Ladies' Three-Quarter Coats.

Ladies' Jackets.

Ladies' Jerseys.

Ladies' Collars and Cuffs.

Girls' Two-Piece Dresses.

FURS.

Fur-Lined Circulars.

SLEIGH ROBES.

Men's Linen Handkerchiefs.

Ladies' Ulsters.

Children's Coats.

Embroideries, Etc.

Ladies' Raglans.

Ladies' Dresses.

Ladies' Toboggan Suits

Ladies' and Children's Shoes.

Men's Custom Work.

SHAWLS.

House-Furnishing Goods.

**JOHN WANAMAKER,**

Chestnut, Market and Thirteenth Streets and City Hall Square.

Philadelphia.

8     THE NORTH AMERICAN, PHILADELPHIA, TUESDAY, FEBRUARY 14, 1899.

*Wanamaker's*    *Wanamaker's*    *Wanamaker's*    *Wanamaker's*    *Wanamaker's*    *Wanamaker's*    *Wanamaker's*

PHILADELPHIA, TUESDAY, FEBRUARY 14, 1899.

The weather today will probably be fair and colder.

# William Penn Has His Old Name Back Again

A century ago the Indians used to call the broad-brimmed Quaker "the White Truthteller."

Yesterday the snow threw a veil of white over the old man's hat, and a lace scarf about his shoulders, and the wind whistled again that old name of his—"the White Truthteller."

If this store had been here in William Penn's lifetime we would have engaged him, had it been possible, to make our business announcements.

When you look up at the colossal figure of the man whose name we bear in this old Commonwealth, please try to think of him as the kind of a man behind our business statements.

## Trustworthy Goods, and Trustworthy Words about them

are two of the cardinal principles of this old-fashioned store.

Whatever is new about the city of Philadelphia, William Penn's method of speech still continues under the shadow of his white face.

*John Wanamaker*

# The Kind of a Store This Is

**Only One Store in Philadelphia**

It is strictly a retail store without any manufacturing rooms or wholesale department to empty their surpluses through the retail section. Every dollar of goods that comes to it is bought with an eye to the needs of Philadelphia. Whatever knowledge or cash we command is put to daily use in bringing together a perfect stock straight from the manufacturers' tables to the customers' hands without "middle-of-the-road-men" to add expenses.

**Size of the Stock**

Seldom less than four millions of dollars, and often as much as five millions of dollars is spread out upon the various floors of this old building, for the selection, not only of Philadelphians, but of people who come here from a hundred miles around. The merchandise is the best that we can buy for money of its kind. It is not the most extravagant or the highest always, though finer and finer goods are constantly coming to Philadelphia because there is demand for them. This is the fact, however, that all the goods we sell are trustworthy and have been bought with all the care, and inspected with all the carefulness, and are presented to the people at the lowest price that goods of their grade can be sold at anywhere.

**The Assortment**

If five of the largest retail stores were to put their stocks together under one roof it would not be so complete as this one, because in such a massing of stocks of five stores there would be the duplication and triplication and quadruplication of great quantities of staples and other goods. This one stock, larger than all of them, furnishes a greater variety and gives opportunity to compare style, and size, and quality, which cannot be done where one must run from store to store and carry quality, sizes and patterns in the eye.

**The Interests of Our Customers**

We never lose sight of the fundamental idea of the Store, which is to serve the people. Whatever will not actually benefit those who entrust their business to us, is of no advantage to us. Whatever is stated in the advertisement we live up to. The goods are here or they would not be advertised, and what we have said about them is true or someone has deceived us. At whatever cost we make good to our customers every offer that we make them. Occasionally lots of goods are sold in an hour or two after the Store opens and people who come late are disappointed, but it is not because the lots were small, but because the demand was early and large. Were we to fix a late hour in the day for the opening of these particular lots of goods it would make such a crowd and occasion so much jostling that we, after trying both plans, have felt obliged to give everybody a chance to take the goods from the moment the Store opens. But every piece of goods that is advertised in the morning is always here when the Store opens.

**An Improving Store**

Lighting a fire in the morning will scarcely keep the house warm all day; some one must keep on caring for it. There is more thinking and relighting of the fires of the purpose and profit of this store than ever before. There is not a day of a step backward, and there are hundreds of days of stepping forward.

**The New York Store**

It certainly has a better building, but it is not so large as this old Philadelphia structure that does not put much cost or expense upon the people who like to be customers here. The outside of the building is not much to brag of, nor do we even brag about the inside, but it will always be hard to provide more comfortable and convenient facilities than now exist in the larger part of this old store. The New York Store, however, helps us in increased purchasing power which reduces here and there the prices, or if the prices are not reduced, improves the quality of what we sell.

**Things that are lacking**

Please tell us what you think the Store lacks. That will help us to know what we have learned it all, and you may help us if you will try suggestions which we will thank you for.

---

## Present facilities of the store

**The Store's Rest Places**

Main Waiting Room—for ladies—First floor, Thirteenth street side—near the Girard Window.
Men's Waiting Room—Basement, Thirteenth street side.

Ladies' Waiting Room—Basement, Thirteenth street side.
Gallery Rest—Juniper and Market streets—half flight up.
Gallery Rest—near Thirteenth street entrance to Book Store.
Rest Room—Basement, by the dairy.
Picture Store, third floor, Chestnut street, has so much of beauty as to offer a restful stroll.

By the picture store just now—the Munich Art Exhibition. Some seven hundred photographic reproductions of famous art works are shown.

Near by, the Furnished Rooms—suggesting artistic furnishing for the various rooms of the house. These rooms are some of the actual work of our upholstery store.

The Lace Exhibit, second floor, Thirteenth street side, presents a collection of rare lace pieces from one hundred to almost four hundred years old.

**Bureau of Information**

At City Hall corner—by our branch postoffice—are answered all questions as to trains, points of interest in the city, and as more generally than you'd think possible the thousands of queries that occur to visitors.

Every effort is made to be prompt and precise. And courteous, of course—that without effort. We expect our people to be courteous naturally.

**Cable, Telegraph, Telephone and Postal Facilities**

Branch Postoffice No. 19, in the City Hall Corner of the store, offers full postal facilities to all. Letters registered, money orders issued.

Of course, telegraph messages may be sent from here and received.

And cable messages, too.

Long Distance and Local Telephones maintain pay stations here.

Our telephone service within the house has been so extended that one may talk directly with a person in any department of the store without delay. It is convenient to order needed articles this way, when the waiting is bad—and of course most satisfactory to you to talk directly to the person whom you wish to fill your order.

**Check Wraps and Parcels**

One bundles up, these days—needs to. But once in the store, wraps would be uncomfortable, and burdensome even to carry. Don't.

In the Basement, Market and Juniper streets, is a checking room, where wraps and umbrellas are cared for—with no charge, of course.

Any packages may be left there as well.

Same corner for Lost Articles. Every day folks drop things about the store—purses, railroad tickets, veils and what-not. As found by our people or kindly friends, these articles go to "Lost and Found," and are delivered as claimed.

Umbrellas are checked at Waiting Rooms, first floor, Juniper street side, and Basement, Thirteenth street.

## A Thankful Friend on a Snowy Day

Mr. JOHN WANAMAKER.

Dear Sir: I was numbed, disheartened, and if I must own it, a trifle bewildered yesterday, when on alighting from a train, and failing to meet the friends I had expected to find at the station, I found myself lost in the snow. But fortunately the north wind caught me up and blew me into your store. And that hasty note is an expression of my grateful feelings.

I know by the newspapers that you have a Department of Public Safety in Philadelphia, but I know of no Department of Public Comfort, save that afforded by your store; and none anywhere to rival it in the great comfort-essentials.

I found first of all a bearable temperature, which, with the accessories of birds in song and plants in bloom, was more suggestive of a day in Florida than in the heart of snow-bound Philadelphia. Next I found a waiting-room in which to rest, catch my breath and collect my wits. I was laden with wraps, but thanks to a polite attendant I checked them and got them off my back and mind.

In short, by the exercise of eyes and tongue I found close to my hand more conveniences than I have found in some hotels, and as many as modern science has been enabled to provide in any capital of the world. With the help of the telephone I found my friends, who soon afterward found me, and in the meantime I was refreshed and strengthened against the blizzard by a comfortable lunch.

I suppose all these conveniences are familiar enough to Philadelphians, but the case was different with a woman from the country; and I cannot help wondering where I could have turned for rest, refreshment, shelter and time to gather myself together, if it had not been for the refuge of your store. Of course I have heard for years of Wanamaker's as a shopping center. To my mind it has another aspect—as a resting center and a sanctuary from stormy out-doors. It is because of this view I take in the memorable blizzard of yesterday that I sign myself

Gratefully yours,
. . . . . . . .

# JOHN WANAMAKER

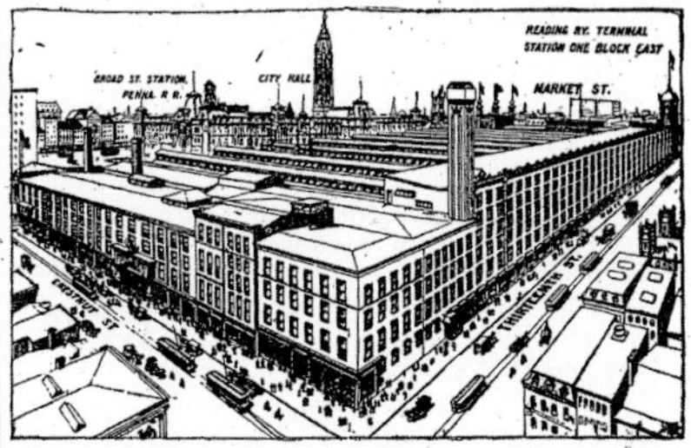

---

# Sending the Goods Home

Of course, with the Storm King's hand on all transportation we had to generally suspend deliveries yesterday. But all will be speedily righted.

Have you an idea of the splendid facilities of our Delivery Service? One hundred and fourteen wagons and trucks are in use, and two hundred and sixty-nine horses are needed to draw them, and furnish necessary relays.

We have sent out very nearly thirty-six thousand packages in a day—and some of them almost half a wagon-load in themselves.

Deliveries direct to the homes of our customers are made in two hundred and ninety-three towns and villages, besides the complete serving of every corner of Philadelphia.

For the delivery service of our New York store two hundred and eight horses, and one hundred and six wagons and trucks are required.

Four hundred and five points are reached by the Parcel Delivery Systems of the railroads—but packages are only delivered to nearest railroad station by this service.

**New Jersey News** — The wagons of our stores deliver goods direct in the following places free of charge: Starting from New York Store—

**Delaware** — The wagons of the store deliver goods direct in Wilmington.

**New York** — Through our New York Store delivery our wagons will deliver goods sold in Philadelphia free of charge throughout New York City and at all rural points traversed by our delivery.

**Pennsylvania News** — The wagons of the store deliver goods direct in the following places free of charge:

**Railroad Deliveries** — The railroads make deliveries of parcels at their stations at these points—following a recent custom we fix the prepay stamps on packages free. We do not pay freight on bales or barrels or on packages weighing over fifty pounds.

8 THE NORTH AMERICAN, PHILADELPHIA, WEDNESDAY, SEPTEMBER 13, 1899.

Wanamaker's Wanamaker's Wanamaker's Wanamaker's Wanamaker's Wanamaker's

The weather today will probably be fair. PHILADELPHIA, Wednesday, September 13, 1899.

# Seventeen Countr... ...ribute the goods that ...he store this Fall

## Exhibit Here

We gather in Orient and Occident New, Useful, Odd Things. They form the

America's Centennial Exposition began in this building when the Franklin Institute, its forerunner, held its exhibit in 1874. Two years later it became a permanent exposition building—for the doors were opened on the new John Wanamaker store. A surprise, rather than an exposition, at first; an audacious upstart that couldn't survive its first year, as many thought. But it did. And today it gives

## Greeting to the National Export Exposition

which formally opens tomorrow.

Commerce sways the world—pessimists say, because men are greedy for gold; optimists say, because it is manifest destiny. Let a broader humanity and thorough good nature say, because we are glad to have whatever of beauty and comfort the world offers—and to get it we institute and carry on exchange. We welcome the Export Exposition with

## An International Exposition here

The regular stocks of the store furnish the window exhibits, which this morning hint of what our own travelers have brought to Philadelphia from

| America | Belgium | Russia | Italy |
| England | Austria | Turkey | Persia |
| Germany | Switzerland | China | Africa |
| France | Holland | Japan | India |

Other countries are large contributors—notably South America.

This store is half as large again as the main building of the Export Exposition. Differently shaped, there are eighteen acres of floor space here as against twelve in that mammoth structure. We are expecting visitors from far and near to these Philadelphia shows, and every one of you is to consider

## this our personal invitation to make the store your headquarters

We have as many conveniences as the best appointed hotel, with an additional Reception Room dedicated especially to the comfort of strangers in Philadelphia. It is supplied with newspapers, writing facilities, telephone and telegraph offices and a lot of restful chairs. Yours to enjoy as you will. Mail can be sent to you "care of John Wanamaker, Philadelphia."

## Important Guests are announced

### AUTUMN DRESS GOODS

Dress Goods fill the heart of the store and are being most graciously received. It is out of the question to present them individually in the papers, but allow us to introduce five today—

### Women's Autumn Costumes and Wraps

### Men's $3 Shoes at $1.85

### Doubling the China Business

# JOHN WANAMAKER

## 9. Gimbel's Advertisements, 1890s.

GIMBEL BROTHERS.  GIMBEL BROTHERS.  GIMBEL BROTHERS.

# CHRISTMAS AT GIMBEL'S

Milwaukee, Sunday, Dec. 13, 1891.

*POINTER No. 2610: There is but good choice where the whole stock is good.*

**In Search of a Christmas Present!**

Many people who journey from shop to shop for hints will be glad for the few suggestions that Gimbels offer from day to day.

Two announcements:

1. The store will be open every night till Christmas, beginning to-morrow.
2. To-morrow, Monday, a live Santa Claus will be at the store.

He will be seen from 10 o'clock to 11:30 every morning, from 2:30 to 5:00 every afternoon, and from 7:30 to 9:00 every evening.

Bring the children.

Among the proverbs which crystalize for man the experience of centuries is one about the matutinal bird and the worm. It finds a fitting application in Christmas trading. There's profit and comfort in early trading at this time.

The writer's particular duty at this time is to lead you through this store with careful step, and point out to you what this great trade tide has brought up. He will do it carefully, truthfully. This great trade center is exacting. A store possessing the greatest trade wisdom—could there be a more pleasing spot at Christmas time?

The stock is the reflector of your Xmas wants. Pre-eminently that. Acres of delight here.

A Mackintosh for a brother or father. $6.75 to $15.00.

Or Smoking Jackets. Very handsome ones In French material, soft, downy and cheerful in designs.

A quality that sells at 4.50.
A quality that sells at 5.00.
A quality that sells at 7.00.
A quality at $8.00.
A quality at $10.00.
A quality at 12.48.
A quality at 13.98.

In point of variety, the men's counter is a rare gift corner.

*Santa Claus*—Fat, plump, grey old Santa Claus—will be around the Toy Basement every day during the Holidays. Bring the little children

**THE NIGHT BEFORE**

here to see him. It will be a delightful sight for the youngsters. The little ones can address him as they please and tell him of their little hearts' Xmas hopes. This will indeed bring joy to the children.

A stock of Toys to wonder at; a help to every parent. The conquest of the Toy trade by this store is nearly complete.

The world has sounder notions of Christmas gift than ever, more practical, more judicious, more sensible. Thus comes the display of special Dress Goods.

The seeker of the useful will find a list for the coming week.

The great sale that brings to you Santa Claus with his trinkets at lowest prices has attractions greater than you'd think in stuffs for Dresses.

There are Robes—a full-pattern—that may be had thus:

At $12.00 from $18.00.
At 10.00 from 15.00.
At 8.00 from 12.00.

In Broadcloth, embroidered with Soutache braid and jet nail heads.

**BRIC-A-BRAC and PICTURES**

Other Robes in serge and embroidered:

From $25.00 to $38.00.
From 20.00 to 12.00.
From 16.50 to 10.00.

and a lot at $8.98, that were a half more.

In the materials by the yard:

All wool Bedford Cords at 60c, from 75c.
The $1.25 quality is 69c.
The 1.78 quality is $1.25.
The 2.25 quality is 1.75.

And the novelties in French goods, $1.75 from $2.50 and more.

The most pleasant features of the business is the price sagging at this time.

**And the Silks!**

Nearly a hundred pieces of Black, 24 inches wide, at $1.00 a yard—1.25 quality.

There must be somewhere in your list a dear old friend whose heart may be cheered by a Silk Dress gift.

Let her pick her favorite:

Black China Silk 50c to $1.25.
Black Sarah Silk 69c to $1.25.
Black French Faille 98c to $2.00.
Black Bengaline $1.25 to $2.00.
Black Tyrolese Silk $1.25 to $2.00.
Imperial Silk, $1.50.
Rhadames 69c to $2.00.
Peau de Soie $1.00 to $2.00.

Or a sister, perhaps, whose young heart may sigh for a party dress. Let her pick also:

Crepe de Chine $1.00 a yard.
Crinkled Crepe $1.25 a yard.
Fancy Brocaded Silks all tints, $1.25 to $10.00 a yard.
China Silks 50c to $1.50 a yard.

*Handkerchiefs.*

That price ripple you heard a week ago was but the faint whisper of a turbulent price-wave that's here to-day. In sorts they run in the hundred; in quantity, into thousands of dozens.

At 5c each.
At 10c each.
At 15c each.
At 15c each.
At 20c each.
At 25c each.

Just enough to suggest coming to this spot for them.

Nothing told of the hundreds of dozens of silk ones for 15c, for 20c, for 39c and 1.00 each; in Dainty Lace up to 10.00; in Mousseline de Soie up to 5.00 and so on,

**CHRISTMAS MORNING**

Our point is merely that you miss the best stock of the town by skipping this place.

Rare and beautiful things in the *Bric-a-brac* corner; Jap sorts and so brilliant gathering now. but likely to dwindle down in a few days. Many pieces of Jap pottery not to be duplicated. 2.00 to 28.75 for vases and fancy corner pieces.

The picture gallery—a variety that ex-

pands up to the most liberal purses or shrinks down to the lank pocket-books. No picture store humbug to fear.

The picture man is not worried by the presence of a thousand pictures here at this writing. "Never" says he, "were such pictures sold here before for less than twice the money."

Wonder where the girl is that has seen such a doll gathering before. Not a Milwaukee girl unless she were in a warehouse in Montreuil. There are dolls as little priced as 5c, and some as extravagantly put up as to cost $20.00.

Here's a stock of umbrellas—unequaled. Each one deserving a special mention. But six to-day:

$1.19.
$1.98.
$2.25.
$2.98.
$3.50.
$4.00.

Rugs from the land of the Mikado, from the domain of the pig-tails and so on.

$6.90 to $150.00 each.

In our own land the rug makers have done excellently, skillfully.

Door sizes 69c and $1.15.
22x45-inch $1.65.
36x54 $2.25.
80x60 $2.00.
36x72 $3.90.
48x84 $5.00.
9x12 feet $27.50.

White Fur Rugs, selected quality, $2.75.

Large Fur Rugs of various kinds, soft to the foot, an admirable gift, $5.00 to $6.50.

The store comes forward again with the

**TREE-FIXINGS**

best linens to cheer the heart of the good, wise housewife.

On the counters stretch of linen like the whitest snow drifts.

The white sets:

2½ yard German Damask Sets with knotted fringe 7.48.
2½ yard German Damask Sets with knotted fringe and drawn work 12.98.
2½ yard German Damask Hemstitched Sets 8.98.
2 yard German Satin Damask Sets 9.98.
2 yard German Satin Damask Hemstitched Sets 17.98.
2 yard German Damask Sets with knotted fringe 8.98.
2 yard German Damask Sets with knotted fringe and open work 14.48.
2½ yard German Damask Sets with knotted fringe 15.98.
2½ yard German Satin Damask Hemstitched Sets 18.98.

You ought to have enough curiosity to see the needlework corner—the play ground of feminine fancies.

Slumber Pillows.
Chair Cushions.
Dainty Wall Ornaments.
Scarfs for Neck and Chairs.
Bureau Ornaments.
Toilet Sets,
And thousands of fancies.

At the home the making would be double, and chances of inferior work no matter how skillful the fingers or loving the heart.

Sweet scented bags. Use them as may tickle your vanity best. In China silk covered with bolting cloth daintily painted. Some with ivy leaves; some with dreaming posies; some with sweet-faced pansies; all brimful of sweetness and brightness.

98c to $8.00, for prices that you could not produce at home for double the price if at all.

# GIMBEL BROTHERS

THE SENTINEL: SUNDAY MORNING, NOVEMBER 29, 1891.

GIMBEL BROTHERS.  GIMBEL BROTHERS.  GIMBEL BROTHERS.  GIMBEL BROTHERS.  GIMBEL BROTHERS.  GIMBEL BROTHERS.

Milwaukee, Sunday, Nov. 29, 1891.

*POINTER No. 1396: The gallant man needs no drums to rouse him.*

# Christmas Carols At Gimbel's

From day to day merry Christmas jingles will be heard from every corner of the store. An era of bright Christmas trading is dawning for Milwaukeeans. This holiday announcement, this generous use of newspaper space, is leading to it. Great expectations are rising. A holiday stock of surprising proportions is here for you—more complete, more commanding, than any stock within the reach of local customers. The favorablest opportunities are given early to buyers. To-morrow the first of a series of Holiday surprises begin. The decorators are progressing speedily with their work and so from day to day the Christmas carols will grow merrier, cheerier for you and for us. This great trade experience must be productive of marked advantages.

## GIMBEL'S

### Toys.

The store writer makes no pretense of giving a correct census of the Xmas things that the vigilance of the department men have brought here, not a bit. The process would be too wearisome. But to us there is no doubt as to where the Holiday-trade leadership is held. Under this roof is to-day the greatest of toy stocks of the town for local traders to witness. And it is fitting to remark, that the clear result of experience and toy-wit have done for you in prices what is beyond the experience of local traders. The Toy business has been done in Milwaukee very much the same way as every other business—for comfortable profit, at random, without fixed policy, without fixed notions. The Bargain Basement is full. You need not repeat the toy-price extravagances of former years unless you want to. This toy business of ours is great, even now.

The Doll population in the Basement is very nearly twenty thousand. They run from one inch long up, and from a cent apiece to $20.00. Startling figures! Startling indeed. The corner is startling from start to finish where the adult or child may gather happiness and knowledge from.

In detail:
Little bits of Dolls at 5c.
Dolls, undressed, 5c to $15.00.
Dolls, with kid bodies, undressed, 29c to $20.00.
Dolls, well dressed, at 60c, and up to $1.00.
Dolls, with rolling eye and joints that move, $1.25, and up to $20.00.

The happiest lots are $1.25 to $4.50. Dressed very attractively. Such doll-worth as these must impress every comer.

Beyond the dolls—Christmas panorama widens. A wonderland! Imposing scenes everywhere. But it's of the price-charm the pen holds to to-day—the Bargain census.

The toy story takes its key from the doll tune. Numerically there is no gathering of toys anywhere in that can make shadow to this one.

There are the wooden toys of all most attractive sorts.

Little Wagons,
Little Horse-cars,
Little Swings,
Little Fire Department Wagons,
Little Beds,    Little Animals,
    Regiments of Little Soldiers,
    Little Wooden Men that do all tricks.
    Games,
    Steam Cars,
    Barns and Little Animals.
    And so on.

And the great wonder about them is that the prices should be so much your way.

*There are tin affairs* of all sorts, noise and joy makers.

Tops that whiz merry tunes
Horns and Trumpets enough to puzzle Gabriel.
Tin Wagons and Horses and articles that play a tune—if you turn the crank.

Not a day but some novelties come, steam engines that go at a speed, and so on. A clock spring attached to the business—anything—makes an otherwise dull toy attractive and instructive. Toys are educators.

*Games.* Something to puzzle to little brains, to tease them, but not to worry the child and tire the patience out.

All the sorts—the best—McLoughlin's.
From 10c up. Tiddelywinks and the latest sorts.

### Books.

The Toy manager says that the books in his Basement—children's picks—is the greatest book outfit in the land.

10c to $5.00. They are all in sight to leaf over and look at.

But it isn't of Toys alone—the story goes beyond that. The Christmas carols rise to the reach of every ear, meet fancies anywhere. There's an attractive jumble of stuffs among the art needle work. Highest hopes of brush and needle. Weapons for cupid these novelties in dainty satins. Covered with sweet posies, fresh as if the dew had just touched off a smile from them. For Glove, $1.50 to $12.00.

For boudoir use of any sorts, dainty finger work from 50c to $20.00. Milady may choose with freedom.

Tidies in Silks and hand decorated from 50c to $5.00 each; in lace from 10c to $2.00.

If you are a fancy goods worker we have the materials for you:
The Oriental Silk Flosses and the Floss that the Japs use and so on.

The ornaments in plush, in silk, in metal—anything. And there are witty needle workers here also to do the work for you. Designs for stamp-work and all that.

The novelties in plush haven't yet gone out of the gift giver's mind, not yet. Not likely to if the variety here gets at the eye of the gift hunter. Child and parent will look with a cheery heart at the hundred feet of counter. Blossoming hedges never offered the eye more beauty than this, never.

Complete Toilet Set in box of silk plush, 79c and up to $30.00.

Some in oxidized silver, at $3.50 to $25.00.
Some in Oak Wood at $7.48 to $15.00.
Some in plush and embossed celluloid at $7.98 to $29.50.

### Handkerchiefs.

The shifting of the great Christmas cargo has given the greatest Handkerchief stock in the town a room of over a hundred feet shelving and a hundred and fifty feet of counter for display. Where is there another stock like it? At the rear to the left.

One table for silks, plain, 15c to $1.25.
One table for silk, embroidered borders, 25c to $2.00.
One table for linen, embroidered, 75c.
One table for linen, embroidered, 50c.
One table for linen, embroidered, 39c.
Three tables for linen, embroidered and colored borders, 25c.
Three tables for linen, colored and embroidered borders, 15c.
Two tables for colored and embroidered borders, 10c.
Also at 5c.
The values are the most surprising up to date.

You know the prices of Art stores—double your best guess always. You'd rather have bare walls than be robbed—overcharged.

Out of the thought we might be of service to you in home-cheer making, came a stock of pictures that we think much, enough as art work and money saving —also art work.

Have you a doubt where the picture business is going to be done this Christmas? Come and see.

Artists proof etchings, framed, 18x27, at $3.50. Two hundred subjects.

The next in better frames is $3.98.

Prang's Novelties for Christmas, 65c and 75c.

Steel and Wood Engravings that frames to a size of 30x36, very good quality of frame, at $3.25, 3.48, 4.00, 4.50 and 4.98. Over a thousand photogravures of most famous paintings, in frames, size 11x15, at 49c each.

Large etchings in most elegant frames, $10.00, 12.00, 15.00 to 20.00.

The picture gallery is not a spot to skip if you are an art lover.

### Rugs.

The Holiday detachment is on deck. Elevator takes up to the display on third floor. It will remain there up to Christmas, but the selections may be made early. By arrangement with the salesman, any favorite one can be put away for you, and delivered when you choose. Better be quick selecting though.

*Bokaras* from $15.00 to 110.00.
*Anatolians* from $18.00 to 75.00.
*Daghestans*, antique and modern, $9.80 to 30.00.
*Kazacks,* $16.00, 18.00, 22.00.
*Kermans,* $22.00 to 150.00.
And thousands of Smyrna and animal rugs.

It is our hope that the store service shall, during the rush of holiday shopping, equal the most exacting demands of the trade. The weak spots have been strengthened, small corners enlarged. There must be convenience and ease, and comfort here for you. The whole store machinery is tuning up for it.

(Signed)

## GIMBEL BROTHERS

8 And 5 Grand Avenue.
174 and 176 West Water St.

THE SENTINEL: SUNDAY MORNING, NOVEMBER 13, 1898

GIMBEL BROTHERS. GIMBEL BROTHERS. GIMBEL BROTHERS. GIMBEL BROTHERS. GIMBEL BROTHERS.

*POINTER No. 3,543: True friendship like phosphorous shows up best at the darkest hour.*

Milwaukee, Sunday, Nov. 13, 1898.

# Gimbels' Monday trading features

## A partial list of random pickings and pricings.

from a stock of rare *completeness in everything* from practical everyday needs to exclusive novelties designed especially for "the *Gimbel stores*"—all chosen with a care and regard to desirability of styles and fullness of value. The climax of our year's usefulness to you—the pinnacle of your patronage to us—comes in the next six weeks. We already see the glow of Christmas candles. We are ready—a complete and perfect readiness that comes of a year's preparation—but that's for another time. Each event in its place. To-day the store reflects everyday life—and prices whisper *"at little expense."*

## Fashionable ulsters

Notice them at golfing meets, on the promenade—wherever congregate those who dress in the front of the mode. We show the only line of ulsters to be found in the city. To get them made at a tailor's you'd pay—well, say $50 to $75. We give you an idea of how you save by getting tailored styles at Gimbels', read about these:

Box front ulsters of the finest pebble cheviot or English covert cloth **$22.50.**

In imported black, navy or tan kersey **$25.00.**

Pebble cheviot, perhaps one of the most dressy fabrics made; either black or navy, dart fly-front style; black coats are lined with fine black and white taffeta; the navy coats with navy and white plaid taffeta. **$18.00.**

Coaching coat, box front, set off by large white pearl buttons, made of Schnable's celebrated cream tan coaching kersey; lined with heavy quality satin duchesse and tailor strapped on all seams in a most superior manner **$25.00**

## Superb winter jackets

At **$4.95**—Jaunty cut box coat of light tan covert, latest dart sleeves, storm collar, satin lined.

At **$5.95**—Coats of good quality black kersey, box front set off by four large pearl buttons, velvet storm collar or coat collar, rhadame lined.

At **$7.50**—Fly front or box coats of black or navy cheviot or kersey, well tailored and lined with rhadame—an exceptional value.

At **$10**—The ever popular cheviots, kerseys, astrakhan cloths in many pretty styles including new "dip" front, lined with Skinner's guaranteed black satin or fancy taffetas.

At **$12.50**—Good serviceable coat of black unfinished worsted, box front or double-breasted buttoning on a fly, lined with heavy black satin.

At **$14.95**—Jaunty coats in black and navy "patent kersey" of exceedingly good quality, lined with fine satin duchesse, Ascot fly front or box front style.

## Furs, scarfs, coats, etc.

These dainty dress auxiliaries are an essential to finely tailored suits, and coat styles lend themselves to becoming use of these furs

*Neck scarfs:*

At **$2.95**—New rounded shape electric seal, cluster of eight imitation marten tails.

At **$3.95**—Latest shape American marten scarf, new rounded shape, cluster of 8 fine marten tails.

At **$12**, $15 and $20 the finest of real marten scarfs.

At **$6 90**—Stone marten scarfs, made of genuine skins; better ones $10, $15, $22.75 and $25.

Scores of handsome styles in collarettes—wanted furs and combinations of furs at $2.95, $3.95, $4.95, $7.50, $10, $15, $20 and up to **$1.50.**

Electric seal jackets, new shapes, best linings, XXX quality $19.75, XXXX quality at **$25.00.**

## Imported coats and capes

Latest ideas in Berlin made flounce, plain or rich hand-beaded velour coats and capes, from favorite makers whose garments good dressers find satisfaction in wearing.

At **$29.75**—Exquisitely fashioned kersey coats, wide coaching front set off by four hand-carved white pearl buttons, tailor strapped in a most original manner and lined with richest quality silk, in cream, tan, Russian brown, navy and black.

At **$25.00**—Berlin made coat of handsome black unfinished worsted, a most excellent cloth for wear, round cornered box front style, lined with extra quality black silk, entire coat roll bound with fine black braid.

At **$18.75**—Very stylish coat of fine finished cheviot, black or navy, dart fly front style, handsomely lined.

At **$8.95**, to $39.75—Exquisite golf capes.

At **$10**, $8.90, $6.50 and $3.95 are American made kersey capes.

## Queen Quality Shoes $3.00

You'll find this shoe everything its name implies—"*Queen Quality*"—shapes dainty and modern, varying from the dressy Paris to the popular extension sole "roller rink" boot, in more than twenty styles, new toes, cloth or kid tops, button or lace, medium, high or low broad heels. Our intention is to make a "leader" at a popular *price.* We've gathered for the purpose an exceptionally large line. The close price paid for big quantities and our *close selling figure* enables us to provide shoes that are no less desirable in style and quality than those for which most stores charge $5.00.

We have other fine shoes with the same reason for superiority at their various prices, but for good "all around" satisfaction we particularly recommend "*Queen Quality*" at $3.00 a pair.

**Improved higharm Singer Sewing Machine $13.50**

How is it possible, people ask? How was it possible for Gimbel to bring bicycles down to a reasonable price? Let one question answer the other. In the meantime we continue the sale of improved higharm Singer sewing machines with a full set of latest nickel plated attachments at $13.50. Machines warranted 10 years.

## Upholsteries

**at underpricings**

Quantity buying and trade conditions have provided you with a chance to *decorate at little cost.* Let us omit all but the climax, which is simply this—An importer "brought over" more goods than his trade would take—the lot was too large for a single store—our two establishments joined hands and came to his relief. Result—you buy as follows:

$1.00 tapestry, handsome colorings and designs............ 49c

250 yards tapestry, values up to $2.00, at............ 98c

Silk damask, silk tapestry, brocatelles and silk frou-frous, values up to $4.50............ $1.98

Silk effect portieres, handsome line colorings, some fringed top and bottom, others fringed side and bottom, per pair............ $2.98

Tapestry portieres in exact reproductions of Bagdad, Kelim and Renaissance pieces, real values $7 and $8, per pair............ $4.98

100 couch covers, Bagdad and Tapestry effects. $7.50 lot at $3.98; $6 kinds at............ $2.98

$4.00 4-panel Jap screens, 5-6 feet high, black or colored ground with gold embroidered designs, to close at............ $2.98

## Silk and dress goods attractions

We have arranged a special selling of silks and dress goods for the coming week that has not been equalled here or elsewhere this season.

20 pieces taffeta silks, plain glace, fancy checks, stripes and novelty effect; our regular 75c and 89c kind............ 59c

10 pieces taffeta silks in fancy plaids and Roman stripes, handsome new combinations, worth 89c and $1............ 69c

Black taffeta silks, 25 inches wide, Lyons dye, recommended for wearing quality, worth $1.25............ 89c

Ombre striped satins in new fall colorings with black satin stripes, beautiful effects for shirt waists, $1.50 quality............ $1.25

Black satin brocade in beautiful patterns, desirable for dress skirts, worth $2.00, special............ $1.50

40-inch fancy mixed suiting, new stylish combinations, 50c quality............ 35c

40-inch plaids Scotch effects, large variety of combinations, desirable for children's dresses, 50c kind............ 39c

45-inch all-wool two-toned sail cloth in new combinations, very desirable for full costumes, regular 75c value............ 59c

48-inch black all-wool jacquards, new designs, medium and small effects, worth 85c............ 69c

54-inch meltons, new colorings, black hair line stripes—new fabric for tailor-made gowns, worth $1.25............ 89c

## Beautiful silk waists $3.95

Granting you could not make them for the money you still wonder how the manufacturer did—but why care with such savings. The always dressy black in taffeta and satin; other sorts in lavender, cerise, turquoise, etc., a wide choosing of colors; most all sizes in the lot 32 to 44, though perhaps not in some styles—and there's where the early choosers benefit, values such as we have sold regularly at $5, $5.90 and $6.50 with a here and there better worth—choose Monday **$3.95.**

## The new "horse blanket" skirts

Fashion has many freaks—"horse blanket" skirts and suits is one of them. Unlike many innovations it has good reasons for its popularity, not the least of which is "style," for they certainly make a very striking costume, then the wear and the warmth. Ours are direct from New York's best costumers, where they gained instant recognition of swell dressers—full showing Monday.

## "Underwear Monday"

and these are some of the items that will make it underwear here to-morrow.

Children's imported non-shrinkable White Australian wool camel's hair vests and pants, size 16............ 40c
5c rise each size.

Women's fleece-lined combination suits, Oneita or straight button front, 50c and............ 75c

Women's black wool tights, guaranteed fast color **$1.39** and **$1.75** fast black merino tights and women's merino combination suits, finished seams, pearl buttons............ 98c

Women's imported ribbed merino vests and drawers, in white and natural, perfect fitting............ $1.00

Women's ribbed shaped australian wool vests and french band pants, white, natural or black............ $1.25

Women's heavy silk and wool underwear in cream, sky, pink and natural, **$1.75**, **$2.25** and............ $3.50

Women's wool combination suits with cotton lining, white or grey, Oneita or straight button front............ $1.50

# A Monday movement of dinnerware, cut glass, china and lamps

John Maddock & Son's $12.75 royal vitreous English porcelain dinner sets, 100 pieces, gold trimmed, dainty spray decoration in turquoise and yellow............ $7.98

$18.75 set in same decoration and ware, 115 pieces, including large soup tureen and turkey platter............ $12.75

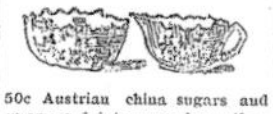

50c Austrian china sugars and creamers, dainty spray decoration, gold traced, large size, per pair............ 25c

Haviland & Co.'s white French white dinner plates doz............ $3.00

Breakfast plates $2.50, and tea plates, per doz............ $2.25

Sauce plates $1.60 doz.; individual butters............ $1.00

Tea cups and saucers, doz............ $3.00

Coffee cups and saucers, per doz............ $4.00

Sauce boats—each............ $1.45

Sauce tureens—each............ $1.50

Dorflinger's American cut glass water bottles, deep chrysanthemum cutting, highly polished, like cut............ $4.00

Cut glass salts and peppers, several shapes and cutting, silver plated tops............ 15c

Cut glass mustards, same style as above, silver plated top............ 35c

Cut glass syrups with silver plated tops, deep notch cutting............ 75c

### Gas Globes--Tea Pots

Cut glass effect gas globes and engraved glass gas globes, each............ 10c

Etched glass gas globes............ 25c

Gibson's fire-proof tea pots, 12c, 15c, 19c, 25c and............ 33c

Gibson's decorated fire-proof tea pots, 25c to............ 65c

Parlor lamps, hand painted floral design, dark ground, center draft burner............ $5.00

Beacon incandescent gas lamps fitted with the best American mantle, regular price 65c............ 48c

Mantles............ 15c Chimneys............ 8c

Welsbach latest improved incandescent gas lamps, complete............ 98c

No. 1 mantles............ 35c

No. 2 mantles............ 25c

### Porcelain chamber sets

English porcelain chamber sets, new shapes, new shaded effects, regular price $8.50, reduced to............ $4.98

English porcelain chamber sets, under glaze decoration, in blue, green and brown, with slop jar............ $3.45

John Maddock & Son's English porcelain sets, Helene shape, heavy gold stippled, complete with slop jar............ $4.98

4½-inch white china vases for decorating............ 9c

6-inch vases, 25c; 6-inch oval vase on feet............ 75c

Openwork fruit bowls, 75c; nut dishes, 58c; olive dishes, 25c, and pin trays............ 12c

Open white china sugars and creamers, a pair............ 25c

English porcelain cuspidors, under-glaze decoration, assorted colors............ 25c

Carlsbad china fern dishes with lining, spray decoration, gold trimmed............ 48c

Egg shell china Japanese tea cups and saucers, in spray decorations, gold trimmed, value 25c............ 19c

A lot decorated bowls and pitchers, blue, green and brown, per pair............ 98c

# GIMBEL BROTHERS

## 10. Wanamaker's Advertisements, 1920s.

Organ plays at 9, 11 and 4.50 — Melody and Chimes at Noon | WANAMAKER'S | STORE OPENS AT 9 — Daylight Saving Time | WANAMAKER'S | STORE CLOSES AT 5 — Daylight Saving Time | WANAMAKER'S | WEATHER — Fair and Warmer

# *What a Day for a Pleasure Trip to Wanamaker's!*

## There Are Few Blessings in Life That Are Equal to

the schoolboy time and the first days in business, when you felt you must have somebody to talk to in vacant hours.

Do you remember how sure we all were of each other? Possibly we might do well to chase up those old friendships within and without our families to the advantage of both parties.

Mark Twain said to get the full of joy you must have somebody to divide it with.

[Signed] John Wanamaker

*July 7, 1922.*

### *The Wanamaker Store Will Be Closed All Day Tomorrow—Summer Saturday Holiday*

## Women's Sports Frocks of Crepe de Chine

The sort of simple frock which will serve for almost any daylight hour, smart in cut and delightful in color and texture.

Some are gayly striped—blue-and-white, orange-and-white, green-and-white, rose-and-white—and some are printed in foulard patterns and foulard colors—dark blue, rose, and so on.

The sleeves are long or short and altogether the dresses are as charming as they are inexpensive—$25.

(First Floor)

### *A Clearaway of Women's Skirts at Half*

Precisely the kind of things most wanted by Summer travelers.

At $5 fine checked velours, plaids and plain homespuns with fringe.

At $10 are wool eponges, novelty checks, jersey cloths in white with colored stripes and fancy striped flannels.

(East Aisle)

## Young Women's Silk Capes Have Shorter Prices

Every silk cape here is included. Mostly black Canton crepe with colored silk linings. A number have black caracul collars, others are corded or beautifully embroidered. Some have deep silk fringe.

Not only are they new in fashion, having only been here a comparatively short time, but they are all capes of the handsomer kinds.

New prices are $25 to $65 and sizes go from 14 to 20 years.

(Second Floor)

## Wanamaker Chamois Lisle Gloves Are Famous

Nothing else as good at the price, and none better at any price, in material, making, color and fit.

Two-clasp at 85c a pair; strap-wrist and eight-button length, each $1 a pair; twelve-button length at $1.25, and sixteen-button length at $1.50.

Black and colors.

(Main Floor)

### *Sheer Striped Dress Linen in Black-and-White Only at 50c*

Fine Irish linen of the sheer "handkerchief" variety.

The most fashionable effect of the season—white with black stripes. Six different patterns, including cluster and single stripes, and varying from hairline to half-inch width.

An importer's overlot, comprising but 1900 yards of a quality that all season has been three times the price. 36 inches wide.

(West Aisle)

## An Important Consignment of Laces From China

A direct importation of the laces in Irish patterns which the Chinese make so beautifully.

There are many designs, and the prices on edges run from 25c for picots to $2.75 for four-inch widths, while prices on insertions are from 75c for a ¼-inch width to $2.25 for a three inch.

(Main Floor)

### *Every One Asks for the New Printed Crepes de Chine*

So light and dainty, so soft and cool and Summery, it is no wonder so many charming gowns are made of them.

New patterns include white grounds printed in pink or red, blue, brown, tan, lavender and other colors. The designs are small and the ground well covered.

40 inches wide, all-silk, and priced $3.25 a yard.

(First Floor)

## Girls' Smocked Dresses Special, $4.75

Newly arrived and wonderfully pretty for such a modest price! They are made of white lawn, dimity or voile with hand smocking in color and perhaps a touch of hand embroidery. Some open in the back, others in front and one style has tucks.

There are also white lawn dresses with tucking and sash and without smocking at $4.75. Sizes, six to 10 years.

(Second Floor)

## Women's Better Pumps Down to $7.75

A clearing-out price on several desirable kinds that were higher.

Plain pumps of black suede; Louis heels and turned soles.

Plain pumps of light-weight calf in tan or black; also, black patent leather. High or low French heels, and turned soles.

One-strap street pumps of grained tan calf with round toe, wing tip and perforations; heavy welted sole and flat, broad heel.

(First Floor)

### Quaint Candle Sconces

Old in design, but modern in use and charming for the right room are a pair of fine old carved and gilded French candle sconces, wired for electricity.

Antiques prices them at $150 the pair.

(Fifth Floor)

## New Summer Fashions in Mourning Millinery

Women are generally agreed that mourning millinery above everything else needs to be of the best materials and most carefully made. Perhaps this is the reason that so many women will go nowhere else for all-black hats.

There are many of the newest and most charming hats made up in Canton crepe, Georgette crepe, silk moire, taffeta and straw or straw and silk combined. Sometimes the entire trimming consists of a softly draped scarf of Georgette crepe which hangs down one side. Prices begin as far down the scale as $10.

(Second Floor)

## Those Gay Bathing Capes of Cretonne

More have arrived—rose and blue effects mostly, and made like the earlier shipments, with reinforced armholes and shoulder yokes. Price, $5.

(First Floor)

## Handkerchiefs to Match Her Gingham Frock

Or it may be a dimity, lawn, voile or any other colored dress in her Summer wardrobe.

In the loveliest rose, violet, maize, green, Copenhagen or tan, either with striped borders or white centers and colored borders. All-linen, 18c and 25c each.

(West Aisle)

## Tuck Into the Children's Trunk

nice little quilted satin bedroom slippers.

Blue, rose color or pink, quilted inside and out, with soft padded soles, $2.25 and $2.50 a pair, in sizes 7 to 2.

(First Floor)

## Women's Inexpensive Undermuslins

Cross-bar dimity step-ins, vests and envelope chemises, each with hemstitching, are each priced at $1.65.

Nightgowns to match, $2.50.

Nainsook bloomers with hemstitched ruffles, $1. With lace, $1.75.

(Third Floor)

## Children's Undermuslins Made Just Right

Some new arrivals are of cambric or fine nainsook.

Drawers, two to 14 year sizes, 85c to $2.

Combinations (drawers and waist), four to 14 year sizes, $2 to $3.25.

Princess petticoats, eight to 16 year sizes, $2 to $3.85.

(Third Floor)

## Candy Is a Gracious Gift to Take a Hostess

A special "hostess box," a large round tin box with lid is here for week-enders.

It is painted the prettiest blue and tied up with a big ribbon rosette. Inside are delicious Wanamaker candies, paper wrapped. The box is priced $3.50 complete.

At all times and all seasons Wanamaker caramels are favorites. A pound box of mixtures is $1.

(Down Stairs Store)

## Be Sure to Remember Letter Paper

For a short visit, there is a convenient box of note paper, twenty-four sheets and envelopes to match, from 25c to $1.25 a box.

Correspondence cards, twenty-four cards and an equal number of matching envelopes, 50c and 75c a box.

Wanamaker French cambric, 50c a pound and 50c for 100 envelopes.

Deckel-edge letter paper, 75c a pound and $1 for 100 envelopes.

(Main Floor)

### A Set of Old English Crown Derby

comprising a dozen fruit plates, each wearing a different flower, and six compotes decorate an old cupboard in Antiques.

The set is priced $150.

(Fifth Floor)

## Like the Soft Bloom of the Rose

is the complexion powdered with the new barley face powder.

Exceptionally delicate, fine and fragrant; absolutely pure. It stays on so well that frequently one application lasts the entire day.

White, natural and brunette, $1 a box.

(Main Floor)

### A Pair of Old English Fire-Screens

of the Sheraton period, of inlaid mahogany with screen of English glazed chintz, came from a famous old collection to Antiques, where they are priced $150 the pair.

(Fifth Floor)

## Cuff Links at Half

Enameled, gold-filled cuff links at $1 a pair—from one of the best makers and exactly the kind men and women wear with sports shirts.

In varying colors, and several designs.

(Main Floor)

## Hand-Carved Picture Frames

The sort which stand. They are in two finishes—antique gilt and silver, and in sizes from 5 x 7 to 8 x 11 inches, and we are selling them for the rather small sum of $2.50.

Lots of people will buy them for prizes.

(Fifth Floor)

## New Models

of cotton runners and centerpieces and children's dresses, all stamped, are being shown in the Art Needlework Store.

(Second Floor)

## *If You Are Going Abroad*

No place in the world where a woman is more conspicuous than on shipboard. Suspended between sky and water on the deck of an ocean liner, with a merciless light beating down upon her, and the close inspection of thousands of critical eyes from which she can't escape—well, every woman who has tried it knows what it is. She wants to look her best!

Here at Wanamaker's will be found just the right little steamer hat and veil, the correct wraps, the proper shoes, and oh, how footwear does show up on shipboard!—the right apparel of every sort, for deck and dinner and salon.

Steamer and wardrobe trunks, hat trunks and shoe trunks, hand luggage, steamer rugs, cameras the necessary guide-books, and the pleasant reading for the voyage—this busy Store is equipping voyagers in every particular, both for the voyage and for comfort in traveling on the other side.

## Bathing Corselets

that combine a brassiere and hip confiner, are priced $2 to $5.50.

A corselet with brassiere back is marked $1.50.

(Third Floor)

## A Music Roll for a Week-End Trip

Any place one goes nowadays music is almost sure to go and the sheets are carried cleaner and better in a little roll.

They are here in all descriptions from the little black roll style at $2 up to the flat type with a lock, made of fine cowhide or seal in black or gray and priced $20.

(Main Floor)

### *Good Honfleur Toilet Helps at Small Prices*

Honfleur stands for quality and economy. Vacationists will stock up with a Summer's supply of such useful, refreshing and necessary things:

Extracts, rose, violet and l'Empire, 50c.

Toilet waters, violet, l'Empire and Bouquet d'Amour, 50c and 85c.

Cleansing cream, "Youth and Beauty" cream and skin cream, each 40c.

Lemon cleansing cream, 35c and 65c.

Face powder, 35c.

Violet ammonia, 20c a pint, 30c a quart.

Bay rum, 50c a half pint, 85c pint, $1.65 quart.

Witch hazel 35c pint, 65c quart.

Sachets, violet, rose, l'Empire, 35c.

(West Aisle)

## A Little Electric Iron That Travelers Take Along

is as small as an iron well could be and takes up surprisingly little room.

The handle comes off, enabling it to slip in small corners as well as making it invertible for heating water or little things to eat, or a curling iron.

The price is $6.50.

(Fourth Floor)

## Nearly Every Porch Has Its Bamboo Tabourette

Most likely more than one for plants here and there seem to make every place cooler.

Right now there are some bamboo tabourettes here for 85c that are unusual.

Bamboo legs, 18 inches high and a 10 x 10 inch matting top.

(Fourth Floor)

## An Oilcloth Table Cover for the Breakfast Room

Practical—in fact, it is hard to think of anything more practical and it is pretty as well.

Made for a 54-inch table, either round or square, and the ground is white with attractive Japanese landscapes painted in blue.

Right now the price is special—$1.60.

(Fourth Floor)

## There's Really Nothing to Do But to Dance

when the Victrola plays this fox trot:

"You Can Have Every Light on Broadway If You Give Me That One Little Light at Home."

It is on a ten-inch double record and the reverse side offers "Lovey Dove" from "The Rose of Stamboul."

Price, 75c.

(Second Floor)

### When Tea Was Locked Up

housewives used cunning little inlaid mahogany caddies with lock and key, such as are shown in Antiques at $15 and up.

They make attractive trinket boxes.

(Fifth Floor)

## A Hat Box That Carries Clothes Is $9

Shirred pockets under the lid and on the flat side of the hat part hold a world of little bits of finery, while all around the hat there is space to pack light Summer clothes.

And, after all, a hat, slippers and hosiery, a frock and toilet things make up a woman's wardrobe on a week-end jaunt.

In the popular round shape, 18 inches in diameter and bound with either black or russet leather.

(Main Floor)

## Honeycomb Wool Coverlets

New coverlets of that soft old-fashioned weave which is so pleasant to the eye and so comfortable on a couch or as a shoulder wrap. They are in rose-and-white and other combinations of color, and sell at $13.50 each.

(Sixth Floor)

## Nurses' Uniforms

and cloaks to measure, and gowns for clergymen and judges, are an important part of the work of the Women's Custom Tailoring Bureau.

Materials are the best, and prices moderate.

(Second Floor)

## A Drink Stays Cool Through the Long Night

in a little vacuum pitcher that sits cozily and cheerily beside the bed.

Vacuum pitchers are not only a convenience—they are as attractive as anything could be in the boudoir.

In high colors to match the hangings or in darker colors with lighter painted patterns.

There are sets, consisting of a vacuum pitcher, glass and tray, priced between $13.25 and $25.

(Fourth Floor)

## Twice as Many Men

have bought tropical suits this year as last year, up to this time.

This is because tropical suits nowadays look like something. They are in the regular business-suit colors and patterns, they are smartly tailored,

And comfortable in hot weather.

Palm Beach suits, $18 and $20.

Fancy mohairs, $20, $22.50 and $25.

Tropical worsteds, $25 to $32.

(Third Floor)

## Men's Good Shoes at $6.40

A strikingly fine, dark brown calfskin brogue, ornamented with four-row stitchings.

A black brogue with full wing tip and perforations.

A tan brogue of grained calfskin and soft straight tip.

(Main Floor)

## A Fine Shirt for $5.50

is of English poplin with pin stripes, in bright Summer colors. Light, sheer, silky and markedly handsome.

(Main Floor)

### *Beluchistan Rugs, $25 to $32*

Fine little pieces, glowing in dark, soft red and deep blue.

Sizes, about 3 x 4 to 3 x 5.6 ft. Prices are moderate for rugs of such excellent quality.

$25 to $32 each.

(Seventh Floor)

## New Dinner Sets From England Special at $42.50

Finest English semi-china, in seven new border designs, including one with a gold band.

Complete sets of 106 pieces, bought to unusual advantage.

(Fourth Floor)

## Fine Silver-Plated Ware Garnishes Many Summer Tables

Almost, one might say, there is no such thing as wearing out with the right kind of silver-plated ware. There is no breakage, and even the most beautiful and useful articles are inexpensive.

Table mats, round, $1.75 to $5. Oblong, $3 to $6.

Bread trays, $4 to $33.

Roll baskets, $7 to $19.50.

Cheese-and-cracker dishes, $4.50.

Sandwich trays, $3 to $5.50.

Covered-vegetable dishes, $10 to $68.

Water pitchers, $11.50 to $44.

Meat platters, $14 to $100.

(Main Floor)

## Thousands of Dollars' Worth of Rugs, Carpets, Linoleums and Mattings Are Going Out in a July Clearaway

Naturally there are not many of any one pattern, but the assortment is generous, embracing almost all patterns that made up the spring stock.

A high-grade Wilton rug, 9x12 ft., $95.

Axminster rugs, 9x12 ft., $32.50 and $42.50.

Double-faced Smyrna rugs, 9x12 ft., $48.50.

Klearflax rugs in four colors, 4.6x7 ft., $9, and 27x54 inches, $3.

Velvet and Axminster carpets, $1.75 to $3.85 the yard.

Inlaid linoleums, $1.15 to $1.35 square yard.

China mattings, $14.50 for roll of 40 yards.

(Seventh Floor)

## 11. Marshall Field's Advertisement, 1920.

## 12. Macy's Advertisements, 1920s.

## France Sends Period Chairs to the Corner Shop

The frames are exact copies of models now in the *Louvre;* the upholstery, typical period fabrics — chintzes, damasks, brocades, velvets, Directoire stripes and toiles de Jouy, old Normandie skirts — harmonize with the frames.

Directoire Arm Chair (pictured) is offered in soft, white lacquer, or in dull antiqued walnut. Covering would blend with almost any decorative scheme.
$58.50 and $69.50

The same style in easy Side Chairs. Especially desirable for bridge.
Covered to match the arm chairs.
$34.75 and $42.75

*Quaint Bergere, exact copy of Louis XV model, with cream lacquer frame,* is covered in an old Normandie petticoat, perfect for living room or boudoir! The piece illustrated, $129.00

## BULBS ARE NOW SUCCESSFULLY GROWN IN U.S.A.

### Locally Produced Narcissi Good Substitute For Holland Product.

Since January 1, 1926, American growers have been increasingly successful in producing narcissus bulbs. On that date the Federal Horticultural Board of the United States Department of Agriculture prohibited the entry into this country of all varieties of imported narcissus, and the United States was thrown on its own resources for its supply.

The purpose of the board's ruling is protection against the destructive narcissus fly, which formerly was wont to enter the country on many of the narcissus bulbs imported from Holland.

Until the ban was placed by the board it was the popular belief that good narcissus bulbs could be grown only in Holland. But now that the abundant Dutch supply has been eliminated they are being produced successfully in large quantities on Long Island, in southern New Jersey, in Florida and along the Pacific Coast.

Several varieties of these American-grown narcissi are being sold in Macy's basement at prices ranging from eighty-four cents a dozen to fourteen dollars and twenty-four cents a hundred.

Since it is legal and safe to import them, tulips, hyacinths and crocus from Holland are also on sale in Macy's basement.

### Cut Silver Jewelry Seems Diamond Set

SPARKLING as though set with innumerable small diamonds is the new, cut silver jewelry, just arrived from France, on the street floor. It would be superb setting off the dull, satiny richness of a black velvet gown, although little can surpass its attractiveness as it lies in the case. The pieces are so delicately fashioned and carry such an air of distinctive simplicity that reading the modest price tags comes as a distinctly pleasant shock.

## Is a Sound Sleep Worth A Penny a Day?

INSOMNIA, it is said, is frequently caused by a lumpy, uncomfortable mattress. A cure for the disease thus caused is on sale in Macy's Bedding Department on the seventh floor. It is a mattress of such excellent quality, as to insure comfort, and it costs thirty-four dollars and fifty cents for the full size. Since its minimum life, under ordinary conditions, is ten years, its cost per day is considerably less than two cents.

Other mattresses in the same department cost from eight dollars and seventy-four cents to seventy-six dollars and fifty cents.

### Hand Tooling Employed Now in Women's Shoes

Italian tooled leather shoes, made in Florence of Florentine leather, are being sold in the Women's Shoe Department on the second floor. Although hand tooling has long been familiar on covers of fine books, this is the first time it has ever been used on shoes.

## The Sportswoman's Hose Take on Autumn Hues

Diamonds, plaids, checks and clocks take on fall colors and a diversity of ways for the sport of the thing.

The blue of fall haze; the browns, tans and grays of autumn landscapes and costumes lend themselves to the new designs. All hose, of course, are wool.

Soft tan and brown combined in diamonds, $3.69.
Soft woolen cashmere, clocked by hand, $3.19.
Two-toned, broken checks, $3.29.
Broken diamonds on a plain background, $1.84.
Diamonds broken by narrow stripes, $3.69.
Sizes, 8½ to 10.

MACY'S—*Street Floor, East Building*

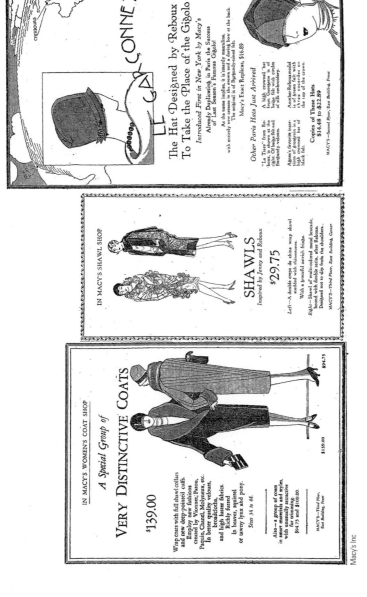

## 13. Marshall Field Promotes Its Image, 1925 and 1927.

# MARSHALL FIELD & COMPANY

MANUFACTURERS · IMPORTERS · WHOLESALERS · RETAILERS    *Retail Store · State, Washington, Randolph and Wabash*

## PROSPERITY AND PROGRESS FOR 1925

A CAREFUL survey of the factors affecting our economic life warrants us in forming the following opinions:

That the United States is now entering upon a new era of industrial expansion, commercial activity, and general prosperity.

That fundamental conditions are today in a better balance than they have been for many years. The assurance of stability, economy, and constructive legislation during the forthcoming administration has given business men everywhere, regardless of party, a definite sense of security and confidence in the future of our country.

That European affairs, so far as they may affect our own economic situation, are improving. The rehabilitation of Europe is now under way and in all reasonable probability will go steadily forward.

That our basic industries, including Agriculture, Steel, Manufacture, Construction, and Merchandising, are now in a favorable condition, with every indication of continued progress in keeping with normal requirements. The financial, banking and mercantile credit situation is especially sound and favorable, with money available for legitimate expansion and conservative enterprises.

Since the first of November there has been a marked improvement in mercantile activities. A vast volume of merchandise is now moving steadily from producer to consumer through the various channels of distribution. Our own business, both wholesale and retail, for the last two months has been largely in excess of the corresponding period in 1923.

From almost every point of view the outlook is encouraging. Over-optimism, however, which often produces speculation and inflation, must be vigilantly guarded against. Moreover, too much stress cannot be placed upon wise economy in the affairs of individuals and private business as well as in the affairs of government.

We confidently expect that 1925 will be an exceptionally good year for the business of this Company and we are making all our plans accordingly. We are determined to improve still further the character of our merchandise and the efficiency of our service. While proceeding with due conservatism, we shall strive to develop in our organization a still more potent spirit of enthusiastic progressiveness, which we believe will be characteristic of the best types of American business during the new year now before us.

*This Sketch Shows a Composite View of the Mills and Warehouses Owned and Operated by Marshall Field & Company (Wholesale Building in Center)*

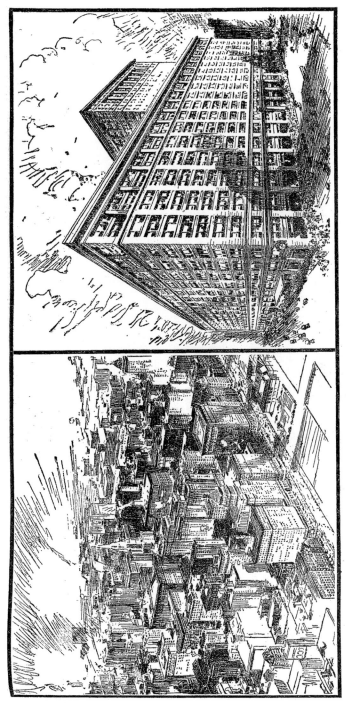

Macy's Inc

✦ C

Selli

Con:

189(

✦ CHAPTER 3

Selling
Consumption,
1890–1930

15. Macy's First 14th Street Location.

Bettmann/Corbis

## 16.  Macy's New 34th Street Store.

17. Marshall Field Department Store, Chicago.

William C. Shrout/Time Life Pictures/Getty Images

## 18. Marshall Field's Interior, ca. 1902.

## 19. Rogers Department Store, Florence, Alabama.

The Landrum Collection.

# Questions to Consider

For convenience, the evidence is divided into three sections. The first (textual) evidence focuses on the business of advertising. These sources are excerpted from an advertising journal, two textbooks, and the autobiography of a famous advertising pioneer. *Printer's Ink* was a weekly journal founded in the second half of the nineteenth century. What kinds of photographs does the author recommend using? Why? What is the relationship between the photographs and the item being sold? Earnest Calkins wrote the textbook *The Business of Advertising*. How does he define advertising? In what ways does he believe that advertising affects people? S. Roland Hall worked as an advertiser and later taught sales and advertising. Why does he believe that the names of products are important? What does he think are the major differences between men and women? How might these differences affect people who created advertisements? Finally, Claude Hopkins was a self-made man who became one of the highest-paid advertising copywriters of the late nineteenth and early twentieth centuries. In this excerpt from his autobiography, he explains the basic elements in his approach to advertising. How does he explain his success?

The second segment of evidence consists of department store advertisements. Advertising, of course, does not simply display, it entices. If it works— and the growth of these companies indicates that it did—advertising sold not simply a product but an image and an identity. Advertisements, therefore,

offer a revealing window into culture. The careful viewer can see underlying assumptions, messages, and appeals. As you read each advertisement, first try to determine the intended message. What is the advertiser trying to sell? What emotions does the advertisement appeal to? What desires? Then ask what the advertisement tells you about society during that time. Many of the advertisements were intended to appeal to women, who increasingly oversaw family shopping and made decisions about fashion and desirability. What can you learn about gender roles? About relationships between men and women? About class distinctions? About urban society? How does all this change over time? Compare the advertisements from the late nineteenth century with those from the 1920s.

Finally, photographs in the last grouping of sources allow you to study the buildings which housed some of America's most successful retail empires. What image did the physical spaces convey? How did structural design advance the commercial aims of department store magnates? How and why did they use architecture to brand themselves? What do you think these spaces meant to Americans in this era? Why would these designs attract customers?

To conclude, consider what you have learned from the evidence as a whole. How did department stores shape consumer behavior? What does the success of these businesses reveal about values, particularly white middle-class values, during this era of thoroughgoing change? Did advertising challenge or reinforce gender norms? Did department stores increase or undermine individualism? What do the merchandise, the pricing system, and the services offered say about the clientele? What is the relationship between urbanization, industrialization, and conspicuous consumption? What can downtown department stores tell us about this generation of Americans?

◆

## Epilogue

The heyday of stylish downtown department stores peaked in the 1920s. Many companies continued to thrive during the twentieth century, but most did so by geographic diversification and by ratcheting back expenditures at their flagships. A number of factors brought their centrality in urban life to a close. The Great Depression severely curtailed conspicuous consumption, as did World War II. Urbanization inextricably led to suburbanization. In 1900, less than 6 percent of Americans lived in suburbs; by 1990, over 46 percent did. Suburban dwellers did not usually return to their city center to shop. White flight—the outmigration of middle-class whites to the suburbs—eroded the customer base for the commercial centers of America's major cities as well as small towns and county seats. The expansion of automobile culture sped the demise of downtown shopping. By the 1970s, Americans owned more than 100,000,000 registered cars. They preferred to drive to new suburban malls, with vast, free parking lots.

The culture that underlay the success of grand department stores changed as well. The early twentieth century saw the captains of industry come under attack for what many came to believe were excesses. Evidence of their maltreatment of workers, strong-arming of politicians, and ruthless business practices came to light due to the efforts of reformers and journalists. The society that once had venerated industrial barons began to fear that they had too much power and believe that such power should be curtailed. Progressive muckrakers likewise criticized advertising, and consumers became more savvy and skeptical about marketing promises. Although its image was also tarnished by the disillusionment accompanying the Great Depression, advertising rebounded. It helped "sell" World War II to the American public by encouraging conservation of scarce resources, and it emerged stronger and more pervasive than ever in the 1950s. Americans were starved for consumer goods after wartime rationing, and their rapid acceptance of a new medium blending entertainment and advertisement—television—greatly expanded marketing opportunities.

In the post-World War II era, suburban malls supplanted downtown department stores as the centers of consumerism. Victor Gruen, an Austrian-born architect, began to design suburban shopping malls in the 1950s—first open-air facilities and then enclosed pedestrian shopping centers. Southdale Mall in Minnesota, the first of its kind in the United States, was his invention. Today there are around 1100 enclosed shopping malls in the United States (and over 45,000 shopping centers). The largest, Mall of America (also in Minnesota), contains over 500 stores, 20,000 parking spaces, 4.3 miles of storefront, an aquarium, a 14-screen multiplex, and an amusement park. As the mall's website proclaims, a person browsing just 10 minutes in each store would spend more than 86 hours during their visit. Seven Yankee Stadiums would fit inside.

Mall of America notwithstanding, the ubiquitous sprawling suburban mall, with its ring of asphalt parking lots, appears to be on the wane. The trend now is toward open-air commercial developments and "Big Box" retailers—20,000- to 100,000-square-foot stores that specialize (in pet supplies, electronics, toys, office supplies) and seek to monopolize their sectors. One writer dubbed these corporations "category killers" pushing "retail Darwinism."[7] As a result of these trends, only one enclosed mall has been built in the U.S. since 2006.

Dozens of traditional malls sit vacant, blighting the landscape and damaging the local economy, and scores more are slowly dying. The 2008–2009 housing crash and subsequent economic slump derailed many Americans' capacity to shop for entertainment, either at suburban malls or in revitalizing downtowns.

Rogers Department Store in Florence, Alabama, lasted longer than most downtown independent retailers. The family opted not to join retail conglomerates, although many independent operators made the choice to consolidate in the mid-twentieth century. The company weathered the economic storms of the 1970s and the construction of malls throughout north Alabama, including one in Florence's eastern suburbs. Rogers expanded into shopping malls in the 1960s and 1970s, and as late as the early 1990s, turned profits at its still-popular flagship store on Court Street. But in 2001, Rogers closed its downtown Florence store. Two bookstores, a men's clothier, and several other small retailers followed. The building that Thomas Rogers II completed in the 1940s—on the same site as his grandfather's "Surprise Store"—remains vacant.

7. Robert Spector, *Category Killers: The Retail Revolution and Its Impact on Consumer Culture* (Boston: Harvard Business School Press, 2005), xii–xiii.

# 4

# Child Labor Reform and the Redefinition of Childhood, 1880–1920

✦

## The Problem

Published in 1890, Jacob Riis's enormously popular book, *How the Other Half Lives*, showed middle-class Americans precisely that. Combining personal stories, photographs, statistics, and social criticism, he carried his readers into the slums, tenement houses, saloons, and alleyways where impoverished families struggled to survive. Riis shone a light on the lives of the urban poor and inspired middle-class reformers to try to improve—in ways they deemed appropriate—city slums and the people who lived there.

Born in Denmark in 1849, Riis immigrated to the United States at the age of twenty-one. He tried his hand at carpentry, iron works, and farming but fell on hard times and wound up destitute and homeless. He eventually secured a job as a newspaper reporter, covering the police beat in an office on Mulberry Street, near Five Points, one of New York's poorest and most dangerous neighborhoods. He soon found himself drawn to Progressive reform campaigns, and married his two passions,

activism and writing. In addition to writing *How the Other Half Lives*, Riis lectured widely on the perils of poverty and published extensively, principally books and articles about the slums of New York City. His titles reveal his agenda: *Children of the Poor* (1892), *Out of Mulberry Street* (1896), *The Battle with the Slum* (1901), and *Children of the Tenements* (1903). A skilled photographer, Riis illustrated his works with heartbreaking pictures of the desperately poor.

Riis felt particularly sympathetic to the plight of impoverished children. His photographs showed these children in their homes, at their jobs, and on the streets where many basically lived. His books recounted stories of drunken and abusive parents, hunger, cruelty, violence, and early deaths.

Middle-class women already undertaking social reforms related to women's and children's well-being found Riis's work inspiring. The conditions under which children of the urban poor lived and worked particularly appalled these women. Their own middle-class children lived far more protected lives, and these mothers believed all children deserved to have their innocence guarded—that should be the "normal" situation in childhood. As a result of Progressive era reformers, ideas about children and childhood gradually yet profoundly shifted.

How did children's lives and societal attitudes about childhood change during the Progressive era?

◆

## Background

Progressivism encompassed a wide range of reforms that swept through the United States in the late nineteenth and early twentieth centuries. Typically associated with the presidencies of Theodore Roosevelt and Woodrow Wilson, Progressivism first emerged in the 1880s, peaked in the 1900s and 1910s, and declined throughout the 1920s. Progressive reformers tackled social inequities, corporate corruption, and urban and labor controversies. Some Progressive campaigns lobbied for federal regulation of food and drugs. Others encouraged the democratization of government by supporting the adoption of referendum, ballot initiative, and recall laws. Progressives fought for women's suffrage, and they formed organizations such as the National Association for the Advancement of Colored People (NAACP). They advocated for better wages and healthy work environments, lower tariffs, and governmental regulation of corporations and industry.

Progressives belonged to both national political parties, the Democrats and the Republicans. Both parties also contained members who believed in social Darwinism. These conservatives thought that the "fittest" people would thrive and that reformers and government should not interfere with the consequences of this "natural" social hierarchy. Progressives countered that the United States could and should be improved, that communities and government could remedy economic, political, and social problems.

Most Progressives came from Protestant, white backgrounds; most had been born in small towns but moved to cities. They put their faith in individuals, especially when they acted together in organizations, to bring about change. The first step, Progressives maintained, was educating the American public about societal problems. Experts such as social workers and social scientists collected information and circulated their findings among the general public in an easily understandable, compelling way. Progressives believed that once properly informed, the American public would support whatever action, policy, or law seemed necessary to solve the problem.

White, middle-class women participated in the whole gamut of Progressive reforms, but many felt especially drawn to issues concerning the vulnerable, impoverished women and children living in urban slums and described

✦ CHAPTER 4
Child Labor
Reform and the
Redefinition of
Childhood,
1880–1920

by Jacob Riis and others. Settlement houses, such as Jane Addams's Hull House in Chicago, emerged in the Progressive era out of the desire, in Addams's words, to "aid in the solutions of life in a great city, to help our neighbors build responsible, self-sufficient lives for themselves and their families." Addams and her colleagues did not simply visit the poor and hope to help them; they lived where they worked—in poor, immigrant neighborhoods. These female Progressives believed that crime, illiteracy, and disease derived from lack of economic opportunity, not any inherent moral failing. If people could have access to the tools to lift themselves out of poverty, most of the problems associated with urban poverty would disappear, and all of society would benefit.[1] Public health nurses and social workers shared with settlement house residents a desire to alleviate the suffering of children and families, but they typically visited slums and returned to their own middle-class neighborhoods after work.

Other Progressive reformers focused on children laboring in textile mills and coal mines. The idea that children should work did not emerge in the industrial age. From the colonial period forward, children often labored on farms, in artisan shops, and as apprentices in trades. Both African American children held in bondage and the offspring of free white families often entered the work force as young as age

six or seven. It was not at all unusual for children that age to help farm and tend animals, to begin learning a trade, or to be hired out or apprenticed.

But industrialization and urbanization, which increased dramatically in the late nineteenth century, intensified socioeconomic class differences and the plight of poor, working children. Homeless families filled urban almshouses to capacity; cities created special institutions—orphanages—for indigent children. Historians estimate that in the late nineteenth century only 20 percent of the children living in orphanages had actually lost both parents. The rest had one or two living parents who simply could not care for them because of extreme poverty, alcoholism, illness, or hopelessness. "We wuz six . . . and we ain't got no father. Some of us had to go," a twelve-year-old boy who shined shoes for a living told Jacob Riis.[2] That boy paid eighteen cents a day for a bed and two meals at the Newsboys' Lodging House in New York City. He and the other boys who lived there numbered among the more fortunate; many children lived on the streets, sleeping in doorways and boxes, with no promise of a next meal and little prospect of a better future.

Progressives undertook myriad campaigns to "save" these homeless and abandoned children. The Children's Aid Society of New York City sent more than 200,000 children on "orphan trains" to the New York state countryside or even the Far West. Sometimes the children

1. For more on Jane Addams's philosophy and her work, see her autobiography, *Twenty Years at Hull-House*. In 1931, she became the first American woman to win the Nobel Peace Prize.

2. Jacob A. Riis, *How the Other Half Lives*, edited by David Leviatin (Boston: Bedford Books, 1996), 191.

were simply dumped at the end of the railroad line, their fates randomly determined by whoever met the train and wanted a child. Some of the children certainly enjoyed better lives, but others were exploited by their new families. Few were legally adopted. Adoption procedures varied from state, to state, and the exchange of money for children remained commonplace.[3]

The New York Foundling Hospital, run by the Sisters of Charity, oversaw a more systematic program of matching orphans with suitable western families, but that too posed unanticipated problems. In 1904, the Sisters became embroiled in a controversy that ended up in the United States Supreme Court. The nuns sent New York orphans, most of Irish Catholic backgrounds, to live with Mexican Catholic families in Arizona. When white Arizona residents found out that Mexican families were raising "white" orphans, they undertook a massive abduction of the children—which the Supreme Court supported.[4]

To aid the poverty-stricken urban mothers who tried to keep their families together, Progressives undertook campaigns to promote pre-natal and early childhood health. They found plenty of problems to remedy: high maternal and infant death rates, tainted food supplies, poor hygiene, and malnutrition. In 1900, 90 percent of American women gave birth at home; only half had access to a doctor. The maternal death rate was thirty times higher between 1900 and 1920 than it is today, owing largely to post-delivery infections. Poor mothers, often malnourished themselves, frequently could not nurse their babies and had to supplement with cow's milk. But most milk in that era was not regulated and not pasteurized. Thus, children in the countryside drank raw milk containing dangerous bacteria. Children in cities fared even worse. Suppliers watered down their milk, so it lacked adequate nutritional value. And they adulterated spoiled milk with sweeteners to cover the bad taste. Malnutrition and diarrhea caused by tainted milk killed large numbers of infants and toddlers in the late nineteenth and early twentieth centuries. Furthermore, poor mothers often fed their infants the same table food they ate, only chewed or mashed up. Working mothers depended on children to take care of infants, which sometimes led to accidents. As a result of all these issues, one in six children died before reaching the age of five—a statistic that inspired Progressive action.

Progressives also fought for legal changes to curb exploitative child labor. Florence Kelley stood at the forefront of the campaign against sweatshops and for children's rights. A stalwart advocate of women's suffrage, African American civil rights (she was one of the founders of the NAACP), and workers' rights, Kelley was living at Hull House and working with Jane Addams when the governor of Illinois appointed her the state's chief factory inspector.

---

3. For more on the history of adoption, see E. Wayne Carp, *Family Matters: Secrecy and Disclosure in the History of Adoption* (Cambridge, MA: Harvard University Press, 1998); and Barbara Melosh, *Strangers and Kin: The American Way of Adoption* (Cambridge, MA: Harvard University Press, 2002).

4. For a full description of this fascinating case, see Linda Gordon, *The Great Arizona Orphan Abduction* (Cambridge, MA: Harvard University Press, 2001).

✦ CHAPTER 4
Child Labor
Reform and the
Redefinition of
Childhood,
1880–1920

In both her volunteer work and her government appointment, Kelley fought for the eight-hour workday, the minimum wage, and safe working conditions. Children laboring in dangerous industrial jobs for a pittance particularly prompted her into action. She was indomitable and imaginative. When she struggled to get her sweatshop suits properly litigated, she decided to become a lawyer herself, earning her law degree from Northwestern University.[5]

In 1912, after years of effort by Progressives such as Florence Kelley, the federal government established the Children's Bureau. Headed first by Julia Lathrop and then by Grace Abbot, both skilled, experienced reformers, the Bureau tried to educate mothers by providing free pamphlets such as "Infant Care." Instrumental in establishing better standards for birth and death registration of children, the Bureau collected the first reliable statistics on the causes of infant mortality. Because it was chronically under-funded, the Children's Bureau depended on large numbers of mostly female volunteers who interviewed mothers and collected data on children to be analyzed by the Bureau's small professional staff.

Progressives believed that education would allow poor children to expand their opportunities, to escape exploitative labor and life in urban slums. The Children's Bureau represented this agenda by lobbying for stricter policing of compulsory education laws. By 1918, most states had school attendance laws

on the books, but municipalities often ignored them. Some states adopted only minimal education laws. North Carolina, for example, required children between the ages of eight and thirteen to attend school only four months per year. In addition to fighting for stricter enforcement of state statutes, the Children's Bureau also sought to raise the age in education laws to ensure that children stayed in school longer. And they encouraged the construction of playgrounds and parks for urban children.

More controversially, the Children's Bureau (and Progressives in general) worked with the National Child Labor Committee to regulate or even abolish children's work. Their activities revealed the wide range of dangerous jobs children held, particularly in the canning industry, coal mines, and textile mills. They also worked to regulate the workloads of children who labored alongside their mothers doing piecework in tenement houses, and on the streets as newsboys, bootblacks, and peddlers.

All of these various reforms aimed at protecting and improving the lives of poor children. But there were clear limits to the Progressive agenda. Religious and class biases sometimes influenced these reforms. Progressives also tended to idealize farm life, missing the fact that farm children worked similarly dangerous jobs for long hours and with commensurately little opportunity for education, as did children who labored in urban factories. White Progressives did little or nothing to ameliorate the conditions African American children endured in the South. Finally, they often underestimated how much poverty limited

5. For more on Florence Kelley, see Kathryn Kish Sklar, *Florence Kelley and the Nation's Work: The Rise of Women's Political Culture, 1830–1900* (New Haven, CT: Yale University Press, 1995).

the choices available to immigrant and working-class families, and assumed that their middle-class ideals should be the norm. In spite of these limitations, the Progressive reformers brought to light the shameful plight of poor, working children, and they helped to redefine Americans' perception of society's collective responsibility to children.

---

## The Method

As you practice your skills as an historian, it is important to remember that, generally speaking, words and concepts do not have fixed, absolute meanings, but rather change over time. For example, the word "family" meant something different at various times in the American past. In the colonial era, most Indian nations organized not around conjugal units but clans, which were often matrilineal. Biological fathers mattered less in children's lives than did maternal uncles. Slavery altered perceptions of family among both enslaved people and slave owners. In the eighteenth century, high mortality rates and importation patterns forced African slaves to broaden their definition of family: for example, "brothers" and "sisters" might be affective rather than biological. In the early nineteenth century, paternalist white slaveholders often referred to "our family" meaning both their biological relations and their slaves. In the late twentieth century, medical advancements transformed the most fundamental elements of family-making: sexual intercourse is no longer a prerequisite to pregnancy, and surrogate "mothers" can deliver children with whom they share no DNA.

Conceptions of being a "man" or a "woman" also shifted at different periods, for different people, and in different parts of the country. For much of U.S. history, white Americans inextricably linked manhood with race; African Americans and Native Americans rejected that view. The age at which a "woman" could legally marry changed over time; and "feminine" duties varied depending on region and class.

Americans' understanding of "childhood" has also changed over time— slowly, perhaps, but profoundly. Just as we might struggle to understand colonial Americans apprenticing out seven-year-olds, they would be nonplussed by our treatment of "tweens" and "teenagers" today. Understanding these changing conceptions of childhood rests on realizing that attitudes toward children are *socially constructed*; that is, they derive from the values and culture of a particular point in history. Between 1880 and 1920, as they became increasingly aware of child labor and poverty, Americans rethought some of their basic assumptions about childhood. What did Progressives think about children and society's responsibility to them? What problems related to childhood poverty and labor did they highlight, and what solutions did they propose? How and why did ideas about childhood change in the Progressive era?

◆ CHAPTER 4
Child Labor
Reform and the
Redefinition of
Childhood,
1880–1920

◆
## The Evidence

**PHOTOGRAPHS OF WORKING AND IMPOVERISHED CHILDREN**

Source 1 from Lewis Hine, 1908 Photograph of Mill Workers in Newton, North Carolina.

## 1. Mill Workers, 1908.

Library of Congress

Source 2 from Lewis Hine, 1912 photograph, Clayton, North Carolina Cotton Mills.

## 2. Mill Workers, 1912.

Library of Congress

♦ CHAPTER 4

Child Labor
Reform and the
Redefinition of
Childhood,
1880–1920

Source 3, from Lewis Hine, 1911 photograph, S. Pittston, Pa., Pennsylvania Coal
Company.

## 3. Breaker Boys Sorting Slate and Rock from Coal.

National Archives

Source 4 photograph by Lewis W. Hine, from Bremner, ed., *Children and Youth in America*, ff. p. 686.

## 4. Coal Miners.

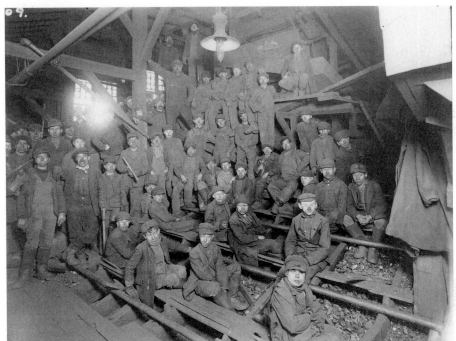

© Lewis Hine/CORBIS

◆ CHAPTER 4

Child Labor
Reform and the
Redefinition of
Childhood,
1880–1920

Source 5 photograph by Lewis W. Hine.

## 5. Newsboys.

© Lewis Hine/CORBIS

Source 6 from Elliot West, *Growing Up in Twentieth Century America: A History and Reference Guide* (Westport, Conn.: Greenwood Press, 1996), p. 50.

## 6. Slum Children Playing in the Street.

◆ CHAPTER 4
Child Labor
Reform and the
Redefinition of
Childhood,
1880–1920

Source 7 photograph by Lewis W. Hine, from West, *Growing Up in Twentieth Century America*, p. 14.

## 7. A Young Girl at an Orphanage.

Lewis Hine/Library of Congress

Source 8 from Jacob A. Riis, *How the Other Half Lives,* David Leviatin, ed. (Boston: Bedford/St. Martin's, 1996), p. 94.

## 8. A Poor Mother and Child.

✦ CHAPTER 4
Child Labor
Reform and the
Redefinition of
Childhood,
1880–1920

**REPORTS FROM URBAN AMERICA**

Source 9 from Jacob A. Riis, *How the Other Half Lives: Studies Among the Tenements of New York* (New York: Charles Scribner's Sons, 1914), pp. 179–185.

## 9. Jacob Riis Describes How Slum Life Affects Children.

### THE PROBLEM OF THE CHILDREN

The problem of the children becomes, in these swarms, to the last degree perplexing. Their very number makes one stand aghast. I have already given instances of the packing of the child population in East Side tenements. They might be continued indefinitely until the array would be enough to startle any community. For, be it remembered, these children with the training they receive—or do not receive—with the instincts they inherit and absorb in their growing up, are to be our future rulers, if our theory of government is worth anything. More than a working majority of our voters now register from the tenements. I counted the other day the little ones, up to ten years or so, in a Bayard Street tenement that for a yard has a triangular space in the centre with sides fourteen or fifteen feet long, just room enough for a row of ill-smelling closets at the base of the triangle and a hydrant at the apex. There was about as much light in this "yard" as in the average cellar. I gave up my self-imposed task in despair when I had counted one hundred and twenty-eight in forty families. Thirteen I had missed, or not found in. Applying the average for the forty to the whole fifty-three, the house contained one hundred and seventy children. It is not the only time I have had to give up such census work. I have in mind an alley—an inlet rather to a row of rear tenements—that is either two or four feet wide according as the wall of the crazy old building that gives on it bulges out or in. I tried to count the children that swarmed there, but could not. Sometimes I have doubted that anybody knows just how many there are about. Bodies of drowned children turn up in the rivers right along in summer whom no one seems to know anything about. When last spring some workmen, while moving a pile of lumber on a North River pier, found under the last plank the body of a little lad crushed to death, no one had missed a boy, though his parents afterward turned up. The truant officer assuredly does not know, though he spends his life trying to find out, somewhat illogically, perhaps, since the department that employs him admits that thousands of poor children are crowded out of the schools year by year for want of room. There was a big tenement in the Sixth Ward, now happily appropriated by the beneficent spirit of business that blots out so many foul spots in New York—it figured not long ago in the official reports as "an out-and-out hog-pen"—that had a record of one hundred and two arrests in four years among its four hundred and seventy-eight tenants, fifty-seven of them for drunken and disorderly conduct. I do not know how many children there were in it, but the inspector reported that he found only seven in the whole house who owned that they went to school. The rest gathered all the instruction they received running for beer for their elders. Some of them claimed the "flat" as their home as a mere matter of form. They slept in the streets at night. The official came upon a little party of four drinking beer out of the cover of a milk-can in the hallway. They were of the seven good boys and proved their claim to the title by offering him some. . . .

. . . The old question, what to do with the boy, assumes a new and serious phase in the tenements. Under the best conditions found there, it is not easily answered. In nine cases out of ten he would make an excellent mechanic, if trained early to work at a trade, for he is neither dull nor slow, but the short-sighted despotism of the trades unions has practically closed that avenue to him. Trade-schools, however excellent, cannot supply the opportunity thus denied him, and at the outset the boy stands condemned by his own to low and ill-paid drudgery, held down by the hand that of all should labor to raise him. Home, the greatest factor of all in the training of the young, means nothing to him but a pigeon-hole in a coop along with so many other human animals. . . . Rough as he is, if any one doubt that this child of common clay have in him the instinct of beauty, of love for the ideal of which his life has no embodiment, let him put the matter to the test. Let him take into a tenement block a handful of flowers from the fields and watch the brightened faces, the sudden abandonment of play and fight that go ever hand in hand where there is no elbow-room, the wild entreaty for "posies," the eager love with which the little messengers of peace are shielded, once possessed; then let him change his mind. . . .

. . . [T]he children of the poor grow up in joyless homes to lives of wearisome toil that claims them at an age when the play of their happier fellows has but just begun. Has a yard of turf been laid and a vine been coaxed to grow within their reach, they are banished and barred out from it as from a heaven that is not for such as they. I came upon a couple of youngsters in a Mulberry Street yard a while ago that were chalking on the fence their first lesson in "writin'." And this is what they wrote: "Keeb of te Grass." They had it by heart, for there was not, I verily believe, a green sod within a quarter of a mile. Home to them is an empty name. . . .

. . . A little fellow who seemed clad in but a single rag was among the flotsam and jetsam stranded at Police Headquarters one day last summer. No

✦ CHAPTER 4
Child Labor
Reform and the
Redefinition of
Childhood,
1880–1920

one knew where he came from or where he belonged. The boy himself knew as little about it as anybody, and was the least anxious to have light shed on the subject after he had spent a night in the matron's nursery. The discovery that beds were provided for boys to sleep in there, and that he could have "a whole egg" and three slices of bread for breakfast put him on the best of terms with the world in general, and he decided that Headquarters was "a bully place." He sang "McGinty" all through, with Tenth Avenue variations, for the police, and then settled down to the serious business of giving an account of himself. The examination went on after this fashion:

"Where do you go to church, my boy?"

"We don't have no clothes to go to church." And indeed his appearance, as he was, in the door of any New York church would have caused a sensation.

"Well, where do you go to school, then?"

"I don't go to school," with a snort of contempt.

"Where do you buy your bread?"

"We don't buy no bread; we buy beer," said the boy, and it was eventually the saloon that led the police as a landmark to his "home." It was worthy of the boy. As he had said, his only bed was a heap of dirty straw on the floor, his daily diet a crust in the morning, nothing else.

Into the rooms of the Children's Aid Society were led two little girls whose father had "busted up the house" and put them on the street after their mother died. Another, who was turned out by her step-mother "because she had five of her own and could not afford to keep her," could not remember ever having been in church or Sunday-school, and only knew the name of Jesus through hearing people swear by it. She had no idea what they meant. These were specimens of the overflow from the tenements of our home-heathen that are growing up in New York's streets to-day. . . .

. . . In thirty-seven years the Children's Aid Society, that came into existence as an emphatic protest against the tenement corruption of the young, has sheltered quite three hundred thousand outcast, homeless, and orphaned children in its lodging-houses, and has found homes in the West for seventy thousand that had none. . . . In the last fifteen years of this tireless battle for the safety of the State the intervention of the Society for the Prevention of Cruelty to Children has been invoked for 138,891 little ones; it has thrown its protection around more than twenty-five thousand helpless children, and has convicted nearly sixteen thousand wretches of child-beating and abuse. Add to this the standing army of fifteen thousand dependent children in New York's asylums and institutions, and some idea is gained of the crop that is garnered day by day in the tenements, of the enormous force employed to check their inroads on our social life, and of the cause for apprehension that would exist did their efforts flag for ever so brief a time. "Nothing is now better understood than that the rescue of the children is the key to the problem of city poverty, as presented for our solution to-day; that character may be formed where to reform it would be a hopeless task.

Source 10 from "Florence Kelley's Testimony on the Sweating System," in *Report and Findings on the Joint Committee to Investigate the "Sweat Shop" System* (Springfield, Illinois: H.W. Rokker, 1983), pp. 135–139. Reprinted at Kathryn Kish Sklar and Thomas Dublin, eds., *Women and Social Movements in the United States, 1600–2000* (Scholar's Edition), website available through www.alexanderstreet.com.

## 10. Florence Kelley Describes Chicago Sweat Shops.

Mrs. Florence Kelly [sic], having been sworn, testified as follows:

Examined by Mr Noonan:

Q. Please state your name, occupation, and place of residence?

A. My name is Florence Kelly [sic]; I live at 335 South Halsted street, Chicago, and I am now an expert of the department of labor at Washington, but I was, last summer, special agent of the Illinois Bureau of Labor Statistics, appointed expressly for the purpose of investigating the sweating shops, and the home finishers for the sweating shops here in the city.

Q. Will you please state your knowledge of the existence of the so called sweating shop evil, and what, if any, suggestions have you to offer for the remedy thereof?

A. Well, while in that capacity, I made a room to room investigation, a canvass of the regions in which clothing was being made. I found employed Russians, Germans, Bohemians, Italians, Scandinavians, but when I looked over my record of people with whom I had spoken, or whose signatures I had got for the purpose of assuring myself of their nationality, I did not find one native American employed either in a shop or as a home finisher. I had nothing to do with the inside shops, only with the sweat shops. The first thing which I noticed in my investigation was the uniformity of filthy surroundings. The first afternoon that I entered upon the work, I came upon a home finisher at 98 Ewing street—it was the second Saturday afternoon in June. The woman had on her lap a baby, wrapped in Italian fashion, with a swelling in its neck, which the mother told me was a scarlet fever swelling; and spread upon the baby, and partly covering it, and coming in contact with its head, was a cloak, which this mother was sewing, which bore the tag "M.F. & Co." It was being finished for a sweater in the neighborhood. I have kept a record of cases of infectious diseases which I found, and they include seven cases of unmistakable infectious diseases, and those were all its finishers families. It is important to

✦ CHAPTER 4

Child Labor
Reform and the
Redefinition of
Childhood,
1880–1920

note that there is constantly a doubt expressed as to whether it is possible to limit the work of people at home in their own rooms, and not directly in a shop, and not employing persons who are not members of their own families. Now, I will give you a copy from my note book, which I took at the time; I will give you these seven cases. The first Saturday afternoon in June I found this scarlet fever case at 98 Ewing street, the following week, I found a case, in a Sicilian family, where four children were just recovering from scarlet fever, and cloak making had been carried on continuously throughout the illness. On the second Sunday afternoon in July I found, at 145 Bunker street, a Bohemian customs' tailor, sewing a fine, customs cloak, not more than six feet from the bed; and on this bed his little boy lay dying of typhoid fever, and I ascertained that the child died of typhoid fever the following week. At 128 Ewing street I found a diphtheria notice posted, and the patient suffering on the ground floor, in a rear room, with cloaks being finished in the room in front, and knee pants in the room overhead. At 365 Jefferson street I found a case of measles, with women finishing cloaks in the same room with the patient. This was the case to which Dr. Alderson called my attention. At 136 Ewing street I found two children, Francisco and Mary Sergello, finishing knee pants in their mother's bedroom, while suffering from a most aggravated case of scabaies [sic]—the itch. This was so aggravated that they had been banished from the children's clubs, because it was dangerous for them to come in contact with other children and I saw them rubbing their faces and the scales falling on the clothing that they sewed.

Q. What quality of clothing was that?

A. Very poor clothing. At 11 Polk street, on the 15th of September, a child died of malignant diphtheria. The work of cloakmaking and knee pants finishing went on in the room with the patient, and in the adjacent rooms, and I myself saw bundles of knee pants carried out of an adjacent room to the sweaters' shop at 257 Polk street. I think that makes seven cases, and it is of importance to note that none of those cases of infectious disease was in a sweater's shop, and each of them was in a family where the family alone worked without employing other help. I also observed in the manufacture of plush cloaks and of expensive fur-trimmed cloaks some of the filthiest places which I visited, and those cloaks are wholly incapable of disinfection by pressing, even if pressing were a disinfecting means, because fur cloaks are never pressed, that is fur-trimmed cloaks, and plush cloaks are never pressed; and throughout the time during which my inspection was made it was principally heavy winter cloaks that I found in process of manufacture among those home finishers. Now, as to the health of the employés, they suffer intensely. The people employed at the sweat shops suffer not only from coming in contact with the clothing which has been finished in the finishers' homes, and from working in ill-ventilated shops, frequently underground, but they also suffer from the excessive speed at which they are compelled to work foot-power machines, and this is true not only of young girls and growing boys, but also of men, in those shops in which any such men are employed. I can't swear that I found in any shop a man able to keep up the regular speed who was over 40 years old. When I inquired as to the age of the employés, I constantly found that the men who looked old and broken-down, and as though they might be well on towards sixty, were early in the thirties. One case which I have since found to be typical came to my attention of a young man about 33, named David Silverman. He had been operating a machine in the ordinary sweaters' shops since he was 14 years old, and was entirely incapacitated by exhaustion from further work. The physicians who examined him agreed in stating that he was suffering from premature old age, and at 33 he was superannuated and wholly dependent upon charity for supporting himself and his five children. I found a large number of cases in which the children were supporting fathers who ranged in age from 38 to 45 years, and were incapacitated purely by reason of having speeded the machine from fifteen to twenty years. The effect of the machine work on young girls and boys was very conspicuous. The effect of speeding machines was seen in the prevailing waxy color of the children's faces, both in the shops and in their homes. I constantly found young people between 15 and 20 who were temporarily disabled by exhaustion, consequent upon speeding their machines; they were weak from exhaustion. So that the poverty of the sweaters' victims results not only from the low wages which they actually receive while at work, but from the fact that the work wears them out so that their earnings are limited to a very few years of their life.

Q. How about the wages paid in those places?

A. I found that the wages for girls ranged from nothing to the highest that I found—I found one girl for one week in the height of the season to be working 15 hours a day for seven consecutive days at seam binding, which is the heaviest work in the trade, and is usually done by strong men, she earned $18. I found an able-bodied girl speeding a machine making knee pants for nothing, and she told me, and the man beside her corroborated her statement, that she had been working three weeks for nothing; and three men in the shop told me that they had earned their places by working six weeks for nothing. In the same shop, at the southwest corner of Jefferson and Taylor streets, on the fourth floor, over a saloon, I found three little girls, who were absolutely illiterate, sewing on buttons and finishing knee pants for nothing, they were said to be learning the trade. The lowness of the wages is further enhanced by the habit of the sweaters of running away, and paying none. A man who is going into the sweating business frequently rents

◆ CHAPTER 4
Child Labor
Reform and the
Redefinition of
Childhood,
1880–1920

a room for a week, hires his hands for a week, requires them to supply sewing machines, and gets a contract of work which will employ them about a week. At the end of the week he turns in the goods, gets the money and leaves the neighborhood. In one case, a week after seeing such a sweater in a shop in the 19th ward, I found the same sweater working in the same temporary manner in the neighborhood of Dickson street and Milwaukee avenue. I found dozens of cases in which sweaters had moved away and had paid none of the wages which they owed their employés. In one case I found a debt of $40 to a single family, on the part of a sweater who left in this way and went to Brooklyn. The municipal ordinances are partly incapable of enforcement, and partly unenforced by reason of the inadequacy of the staff, and there is no hope of any improvement in the activity of the board of health by reason of simple agitation of the subject, for agitation has been thoroughly tried during the past year, and the committee has seen the results of it. The only hope of an improvement in the condition of the people engaged in the manufacture of clothing in this city is in stringent legislation and the further organization of the victims of the clothing manufacturers. Those victims themselves, so far as they are organized at all, unanimously endorse the cloak makers' bill and urge its passage at the earliest possible date. And it is the judgment of the employés in the trade, whom I know very thoroughly by reason of my canvass amongst them, and it is most emphatically my own judgment, that any measure which does not prohibit the manufacture of clothing in any dwelling by any woman or child, will wholly fail of its object.

Source 11 from "Filthy Shops" and "Injurious Employments," in *First Annual Report of the Factory Inspectors of Illinois* (Springfield, Illinois: H.W. Rokker, 1894), pp. 10–11. Reprinted at Kathryn Kish Sklar and Thomas Dublin, eds., *Women and Social Movements in the United States, 1600–2000,* (Scholar's Edition), website available through www .alexanderstreet.com.

## 11. Florence Kelley Reports on Child Labor in Illinois Factories.

### *Filthy Shops.*
The medical examinations made in this office preliminary to granting health certificates reveal an incredible degree of filth of clothing and person. The children taken from the candy factories were especially shocking in this respect, and demonstrated anew, the urgent need of bathing facilities both in the workingman's home, where bath-tubs seem to be unknown, and in numerous and accessible swimming-baths, where a plunge can follow the day's work.

Boys are found handling candy with open sores upon their hands, and girls wrapping and packing it whose arms were covered with an eruption which is a direct consequence of filth. Boys from knee-pants shops have presented themselves so covered with vermin as to render a close examination almost impossible.

### *Injurious Employments.*

The reckless employment of children in injurious occupations also is shown in the record of these medical examinations. A glaring example of this is Jaroslav Huptuk, a feeble-minded dwarf, whose affidavit shows him to be nearly sixteen years of age. This child weighs and measures almost exactly the same as a normal boy aged eight years and three months. Jaroslav Huptuk cannot read nor write in any language, not speak a consecutive sentence. Besides being dwarfed, he is so deformed as to be a monstrosity. Yet, with all these disqualifications for any kind of work, he has been employed for several years at an emery wheel, in a cutlery works, finishing knife-blades and bone handles, until, in addition to his other misfortunes, he is now suffering from tuberculous. Dr. Holmes, having examined this boy, pronounced him unfit for work of any kind. His mother appealed from this to a medical college, where, however, the examining physician not only refused the lad a medical certificate, but exhibited him to the students as a monstrosity worthy of careful observation. He was finally taken in charge by an orthopedist, and after careful treatment will be placed in a school for the feeble-minded. The kind of grinding at which this boy was employed has been prohibited in England for minors since 1883, by reason of the prevalence of "grinders' pthisis" among those who begin this work young.

Another occupation conspicuously injurious to children is the running of button-hole machines by foot-power. As a typical case: Joseph Poderovsky, aged fourteen years, was found by a deputy inspector running a heavy button-holer at 204 West Taylor street, in the shop of Michael Freeman. The child was required to report for medical examination, and pronounced by the examining physician rachitic and afflicted with a double lateral curvature of the spine. He was ordered discharged, and prohibited from working in any tailor shop. A few days after he was found at work at the same machine. A warrant was sworn out for the arrest of the employer, under Section Four of the law, but before it could be served the man left the State. This boy has a father in comfortable circumstances, and two adult able-bodied brothers.

Bennie Kelman, Russian Jew, four years in Chicago, fifteen years and four months old, father a glazier, found running a heavy sewing

✦ CHAPTER 4

Child Labor
Reform and the
Redefinition of
Childhood,
1880–1920

machine in a knee-pants shop. A health certificate was required, and the examination revealed a severe rupture. Careful questioning of the boy and his mother elicited the fact that he had been put to work in a boiler factory, two years before, when just thirteen years old, and had injured himself by lifting heavy masses of iron. Nothing had been done for the case, no one in the family spoke any English or knew how help could be obtained. The sight test showed that he did not know his letters in English, though he claimed that he can read Jewish jargon. He was sent to the College of Physicians and Surgeons for treatment, and forbidden work until cured.

When the law went into operation, every tin-can and stamping works in Illinois was employing minors under sixteen years of age, at machines known to be liable to destroy the fingers, hands, and even the whole arm of the operator. The requirement of a medical certificate for all minors so employed has materially reduced their number, but the law should be so amended as to give the inspector power to prohibit the employment of minors at this and all kindred occupations. Until such power is conferred, the mutilation of children will continue to be a matter of daily ocurrence.

The working of the law, even in its present inadequate form, is exemplified in its application to the tin-can industry by Norton's tin-can factory at Maywood. Here a very large number of boys are employed, a score having been found under fourteen years of age. In one part of the factory twenty to thirty boys work upon a shelf suspended between the first and second floors of the building. These unfortunate lads crouch, lie on their sides, sit on their feet, kneel, in short, assume every possible attitude except the normal, straight, sitting or standing posture of healthful employment. Their work consists in receiving pieces of tin sent to them by boys on the second floor, sorting them and poking them into slits in the shelf, whence the pieces of tin are conveyed to the machines on the ground floor for which they are destined. The atmosphere of the room at the height of the shelf is such that the inspector could endure it but a few minutes at a time. The noise of the machinery was so overpowering that it was impossible to make the boys hear questions until after two or three repetitions. The pieces of tin being sharp, the lad's fingers were bound up in cloths to prevent cutting, but in many cases these cloths were found to be saturated with blood. Altogether, the situation of these tin can boys was among the most deplorable discovered. Four inspections were made, and literal compliance with the wording of the law in all respects required. When the season ended, it was with the assurance upon the part of the Norton Bros. that they will open next year with no minors employed on their Maywood premises under sixteen years of age.

Source 12 from Massachusetts Society for the Prevention of Cruelty to Children, *Twenty-First Annual Report* (Boston, 1901), pp. 23–25. Found in Robert H. Bromner, ed., *Children and Youth in America: Documenting History* (Cambridge, MA: Harvard University Press, 1971), Vol. II, 1866–1932, Parts 1–6, pp. 211–212.

## 12. Child Neglect Cases.

23705.   Parents and six children, ages from one year to twelve. Both parents drink badly. A girl of four was suffering from an injured knee, and could not leave her bed. The city physician was notified, but was refused admittance by the parents, who were drinking at the time. Our agent visited, and removed the injured child at once to the hospital. The baby, which appeared in a dying condition, was taken by an aunt to her home, also two of the other children. . . .

13321.   A mother and four children. The youngest, a babe of five months, was found very emaciated and apparently dying from starvation. The mother had offered to give the child to any one who would take it. Its body was completely raw from neglect. A boy of three was nearly naked. . . .

15278.   The father worked steadily, and yet the house was as desolate as it was possible for a house to be. Filth reigned everywhere. There was but one bed for the entire family. . . . Neighbors testified that the children were in the habit of eating from their swill barrels. Children were in a terrible condition,—with heads sore from vermin, and with little clothing. A warrant was secured, and the children promptly removed. The family bed was black with dirt, the floors looked as though water had never touched them; and the breakfast table dirty, and with no food, was a sad sight. . . .

20735.   Father earning $3 per day, and with his wife and four children living in the utmost condition of filth. But one bed, the children burrowing in a pile of feathers on the floor. They were so foul that, when they went to school, the teacher had to burn sticks to fumigate the room. A complaint of neglect was made.

✦ CHAPTER 4

Child Labor
Reform and the
Redefinition of
Childhood,
1880–1920

**EXPERT ADVICE**

Source 13 from Molly Ladd-Taylor, *Raising a Baby the Government Way: Mothers' Letters to the Children's Bureau, 1915–1932* (New Brunswick, N.J.: Rutgers University Press, 1986). Copyright © 1986 by Molly Ladd-Taylor. Reproduced by permission from the author.

## 13. Letters to the Children's Bureau.

Mrs. A.P., Wyoming (October 19, 1916)

Dear Miss Lathrop,

 . . . I live sixty five miles from a Dr. and my other babies (two) were very large at birth, one 12-lbs the other 10½ lbs. I have been *very* badly torn each time, through the rectum the last time. My youngest child is 7½ (and when I am delivered this time it will be past 8½ yrs). I am 37 years old and I am so worried and filled with perfect horror at the prospects ahead. So many of my neighbors die at giving birth to their children. I have a baby 11 months old in my keeping now whose mother died—when I reached their cabin last Nov., it was 22 below zero and I had to ride 7 miles horse back. She was nearly dead when I got there and died after giving birth to a 14 lb. boy. It seems awfull to me to think of giving up all my work and leaving my little ones. . . .

 Will you please send me all the information for the care of my self before and after and at the time of delivery.

Mrs. H.R., Georgia (June 14, 1920)

Dear Madame

 I need advise. I am a farmers wife, do my household duties and a regular field hand too. The mother of 9 children and in family way again. I am quar[re]lsome when tired & fatigued. . . .

 What shall I do? My Husband wont sympathise with me one bit but talks rough to me. . . . Does it make a Mother unvirtuous for a man physician to wait on her during confinement? Is it Safe for me to go through it Without aid from any one? Please give me Some advise. There isent any mid wives near us now. I am not friendless but going to you for advise too keep down gossip. Yours.

Mrs. C.T., Tennessee (June 29, 1921)

I am a farmers wife only thirty three years of age, the mother of seven children. This is the eighth pregnancy, and I am in real bad health and am quite unable to have proper medicine, diet or clothing.

My husband does not see any necessity of any extra care of my health now, and says it is only foolishness. So I am quite at a loss to know what to do. [I] have been in bed most of the time for 6 or 7 weeks without much care, as it takes quite all my little girl's (who is fifteen years old) time to do the housework and care for the smaller little one. Please send me any reading matter that might help me as I like to read. Your friend.

Mrs. W.D., Brooklyn, New York (September 10, 1917)

My Dear Mrs. M. West.

A year ago last Mar. I gave birth to a beautiful fat boy and it lived but 3 days. The Drs. claimed the baby had a leaking heart; he died in convulsions. I would like to know if the injection the *woman* gave him of soap & water threw him in these convulsions as he just moaned like a pigeon & his whole body shook after that & at night he was dead. This was the first time I became pregnant in 4 yrs and you can imagine how glad & happy I was, only instead of having him at my breast, the third day they brought him to the door in his little casket. My heart was broke. I wish that I too was taken, as I suffer terrible with my head during the 9 mths and then I am always in labor from 10 to 12 hrs at a stretch before I can bear my babies. It was only 3 mts again until I was to become a mother again, so I had another babe the next Feb., this making 2 in 1 yrs. I raised him until he was 1 yr and 11 days. He was an angel, never cried, to[o] good I guess to be left on earth. I washed and put his night drawers on and put him to bed well & healthy. He played about the floor that night, laughing and as happy as could be. I nursed him at 3 o'clock in the morning and I awoke at 7 am and found him dead along side of me. You can think how I feel. I cry night and day for my big fat baby, [taken] from me like that.

I try and live a good honest life and my home is my heaven and babies are my idols. I love them but I am afraid something will happen to this one again. I am stout and as a rule healthy. I can't understand why my babies should have weak hearts; that is why I am asking for your books. Maybe I can be spared that terrible long labor and my babies will be spared.

Mrs. M.T., Texas (June 23, 1916)

I have had nine children, but there is much in these booklets I never heard, no, nor even thought of. I have one little girl nearly 10, but I do not know how or what to teach her hardly: in fact, I have so much to do, I have no time to teach, only to scramble through some way. If you have booklets which will be helpful to me, I would thank you to tell me of them or just send them. My mother taught *me nothing*. I am *still* paying the penalty of ignorance. Thanking you again, I am yours sincerely.

◆ CHAPTER 4

Child Labor
Reform and the
Redefinition of
Childhood,
1880–1920

Mrs. M.R., Idaho (January 4, 1916)

Dear Madame.

I would like to know if your people can give me a answer on this. What I am to do I dont know. I am living 25 miles away from any Doctor. We have 4 small children, my Husband is only making 1.35 a day, and every thing is so high it takes all he makes to keep our babys in cloth[e]s and food, as we have ev[e]ry thing we put in our mouths to buy. I am looking for the stork about the 19 of aprial. . . . How am I going to get 35 dollar to have a doctor, for he will not come for less and not unless we have the cash. Talk about better babys, when a mother must be like some cow or mare when a babys come. If she lives, all wright, and if not, Just the same.

So please answer me if you can. You may send me a copie of Bulletin and if I live [through] it, then I will try to [follow] it as close as I can.

Yours truly, answe[r] at [once].

Mrs. W.S., Brooklyn, New York (January 30, 1918)

Dear Madam,

I read this mornings article in the New York American about the campaign to save babies. I fear my baby will be born too soon to have such wonderful help as you propose. My babies come fast and where I am going to meet the Doctors bills I cannot see. I have a daughter one year old this Jan. . . . I can and would gladly do sewing to earn some money but can find no work like that in these times. Can you show me a way out or a way I can help my self? I expect my baby the first of March. I hope I have not done anything wrong in writing to you like this. I am very respectfully.

Source 14 from Winfield Scott Hall and Jeanette Winter Hall, *Counsel to Parents* (Howard-Severance Company, 1917), pp. 61, 63, 65–66.

## 14. Advice to Parents.

The problem of securing pure air for the baby to breathe and at the same time having this air sufficiently warm for a very young child, and of securing free access of the air to the room in which the child is kept without causing draughts, is really a very delicate and serious problem of domestic hygiene. . . .

Quiet should pervade the household where a very young child is. . . .

If the mother is nursing her child at the breast, it goes without saying that her own health is a matter of the greatest importance for the well-being of her child. Not only should the nursing mother be in as nearly perfect health, and should maintain as nearly a perfect state of nutrition, as is possible, but it is a matter of no small importance that the mother maintains a happy frame of mind. . . .

At this place we need only call attention to the general importance of cleanliness as a matter of household hygiene, and emphasize the fact that the infant is especially sensitive to uncleanliness. Not only its person and its food, but also its clothing and bedding, and everything that comes in any way in contact with the child, should be kept spotlessly clean. . . .

## LEGAL CHANGES

Source 15 from Ch. 432, U.S. Statutes at Large, XXXIX, Part I, pp. 675–676. Found in Bremner, ed., *Children and Youth in America*, pp. 703–704.

### 15. Keating Owen Act.

*Be it enacted by the Senate and House of Representatives of the United States of America in Congress assembled,* That no producer, manufacturer, or dealer shall ship or deliver for shipment in interstate or foreign commerce any article or commodity the product of any mine or quarry, situated in the United States, in which within thirty days prior to the time of the removal of such product therefrom children under the age of sixteen years have been employed or permitted to work, or any article or commodity the product of any mill, cannery, workshop, factory, or manufacturing establishment, situated in the United States, in which within thirty days prior to the removal of such product therefrom children under the age of fourteen years have been employed or permitted to work, or children between the ages of fourteen years and sixteen years have been employed or permitted to work more than eight hours in any day, or more than six days in any week, or after the hour of seven o'clock postmeridian, or before the hour of six o'clock antemeridian. . . .

Sec. 3. That for the purpose of securing proper enforcement of this Act the Secretary of Labor, or any person duly authorized by him, shall have authority to enter and inspect at any time mines, quarries, mills, canneries, workshops, factories, manufacturing establishments, and other places in which goods are produced or held for interstate commerce; and the Secretary of Labor shall have authority to employ such assistance for the purposes of this Act as may from time to time be authorized by appropriation or other law.

Source 16 from 247 U.S. 251, 268–281. Found in Bremner, ed., *Children and Youth in America*, pp. 712–714.

### 16. *Hammer v. Dagenhart.*

Opinion of the Court, delivered by MR. JUSTICE DAY, as follows:
A bill was filed in the United States District Court for the Western District of North Carolina by a father in his own behalf and as next friend of his two

✦ CHAPTER 4

Child Labor
Reform and the
Redefinition of
Childhood,
1880–1920

minor sons, one under the age of fourteen years and the other between the ages of fourteen and sixteen years, employees in a cotton mill at Charlotte, North Carolina, to enjoin the enforcement of the act of Congress intended to prevent interstate commerce in the products of child labor. . . .

The District Court held the act unconstitutional and entered a decree enjoining its enforcement. This appeal brings the case here.

The controlling question for decision is: Is it within the authority of Congress in regulating commerce among the States to prohibit the transportation in interstate commerce of manufactured goods, the product of a factory in which, within thirty days prior to their removal therefrom, children under the age of fourteen have been employed or permitted to work, or children between the ages of fourteen and sixteen years have been employed or permitted to work more than eight hours in any day, or more than six days in any week, or after the hour of seven o'clock P.M. or before the hour of six o'clock A.M.? . . .

In interpreting the Constitution it must never be forgotten that the Nation is made up of States to which are entrusted the powers of local government. And to them and to the people and the powers not expressly delegated to the National Government are reserved. . . .

To sustain this statute would not be in our judgment a recognition of the lawful exertion of congressional authority over interstate commerce, but would sanction an invasion by the federal power of the control of a matter purely local in its character, and over which no authority has been delegated to Congress in conferring the power to regulate commerce among the States. . . .

. . . if Congress can thus regulate matters entrusted to local authority by prohibition of the movement of commodities in interstate commerce, all freedom of commerce will be at an end, and the power of the States over local matters may be eliminated, and thus our system of government be practically destroyed.

For those reasons we hold that this law exceeds the constitutional authority of Congress.

✦

## Questions to Consider

The evidence in this chapter is grouped into four sections, representing three approaches Progressives typically used in their reform efforts. First and most importantly, they gathered and disseminated information about the problem. The first 12 sources allow you to consider two forms of information: visual and literary. Sources 1–8 are photographs of impoverished and working children. In Sources 9–12, Progressives offer graphic descriptions of the wages of childhood poverty and labor.

What do the visual images convey about children in this era? What do they reveal about the effects of poverty and labor on childhood?

In their reports on urban life, what did Progressive reformers say about the effects of poverty and labor on children? What did they believe society should do for these children?

What do these sources reveal about the agendas of photographers and writers? Why were they effective in shaping public opinion?

Jacob Riis (Source 9), Florence Kelley (Sources 10 and 11), and the social workers describing child neglect cases (Source 12) also move beyond providing documentation to making assessments. Riis and Kelley understood that children offered industries a cheap, steady source of labor; but they wanted Americans to understand the societal cost of that labor. Social workers entered poor homes and interceded in what they considered dangerous, abusive situations. Their writings therefore form a bridge between gathering information and providing *advice*—a second common tactic among Progressive reformers. Sources 13 and 14 present advice sought by and offered to mothers, from the U.S. government's Children's Bureau (Source 13) and a Progressive doctor and writer (Source 14).

What do the problems described in letters to the Children's Bureau (Source 13) and the advice offered by the Progressive writer (Source 14) convey about children in this era? What do they reveal about the effects of poverty on childhood? The Children's Bureau received thousands of similar letters from mothers, and expert advice proliferated in this era. What does the content and the volume of this advice say about Americans' attitudes toward childhood and society's responsibility to protect children?

Finally, Progressives tried to change *laws*, sometimes in localities or states but more often on the national level, in order to remedy the problems they identified. On the subject of children, Progressives wanted government to protect children, both for their own sakes and for the good of society. Legal changes and court rulings dealing with child labor proliferated during this period. Sources 15 and 16 provide just a sampling. Source 15 is an excerpt from an important piece of Progressive legislation, the Keating Owen Act of 1916. Source 16 comes from the Supreme Court ruling that declared that act unconstitutional. What did the Act do? Why did the Court overturn it? What do these two documents tell you about the changes forged by Progressive activism and the limits of those changes?

Now that you have considered the *information*, *advice*, and *laws* associated with the Progressive campaign on behalf of poor children, return to the central questions of the chapter: What problems related to child labor and poverty did the Progressive see? What solutions did they offer? What did their campaigns reveal about their perceptions of childhood? In sum, how did children's lives and societal attitudes about childhood change during the Progressive era?

♦ CHAPTER 4
Child Labor
Reform and the
Redefinition of
Childhood,
1880–1920

♦

# Epilogue

The Progressives achieved many of their goals between the 1890s and 1920s, and other successes came with New Deal legislation in the 1930s. For example, the Seventeenth and Nineteenth Amendments to the Constitution provided for the direct election of senators and gave women the right to vote, respectively. Although the Supreme Court declared the Keating Owen Act unconstitutional, child labor in manufacturing and mining declined significantly during the 1920s. Progressive campaigns to document the harmful effects of child labor influenced public opinion; in response, states raised the age of compulsory school attendance and prohibited child labor in the most dangerous industries. In 1921, Progressives succeeded in getting the federal government to help poor mothers and their babies. The Sheppard Towner Act appropriated money to be used by the states for improving maternal and child welfare. Although the act expired in 1929, the number of infant deaths declined precipitately in the 1920s. Childhood health further improved with the growing availability of pasteurized milk in the 1930s, along with greater knowledge about vitamins and nutritional health. Finally, the Progressives call for society to help poor mothers received a major endorsement with the passage of the New Deal's Social Security Act.

Far less progress occurred in the South, however (see Chapters 7 and 9). And throughout the nation, "invisible" child workers continued to labor in home production, door-to-door sales, domestic service, and agriculture. Not until the New Deal did the federal government pass legislation restricting most child labor.

Today, childhood poverty and child labor remain both national and international problems. At the turn of the twentieth century, an estimated one in fifty children in the United States experience homelessness, living in motels, cars, shelters or other transitory housing, or waiting for foster care placement. Throughout the twentieth century and into the twenty-first, some American children continued to suffer in poverty and exploitative work environments. Still, networks of state and federal laws, government agencies, faith-based institutions, and non-profit foundations seek to protect children, and Americans generally agree that childhood should be a distinct, sheltered time of life—a legacy of the Progressive agenda.

# 5

# Homogenizing a Pluralistic Nation: Propaganda During World War I

✦

## The Problem

One week after Congress approved the war declaration that brought the United States into World War I,[1] President Woodrow Wilson signed Executive Order 2594, which created the Committee on Public Information, a government agency designed to mobilize public opinion behind the war effort. Wilson selected forty-one-year-old journalist and political ally George Creel to direct the committee's efforts. By war's end in late 1918, Creel's committee had a staff of over 150,000 full-time employees and volunteers who had affected the lives of nearly every man, woman, and child in the United States. "There was no part of the great war machinery that we did not touch," Creel boasted, "No medium of appeal that we did not employ."[2]

Although Creel himself opposed government-imposed censorship and repression of information and opinions, the Committee on Public Information did construct a system of *voluntary* censorship, while at the same time employing all the appeals and tools used by private agencies in the relatively new field of mass advertising. During the twenty months that the United States was at war, the committee produced millions of press releases, books, pamphlets, scripts for speeches by Four Minute Men, and films.[3] In addition, the nation's best

1. Wilson delivered his war message on April 2, 1917. The Senate declared war on April 3 and the House of Representatives followed suit on April 6.

2. Walton Rawls, *Wake Up, America: World War I and the American Poster* (New York: Abbeville Press, 1988), p. 137.
3. The Four Minute Man speeches originally were intended to be used at moving picture theaters during the roughly four minutes that the reels were being changed. They soon expanded to civic clubs, theaters, and so on. Approximately 75,000 volunteers (men and

◆ CHAPTER 5

Homogenizing a
Pluralistic Nation:
Propaganda
During
World War I

artists and illustrators donated their talents to the committee by producing full-color posters that played a major propaganda role.[4] In all, then, United States citizens were almost literally inundated with propaganda commissioned by the Committee on Public Information as well as by news stories, films, songs, and other types of mass communication that the committee oversaw and approved.

Why did the federal government believe that such a massive propaganda appeal by the Committee on Public Information was necessary? For one thing, since the war broke out in Europe in 1914, the Wilson administration had promised that the United States would remain neutral and non-involved—a policy supported strongly by the American people. It was feared, therefore, that a relatively swift shift from neutrality to full engagement would not be supported. Also, a number of well-known and respected Americans (including Senators Robert LaFollette of Wisconsin and George Norris of Nebraska, industrialists Andrew Carnegie and Henry Ford, and reformer Jane Addams), as well as practically the entire American left (led by socialist Eugene Debs), vehemently opposed American involvement and might affect public opinion. Finally, many government officials feared that large ethnic blocs of Americans would

not support the United States' entry into the conflict. In 1917, the Census Bureau had estimated that approximately 4.7 million people living in the United States had been born in Germany or in one of the other Central Powers.[5] It was also known that the nation contained a large number of Irish Americans, many of whom were vehemently anti-British and thus might be expected to side with the Central Powers.[6] Could such a heterogeneous society be persuaded to support the war effort voluntarily? Could Americans of the same ethnic stock as the enemies be rallied to the cause?

The purpose of the Committee on Public Information was to use every means at its disposal to garner support for the United States' war effort. Not only did the committee create its own propaganda, but it also either discouraged or banned outright speeches, news reports, editorials, and films that expressed conflicting opinions.

Although examples of propaganda are nearly as old as society itself, by World War I the combination of government propaganda and modern communications technology made the manipulation of collective attitudes and opinions considerably more pervasive and doubtless more effective than earlier efforts. Indeed, some liberal intellectuals began to fear that propaganda techniques exploited

women, in spite of their name) delivered over seven million of these talks, written by the Committee on Public Information.
4. The committee engaged 279 artists to create several hundred poster designs. Some of the best-known illustrators were James Montgomery Flagg, Charles Dana Gibson, Joseph Christian Leyendecker, Haskel Coffin, and Alonzo Earl Foringer. Female illustrators included Lucille Patterson and Laura Brey.

5. The actual figure was closer to 4.27 million people. See U.S. Bureau of the Census, *Historical Statistics of the United States* (Washington, D.C.: U.S. Government Printing Office, 1975), Pt.I, p. 117.
6. According to the U.S. census of 1920, there were 1.04 million Americans who had been born in Ireland and 3.12 million native-born Americans who had one or both parents of Irish birth.

latent prejudices, created a kind of mob psychology, and used lies and half-truths to sway the crowd. For these increasingly concerned individuals, the word *propaganda* itself began to take on sinister connotations. Thus Socialist leader Eugene V. Debs was not completely alone when he recognized the "irony of free speech suppressed by a nation allegedly fighting for democracy." Yet these doubters and worriers were in the distinct minority, and the Committee on Public Information for the most part not only successfully marshaled American public opinion in support of the war effort, but in doing so helped create a climate of mass fear and suspicion.[7]

In this chapter, you will be examining and analyzing the propaganda techniques of a modern nation at war. The Evidence section contains material sponsored or commissioned by the Committee on Public Information (posters, newspaper advertisements, excerpts from speeches by Four Minute Men) as well as privately produced works (song lyrics and commercial film advertisements) that either were approved by the committee or tended to parallel its efforts. After examining the evidence, you will work to answer the following questions:

1. How did the government attempt to mobilize the opinion of a diverse American public in support of a united war effort?
2. What were the consequences—positive and negative—of this effort?

On a larger scale, you should be willing to ponder other questions as well, although they do not relate directly to the evidence you will examine. To begin with, is government-sponsored propaganda during wartime a good thing? When it comes into conflict with the First Amendment's guarantees of freedom of speech, which should prevail? Finally, is there a danger that government-sponsored propaganda can be carried too far? Why do you think that was (or was not) the case during World War I?

## Background

By the early twentieth century, the United States had worldwide economic interests and even had acquired a modest colonial empire, but many Americans wanted to believe that they were insulated from world affairs and impervious to global problems. Two great oceans seemed to protect the nation from overseas threats, and the enormity of the country and comparative

7. For three especially interesting studies of propaganda during World War I, see J. Michael Sproule, *Propaganda and Democracy: The American Experience of Media and Mass Persuasion* (Cambridge: Cambridge University Press, 1997), esp. pp. 1–14; Brett Gary, *The Nervous Liberals: Propaganda Anxieties from World War I to the Cold War* (New York: Columbia University Press, 1999), esp. pp. 1–23; and Philip M. Taylor, *Munitions of the Mind: A History of Propaganda from the Ancient World to the Present Era* (Manchester, U.K.: Manchester University Press, 2003), esp. pp. 177–185.

✦ CHAPTER 5

Homogenizing a
Pluralistic Nation:
Propaganda
During
World War I

weakness of its neighbors appeared to secure it against all dangers. Let other nations waste their people and resources in petty wars over status and territory, Americans reasoned. The United States should stand above such greed or insanity, and certainly should not wade into foreign quagmires.

To many Americans, Europe was especially suspect. For centuries, European nations had engaged in an almost ceaseless round of armed conflicts—wars for national unity, territory, or even religion or empire. Moreover, in the eyes of many Americans, these bloody wars appeared to have solved little or nothing, and the end of one war seemed to be but a prelude to the next. Ambitious kings and their plotting ministers seemed to make Europe the scene of almost constant uproar, an uproar that many Americans saw as devoid of reason and morality. Nor did it appear that the United States, as powerful as it was, could have any effect on the unstable European situation.

For this reason, most Americans greeted news of the outbreak of war in Europe in 1914 with equal measures of surprise and determination not to become involved. They applauded President Wilson's August 4 proclamation of neutrality, his statement (issued two weeks later) urging Americans to be impartial in thought as well as in deed, and his insistence that the United States continue neutral commerce with all the belligerents. Few Americans protested German violation of Belgian neutrality. Indeed, most Americans (naively, as it turned out) believed that the United States both should and could remain aloof from the conflict in Europe.

Many factors pulled the United States into the conflict that later became known as World War I.[8] America's economic prosperity to a large extent rested on commercial ties with Europe. In 1914, U.S. trade with the Allies (England, France, Russia) exceeded $800 million, whereas trade with the Central Powers (Germany, Austria, Turkey) stood at approximately $170 million. Much of the trade with Great Britain and France was financed through loans from American banks, something President Wilson and Secretary of State William Jennings Bryan openly discouraged because both men believed that those economic interests might eventually draw the United States into the conflict. Indeed, Wilson and Bryan probably were correct. Nevertheless, American economic interests were closely tied to those of Great Britain and France. Thus a victory by the Central Powers might damage U.S. trade. As Wilson drifted to an acceptance of this fact, Bryan had to back down.

A second factor pulling the United States into the war was the deep-seated feelings of President Wilson himself. Formerly a constitutional historian (Wilson had been a college professor and university president before entering the political arena as a reform governor of New Jersey), Wilson had long admired the British people and their form of government. Although technically neutral, the president strongly, though privately, favored the Allies and viewed a German victory as unthinkable. Moreover, many of Wilson's key advisers and the people

8. Until the outbreak of what became known as World War II, World War I was referred to as the Great War.

close to him were decidedly pro-British. Such was the persuasion of the president's friend and closest adviser, Colonel Edward House, as well as that of Robert Lansing (who replaced Bryan as secretary of state)[9] and Walter Hines Page (ambassador to England). These men and others helped reinforce Wilson's strong political opinions and influence the president's changing position toward the war in Europe. Hence, although Wilson asked Americans to be neutral in thought as well as in deed, in fact he and his principal advisers were neither. More than once, the president chose to ignore British violations of America's neutrality. Finally, when it appeared that the Central Powers might outlast their enemies, Wilson was determined to intercede. It was truly an agonizing decision for the president, who had worked so diligently to keep his nation out of war.

A third factor pulling the United States toward war was the strong ethnic ties of many Americans to the Old World. Many Americans had been born in Europe, and an even larger number were the sons and daughters of European immigrants. Although these people considered themselves to be, and were, Americans, some retained emotional ties to Europe that they sometimes carried into the political arena—ties that could influence America's foreign policy.

Finally, as the largest neutral commercial power in the world, the United States soon became caught in the middle of the commercial warfare of the belligerents. With the declaration of war, both Great Britain and Germany threw up naval blockades. Great Britain's blockade was designed to cut the Central Powers off from war materiel. American commercial vessels bound for Germany were stopped, searched, and often seized by the British navy. Wilson protested British policy many times, but to no effect. After all, giving in to Wilson's protests would have deprived Britain of its principal military asset: the British navy.

Germany's blockade was even more dangerous to the United States, partly because the vast majority of American trade was with England and France. In addition, however, Germany's chief method of blockading the Allies was the use of the submarine, a comparatively new weapon in 1914. Because of the nature of the submarine (lethal while underwater, not equal to other fighting vessels on the surface), it was difficult for the submarine to remain effective and at the same time adhere to international law, such as the requirement that sufficient warning be given before sinking an enemy ship.[10] In 1915, hoping to terrorize the British into making peace, Germany unleashed its submarines in the Atlantic with orders to sink all ships flying Allied flags. In March, a German submarine sank the British passenger

9. Bryan resigned in 1915, in protest over what he considered Wilson's too sharp note to Germany over the sinking of the passenger liner *Lusitania*. Wilson called the act "illegal and inhuman." Bryan sensed that the Wilson administration was tilting away from neutrality.

10. International laws governing warfare at sea, as well as neutral shipping during wartime, were written in the mid-eighteenth century, more than one hundred years before the submarine became a potent seagoing weapon.

✦ CHAPTER 5

Homogenizing a
Pluralistic Nation:
Propaganda
During
World War I

ship *Falaba*. Then on May 7, 1915, the British liner *Lusitania* was sunk with a loss of more than 1,000 lives, 128 of them American. Although Germany had published warnings in American newspapers specifically cautioning Americans not to travel on the *Lusitania*, and although it was ultimately discovered that the *Lusitania* had gone down so fast (in only eighteen minutes) because the British were shipping ammunition in the hold of the passenger ship, Americans were shocked by the Germans' actions on the high seas. Most Americans, however, continued to believe that the United States should stay out of the war and approved of Wilson's statement, issued three days after the *Lusitania* sank to the bottom, that "there is such a thing as a man being too proud to fight."

Yet a combination of economic interests, German submarine warfare, and other events gradually pushed the United States toward involvement. In early February 1917, Germany announced a policy of unrestricted submarine warfare against all ships—belligerent and neutral alike. Ships would be sunk without warning if found to be in what Germany designated as forbidden waters. Later that month, the British intercepted a secret telegram intended for the German minister to Mexico, stationed in Mexico City. In that telegram, German Foreign Secretary Arthur Zimmermann offered Mexico a deal: Germany would help Mexico retrieve territory lost to the United States in the 1840s if Mexico would make a military alliance with Germany and declare war on

the United States in the event that the United States declared war on Germany. Knowing the impact that such a telegram would have on American public opinion, the British quickly handed the telegram over to Wilson, who released it to the press. From that point on, it was but a matter of time before the United States would become involved in World War I.

On March 20, 1917, President Wilson called his cabinet together at the White House to advise him on how to proceed in the deteriorating situation with Germany. Wilson's cabinet officers unanimously urged the president to call Congress into session immediately and ask for a declaration of war against Germany. When the last cabinet member had finished speaking, Wilson said, "Well, gentlemen, I think there is no doubt as to what your advice is. I thank you," and dismissed the meeting without informing the cabinet of his own intentions.

Yet even though Wilson had labored so arduously to keep the United States out of the war in Europe, by March 20 (or very soon after) his mind was made up: the United States must make war on Germany. Typing out his war message on his own Hammond portable typewriter, Wilson was out of sorts and complained often of headaches. The president, devoted to peace and Progressive reform, was drafting the document he had prayed he would never have to write.

On April 2, 1917, President Wilson appeared in person before a joint session of Congress to deliver his war message. Congress was ready. On April 4, the Senate approved a war declaration (the vote was 82–6). The House of Representatives followed suit two days later (by a vote of 373–50).[11]

As noted earlier, at the outset of the United States' entry into the war, the Wilson administration feared that the ethnically diverse American public might not unite in support of the nation's involvement in the Great War. Without a decisive event to prompt the war declaration (some Americans even suspected the Zimmermann telegram was a British hoax), would the American people support the war with sufficient unanimity? No firing on Fort Sumter or blowing up of the battleship *Maine* would force America's entrance into this war, nor would the *Lusitania* sinking, which had occurred two years before the 1917 war declaration. Without the obvious threat of having been attacked, would the American people rally to the colors to defeat a faraway enemy? Could isolationist and non-interventionist opinion, very strong as late as the presidential election of 1916, be overcome? Could an ethnically heterogeneous people stand together in time of war? To bind together a diverse people behind the war effort, President Wilson created the Committee on Public Information.

## The Method

For George Creel and the Committee on Public Information, the purposes of propaganda were very clear:

1. Unite a multiethnic, pluralistic society behind the war effort.
2. Attract a sufficient number of men to the armed services and elicit universal civilian support for those men.
3. Influence civilians to support the war effort by purchasing war bonds or by other actions (such as limiting personal consumption or rolling bandages).
4. Influence civilians to put pressure on other civilians to refrain from antiwar comments, strikes, antidraft activities, unwitting dispersal of information to spies, and other public acts that could hurt the war effort.

To achieve these ends, propaganda techniques had to be used with extreme care. For propaganda to be effective, it would have to contain one or more of the following features:

1. Portrayal of American and Allied servicemen in the best possible light.
2. Portrayal of the enemy in the worst possible light.

11. The fifty-six votes in the Senate and House against the declaration of war essentially came from three separate groups: senators and congressmen with strong German and Austrian constituencies, isolationists who believed the United States should not become involved on either side, and some Progressive reformers who maintained that the war would divert America's attention from political, economic, and social reforms. Interestingly, Jeannette Rankin (Republican, Montana), the first woman elected to Congress, was the only member of Congress who voted against America's entry into World War I *and* World War II. During the Vietnam War, she led a demonstration against that conflict in front of the U.S. Capitol.

◆ CHAPTER 5

Homogenizing a
Pluralistic Nation:
Propaganda
During
World War I

3. Portrayal of the American and Allied cause as just and the enemy's cause as unjust.
4. Message to civilians that they were involved in the war effort in important ways.
5. Communication of a sense of urgency to civilians.

In this chapter, you are given the following six types of World War I propaganda to analyze, some of it produced directly by the Committee on Public Information and some produced privately but examined and approved by the committee:

1. One popular song, perhaps the most famous to come out of World War I, performed in music halls and vaudeville houses (Source 1). Although the Committee on Public Information did not produce this kind of material, it could—and did—discourage performances of "unpatriotic" popular songs.
2. Three newspaper and magazine advertisements produced directly by the Committee on Public Information (Sources 2 through 4).
3. Eleven posters commissioned by the committee to be used for recruiting, encouraging the purchase of liberty bonds and liberty loans, calling for sacrifices by civilians, and urging unity and patriotism (Sources 5 through 15).
4. Two cartoons, one an editorial cartoon and the other a prize-winning cartoon in a contest sponsored by a U.S. Army camp publication (Sources 16 and 17).
5. Two excerpts of speeches by Four Minute Men and one poem by a Four Minute Man. (Sources 18 through 20).

6. Material concerning committee or commercial feature films, including suggestions to theater owners on how to advertise the film *Kultur*, two film advertisements, and one still photograph used in advertising the film, *The Kaiser, the Beast of Berlin* (Sources 21 through 24).

As you examine the evidence, you will see that effective propaganda operates on two levels. On the surface, there is the logical appeal for support to help win the war. On another level, however, certain images and themes are used to excite the emotions of the people for whom the propaganda is designed. As you examine the evidence, ask yourself the following questions:

1. For whom was this piece of propaganda designed?
2. What was this piece of propaganda trying to get people to think? To do?
3. What logical appeals were being made?
4. What emotional appeals were being made?
5. What might have been the results— positive and negative—of these kinds of appeals?

In songs, speeches, advertisements, and film reviews, are there key words or important images? Where there are illustrations (ads, posters, cartoons), what facial expressions and images are used? Finally, are there any common logical and emotional themes running through government-sponsored propaganda during World War I? How did the United States use propaganda to mobilize public opinion during the war?

◆

# The Evidence

Source 1 is a popular song by George M. Cohan, 1917.

## 1. "Over There."

Johnnie, get your gun,
Get your gun, get your gun,
Take it on the run,
On the run, on the run.
Hear them calling you and me,
Every son of liberty.
Hurry right away,
No delay, no delay.
Make your daddy glad
To have had such a lad.
Tell your sweetheart not to pine,
To be proud her boy's in line.

*Chorus (repeat chorus twice)*
Over there, over there,
Send the word, send the word over there—
That the Yanks are coming,
The Yanks are coming,
The drums rum-tumming
Ev'rywhere.
So prepare, say a pray'r,
Send the word, send the word to beware.
We'll be over, we're coming over,
And we won't come back till it's over
Over there.

✦ CHAPTER 5

Homogenizing a
Pluralistic Nation:
Propaganda
During
World War I

Sources 2 through 4 from James R. Mock and Cedric Larson, *Words That Won the War: The Story of the Committee on Public Information* (Princeton: Princeton University Press, 1939), pp. 64, 169, 184.

## 2. "Spies *and* Lies" Advertisement Urging Americans to Report the Enemy.

# Spies *and* Lies

German agents are everywhere, eager to gather scraps of news about our men, our ships, our munitions. It is still possible to get such information through to Germany, where thousands of these fragments—often individually harmless—are patiently pieced together into a whole which spells death to American soldiers and danger to American homes.

But while the enemy is most industrious in trying to collect information, and his systems elaborate, he is *not* superhuman—indeed he is often very stupid, and would fail to get what he wants were it not deliberately handed to him by the carelessness of loyal Americans.

Do not discuss in public, or with strangers, any news of troop and transport movements, or bits of gossip as to our military preparations, which come into your possession.

Do not permit your friends in service to tell you—or write you—"inside" facts about where they are, what they are doing and seeing.

Do not become a tool of the Hun by passing on the malicious, disheartening rumors which he so eagerly sows. Remember he asks no better service than to have you spread his lies of disasters to our soldiers and sailors, gross scandals in the Red Cross, cruelties, neglect and wholesale executions in our camps, drunkenness and vice in the Expeditionary Force, and other tales certain to disturb American patriots and to bring anxiety and grief to American parents.

And do not wait until you catch someone putting a bomb under a factory. Report the man who spreads pessimistic stories, divulges—or seeks—confidential military information, cries for peace, or belittles our efforts to win the war.

Send the names of such persons, even if they are in uniform, to the Department of Justice, Washington. Give all the details you can, with names of witnesses if possible—show the Hun that we can beat him at his own game of collecting scattered information and putting it to work. The fact that you made the report will not become public.

You are in contact with the enemy today, just as truly as if you faced him across No Man's Land. In your hands are two powerful weapons with which to meet him—discretion and vigilance. *Use them.*

COMMITTEE     ON     PUBLIC     INFORMATION

8 JACKSON PLACE, WASHINGTON, D. C.

*Contributed through Division of Advertising*          *United States Gov't Comm. on Public Information*

George Creel, *Chairman*
*The Secretary of State*
*The Secretary of War*
*The Secretary of the Navy*

### 3. "Bachelor of Atrocities" Advertisement for Fighting the Enemy by Buying Liberty Bonds.

**Bachelor of Atrocities**

IN the vicious guttural language of Kultur,[12] the degree A. B. means Bachelor of Atrocities. Are you going to let the Prussian Python strike at your Alma Mater, as it struck at the University of Louvain?[13]

The Hohenzollern[14] fang strikes at every element of decency and culture and taste that your college stands for. It leaves a track so terrible that only whispered fragments may be recounted. It has ripped all the world-old romance out of war, and reduced it to the dead, black depths of muck, and hate, and bitterness.

You may soon be called to fight. But you are called upon right now to buy Liberty Bonds. You are called upon to economize in every way. It is sometimes harder to live nobly than to die nobly. The supreme sacrifice of life may come easier than the petty sacrifices of comforts and luxuries. You are called to exercise stern self-discipline. Upon this the Allied Success depends.

Set aside every possible dollar for the purchase of Liberty Bonds. Do it relentlessly. Kill every wasteful impulse, that America may live. Every bond you buy fires point-blank at Prussian Terrorism.

**BUY U. S. GOVERNMENT BONDS FOURTH LIBERTY LOAN**

Contributed through Division of Advertising

United States Gov't Comm. on Public Information

*This space contributed for the Winning of the War by*
A. T SKERRY, '84, and CYRILLE CARREAU, '04.

*Appeal to the Symbols of Education*
Two Graduates of New York University Contributed the Space for This CPI Advertisement in Their "Alumni News"

National Archives

12. Germans often asserted that they had *Kultur,* or a superior culture, in contrast to *civilization,* which they viewed as weak and effeminate.
13. *The University of Louvain,* in Belgium, was pillaged and partially destroyed by German troops. Some professors were beaten and others killed, and the library (containing 250,000 books and manuscripts, some irreplaceable) was totally destroyed. The students themselves were home for summer vacation.
14. *Hohenzollern* was the name of the German royal family since the nation's founding in 1871. It had been the Prussian royal family since 1525.

◆ CHAPTER 5

Homogenizing a
Pluralistic Nation:
Propaganda
During
World War I

## 4. Advertisement Appealing to History Teachers, April 4, 1917.

# The Committee on Public Information

### Established by Order of the President, April 4, 1917

Distribute free *except as noted* the following publications :

### I. Red, White and Blue Series :

No. 1. How the War Came to America (English, German, Polish, Bohemian, Italian, Spanish and Swedish).

No. 2. National Service Handbook (primarily for libraries, schools, Y. M. C. A.'s, Clubs, fraternal organizations, etc., as a guide and reference work on all forms of war activity, civil, charitable and military).

No. 3. The Battle Line of Democracy. Prose and Poetry of the Great War. Price 25 cent. Special price to teachers. Proceeds to the Red Cross. Other issues in preparation.

### II. War Information Series :

No. 1. The War Message and Facts Behind it.

No. 2. The Nation in Arms, by Secretaries Lane and Baker.

No. 3. The Government of Germany, by Prof. Charles D. Hazen.

No. 4. The Great War from Spectator to Participant.

No. 5. A War of Self Defense, by Secretary Lansing and Assistant Secretary of Labor Louis F. Post.

No. 6. American Loyalty by Citizens of German Descent.

No. 7. Amerikanische Bürgertreue, a translation of No. 6.

Other issues will appear shortly.

### III. Official Bulletin :

Accurate daily statement of what all agencies of government are doing in war times. Sent free to newspapers and postmasters (to be put on bulletin boards). Subscription price $5.00 per year.

### *Address Requests to*

## Committee on Public Information, Washington, D. C.

# What Can History Teachers Do Now?

You can help the community realize what history should mean to it.

You can confute those who by selecting a few historic facts seek to establish some simple cure-all for humanity.

You can confute those who urge that mankind can wipe the past off the slate and lay new foundations for civilization.

You can encourage the sane use of experience in discussions of public questions.

You can help people understand what democracy is by pointing out the common principle in the ideas of Plato, Cromwell, Rousseau, Jefferson, Jackson and Washington.

You can help people understand what German autocracy has in common with the autocracy of the Grand Mogul.

You can help people understand that democracy is not inconsistent with law and efficient government.

You can help people understand that failure of the past to make the world safe for democracy does not mean that it can not be made safe in the future.

You can so teach your students that they will acquire "historical mindedness" and realize the connection of the past with the present.

You can not do these things unless you inform yourself, and think over your information.

You can help yourself by reading the following :

"History and the Great War" bulletin of Bureau of Education.

A series of articles published throughout the year in THE HISTORY TEACHER'S MAGAZINE.

You can obtain aid and advice by writing to

The National Board for Historical Service, 1133 Woodward Building, Washington, D. C.

United States Bureau of Education, Division of Civic Education, Washington, D. C.

Committee on Public Information, Division of Educational Co-operation, 10 Jackson Place, Washington, D. C.

The Committee on Patriotism through Education of the National Security League, 31 Pine Street, New York City.

Carnegie Endowment for International Peace, 2 Jackson Place, Washington, D. C.

National Committee of Patriotic and Defense Societies, Southern Building, Washington, D. C.

The World Peace Foundation, 40 Mount Vernon St., Boston, Mass.

American Association for International Conciliation, 407 West 117th Street, New York City.

The American Society for Judicial Settlement of International Disputes, Baltimore, Md.

The Editor, THE HISTORY TEACHER'S MAGAZINE, Philadelphia.

4

Source 5 from *The James Montgomery Flagg Poster Book*, introduction by Susan E. Meyer (New York: Watson-Guptill Publications, 1975).

## 5. The Famous Uncle Sam Poster.

✦ CHAPTER 5

Homogenizing a
Pluralistic Nation:
Propaganda
During
World War I

Source 6 from Peter Stanley, *What Did You Do in the War, Daddy?* (Melbourne: Oxford University Press, 1983), p. 55.

**6. Poster Portraying Germany as a Raging Beast.**

Source 7 from Anthony Crawford, *Posters in the George C. Marshall Research Foundation* (Charlottesville: University of Virginia Press, 1939), p. 30.

## 7. "Joan of Arc Saved France" (Haskell Coffin).

Source 8 from Walton Rawls, *Wake Up, America! World War I and the American Poster* (New York: Abbeville Press, 1988), p. 232.

## 8. "Our Boys Need Sox" (Anonymous).

◆ CHAPTER 5

Homogenizing a
Pluralistic Nation:
Propaganda
During
World War I

12. "Here He Is, Sir" (Charles Dana Gibson).

13. "Americans All!" Poster (Howard Chandler Christy).

✦ CHAPTER 5

Homogenizing a
Pluralistic Nation:
Propaganda
During
World War I

14. **Jewish Welfare Board Poster, 1918 (Sidney Reisenberg).**

Sidney H. Riesenberg/Library of Congress

## 15. "Colored Man Is No Slacker" Poster (Anonymous).

COLORED MAN IS NO SLACKER

◆ CHAPTER 5

Homogenizing a
Pluralistic Nation:
Propaganda
During
World War I

Source 16 from John Higham, *Strangers in the Land: Patterns of American Nativism, 1860–1925* (New Brunswick, N.J.: Rutgers University Press, 1955), p. 210.

**16. *New York Herald* Editorial Cartoon: German American Dr. Karl Muck, Conductor of the Boston Symphony Orchestra, Needed a Police Escort When He Conducted a Concert in March 1918 in New York City.**[15]

John Higham/Rutgers University Press

15. Dr. Karl Muck, a native of Germany and conductor of the Boston Symphony Orchestra since 1912, was accused of sympathizing with the enemy for conducting German music. When he declined a request to lead the orchestra in "The Star Spangled Banner," he was arrested and imprisoned in Georgia for the duration of the war. After the war he was deported to Germany, where he lived until his death in 1940.

Source 17 from *New York Times,* January 6, 1918.

## 17.  Hines's Prize-Winning Cartoon in the 1918 *Trench and Camp* Cartoon Contest.[16]

The New York Times

16. *Trench and Camp* was a weekly publication of the United States Army for its thirty-two training centers in the United States. For this prize-winning cartoon, Frank Hines won a wristwatch. In the cartoon, the American soldier is holding a *pickelhaube,* a German spiked helmet.

◆ CHAPTER 5

Homogenizing a
Pluralistic Nation:
Propaganda
During
World War I

Sources 18 through 20 from Alfred E. Cornbise, *War as Advertised: The Four Minute Men and America's Crusade, 1917–1918*, pp. 72–73, 122, 60. Copyright © 1984 American Philosophical Society. All rights reserved. Reproduced by permission.

### 18. Excerpt of a Speech by a Four Minute Man.

Ladies and Gentlemen:

I have just received the information that there is a German spy among us—a German spy watching *us*.

He is around here somewhere, reporting upon you and me—sending reports about us to Berlin and telling the Germans just what we are doing with the Liberty Loan. From every section of the country these spies have been getting reports over to Potsdam[17]—not general reports but details—where the loan is going well and where its success seems weak, and what people are saying in each community.

For the German government is worried about our great loan. Those Junkers[18] fear its effect upon the German *morale*. They're raising a loan this month, too.

If the American people lend their billions now, one and all with a hip-hip-hurrah, it means that America is united and strong. While, if we lend our money half-heartedly, America seems weak and autocracy remains strong.

Money means everything now; it means quicker victory and therefore less bloodshed. We are *in* the war, and now Americans can have but *one* opinion, only *one* wish in the Liberty Loan.

Well, I hope these spies are getting their messages straight, letting Potsdam know that America is *hurling back* to the autocrats these answers:

For treachery here, attempted treachery in Mexico, treachery everywhere—*one billion*.

For murder of American women and children—*one billion more*.

For broken faith and promise to murder more Americans—*billions and billions more*.

And then we will add:

In the world fight for Liberty, our share—*billions and billions and billions and endless billions*.

Do not let the German spy hear and report that *you* are a slacker.

---

17. *Potsdam* (a suburb of Berlin) was where the Kaiser lived.
18. *Junkers* were the Prussian nobility.

## 19. Part of a Speech by a Four Minute Man.

German agents are telling the people of this . . . race[19] through the South that if they will not oppose the German Government, or help our Government, they will be rewarded with Ford automobiles when Germany is in control here. They are told that 10 negroes are being conscripted to 1 white man in order that the Negro race may be killed off; and that the reason Germany went into Belgium was to punish the people of that country for the cruel treatment of the negroes in the Congo.

## 20. "It's Duty Boy," a Poem Read by Four Minute Men.

My boy must never bring disgrace to his immortal sires—
At Valley Forge and Lexington they kindled freedom's fires,
John's father died at Gettysburg, mine fell at Chancellorsville;
While John himself was with the boys who charged up San Juan Hill.
And John, if he was living now, would surely say with me,
"No son of ours shall e'er disgrace our grand old family tree
By turning out a slacker when his country needs his aid."
It is not of such timber that America was made.
I'd rather you had died at birth or not been born at all,
Than know that I had raised a son who cannot hear the call
That freedom has sent round the world, its precious rights to save—
This call is meant for you, my boy, and I would have you brave;
And though my heart is breaking, boy, I bid you do your part,
And show the world no son of mine is cursed with craven heart;
And if, perchance, you ne'er return, my later days to cheer,
And I have only memories of my brave boy, so dear,
I'd rather have it so, my boy, and know you bravely died
Than have a living coward sit supinely by my side.
To save the world from sin, my boy, God gave his only son—
He's asking for my boy, to-day, and may His will be done.

19. At the front lines in France, Germans barraged America's African American soldiers with leaflets urging them to desert (none did). One of those propaganda leaflets said, in part, "Do you enjoy the same rights as the white people do in America ... or are you rather not treated over there as second-class citizens?" As to the charge of discrimination against African Americans by draft boards, there were numerous complaints that African Americans found it almost impossible to get exemptions from military service. In the end, about 31 percent of the African Americans who registered were called into service, as opposed to 26 percent of the registered whites. To counteract German propaganda, prominent African Americans were sent to France to lecture to the African American troops.

◆ CHAPTER 5

Homogenizing a
Pluralistic Nation:
Propaganda
During
World War I

Source 21 from *The Moving Picture World,* September 28, 1918.

## 21. Promotional Tips to Theater Managers, 1918.

# ADVERTISING AIDS FOR BUSY MANAGERS
### "KULTUR."

**William Fox Presents Gladys Brockwell in a Typical Example of the Brutality of the Wilhelmstrasse to Its Spy-slaves.**

#### Cast.

| | |
|---|---|
| Countess Griselda Von Arenburg, | Gladys Brockwell |
| Eliska | Georgia Woodthorpe |
| René de Bornay | William Scott |
| Baron von Zeller | Willard Louis |
| Archduke Franz Ferdinand | Charles Clary |
| Danilo | Nigel de Brullier |
| The Kaiser | William Burress |
| Emperor Franz Josef | Alfred Fremont |

Directed by Edward J. Le Saint

**The Story:** The Kaiser decides that the time is ripe for a declaration of war, and sends word to his vassal monarch of Austria. René de Bornay is sent by France to discover what is being planned. He meets the Countess, who falls in love with him. She sickens of the spy system and declares that she is done with it, but is warned that she cannot withdraw. She is told to secure René's undoing, but instead procures his escape and in her own boudoir is stood against the wall and shot for saving the man whom she loves better than her life.

**Feature** Gladys Brockwell as Countess Griselda Von Arenburg and William Scott as René de Bornay.

**Program and Advertising Phrases:** Gladys Brockwell, Star of Latest Picture, Exposing Hun Brutality and Satanic Intrigue.

How An Austrian Countess Gave Her All for Democracy.

She Was an Emperor's Favorite Yet She Died for World Freedom.

Story of an Emperor's Mistress and a Crime That Rocked the World.

Daring Exposure of Scandals and Crimes in Hun Court Circles.

Astonishing Revelations of Hun Plots to Rape Democracy.

**Advertising Angles:** Do not offer this as a propaganda story, but tell that it is one of the angles of the merciless Prussian spy system about which has been woven a real romance. Play up the spy angle heavily both in your newspaper work and through window cards with such lines as "even the spies themselves hate their degradation." Miss Brockwell wears some stunning and daring gowns in this play, and with these special appeal can be made to the women.

**22.  Advertisement for the Feature Film *The Kaiser, the Beast of Berlin* (1918), Described by Some as the Most Famous "Hate Picture."**

◆ CHAPTER 5

Homogenizing a
Pluralistic Nation:
Propaganda
During
World War I

Source 23 from Rawls, *Wake Up, America!*, p. 234.

### 23. "Pershing's Crusaders" Film Poster (Anonymous).

**24. Still Photograph from *The Kaiser, the Beast of Berlin* (1918). Used in Advertising.**

♦ CHAPTER 5

Homogenizing a
Pluralistic Nation:
Propaganda
During
World War I

♦

## Questions to Consider

Keep in mind that the "target audience" of the Committee on Public Information propaganda was America's civilian population—those men and women who were expected to support military enlistments, buy liberty bonds and liberty loans, report suspicious or unpatriotic individuals, cut back on consumption of food, fuel, and other commodities needed for the war effort, and support civilian unity and patriotism. To achieve these goals, the committee virtually bombarded the civilian population with propaganda.

Source 1, George M. Cohan's enormously popular song, "Over There," was familiar to almost every American in 1917 to 1918. What is the song urging young men to do? What emotions are the song's lyrics trying to arouse? How would you interpret the lines, "Make your daddy glad" and (speaking of sweethearts) "To be proud her boy's in line"? Recordings of the song "Over There" are readily available. As you listen to the song, how does it make you feel?

The advertisements shown in Sources 2 through 4 were produced by the Committee on Public Information. How are the Germans portrayed in the "Spies *and* Lies" ad (Source 2)? in the "Bachelor of Atrocities" ad (Source 3)? Source 4 is an appeal to history teachers. Did the Committee on Public Information ask history teachers to "tilt" their treatments of the past? If so, how? Were there any dangers inherent in the kinds of activities the committee was urging on patriotic Americans?

In some ways, poster art (Sources 5 through 15) is similar to editorial cartoon art (Sources 16 and 17), principally because the artist has only one canvas or frame on which to tell his or her story. Yet the poster must be more arresting than the cartoon, must convey its message rapidly, and must avoid ambiguities and confusion. Posters commissioned or approved by the Committee on Public Information were an extremely popular form of propaganda during World War I. Indeed, so popular were the posters of James Montgomery Flagg (1877–1960) that he helped sell $1,000 of liberty bonds by performing (in his case, painting posters) in front of the New York Public Library.

Source 5, Flagg's Uncle Sam poster, probably is the most famous poster ever created. The idea was taken from a British poster by Alfred Leete, and Flagg was his own model for Uncle Sam. The poster is still used by the United States Army. What feeling did the poster seek to elicit?[20]

The poster "Destroy This Mad Brute" by illustrator H. R. Hopps is a classic example of a recruiting appeal. How is the enemy portrayed? What darker emotions or fears does the poster hope to elicit?

A surprisingly large percentage of the posters were appeals to women

20. For a photograph of Flagg painting a recruiting poster on the steps of the New York Public Library, see his autobiography, *Roses and Buckshot* (New York: G.P. Putnam's Sons, 1946), facing p. 159.

(Sources 7, 8, 10, and 12). How are women portrayed in each poster? What are American women expected to contribute to the war effort (consider especially the emotions in Source 12)? Do these four posters tell you anything about World War I era gender roles and stereotypes? As you examine Alonzo Earl Foringer's poster "The Greatest Mother in the World" (Source 10), what famous statue does that poster remind you of? Do you think Foringer hoped that those who saw the poster would make that connection?

The posters in Sources 7, 9, and 11 are appeals to civilians to purchase liberty bonds and liberty stamps. What appeal does each poster make? Do the posters attempt to elicit deeper emotions?

Sources 13 through 15 are extremely interesting in light of the government's fears and the role President Wilson assigned to the Committee on Public Information. What emotion does the extraordinary "Americans All!" poster (Source 13) attempt to elicit? What is the poster's intended "message"? How do Sources 14 and 15 seek to bolster that message? If the goal of the committee was to *unite* Americans behind the war effort, why do you think it chose to target appeals to specific groups?

Speaking of cartoons, nineteenth-century New York political boss William Marcy ("Boss") Tweed once exclaimed, "Let's stop these damn pictures. I don't care so much what the papers say about me—my constituents can't read; but damn it, they can see the pictures!" The editorial cartoon from the *New York Herald* (Source 16) is fairly self-explanatory. What emotions does the cartoon seek to elicit? What actions, intended or unintended, might have

resulted from those emotions? Frank Hines's prize-winning cartoon (Source 17) seeks to elicit very different emotions, primarily in men. Compare the cartoon with Cohan's lyrics (Source 1) and the recruiting poster (Source 6).

Sources 18 through 20, speeches and a poem by Four Minute Men, also were published in the Committee on Public Information's *Bulletin*, which was distributed to all volunteer speakers. Not a few of the Four Minute Men were women, but most of them delivered their speeches to women's organizations. All speakers received certificates from President Wilson after the war. What appeals are made in Source 18? How are appeals to African Americans (Source 19) similar or different? Compare to the poster in Source 15. The poem in Source 20 is particularly painful to read. Why is that so? How can this poem be compared to Sources 1, 12, and 17?

From 1917 to 1918, the American film industry and the Committee on Public Information produced over 180 feature films, 6 serials, 72 short subjects, 112 documentaries, 44 cartoons, and 37 liberty loan special films. Unfortunately, the vast majority of those motion pictures no longer are available, principally because the nitrate film stock on which the films were printed was extremely flammable and subject to decomposition.[21]

---

21. In 1949, an improved safety-based stock was introduced. Those films that do survive, except in private collections, are in the Library of Congress; the American Film Institute Library in Beverly Hills, California; the Academy of Motion Picture Arts and Sciences in Los Angeles; the Museum of Modern Art in New York; the National Archives in Washington, D.C.; the New York Public Library; and the Wisconsin Center for Theater Research in Madison.

♦ CHAPTER 5

Homogenizing a
Pluralistic Nation:
Propaganda
During
World War I

No sound films were produced in the United States before 1927. Until that time, a small orchestra or (more prevalent) a piano accompanied a screening. What dialogue there was—and there was not much—was given in subtitles.

The advertising tips for the film *Kultur* (Source 21) suggest a number of phrases and angles designed to attract audiences. What are the strongest appeals suggested to theater owners? Do those same appeals also appear in the song, advertisements, posters, cartoons, and speeches?

Sources 22 and 24 are advertisements for *The Kaiser, the Beast of Berlin,* produced in 1918. What appeal do the advertisements intend to make? How effective do you think such an appeal would be? Source 23, however, is an advertisement for a government-produced film. Note the committee's seal at the upper right of the advertisement. How is the appeal in Source 23 similar to or different from that in Source 24? How are Germans depicted in Source 21? How can Source 21 be compared with Sources 6 and 7? How can Source 22 be compared with those sources as well?

You must now summarize your findings and return to the central questions: How did the United States use propaganda to mobilize public opinion in support of the nation's participation in World War I? What were the consequences—positive and negative—of the mobilization of public opinion?

♦

## Epilogue

The creation of the Committee on Public Information and its subsequent work show that the Wilson administration had serious doubts concerning whether the American people, multiethnic and pluralistic as they were, would support the war effort with unanimity. And, to be sure, there was opposition to American involvement in the war, not only from socialist Eugene Debs and the left but also from reformers Robert La Follette, Jane Addams, and others. As it turned out, however, the Wilson administration's worst fears proved groundless. Americans of all ethnic backgrounds overwhelmingly supported the war effort, sometimes rivaling each other in patriotic ardor. How much of this unanimity can be attributed to patriotism and how much to the propaganda efforts of the Committee on Public Information will never really be known. Yet, for whatever reason, it can be said that the war had a kind of unifying effect on the American people. Women sold liberty bonds, worked for agencies such as the Red Cross, rolled bandages, and cooperated in the government's effort to conserve food and fuel. Indeed, even African Americans sprang to the colors, reasoning, as did the president of Howard University, that service in the war might help them achieve long-withheld civil and political rights.

However, this homogenization was not without its price. Propaganda was so effective that it created a kind of national hysteria, sometimes with terrible results. Vigilante-type groups often shamefully persecuted German Americans, lynching one German American man of draft age for not being in uniform (the man was physically ineligible, having only one eye) and badgering German American children in and out of school.[22] Many states forbade the teaching of German in schools, and a host of German words were purged from the language (sauerkraut became liberty cabbage, German measles became liberty measles, hamburgers became liberty steaks, frankfurters became hot dogs). The city of Cincinnati even banned pretzels from saloons. In such an atmosphere, many Americans lived in genuine fear of being accused of spying or of becoming victims of intimidation or violence. In a society intent upon homogenization, being different could be dangerous.

During such hysteria, one would expect the federal government in general and the Committee on Public Information in particular to have attempted to dampen the more extreme forms of vigilantism. However, it seemed as if the government had become the victim of its own propaganda. The postmaster general (Albert Burleson), empowered to censor the mail, looking for examples of treason, insurrection, or forcible resistance to laws, used his power to suppress all socialist publications, all anti-British and pro-Irish mail, and anything that he believed threatened the war effort. One movie producer, Robert Goldstein, was sentenced

to ten years in prison for releasing his film *The Spirit of '76* (about the American Revolution) because it portrayed the British in an unfavorable light.[23] Socialist party leader Eugene Debs was given a similar sentence for criticizing the war in a speech in Canton, Ohio, on June 16, 1918. Debs announced at the outset of his remarks that he might be arrested for what he had to say, and then declared that "the working class who fight all the battles, the working class who make the supreme sacrifices, the working class who freely shed their blood and furnish the corpses, have never yet had a voice in either declaring war or making peace. It is the ruling class that invariably does both."[24] The left-wing Industrial Workers of the World (IWW) was falsely accused of advocating draft evasion and was the victim of considerable violence, and many of its leaders were either imprisoned or deported. Freedom of speech, press, and assembly were violated countless times, and numerous lynchings, whippings, and tar-and-featherings occurred. Excesses by both government and private individuals were as effective in *forcing* homogeneity as were the voluntary efforts of American people of all backgrounds.

Once the hysteria had begun, it is doubtful whether even President Wilson

22. The mother of one of the authors of this volume, who was ten years old in 1917, was chased home from school by rock-throwing boys because she was of German descent.

23. This gave rise to a court case with the improbable title *United States v. The Spirit of '76.*
24. Debs actually was indicted the day before he made the speech. He spent three years in prison and in 1921 his sentence was commuted by President Warren Harding. See Ernest Freeberg, *Democracy's Prisoner: Eugene V. Debs, the Great War, and the Right to Dissent* (Cambridge, MA: Harvard University Press, 2008), pp. 72–77, 289–296.

✦ CHAPTER 5

Homogenizing a
Pluralistic Nation:
Propaganda
During
World War I

could have stopped it. Yet Wilson showed no inclination to do so, even stating that dissent was not appreciated by the government. Without the president to reverse the process, the hysteria continued unabated.

Before the outbreak of World War I, anti-immigrant sentiment had been growing, although most Americans seem to have believed that the solution was to Americanize the immigrants rather than to restrict their entrance into the country. But the drive toward homogenization that accompanied America's war hysteria acted to increase cries for restricting further immigration and to weaken champions of the "melting pot." As restriction advocate Madison Grant wrote in 1922, "The world has seen many such [racial] mixtures and the character of a mongrel race is only just beginning to be understood at its true value. . . . Whether we like to admit it or not, the result of the mixture of two races . . . gives us a race reverting to the more ancient, generalized and lower type." Labor leaders, journalists, and politicians called for immigration restrictions, and a general immigration restriction (called the National Origins Act) became law in 1924.

This insistence on homogenization also resulted in the Red Scare of 1919, during which Attorney General A. Mitchell Palmer violated many people's civil liberties in a series of raids, arrests, and deportations directed largely against recent immigrants. As seen, the efforts to homogenize a pluralistic nation could have an ugly side.

As noted in the Problem section of this chapter, some liberal intellectuals were both shocked and frightened by the relative ease with which the Com-

mittee on Public Information was able to manipulate public opinion and create a climate of mass patriotic hysteria. How, they asked, could "the people" be trusted if they could be swayed and stampeded so easily? And yet, open criticism of the government or the American people themselves still could be dangerous. As one minor example, noted historian Charles Beard resigned from Columbia University in protest over the firings of antiwar faculty members. As a result, sales of Beard's books plummeted.[25]

As Americans approached World War II, some called for a revival of the Committee on Public Information. Yet President Franklin Roosevelt rejected this sweeping approach. The Office of War Information was created, but its role was a restricted one. Even so, as you will see in Chapter 8, Japanese Americans were subjected to relocation and humiliation in one of the mostshameful episodes of recent American history. (see Chapter 8). And although propaganda techniques were sometimes more subtle, they nevertheless displayed features that would cause Americans to hate their enemies and want to destroy them. Japanese people especially were portrayed as barbaric. Two good examples of this can be seen in Sources 25 and 26. Compare these posters to the examples of World War I posters in Sources 5 through 15. In general, however, a different spirit pervaded the United States during World War II, a spirit generally more tolerant of American pluralism

25. On liberals' fear, see Walter Lippmann's columns in the November and December 1919 issues of *Atlantic Monthly*, cited in Gary, *Nervous Liberals*, p. 2. On Beard, see Sproule, *Propaganda and Democracy*, p. 14.

and less willing to stir Americans into an emotional frenzy.

And yet the possibility that propaganda will create mass hysteria and thus endanger the civil rights of some Americans is present in every national crisis, especially in wartime. In the "total wars" of the twentieth century, in which civilians played as crucial a role as soldiers (in factories, military training facilities for soldiers, and in shipping men and materiel to the front), the mobilization of the home front was a necessity. But could that kind of mobilization be carried too far?

◆ CHAPTER 5

Homogenizing a
Pluralistic Nation:
Propaganda
During
World War I

**25. United States Army Poster from World War II.**

Library of Congress

**26. "Pvt. Joe Louis says. . ." (Office of Facts and Figures).**[26]

David Pollack/Corbis

26. Joseph Louis Barrow, better known as Joe Louis (1914–1981), was the world heavyweight boxing champion from 1937 to 1949 and is generally regarded as the first African American to achieve status as a national hero. His nickname was "The Brown Bomber."

# 6

# The "New" Woman: Debating Women's Roles in the 1920s

◆

## The Problem

In 1920, the Nineteenth Amendment to the Constitution, granting women the right to vote, was finally ratified. Seventy-five years in the making, ratification came too late for women such as Susan B. Anthony and Elizabeth Cady Stanton; both had died in the prior decade after working for over half a century on behalf of women's rights. "Few people live to see the actual and final realization of hopes to which they have devoted their lives," announced Carrie Chapman Catt to the two thousand women attending the National American Woman Suffrage Association (NAWSA). "That privilege is ours." After more than an hour of singing and waving banners, the delegates turned their attention to the business of converting the NAWSA into the League of Women Voters (LWV). "A dream has come true," proclaimed the new LWV president and long-time suffragist, Maude Wood Park.[1] But that dream of women's citizenship proved disappointing to many in the ensuing decade. The

female solidarity fostered during the long fight for suffrage—at least among white middle-class women—waned as women practiced that right as individuals, alone in the voting booth. Women turned out to be as diverse in their political agendas and as readily factionalized as their male countrymen.

But the biggest change that women such as Maude Wood Park and Carrie Chapman Catt witnessed was the disinterest of their daughters and granddaughters. Politics struck many young women in the 1920s as boring; the LWV effort to educate citizens and promote voter turnout seemed out of step with the emerging youth culture.

A "new" woman emerged in the 1920s: the flapper, best symbolized by the original "it" girl, silent film actress Clara Bow.[2] Bow was vivacious, sensuous, and bohemian. She wore her hair and her

1. Barbara Stuhler, ed., *For the Public Record: A Documentary History of the League of Women Voters* (Westport, Conn.: Greenwood Press, 2000), pp. 31, 43.

2. The term "silent" film is actually misleading. Films, though lacking soundtracks in the modern sense, were often accompanied by musicians, especially organists; gramophone disks; local actors who performed dialog; and even entire orchestras. The first "talkie"—a feature film with sound—was *The Jazz Singer*, released in 1927. Bow, a Brooklyn native who

skirts short. On the screen and in life, she flaunted her relationships, her freedom, and her sexuality. She was wildly popular in the 1920s. In those days, fifty million Americans—half the population—went to the movies every week. Theatre owners ran over twenty thousand movie houses. Hollywood studios released eight hundred feature films a year in the 1920s—it was the greatest film output in American history. (Today, studios rarely release five hundred films per year.) Producers and studio heads were constantly looking for new talent, which is how Clara Bow was discovered: she won a nationwide talent contest in 1922 at the age of sixteen. Her rise to fame was meteoric. In 1924 and 1925, she starred in no less than twenty-three feature films. By 1928, she was the highest-paid movie star in Hollywood. Fans flocked to see her films; young women emulated her haircut, fashion choices, even the way she applied her lipstick (in a heart-shape).

The women who cultivated this flapper self-image through dress and hairstyle often went further than simply making superficial changes. They typically did not identify with reform

efforts, including the feminist advocacy of organizations such as the LWV. They often criticized feminism as old-fashioned, and many rejected Victorian attitudes toward sexuality. These "new" women also argued that they would be the first generation of women to have it all: education, career, marriage, and children.

Experts, primarily social scientists such as sociologists, psychologists, economists, political scientists, home economists, and anthropologists, attempted to help American women negotiate this new age. They counseled women on how to act— in relationships, the workplace, and their homes. These experts, however, often disagreed about *how* or even *whether* changes in women's roles should occur. In this chapter, you will read several selections from some of the vast social science literature of the 1920s in order to identify and understand the issues surrounding the redefinition of "new" women's roles. What was at stake in these arguments about womanhood? What assumptions and recommendations did social scientists make? What can "experts" tell us about American society in the 1920s?

◆

# Background

The debates that raged over the proper roles of American women in the 1920s had a long, complicated history. During

never shed her thick accent, struggled in the transition to talkies. She also suffered a series of mental breakdowns and public scandals, and her career was over by 1933. F. Scott Fitzgerald's novels and short stories captured this era, which he termed the Jazz Age.

their lengthy battle for the right to vote, suffragists themselves were sharply divided over what they should do. From the months after the Seneca Falls Convention in 1848 through the ratification campaigns of 1920, feminist leaders fiercely debated the proper and effective approach. Should the suffragists focus on changing state constitutions,

artists, and intellectuals, most African Americans still endured abject poverty and political disfranchisement in the rural South. Two famous trials of the decade—the Sacco and Vanzetti case against Italian anarchists convicted of committing a murder during a payroll robbery, and the Scopes case involving a teacher found guilty of breaking Tennessee state law by teaching evolution—highlights the growing societal rift between older values of rural and small-town America and the newer values of twentieth-century modernism.

But perhaps nowhere were the cultural and social strains of the decade more evident than in the fierce debates about the proper place of white women. There was no doubt in the minds of contemporary observers that women's experiences were changing, and a great deal of public concern swirled around these modern, or "new," women.

Between 1920 and 1930, one in four American women worked outside the home—a pattern that had emerged over the prior twenty years. But the 1920s were different: that era glamorized working women in magazines and the movies. Clara Bow's character worked in a department store in the 1927 film *It*—which is where she got her moniker. In particular, modern women were associated with retail sales and clerical work; the secretary was the most popular image of new, working womanhood. Before 1900, secretaries were overwhelmingly men. In the 1920s, corporate America decided that successful businessmen needed "in the office something as much like the vanished wife of his father's generation as could be arranged—someone to balance his checkbook, buy his railroad tickets, check his baggage, get him seats in the fourth row, take his daughter to the dentist, listen to his side of the story, give him a courageous look when things were the blackest, and generally know all, understand all."[5] While popular culture increasingly depicted working women as desirable and glamorous, they were certainly not feminists in the tradition of either Carrie Catt or Alice Paul.

The expansion of higher education and particularly of co-education—an innovation at American colleges in the early twentieth century—fostered familiarity between young women and men and advanced a different youth culture than earlier generations of Americans had experienced. New courtship values encouraged young people to seek passion and sexual gratification. Smoking and drinking in public, dating casually, and dancing all night in jazz clubs, young women known as flappers embodied the most extreme, sometimes shocking, changes in behavior. Clothing and hairstyles shifted dramatically, at first among urban young women. The movies, department stores, and mail-order catalogues made these fashions available to women across the country. The influences of "new" womanhood quickly spread far beyond the college girls emulating Clara Bow.

The "new" woman and the urban, youth culture that pushed this image of womanhood emphasized pleasure, individualism, conspicuous consumption, and innovation. These values were embraced by middle-class Americans, including the daughters and wives

5. *Fortune*, August 1935, quoted in Evans, *Born for Liberty*, 183.

of businessmen, skilled laborers, and professionals. Even for white women who remained in traditional roles as wives and mothers, the 1920s brought profound changes. Technological innovations, particularly new and affordable household appliances, altered the responsibilities of middle-class housewives. Consumption became a female responsibility and was read as evidence of wives' savvy and efficiency.

What impact would these changes have on the home and family, long considered the basis of American society? Advice literature sought to answer this question and to define the proper role of American women. Beginning in the late nineteenth century as a response to massive immigration, rapid industrialization, and widespread urbanization, researchers began investigating the societal consequences of these changes. Borrowing some of their methods from natural science but focusing their works on society, new social scientists began to emerge in universities and government service. Sociologist Thorstein Veblen wrote *The Theory of the Leisure Class* (1899) while teaching at the University of Chicago; Richard Ely was head of the Economics Department at the University of Wisconsin when he wrote *Monopolies and Trusts* (1900). Both men were interested in the analysis of the formation and functions of great wealth during the period. In contrast, anthropologist Elsie Clews Parsons was teaching at Columbia University when she wrote *The Family* (1906), followed by five other books during the next ten years in which she compared contemporary American social attitudes and conventions to those of other, preindustrial cultures.

This trend in the social sciences—especially in sociology, political science, psychology, economics, and home economics—grew out of the Progressive movement. Turn-of-the century Progressive reformers generally believed that if Americans were properly educated about social problems they could and would find solutions. Gathering data, interviewing individuals, and compiling statistics provided the material with which reformers could inform citizens, formulate social policy, and convince government officials of the need for legislative changes. Social scientists saw themselves as practical researchers and writers whose work could form the basis for important social and economic reforms. Widely accepted as experts in their specialized fields, in the 1920s they published their research findings and recommendations not only in scholarly journals but in popular middle-class books and magazines as well. Borrowing the language and style of social scientists, "experts" of every vein wrote advice columns in magazines, public policy manuals, books, and newspaper op-ed pieces.

This proliferating advice literature promised to help women negotiate the overwhelming changes occurring in 1920s America. And it reached into the most intimate part of women's lives. Writers counseled couples on the legitimate bases for marriage, although the experts often disagreed about the exact criteria. Experts sought to counsel homemakers on the most professional, up-to-date means of completing their work. Nutrition, decorating, entertaining— all became specialized, advice-laden enterprises. Motherhood was likewise to be professionally managed, from pregnancy to infant nutrition to toddlers' playtime. Political scientists were very interested in the impact of the newly enfranchised women voters in the first half of the decade. That interest waned, however, as the decade progressed, and political questions were replaced by concerns about women's roles in the work force and the family. Home economists investigated the rates at which women were entering high schools and universities, preparing for professions, and entering the work force, especially in the expanding service sector. Although the typical woman worker was single, there was a definite increase in questions concerning marriage that home economists, psychologists, and sociologists all tried to answer. As more women pursued jobs and careers, the role of homemaker seemed to become less important to American women. This in turn raised important questions about women's traditional roles in the family.

In this chapter, you will read selections from the social science and advice literature of the 1920s about the roles of modern women in order to answer several questions: What did these researchers identify as the most important issues confronting modern women? What ethnic groups and social classes most concerned these writers? What assumptions did they make about their readers? To what image of proper womanhood did they ascribe? What did they understand to be the foundations of women's happiness and success? To what degree did they suggest redefining women's roles? What can we learn about America in the 1920s from advice experts?

## The Method

Historians who use evidence such as social science literature from the early twentieth century do so with caution. Although these writers and researchers believed themselves to be truly objective, the great majority came from middle- or upper-class backgrounds. Most were Protestants whose families had lived in the United States for many generations. Most of them were white and—an important point to note—most of them had been directly or indirectly involved in various urban reform activities. Generally for these scholars and experts the obvious problems of the 1920s were related to immigration, industrialization, and urbanization; they chose which problems they studied. Thus, we certainly cannot say that the social science literature of this era was objective.

This does not mean that such evidence is worthless to the historian. Rather, it must be read with nuance and care, and with a thoughtful appreciation of the context of its production. None of the evidence available to historians is perfect; every form of primary source comes with both virtues and problems. Because of this, historians avoid taking any evidence literally or at face value. Rather, they approach their evidence critically, aware of its imperfections and limits with regard to answering historical questions.

In analyzing the social science literature presented in the Evidence section, you should focus on three specific tasks:

1. Summarize the *message* of each excerpt. What does it describe, criticize, praise, or recommend? What issues are revealed?
2. Identify the author's underlying *assumptions*. Does the writer assume readers are male or female? What class does the writer address? Does the writer seem to have fixed or flexible beliefs about women's roles? What sorts of solutions does the author find valuable? How do these assumptions affect the author's message?
3. Determine what the evidence reveals about the *debate* surrounding the redefinition of women's roles during the 1920s. What controversies does the author engage? Does the author support or regret changes in women's roles? What underlying contests over womanhood can you see in the advice offered?

Social science literature is only one of several types of evidence that help us understand the degree to which women's roles were redefined in the 1920s. But a careful analysis of this literature can give us valuable insight into the story.

◆

# The Evidence

## ADVICE TO GIRLS

Source 1 from Alyse Gregory, "The Changing Morality of Women," *Current History* 19 (1923): 298, 299.

## 1. Alyse Gregory on Sex and the New Woman.

*[Alyse Gregory was a feminist, a statistical researcher for the Carnegie Educational Foundation, a "new" woman herself.]*

### Girls' New Habits

Then suddenly all was changed again. The war [World War I] was over and women were admonished to hurry once more home and give the men back their jobs. It was too late. The old discipline had vanished in the night. There was neither an avenging God nor an avenging father to coerce women back into their old places at the family board. They took flats or studios and went on earning their livings. They filled executive offices, they became organizers, editors, copywriters, efficiency managers, artists, writers, real estate agents, and even in rare instances brokers. . . . However unwilling one may be to acknowledge it, girls began to sow their wild oats. Women of the aristocratic upper classes and the poorest women had never followed too rigidly the cast-iron rules of respectability because in neither instance had they anything to lose by digressing. But for the first time in the memory of man, girls from well-bred, respectable middle-class families broke through those invisible chains of custom and asserted their right to a nonchalant, self-sustaining life of their own with a cigarette after every meal and a lover in the evening to wander about with and lend color to life. If the relationship became more intimate than such relationships are supposed to be, there was nothing to be lost that a girl could not dispense with. Her employer asked no questions as to her life outside the office. She had her own salary at the end of he month and asked no other recompense from her lover but his love and companionship. Into the privacy of her own snug and pleasant rooms not even her mother or her oldest brother could penetrate, for she and she alone, unless perhaps one other, carried the only key that would fit the lock.

Profoundly shocking as such a state of affairs may seem to large numbers of people, there is no use pretending that it does not exist. There are too many signs abroad to prove that it does. Ministers may extol chastity for women from pulpit rostrums and quote passages from the Old and New Testaments to prove that purity and fidelity are still her most precious assets, but this new woman only shrugs her shoulders and smiles a slow, penetrating, secret smile.

Source 2 from Ernest Groves, *Personality and Social Adjustment* (New York: Longman, Green, 1925), pp. 204, 213, 214.

## 2. Ernest Groves on the Psychological Development of Girls.

*[Ernest Groves, deeply affected by Freudian psychology, was a professor of social science and the author of numerous college textbooks on child and family studies.]*

The development of the girl's affection is not so simple as that of the boy's. It also has greater opportunities for emotional disturbances. The girl begins, as does the boy, with a fixation upon the mother. But this in the case of the girl is a homosexual experience and thus at the very start of the evolution of affection of the girl there is satisfaction in a relationship which does not require cognizance of sex differences. It is easier therefore for the girl to continue the expression of affection upon members of her own sex straight through childhood into the adult period. Even if the boy has only the dimmest of ideas of the differences between his mother and himself he nevertheless has some slight misunderstanding that he belongs to the class to which his father belongs and not to that of his mother.

It is fortunate that most girls, as if by instinct, tend as they pass the first years of the infantile period to turn their affection to their fathers. . . .

The period that covers the daughter's greatest need of her father's help is necessarily brief. She normally passes quickly on to the next adventure in affection and her impulses turn all the deep interests of her life toward men of her own age. Her emotions and her thought are concentrated upon her new experiences in heterosexual association. It is easy for the adult to forget how tremendous these reactions are in the average girl. What she wears, where she goes, what she does, all her behavior is primarily related to "man." Her feeble efforts to conceal this fact frequently make it all the more noticeable. She is like an actress playing a part with her consciousness fixed upon her audience.

If her new attention to men receives a favorable response her emotional life is wont to flow smoothly. She may still err, to be sure, in her judgment and may consequently make an unwise choice for a life-mate, but she has at least passed through all the various phases of the love experience that precedes adulthood.

Source 3 from *Happy, Healthy Womanhood* (New York: Social Hygiene Press, 1920), pp. 3–5, 11–13, 15–16.

### 3. The United States Public Health Service Healthy Living and Sexual Restraint.

**HEALTHY, HAPPY WOMANHOOD**

Throughout France and in many different countries of the world there stands the statue of a great, heroic Frenchwoman, Joan of Arc. This humble peasant girl of Brittany, aroused by the misfortunes of her countrymen, helped to free them from the hands of a foreign foe. But today she has come to represent far more than this. She has come to stand for the woman with a vision, the woman who is seeking to do her part in the betterment of the world. Wherever her figure appears, it is always looking forward, the light of a great purpose in her eyes, the will for a large achievement in the lines of her face. As she raises her standard aloft there seem to gather behind it innumerable hosts of those who would follow her lead. A daughter of war-ridden fifteenth-century France, she nevertheless symbolizes the woman of the twentieth century, eager to take a part in the work of the world and in the great life-giving enterprises of peace.

## HEALTH, THE FOUNDATION

You who aspire to take part in the work of the world should assure yourself of good health. Without it all other preparation may be in vain. Today, in addition to the more familiar duties of the home, new occupations in factory and office are open to you. In many fields you may now compete with men. But only if you possess good health—a vigorous body and a clear brain—can you expect to undertake the new and trying work successfully. No matter how thoroughly you are trained, such training will be of little value unless it rests upon a foundation of good health.

Good health is even more important from the point of view of motherhood. In some of the war-ravaged countries of Europe more than half of the babies who are born die during the first year of life. Thousands of others begin their lives under tremendous handicaps. Why? Largely because the strength of the mothers has been sapped by food shortage and over-work so that they cannot give their babies proper nourishment. The dream of these mothers of chubby, rosy-cheeked babies, who were to have been their joy, has vanished. Upon healthy womanhood depends to a large extent happy motherhood.

Physical fitness during youth is the best foundation for healthy, happy womanhood. It is an asset of which you may rightly feel proud. With health, you can look forward to the time when you can participate actively in the work of the world; with health, happy motherhood becomes a well-grounded hope for the future.

## BEAUTY AND POPULARITY

Besides fitting you more effectively for your life's work, good health will incidentally increase your beauty and attractiveness. True beauty comes from within; it cannot be put on from without. Good health gives such beauty, a beauty that will wear. Its foundation is health of mind and body; its expression is a sparkling eye, a clear complexion, a graceful body, an active brain.

Every girl wants to be popular with her companions. Today the popular girl is the girl who glows with life, who can swim and dance and play outdoor games, who has plenty of energy for fun when she has finished her daily tasks. Good health, since it produces high spirits, vitality, cheerfulness, and leadership, will help to make you popular. Every girl likes to enjoy herself. She likes to go to parties and picnics, to find the real joys of living. Physical fitness, by enlarging your opportunity for enjoyment and your power to enjoy, makes more such occasions possible.

## HOW FITNESS IS ATTAINED

Plenty of physical exercise, fresh air, sufficient sleep, frequent bathing, three well-balanced meals a day, erect carriage, and comfortable clothing will help to make you strong and well. . . .

## MISUSE OF SEX

After centuries of experience, the marriage of one man with one woman has come to be considered the best method of carrying on the life of the race. Through such a relationship the sex instinct finds its most wholesome satisfaction. A man and a woman who bring children into the world of whom they are unwilling to take care, endanger their own happiness as well as the welfare of the community. They miss the finer joys of human love, and fail to appreciate what such love may mean in their lives.

More than this. Indulgence in sex relations among persons who are not married to each other exposes them to a serious physical danger. They are likely to become infected with a venereal disease. These diseases are called syphilis (pox) and gonorrhea (clap). They are germ diseases.

To the man a venereal disease may mean lifelong suffering, unless by proper treatment the germs are destroyed. Syphilis often causes heart disease, paralysis, and some forms of insanity. Gonorrhea may cause blindness, chronic rheumatism, incurable disorders of the sex organs, and inability on the man's part to become a father.

A man who has one of these diseases is likely to give it to his wife. While syphilis affects her much as it does a man, gonorrhea often afflicts her even more seriously. Many operations upon women's reproductive organs are made necessary by gonorrhea. Many women are lifelong invalids as a result of this disease. Some die. Many babies are blinded at birth by gonorrhea in the mother. Fortunately, simple medical treatment given the baby immediately after birth will prevent blindness of this kind. Syphilis causes many miscarriages (the birth of babies before they can live outside the mother's body). Many babies are defective in various ways because of syphilis.

It is important to remember, however, that these results—blindness, sores, invalidism, and operations upon women—are often due to causes other than syphilis and gonorrhea.

These diseases are contagious or "catching." Usually they are passed from person to person through sexual intercourse. Occasionally, however, a person is infected through using a towel or public drinking cup or from being kissed by a diseased person. Accusations should never be made, therefore, against any one who appears to be suffering from the effects of gonorrhea or syphilis. If one of these diseases has actually been contracted, the infection may have occurred in an entirely innocent way.

Syphilis and gonorrhea can be cured if treated by a competent physician. There are many good clinics for those who cannot afford a private physician. If the treatment is not thorough and continued long enough, the disease may reappear years after the patient believes the cure to be complete. This is especially true when the infected person relies on patent medicines or "quack" doctors. Advertising doctors seldom cure and generally do more harm than good.

Because the sex instinct, which may bring the individual the greatest joy, is sometimes misused, a girl should exercise great care in the choice of the men with whom she associates. Chance acquaintances often invite girls on automobile rides, to movies and cafés with the intention of leading them into sex relations. Such invitations should be refused. A girl does not wish to be considered an easy mark, or to put herself in a position where a man may take advantage of her. . . .

## A CHALLENGE TO THE PRESENT

In the development of America, women have made a splendid record. Three hundred years ago when the Pilgrims landed on the stern and rock-bound New England coast it was the women—the Anns and the Priscillas—who kept hope and faith alive as the number of graves beneath the Plymouth corn fields grew and grew. During pioneer days in solitary log cabins, women shared with their husbands the constant danger of attack from hostile Indians. They were not spared when the redskins descended upon the settlements with tomahawk and torch, as the stories of Ann Hutchinson, Hannah Dustin, and many others indicate. At the time of the Revolution, Molly Pitcher, taking her husband's place in the fighting when he was grievously wounded, was not the only woman who showed courage and endurance. Through the terrible winter at Valley Forge, when the cause of Washington and Jefferson seemed all but lost, women in homes from Massachusetts to Georgia helped to keep the light of liberty burning. Women bore their share of the burden in the settlement of the lands across the Alleghenies, in the fertile valleys of the Ohio and the Mississippi. And in the tragic days of the Civil War, in homes north and south, in hospitals and on battlefields, women took their part earnestly and courageously. Never in any period of the country's history have they been found wanting.

Today the opportunities for woman's development and her ability to contribute toward the creation of a better world are greater than ever before. At last all activities of life are open to her. She is now free to choose the part she will play in the world's work. Whatever part it may be, good health is essential. Only because the women of pioneer days possessed clear minds and vigorous bodies were they able to take such an active part in the settlement of this country. Their record is a challenge to you, a woman of the new century. But only as you are similarly qualified can you in the home and in the larger world outside meet this challenge of a glorious past by your achievement.

Source 4 from S. Dana Hubbard, *Facts about Marriage Every Young Man and Woman Should Know* (New York: Claremont Printing Company, 1922), pp. 2–5. Accessed at http://asp6new.alexanderstreet.com.proxy.lib.utk.edu:90/adli/adli.image.gallery.aspx?view=galleryplusimage&dorpid=1001155127&abspage=8

### 4. S. Dana Hubbard on Choosing a Spouse.

*[S. Dana Hubbard was a physician from New York who wrote extensively about sex education, including pamphlets on "Sex Education for Young Men" and "Facts about Motherhood."]*

. . . Marriage naturally implies motherhood. There is no nobler word in any language than MOTHER. The young mother with her first born is a picture of joy and accomplishment that fills us with wonder and approbation. If there is a perfect home atmosphere—"the rallying place of affections"—every one does the utmost to make this place the happiest on earth.

There is a definite physical side to marriage, and if all husbands and wives were experts in gentleness and kindness the world would be spared many tragedies.

Maternity neither dims nor diminishes the energy, nor the intellectual faculties of the mother. On the contrary it acts positively on the virtues necessary for a proper membership in human society.

"Marriage is the beginning and the summit of all earthly civilization."

The union of a young man and woman in the holy tie of matrimony is the most important step in life. The entire future of both depends upon whether this step is taken seriously and after proper contemplation, because success and happiness depends upon wise selection. Marriage carries with it responsibilities far greater than the average person realizes.

Some marry for a home, some marry for money, some for position, some simply because it is fashionable. Foolish people. The person that marries for money, as the wag says humorously, earns it often times before he gets it.

Marriage should be only for love. Happy married life must be built upon mutual trust and devotion, not forgetting that there will be both happiness and trial and that come what may it is a case of mutual sacrifice and helpfulness.

No undertaking in life should cause more careful consideration and it is ever an undertaking which affects both health and is worthy of seeking advice and the opinion of others' happiness nothing should be overlooked in making this step.

The man a woman should marry should be healthy, clean minded and strong, not a weakling—because the husband will be the father of the children and the offspring inherit mental and physical traits of the parents. Don't help perpetuate bad traits and bad character. You cannot go against nature in heredity.

Don't marry a man who cannot provide you with a home. Insist upon your own home, be it ever so humble a beginning. "Tall oaks from acorns grow." Boarding with either your or his family is unwise. Living in furnished rooms may ruin your life or his.

While it is a delicate subject for a woman to discuss, yet the matter of children is often times a stumbling block. Don't marry a man who does not want children, such a man will not want you very long. If he loves and love truly, he will be eager to be the father of your babies.

In contemplating marriage, health is the first consideration. Have a careful understanding on this point. Insist upon both yourself and himself undergoing a careful medical examination to ascertain your fitness for marriage and parenthood. Never take this for granted. If too delicate for you to undertake have your parent or guardian do so for you. This test is for your protection, because many men "sowing wild oats" before marriage contract disease and so very few of them have their disease cured. If you do not insist upon this test you may some day find yourself with out children, or else the mother of weak, puny, diseased children.

If you are averse to having children, don't marry. You will be committing a sin that Nature will punish you for as surely as God exists. The world holds no more cowardly murderers than those who are involved in committing abortions to prevent child birth.

Do not allow your fiance any liberties with your person before marriage. He may be only testing you to learn if he can have them, but many engagements are ruined by this foolish mistake. Most men figure that if one man can have liberties before marriage other men can have similar liberties after marriage. Confirmed libertines on many occasions have proposed marriage only to deceive and obtain special privileges and this is one of the surest methods of ruining women, especially young women.

If the man you are about to marry loves and respects you, he will not ask you to degrade yourself by being his prostitute before marriage. Should you not refuse, he will surely bring this up in your family bickerings and "twit" you about your weakness, that is if he will marry you after you have allowed him to ruin you.

It is the woman's right to name the wedding day—insist upon doing this. Have a confidential talk with your parents, especially your mother or some other married woman about the obligations of the marriage relation as it affects the wife or mother.

There may be instances when elopements or run-away marriages are advisable but outside of the romance these are dangerous occasions for both man and woman. The vast majority of such hasty unions turn out badly.

Be sure the marriage license is legal. That the person performing the ceremony is duly authorized. Don't take any one's word for these facts but make certain. Make them prove it. This is emphasized to save girls from being victimized by "fake" marriages.

Never marry a chronic alcoholic, you never reform him. Never marry a drug addict. He will lower you to his level and you will never elevate him. Such experiments are failures from the first. If you decide to marry, do so, long engagements are not advisable. The engagement period is a strain on both man and woman. Extravagances that most people can ill afford are usual during this period and it is money wasted that would be most useful in your new home.

Arrange your wedding day according to your menstrual cycle. Ten days after or ten days before. This will save you some embarrassment.

In marrying, make no reservations. If there are reservations it were best not to marry. Wait for the man you are willing to share not only your heart but all your worldly possessions. . . .

## WOMEN WORKING OUTSIDE THE HOME

Source 5 from Gwendolyn Hughes, *Mothers in Industry* (New York: New Republic, 1925), pp. 1, 149, 180–181.

## 5. Gwendolyn Hughes on Working Mothers.

*[Dr. Gwendolyn Hughes was a social research fellow at Bryn Mawr College for women when she prepared* Mothers in Industry, *a massive research project involving twelve thousand households of wage-earning women in Philadelphia.]*

When the mother of young children leaves her traditional place in the home to earn money in a factory she becomes the subject of heated controversy. By some sincere observers she is regarded as a menace to the race and held accountable for the falling birthrate, declining parental responsibility and decadence in home and family life. To others, equally in earnest, her action is entirely commendable and she is regarded as a champion of woman's rights, establishing the greater personal freedom and financial independence of women. . . .

Most of the mothers are working full time in industry. . . . The most common weekly schedule is nine and one-fourth hours or nine and three-fourths hours a day with five and one-fourth hours on Saturday, a total of $52\frac{1}{2}$ or 54 hours. . . .

. . . Although most of these homes have running water in the kitchen, there are no stationary tubs, no washing machines, no mangles,[6] no electric irons. The wage-earning mother does not have the means to purchase these household appliances and must do the washing under conditions which most increase her two great disabilities, exhaustion and lack of time. . . .

On Saturday afternoon and Sunday these mothers who work full time clean house, scrub the steps, wash and iron, bathe the children and do the extra cooking. Practically without exception, they maintain that they give their families home cooking; some of them even bake bread.

Source 6 from Alice Rogers Hager, "Occupations and Earnings of Women in Industry," in *The Annals: Women in the Modern World* (Philadelphia: Sage Publications, 1929), p. 72. Copyright © 1929 by Sage Publications. Reprinted by permission of Sage Publications.

## 6. Alice Rogers Hager on Men's and Women's Factory Pay in the Mid-1920s.

*[Alice Rogers Hager, along with Caroline Manning (Source 7), was a researcher and writer for the Women's Bureau of the U.S. Department of Labor.]*

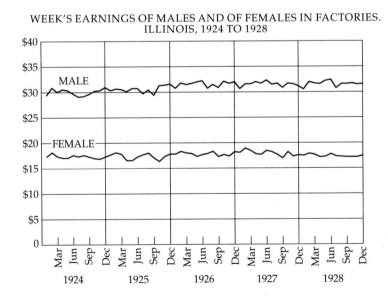

WEEK'S EARNINGS OF MALES AND OF FEMALES IN FACTORIES.
ILLINOIS, 1924 TO 1928

6. Machines for pressing fabrics by means of heated rollers.

Source 7 from Caroline Manning, *The Immigrant Woman and Her Job* (Washington, D.C.: U.S. Government Printing Office, 1930), pp. 40, 50, 59.

## 7. Caroline Manning on Immigrant Women Workers.

*Care during mother's absence.*—The families were large, the children young, and life was especially strenuous for the 500 employed mothers whose youngest child was less than 6. It was not customary for children to begin school before they were 6, and in more than half of the families with five, six, and seven or more children the youngest child was not yet 4 years old. . . .

The opinion was general among the families visited that children of 7 who were in school part of the time certainly knew enough to get something to eat at noon and to take care of themselves when not in school, and that children as old as 12 were quite able to care not only for themselves but for younger children; in fact, the care of a 12-year-old presented few problems. . . .

To the question as to why the women had returned to work after marriage there was repetition in the answers: "Times weren't so good." "Expenses so high." "We were getting behind in everything." "The men were laid off and we needed a slice of bread." "Never know when sickness comes how much it cost." "To pay for my home some day." All "needed to help a little out"—husbands ill, husbands out of work or on part time, rent to pay, and children to feed were indeed common to all. . . .

. . . Yet the conversation often drifted into channels that revealed deeper hopes and ambitions. Though the women did not give such desires as their definite reasons for working, they constituted perhaps the impelling force that directed the lives of these wage earners. At least 700 mothers referred to the plans they had for their children and the problems arising in regard to their education and the kinds of work in which they should be trained. Their comments speak for themselves: "I am still a greenhorn. My little girl must be smart." "She must not do stripping like me." "My boys must go to high school if they have good heads." "He must not work in the mill but be an American." The children of an ambitious woman who was spending her days at the polishing wheel took music lessons. Another mother, recalling her days of "slavery" in the mill, was helping her daughter through a business college.

Women feeling the pinch of hard times were ready to make sacrifices: "We do by our children in school what we can afford." The goal of a widow who worked 10 hours a day was to see her daughter a graduate of the normal school: "I no care how long I work if she can teach in a school."

Source 8 from Ernest Mowrer, *Domestic Discord* (Chicago: University of Chicago Press, 1928), pp. 160–169. Copyright © 1928 by the University of Chicago Press. Reproduced by permission.

## 8. Ernest Mowrer, Notes from Two Social Workers' Visits with Two Immigrant Families, 1928.

"Visited home. Mr. M and children at home. House and children very dirty and the babies half dressed. Mr. M said Mrs. M is working. Goes early in the morning and works ten hours. . . .

"Told him that if he would leave drink alone and work regularly that Mrs. M wouldn't have to work. Compared the neatness and cleanliness of the children when Mrs. M was home and the filth and dirt now. He said she wanted to work. I told him that was because she couldn't see the children without clothes and food."

Then four months later:

"I told the interpreter to explain very carefully to Mr. M that Mrs. M should not be working. That it was her job to stay at home and take care of the children. It is his job to support them, and if he does not do it, we will have to send him to the Bridewell [correctional institution]. . . . I am going to check up his pay every two weeks, and if he does not come up to the standard he will have to give me satisfactory reason, or we will have to bring him into court. . . ."

"Visited the B home. The house was in a terrible condition, the bed was unmade, everything was dusty and dirty, and the children were dirty and half-dressed.

"Mrs. B still wishes to leave her husband as she feels that there will never be any harmony between them. She proposes to leave the two oldest children with Mr. B and take the baby with her. She knows that Mr. B is a dutiful father and will not abuse them. She states "she is still young and can make a living for herself at any time."

"Mrs. B is selfish and is always thinking of her own comfort and pleasure. She has permitted her jealousy to overrule her and is constantly doubting her husband's fidelity. Also finding fault in the unimportant things.

"Worker tried to make Mrs. B realize her responsibility as a wife and mother. Advised her that she ought to keep her house and children clean if she wishes to command the respect of her husband. Also advised her to have her husband's meals ready on time when he comes home from a hard day's work."

### 9. Married Women and Business Careers, 1926.

Fifteen years ago married women stood outside the door opening into the business world. Few of them were allowed to enter. Had the word "flapper" been in common use then, the sign over the door probably would have read: "Only Flappers and Spinsters Admitted Here—No Married Women Wanted."

Some married women, to be sure, managed to squeeze through. But they were usually uncomfortable when they got on the other side. To begin with, their employers quite often did not believe that they were seriously interested in their work. The married woman was expected to jump up and run home the moment her husband caught cold or the children came home ill from school. She was not to be depended upon. The distractions of domesticity would prove too much for her. The married woman, therefore, when she did manage to slip through the door, was only tolerated, she was not welcomed and made a part of the establishment. . . .

Today things are very different. The married woman is no longer the object of ridicule and resentment that she once was. Not only is she now admitted to many business establishments, she is warmly welcomed, also, by some. Interviews with business men, obtained in the course of the past few days, clearly prove this.

The married woman is regarded by some business men as more dependable than many unmarried women. She has settled down and knows what she wants. This is true not only in business, but in some of the professions as well—for example, teaching. The revolution that has occurred in New York City in regard to married women holding positions in the public schools is remarkable. Few people realize the extent of the revolution.

One result of the present situation is that married women do not feel it necessary to practice, as they used to do, the gentle art of prevarication. It is not now so necessary to say that one is not married when one is. Formerly married women did this quite often. They believed that they were justified, because only by pretending to be single could they get their jobs. . . . .

Moreover, women who held positions used to slip out and get married without letting their employers know. A convenient cold supplied the excuse for absence, or perhaps the matrimonial knot was tied while the woman was on her vacation. Returning, she held her position as if nothing had happened.

When the discovery came, she passed it off as best she could. Dubious as these measures were, they were sometimes used.

Now, however, the woman is seldom driven to such extremes. When R. A. Doyle, general manager of James McCreery & Co., was asked whether objections to married women in business was as strong as they used to be, he answered: "No. Married women are much more welcome in business than they used to be. The objections have practically disappeared in some lines of work, and in others they are far less noticeable.

"We welcome married women here. They are sometimes better employes [sic] for us than unmarried women. We want women who have settled down, who have reached some serious purpose in life. It doesn't make any difference to us whether such a woman is married, or whether she is unmarried and has passed through the flapper stage. We like them both; we will give them both jobs. The point is that marriage is a kind of settling or sobering influence. The married woman usually knows what she wants and is willing to work to get it. Many unmarried women are not like that. They are still searching for something.

"Consider the flapper for a moment. She likes to dance late and amuse herself in other lively ways. She is interested in having a good time. Very often she is on the lookout for a husband, or her mind is full of young men. The flapper has difficulty in keeping her thoughts behind the counter. People talk about the distractions in the life of the unmarried woman, too. Of course, when a young woman has passed through this stage and settled down, though she still remains unmarried, she's all right; that's different. But that is one reason why we don't like to employ women under 26. We prefer them after they have passed that mark. . . ."

Source 10 from Willystine Goodsell, *Problems of the Family* (New York: Century Company, 1928), pp. 281, 282.

## 10. Married Women and Academia, 1928.

*[Sociology professor Dr. Willystine Goodsell taught at Teachers College, Columbia University.]*

Perhaps a concrete instance of the situation in which the trained woman often finds herself after marriage may serve to make the problem more real in the minds of the indifferent or the unsympathetic. In one of the issues of the *Journal of the Association of Collegiate Alumnae*, there appeared a few years ago a brief article entitled "Reflections of a Professor's Wife." With her husband, the writer had spent several years in the graduate school of a university where both had earned their doctor's degrees. Then the equality in work and the delightful companionship ceased. The man was appointed assistant professor in a state university at a small salary; and the woman, who had eagerly looked forward to a similar appointment in the same institution, was brought face to face with the ruling, by no means uncommon, which prohibited wives of faculty members from teaching in the university. The comments of the professor's wife, after years spent in housekeeping, are worth quoting, for they reflect the feelings of many other women caught in a similar net of circumstance:

"After an expenditure of several thousand dollars and the devotion of some of the best years of my life to special study, I was cut off from any opportunity to utilize this training. And unless I could earn enough money to pay some one else to do the housework, I was doomed to spend a large part of my time in tasks which a woman with practically no education could do. However, accepting the situation, I put on my apron and went into the kitchen, where for six years I have cooked a professor's meals and pondered over the policy of our university. Can it be in the divine order of things that one Ph.D. should wash dishes a whole life time for another Ph.D. just because one is a woman and the other a man?"

Source 11 from John Watson, "The Weakness of Women." Reprinted with permission from the July 6, 1927 issue of *The Nation*. For subscription information, call 1-800-333-8536. Portions of each week's *Nation* magazine can be accessed at http://www.thenation.com

## 11. John Watson on Married Women and Careers, 1926.

*[Psychologist John Watson was the founder of American behaviorism, a school of thought that maintained that human behaviour was conditioned by the environment and training of the individual.]*

I have never believed that there were any unsuperable difficulties which keep women from succeeding. They have strength enough to paint, yet there has never been a great woman painter. They have strength enough to play the violin and yet there has never been a great woman violinist. They have endurance and strength enough to become great scientists and yet one can count on fewer than the fingers of one hand the women scientists who have achieved real greatness. During the past thirty years thousands of women have taken the degree of Ph.D. and yet scarcely a dozen have come to the front. . . .

Not being trained from infancy to the tradition of incessant manipulative work they drop out of the race as soon as they get comfortable. Marriage is usually the shady spot that causes them to lie down and rest. And when they fail in that, as 80 per cent do, restlessness again sets in, but now it is too late to go back and take up the threads of the old career. Most women who had aspirations for a career have tried to eat their cake and have it too. A career is a jealous all-consuming taskmaster.

Marriage as such should be no barrier to a career. . . . The having of children is almost an insuperable barrier to a career. The rearing of children and the running of a home for them is a profession second to none in its demands for technique.

## PROFESSIONALIZING DOMESTICITY

Source 12 from Christine Frederick, *Efficient Housekeeping, or Household Engineering: Scientific Management in the Home* (Chicago: American School of Home Economics, 1925), pp. 17, 70, 384, 385.

## 12. Christine Frederick on Efficient Housekeeping.

*[As participants in the scientific management movement of the early twentieth century, Christine Frederick (Source 12), an educator, and Dr. Lillian M. Gilbreth (Source 13), a consulting engineer, sought to apply the standards of industrial efficiency to housekeeping. Mildred Maddocks Bentley (Source 14) pursued similar objectives, including as director of the Delineator Home Institute, which, among other undertakings, was a major cookbook publisher in this era.]*

I want you who take this course to feel that you are *not working alone* in your own home kitchen. I want you to feel that when you discover new methods of housework and better ways of management that you can receive the same recognition that a scientist or business investigator receives. Do not think you are working out the problem for your own home only. You are helping solve the problems of countless other women and homes, and *what you do will be passed on*, and help build up a great mass of proved knowledge on housekeeping. . . .

### Schedule for Family of Five

#### Monday

| | |
|---|---|
| 6:00–6:30 | Rise and dress; start water heater |
| 6:30–7:00 | Prepare breakfast |
| 7:00–7:30 | BREAKFAST |
| 7:30–8:30 | Wash dishes; straighten kitchen; inspect icebox; plan meals for Monday and Tuesday |
| 8:30–9:00 | Prepare towards lunch |
| 9:00–10:00 | Bedrooms, bath and hall cleaned; sort and prepare soiled linen and laundry |

| | |
|---|---|
| 10:00–11:00 | Thorough downstairs cleaning |
| 11:00–11:30 | *Rest period* |
| 11:30–12:00 | Serve lunch |
| 12:00–1:00 | LUNCH |
| 1:00–3:00 | Lunch dishes; prepare cooking for Monday and Tuesday; mop kitchen |
| 3:00–4:00 | Sewing and mending |
| 4:00–4:30 | Soak clothes and prepare for next day's washing |
| 4:30–5:30 | *Rest period*; play with children; walk, recreation or market |
| 5:30–6:00 | Prepare supper |
| 6:00–7:00 | SUPPER |
| 7:00–7:30 | Wash dishes |

**Tuesday**

| | |
|---|---|
| 6:00–6:30 | Rise and dress; put on boiler [tub in which to boil dirty clothes] |
| 6:30–7:00 | Prepare breakfast |
| 7:00–7:30 | BREAKFAST |
| 7:30–8:00 | Stack dishes; make beds |
| 8:00–11:30 | Washing |
| 11:30–12:00 | *Rest period* |
| 12:00–1:00 | LUNCH (prepared day before) |
| 1:00–2:30 | Wash breakfast and lunch dishes; clear up laundry |
| 2:30–4:00 | Take in clothes; fold, sprinkle [dampen clothes before ironing], lay away |
| 4:00–5:30 | *Rest period* |
| 5:30–6:00 | Prepare supper |
| 6:00–7:00 | SUPPER |
| 7:00–7:30 | Wash dishes |

In some households where there is no permanent worker, it often happens that the homemaker looks to the husband as a kind of nursemaid, choreman or kitchen assistant. The author's feeling is very much against this view,—that the moment a man comes into the house he should be asked to carry out the slops, hold the baby or wash the dishes. If that father works hard and faithfully at his task of earning money during his work day, it is not more fair to ask him to turn choreman as soon as he comes home, than it would be to ask the woman who has cooked and cleaned all day to turn around and do office or business work after five o-clock. It is not fair to put on a father any housework duties; his hours at home should be hours of recuperation, or so that he can study *his own work*, become more proficient, and thus secure advancement or a better economic position.

There comes to mind the case of a gifted man starting a profession, who, because of his wife's poor management, spent his time after office hours caring for the children and doing chores. He never seemed to "get on" as far as people had expected. Would it not have been better to use his spare time studying and improving in his own profession and thus be eventually able to pay for more service to help his wife, than to neglect his own opportunities by doing the housework?

Source 13 from Lillian M. Gilbreth, *The Homemaker and Her Job* (New York: Appleton-Century, 1927), pp. vii, 50, 51.

### 13. Lillian M. Gilbreth on Making Housework Satisfying.

Home-making is the finest job in the world, and it is the aim of this book to make it as interesting and satisfying as it is important.

Waste of energy is the cause of drudgery in work of any kind. In industry the engineer and the psychologist, working together, have devised means of getting more done with less effort and fatigue and of making everything that is done more interesting. The worker not only spends his working hours more effectively and with more satisfaction, but has more time and more energy freed for other things.

This book applies to the home the methods of eliminating waste that have been successful in industry. To the home-maker it offers a philosophy that will make her work satisfying, a technic [sic] that will make it easy, and a method of approach that will make it interesting.

Source 14 from Mildred Maddocks Bentley, "Labor-Saving Devices," Ch. 1 in *Good Housekeeping's Book on the Business of Housekeeping* (New York: J.J. Little and Ives Company, 1924).

### 14. Mildred Bentley on Technological Innovations in Housekeeping.

#### Labor-Saving Equipment

The new housekeeping is vastly different from the old régime. Largely because well made, efficient machines replace much of the hand labor of our grandmother's time, the modern beginner in household lore must learn a new system of planning and new methods of work.

Many are at a loss to decide just what machines are the indispensable ones for their housework and put off acquiring any because of this uncertainty. Frankly there is ample opportunity for saving both time and labor as well as money in servant hire by the purchase of well constructed and well designed equipment. And it is a fallacy to think that servants cannot learn to use them.

For instance, for the kitchen there are today well planned kitchen cabinet systems either in wood or metal to take the place of the large pantries and to accomplish their work better. This same new housekeeper has her choice of gas or electric ranges with heat regulated ovens, electric fireless cookers and fireless cookers to be used in conjunction with the gas range; pressure cookers and ranges burning oil so efficiently that this quick fuel has revolutionized the country kitchen. There is something for every one of you.

Water heating systems enable her to have an ample supply of hot water at temperatures high enough for the best work, and she can select her fuel—gas, oil, or electricity in the few sections its cost would not make it prohibitive.

Electric refrigeration is more than a dream. It is a real fact of accomplishment. In the larger sizes (250 pounds ice capacity) refrigerators are less costly to operate than with ice service even at high rates for electricity and in both large and small sizes they furnish lower refrigeration and better food conservation with some additional saving in time and labor hitherto involved in cleaning the refrigerator. When the first cost can be assumed they prove indispensable in the well ordered home.

In a single maid household it enables daughter or mother to care for all serving dishes; leaving the cooking dishes to be washed at the kitchen sink by the maid.

Even the linoleum, cemented to the kitchen floor, proves an appreciable labor saver in that it eliminates floor scrubbing and reduces the care to a semi-weekly or weekly cleaning and polishing with liquid wax, and a very occasional mopping followed by the polishing.

Laundry equipment has revolutionized home laundering methods. The indispensables are a washing machine, an ironing machine and a dryer for use on stormy days. The latter however should not take the place of all the "sun and air" drying the weatherman allows to the housekeeper. Ceiling dryer racks are convenient as are also low benches on casters for easy rolling. A well designed wall-hung ironing board for hand work with electric irons of different weights should be provided. Not until one really stops to think, is it possible to realize what these mean as work-savers in comparison with the hand washing methods, the hand wringer and the old-fashioned sad irons.

The vacuum cleaner and the electric sewing machine stand out as indispensable equipment for their several tasks. Tribute must also be paid to the chemically prepared and the wax and oil treated mops, dusters and polishing cloths. These save more work than one credits at first though, because they have revolutionized floor, wood trim and furniture care.

Space does not permit mention of all the excellent special devices for a kitchen, laundry, etc. . . .

**ADVICE ON MARITAL HAPPINESS**

## 15. Ernest and Gladys H. Groves on How to Have a Happy Marriage, 1927.

LIFE PARTNERSHIP. What is the secret of those marriages in which the wedding day seems to be a turning-point that brings the man to the straightaway leading to business success? It would be well to know, if the knowledge could be used to help those for whom the marriage ceremony is but a milestone in a long, slow, uphill climb to financial security.

The answer lies in the reactions of the newly married couple to their new relationship. Normally the man is very proud of his responsibility for the welfare of his family. He takes his business much more seriously than he did before, for now he has two mouths to feed instead of one. It would never do to lose his job, or even to miss an expected promotion.

The young husband "settles down" to his work, determined to make good if it is in him. He is somewhat helped in the settling-down process by the strange, new fact that he is no longer in constant fear of losing his sweetheart. She is his "for keeps" now, and his only anxiety is to be able to do his part well in the establishment of the home life they are entering upon.

This means money, a steady stream of it that can be depended on and promises to grow larger in time. So the young man throws himself into his work whole-heartedly, and the stuff he is made of shows. That is his side of the story. . . .

Of course the wife who helps her husband on to success makes the home life restful and refreshing. Dissatisfaction finds no quarters within the four walls of the house, be it two-room flat or rambling country homestead. Good housekeeping is not enough to turn the trick, but it is an indispensable card. Singleness of purpose, alertness of mind, and a broad outlook on life are all needed.

Then the wife does not put her embroidery, bridge, and tea parties above her husband's peace of mind. She does her best to keep the home life pleasant, that her man may be in tip-top condition for his work outside. Turning and twisting to save a penny, she sees to it that the family lives within its income, so that her husband will not be worried by unpaid bills, when he is trying to increase his earning capacity. Above all she has faith in her husband's ability to better his condition.

Source 16 from Lorine Pruette, "The Married Woman and the Part-Time Job," in *The Annals: Women in the Modern World*, pp. 302, 303, 306, copyright © 1929 by Sage Publications. Reprinted by permission of Sage Publications.

## 16.  Lorine Pruette's Critique of Domesticity, 1929.

*[Dr. Lorine Pruette was an economist whose dissertation,* Women and Leisure, *was published in 1924. Married and divorced twice, Pruette became a freelance consultant in order to try to adapt to her husbands' academic career moves.]*

The worst thing that can be said for the American home is that it ruins so many of its members. It is a disheartening and disillusioning business to survey the middle-aged married women of the country. They have been permanently damaged as persons by the disintegrating influences of the modern home and family life. Conversely, they contribute to the further disintegration of the institution to which they have given their lives.

It is only the rare woman who can pass without deterioration through many years of uninterrupted domesticity. . . . Schemes for coördination and coöperation in women's activities appear predicated on the idea that wives, when freed from minor household responsibilities, will find their satisfactions in helping their husbands get ahead in their vocations. This implies a subordination of self unfashionable in an age where the emphasis is on self-expression and uncommon among the individualistic American women of today. . . .

Not only does part-time employment of the married woman offer the opportunity for the development of a new home life, it lessens or destroys the appalling economic risk taken by every woman who today marries and devotes herself to the traditional role of wife. There is no security in domesticity. It is heart-breaking to see the middle-aged woman, trained for nothing except the duties of the home, venture out into the industrial world. Divorce, death or loss of money may put her in this position, where she has so little to offer organized industry and so much to suffer. The married woman who lets herself go upon the easy tide of domesticity is offering herself as a victim in a future tragedy.

Source 17 from *The Unadjusted Girl*, by William Isaac Thomas, pp. 72, 73. Copyright © 1923 by William I. Thomas. Copyright © renewed 1951 by William I. Thomas. By permission of Little, Brown, and Co., Inc.

## 17.  W. I. Thomas, Case 37: A Married Woman's Despair, 1923.

*[William Isaac Thomas was one of the pioneers in social psychology and the sociological case study. His earliest work centered on immigrant families; later he turned his attention to issues of gender and sexuality. He is particularly noted for the sociology*

*construct known as the Thomas theorem: "If men define situations as real, they are real in their consequences."]*

My husband's career, upon which I spent the best years of my life, is established favorably; our children are a joy to me as a mother; nor can I complain about our material circumstances. But I am dissatisfied with myself. My love for my children, be it ever so great, cannot destroy myself. A human being is not created like a bee which dies after accomplishing its only task. . . .

Desires, long latent, have been aroused in me and become more aggressive the more obstacles they encounter. . . . I now have the desire to go about and see and hear everything. I wish to take part in everything—to dance, skate, play the piano, sing, go to the theatre, opera, lectures and generally mingle in society. As you see, I am no idler whose purpose is to chase all sorts of foolish things, as a result of loose ways. This is not the case.

My present unrest is a natural result following a long period of hunger and thirst for non-satisfied desires in every field of human experience. It is the dread of losing that which never can be recovered—youth and time which do not stand still—an impulse to catch up with the things I have missed. . . . If it were not for my maternal feeling I would go away into the wide world.

## WEIGHING IN ON THE "NEW WOMAN"

Source 18 from David Stern, *Clara Bow: Runnin' Wild* (New York: Cooper Square Press, 2000), pp. 2, 68.

### 18. Clara Bow, the Original "It" Girl.

20th Century-Fox Film Corp/Everett Collection

## 19:  A Typical Flapper

Source 20 from John Watson, "The Weakness of Women." Reprinted with permission from the July 6, 1927 issue of *The Nation*. For subscription information, call 1-800-333-8536. Portions of each week's *Nation* magazine can be accessed at http://www.thenation.com

## 20. John Watson on the Sex Adjustment of Modern Women.

. . . These women were too modern to seek happiness; they sought what? Freedom. So many hundreds of women I have talked to have sought freedom. I have tried to find out diplomatically but behavioristically what they mean. Is it to wear trousers? Is it to vote—to hold office—to work at men's trades—to take men's jobs away from them—to get men's salaries? Does their demand for this mystical thing called freedom imply a resentment against child-bearing—a resentment against the fact that men's sex behavior is different from women's (but not so much any more)? I rarely arrive at a reasonable answer. . . . When a woman is a militant suffragist the chances are, shall we say, a hundred to one that her sex life is not well adjusted? Marriage as such brings adjustment in only approximately 20 per cent of all cases, so poorly have men and women been taught about sex. Among the 20 per cent who find adjustment I find no militant women, I find no women shouting about their rights to some fanciful career that men—the brutes—have robbed them of. They work—they work like a man (than which nothing better can be said about work)—they often quietly achieve careers. Most of the terrible women one must meet, women with the blatant views and voices, women who have to be noticed, who shoulder one about, who can't take life quietly, belong to this large percentage of women who have never made a sex adjustment.

Sources 21–24: *The New York Times* Coverage of Flapper Controversies.
As more and more women embraced the flapper image, ministers, doctors, and judges
weighed in on the phenomenon.
Source 21 from *The New York Times*, 23 May 1922, p. 3.

## 21. Minister Defends Flappers, 1922.

MINISTER DEFENDS FLAPPER
The Rev. Almer Pennewell Predicts Fine Generation of Women.

CHICAGO, May 22.—The modern flapper was defended by the Rev. Almer
Pennewell, pastor of the Covenant Church at Evanston yesterday in a sermon
in which he approved short skirts, bobbed hair, and knickerbockers.

"Flapperism is not a disease, but a diversion," he said. "Bobbed hair,
short skirts and knickerbockers are not signs of sin, but a declaration
of independence. The girls are a jolly lot, and they will give us the finest
generation of women the world has ever known.

"We are passing from the man age, a rough age, and emerging into the age
of culture, the women's age. That is why the flapper exists today. The new
age will be one not ruled by women but one in which their influence will be
felt. Girls in the past have been pretty little birds in cages of husky beasts of
burden."

Source 22 from *The New York Times*, 5 February 1923, p. 26.

## 22. Physicians Defend Flappers, 1923.

DEFEND FLAPPER GARB
Baltimore Physicians Dispute Theory That it Causes Disease

BALTIMORE, Feb. 4.—Along about this season of the year, when influenza,
colds and other Winter diseases spread most rapidly, anti-feminists and other
conservatives regarding apparel contend that a large amount of illness is due
to the clothes women wear. They insist illness is spread by women who wade
through slush in thin stockings and paper-shell slippers and who walk the
streets with their chests bare to the Winter winds or expose their backs to the
draughts of theatres and dance halls.

Opinions expressed today, however, by a number of prominent Baltimore
physicians indicate that such conclusions are not necessarily correct.

Dr. Clairbel Cone declares that instead of exposing herself to disease because of her clothing, the modern girl is actually increasing her powers of resistance.

"I think the clothing the girls of today wear," Dr. Cone said, "is an advantage rather than otherwise, speaking strictly from the health standpoint. It accustoms the body to the various changes of temperature of our climate. You know the savages used to wear very little clothing and they got along very well. What, in my opinion, does tend to spread influenza in Baltimore, is the dirty streets."

Dr. John Fulton, State Health Commissioner; Dr. C. Hampson Jones, City Health Commissioner, and Dr. Albert Bloomfield of the Johns Hopkins Hospital expressed practically the same opinion.

"Ever since I can remember," Dr. Fulton said, "I have been hearing that women's clothes would kill them. But they keep on living. The people who make the styles really have some sense after all. It was not so very long ago that heels were so high a woman couldn't walk down a flight of stairs frontward without running the risk of breaking her neck. Then there was the bustle epoch and the corset era. I am very much of the opinion that the effect of style on health has been greatly exaggerated at all times. I do not think that thin stockings, for instance, induce pneumonia necessarily, though the medical profession is not to be blamed for condemning certain types of clothing."

Source 23 from *The New York Times,* 21 May 1924.

### 23. Wife Allowed to Bob Hair, 1924.

COURT RULES A WIFE IS FREE TO BOB HAIR
Says Husband Has No More Control Over Her Hair-Cut Than Over Her Vote.

CHICAGO, May 20.—Judge Burke, in the Municipal Court today, ruled that a husband has no more control over his wife's hair-cut than he has over her vote.

The ruling was in the case of Jacob Silverman, arraigned on complaint of his wife, Jennie. She said she had her hair bobbed yesterday and when Jacob arrived home he expressed his disapproval by striking her.

"I wouldn't mind a plain bob," said Silverman, "but she is 32 years old and ought to know better than to get one of those what you call King Tuts."

"Times have changed," said the Court. "It is now one of woman's inalienable rights to vote. Surely a person capable of casting a ballot must be presumed capable of choosing a hair-cut. You are placed under peace bonds."

### 24. Student Nurses Allowed to Bob Hair, 1926.

STUDENT NURSES WIN RIGHT TO BOB HAIR
Ban at Hospital in Long Branch Lifted After They Persistently Opposed It.

LONG BRANCH, N. J., June 6.—Long Branch fashioners of the boyish bob were pleased today with the prospect of additions to the number of young women who wear their hair cut short. For the bob has been recognized by the Monmouth Memorial Hospital when it is worn by a student nurse.

The student nurses, nearly fifty of them, sought for some time to get permission to cut their hair short, but Mrs. Martha Scott, Superintendent, refused. She said hospital regulations forbade. But the nurses persisted; bobbed hair, they insisted, was an accepted mode of hairdressing, and certainly the student nurses wanted to be bobbed.

They presented a petition to Mrs. Scott. Mrs. Scott took up the matter with the other hospital officials, and the hospital officials gave their consent. The regulations were abrogated, and business in the barber and beauty shops of Long Branch, accordingly, has been increased.

# Questions to Consider

The evidence is grouped into several broad categories, including coming of age, work inside and outside the home, and marriage. The last selection of materials focuses on images of and reactions to the flapper. There is some unavoidable overlap between the divisions, but the groupings should still allow you to get a better handle on the advice literature and on the debates surrounding new womanhood in the 1920s.

Start by taking note of the *intended* message of the documents. What are the most important issues to these authors? What do they think is at stake? What roles do they think women should fill? What recommendations do they make to their readers? What do they believe will make women fulfilled and successful?

Each section invites its own particular questions:

What is the proper outlet for women's sexual desires? What should intimate relationships offer to young women? How should women go about choosing a husband?

How was the concept of work gendered—what work did women do, and what work did men do? How was women's work understood in society? What was the cost of mothers working outside the home? The benefit? How did class shape work—what kinds of work did middle-class women do as opposed to working-class women?

How did a good, efficient housewife conduct herself? How was domesticity

changing in this era? How could women best adjust to those changes?

What was marriage supposed to offer young women and men? What obligations did a couple have to one another? What gender dynamics were at play in courtship and marriage? What would make marriages emotionally fulfilling and strong?

What self-image did flappers present? How did they challenge tradition? At what cost to themselves? To society? Was adopting new hairstyles and new ways of dress really dangerous? Did physical appearance bespeak character and morality?

Now, think about other, more *subtle* messages within the sources—even messages the authors aren't self-conscious of giving. What do these writers presume about their subjects and their readers? What economic values are reflected in the sources? How did class shape the advice offered? How did race and ethnicity shape the advice? How might age and gender shape the reaction to flappers? In what ways are the situations of all classes and races of women similar? In what ways are they different? What about stage of life? Sexual norms? Women's defining characteristics? Their nature?

Finally, probe the changing image of womanhood conveyed and/or endorsed in these sources. Are attitudes about women's work changing? What about attitudes about women's sexuality? Attitudes about family life? Do the authors endorse or spurn "new" womanhood?

*their*

*honor*

*their*

What is at stake if women embrace the new ideals of womanhood? What is at stake if they reject these changes? Try to pull all the material together to understand the degree to which women's roles in society and the ideals of womanhood (in terms of sexuality, economy, culture, and family) were being redefined in the 1920s—and with what consequences.

◆

# Epilogue

For all practical purposes, the stock market crash of 1929 and the deep depression that lasted throughout the 1930s ended the fascination with the "new woman" and replaced it with sympathy and concern for the "forgotten man." Women who worked, especially married women, were perceived as taking jobs away from unemployed men who desperately needed to support their families. In hard times, people clung to traditional male and female roles: men should be the breadwinners, and women should stay home and take care of the family. Women's fashions changed just as dramatically. Clothing became more feminine, hemlines dropped, and hairstyles were no longer short and boyish.

Yet women, including married women, continued to move into paid employment throughout the 1930s, and women's roles within their families continued to transform. During the 1930s, the age of marriage rose, the number of children women bore decreased, and the percentage of women who intentionally remained childless increased. Birth control was not only frequently used, as these demographic patterns indicate, but it became increasingly widely accepted. The *Ladies Home Journal* conducted a survey in 1938 which found that 79 percent of American women approved of birth control. Divorce rates increased dramatically in the early twentieth century; by 1924, one in every seven marriages legally ended, and the national rate of divorce was fifteen times higher than it had been fifty years before. During the Great Depression this pattern reversed; as fewer couples could afford legal fees, the rate of legal divorces dropped—but desertion rates soared.[7]

With the United States' entry into World War II, millions of women who had never held paying jobs went to work in factories and shipyards, motivated by patriotism and a desire to aid the war effort. By the 1950s, women workers, having been replaced by returning WWII veterans, were once again being urged to stay at home and concentrate on fulfilling traditional roles as wives and mothers. Women's educational achievements and age of marriage dropped; the white middle-class birthrate nearly doubled.

7. John D'Emilio and Estelle B. Freedman, *Intimate Matters: A History of Sexuality in America* (New York: Harper and Row, 1988), 248; and Steven Mintz and Susan Kellogg, *Domestic Revolutions: A Social History of American Family Life* (New York: Free Press, 1988), 108–110, 136–137.

Fashions changed from knee-length tailored suits and dresses and "Rosie the Riveter" pants to puff-sleeved, tiny-waisted, full-skirted, full-skirted dresses.

The resistance to changes in women's roles so prominent in the 1920s was replicated in the 1960s and 1970s. The development and widespread use of the birth control pill, the passage of Title IX in 1972 and the consequent rise of women's athletics, the legalization of abortion following the 1973 *Roe v. Wade* Supreme Court case, and the influx of young women into graduate and professional programs all seemed to threaten both women's traditional role in the family and men's traditional role as breadwinners. In the 1960s and 1970s, the gay rights movement was born, and older assumptions about sexuality were questioned and, in many cases, rejected. These controversial changes, coupled with the perceived radicalism of women's full equality, produced a conservative backlash. Second-wave feminists revived the idea of broad-based women's equality, which they called liberation. They got as far as congressional passage of Alice Paul's dream of an equal rights amendment before stalling in the state ratification campaigns. In a savvy and relentless campaign against the ERA, Phyllis Schlafly painted feminists as dangerous outsiders: "See for yourself the unkempt, the lesbians, the radicals, the socialists." African American women played pivotal roles in the Civil Rights Movement only to find their equality questioned by mainstream leaders, student protest organizations, and the Black Power movement. In 1964, Stokeley Carmichael was asked about the role of women in the Student Non-Violent Coordinating Committee. His reply: "The only position for women in SNCC is prone."

In the second half of the twentieth century, the most intimate aspects of women's lives—their sexuality, their reproductive choices, their family relationships—became increasingly politicized, as people on both the left and the right of the political spectrum struggled to define the proper role of women. In no small measure, the fight was so fierce because conservatives and progressives agreed on at least one thing: the roles women fill in American society shape our families as well as our nation's culture.

# 7

# Understanding Rural Poverty During the Great Depression

✦

## The Problem

Americans financially devastated by the Great Depression and desperate enough to write First Lady Eleanor Roosevelt to personally appeal for help tended to be ashamed of their need. Most begged Mrs. Roosevelt never to disclose their identity, believing they would lose the respect of their neighbors if their circumstances became common knowledge, and, in the case of children, fearing their parents would punish them for revealing their destitution. All we know about E. B., then, is that he[1] was sixteen years old, that he lived in Double Springs, Alabama (in the rural, northwest part of the state), and that his family had fallen on hard times. With debts skyrocketing and farm prices plummeting, E. B.'s parents were about to lose their farm. The family might have been able to hold on—E. B. was willing to work as hard as he could—but both his mother

and father were "in very bad Health." His father and a sister had recently required surgery, so "We owe lots of Hospital Bills." All that stood between this family and homelessness was a little time and, E. B. hoped, the Roosevelt administration.

E. B. supported the political vision of Eleanor's husband, President Franklin Roosevelt, but wished the help he campaigned on providing could come quicker: "We know it is for the poor people good. But," he poignantly added, "it seems it hasn't reached us yet much." E. B. was not asking for money to pay his relatives' medical bills; he wrote to beg for clothes for himself and his siblings. Their situation was that dire, and he did not know where else to turn. We can surmise one other thing from E. B.'s letter: since it was dated December 27, 1934, Christmas must have been very bleak for the forlorn teenager and his siblings.

That 1934 letter sent from "your friend that lives in Ala." was one among tens of thousands received by Eleanor and Franklin Roosevelt during his administration. She received 300,000 pieces of mail in the first year alone—far

---

1. E. B. does not identify by gender. The authors infer that the person who wrote the letter was a boy, because girls tended to self-identify in their letters to Eleanor Roosevelt and because of other tonal hints in the letter. But this is speculation. The letter is reprinted in Source 3 so you can decide for yourself.

more than any other first lady. And he received three times the amount of mail of any previous president.[2]

Appeals for food, clothing, money, and sympathy flooded the White House during the 1930s, and for good cause. Nationally, unemployment stood at 25 percent for most of the decade. In pockets of the country that figure could be double or higher. Between 1929 and 1932, farm prices in the United States fell by half, and the net income of farm families dropped by 66 percent. In his second inaugural address, President Roosevelt observed that one-third of the nation remained "ill-housed, ill-clad, and ill-nourished." It was no exaggeration.

President Roosevelt also said in that same speech: "[T]he test of our progress is not whether we add more to the abundance of those who have much; it is whether we provide enough for those who have little." But his plan to aid the poor, to raise Americans out of the economic devastation of the Great Depression, known as the New Deal, was radical and controversial.

New Deal proponents understood that if the United States was going to help the E. B.'s of the world their living conditions could not be concealed. Americans of all classes would have to truly understand what poor farm families faced in order to be moved to support New Deal legislation.

A host of efforts were undertaken in the 1930s to sway public opinion in favor of controversial government programs such as rural electrification and Social Security. Interestingly enough, one of the most powerful tools for creating support for these and other New Deal programs was photography. The Historical Section of the Farm Security Administration (FSA) sent professional photographers into rural America to document the lives of people like E. B. of Double Springs, Alabama. These powerful images graphically captured rural poverty, dislocation, and suffering. They remain iconic today.

In this chapter you will analyze letters sent from poor children to Eleanor Roosevelt alongside photographs taken by FSA employees in order to address two related issues: What did the Great Depression mean in rural America? How did the FSA photographs build support for President Roosevelt's New Deal?

---

## Background

Despite the popular cliché, the stock market crash of 1929 did not cause the Great Depression. October 29, 1929, certainly dealt a blow to America's

2. Robert Cohen, ed., *Dear Mrs. Roosevelt: Letters from Children of the Great Depression* (Chapel Hill: University of North Carolina Press, 2002), p. 5.

economy; within a month the stock market lost half its value. But the trouble ran deeper than the stock market. "Black Tuesday" revealed those underlying problems. And it portended what lay ahead for Americans.

Economists in the 1930s debated (as do historians today) the causes of the depression. While there is no firm consensus, experts point to a number of interrelated issues. America was shifting from an economy built around heavy industry (coal, railroads, steel) to one increasingly dependent on consumerism (cars, clothes, radios)—which was more volatile. When the stock market collapsed, so did consumer purchasing. Banks were virtually unregulated and often failed, even in periods of economic stability. The federal government generally did not regulate corporations either, despite their sometimes suspect and erratic fiscal dealings. The American economy was weakened by European downturns, particularly in Germany in the wake of the Great War.

The Republican President Herbert Hoover believed that government intervention in the faltering economy would destroy American capitalism. Hoover was at first bewildered and then defensive about the rapid downward spiral of the nation's economy in 1930. The president, like many Americans, believed in the basic soundness of capitalism, and he prized individualism as a core American value. In Hoover's mind, federal intervention compromised both. While he tried to get corporations, bankers, and industrial leaders to cooperate to stabilize the economy, government intervention was antithetical to his political philosophy.

Between 1929 and 1933, when President Franklin D. Roosevelt took office, every sector of the nation's economy was in a virtual freefall: farm prices, wages, exports, imports, gross national product (GNP). Bank failures and farm foreclosures skyrocketed, followed inevitably by joblessness and homelessness. The poorest Americans were hit hardest: tenant and sharecropping families in the South, migrant workers in the West, rural farmers. Ecological problems, including a massive drought in the South and Southwest in the first years of the 1930s, rendered farmland useless. The southern plains became the Dust Bowl. Terrifying dust storms, caused by over-farming and persistent drought, blotted out the sun, blew away the topsoil, and buried some farms in dust.

Private charities and churches simply could not meet the pervasive and continuing needs of all these people. Nor could municipalities: many cities faced bankruptcy as their tax base collapsed. Only eight states offered any sort of unemployment insurance. Increasingly Americans looked to the federal government as their last, best hope.

Roosevelt was swept into office in a landslide victory. In 1932, he won 89 percent of the electoral votes and carried every state in the South, Midwest, and West, losing only six states.[3] Roosevelt had campaigned on a "new deal" for Americans—and he undertook a massive number of governmental innovations during his first hundred days in office. On his first day on the job, President Roosevelt declared a national bank holiday, temporarily forbidding investors from pulling their money out of banks and causing them to fail. Under the Emergency Banking Act, the Secretary of the Treasury exercised the authority to determine when banks could reopen or, if they were insolvent, how they might be reorganized. The Emergency Banking Act passed both houses of Congress in a single day with

3. Hoover won Pennsylvania, Delaware, Connecticut, Vermont, New Hampshire, and Maine.

the support of all but seven members of the U.S. Senate.

New Deal legislation sought to provide both immediate relief for the needy and legislation to ensure the nation's long-term recovery. The president and Congress created reforms focused on banking, business, the stock market, unemployed workers, farmers, and young people. In his fireside radio chats, as well as in his other speeches, Roosevelt consistently reassured the American public that the country's economic institutions remained sound and that the nation would recover. Meanwhile, he listened to a wide range of expert opinions, remained open to experimentation and innovative ideas, and led his administration by the example to "above all, try something."

Like her husband, First Lady Eleanor Roosevelt worked tirelessly to mitigate the effects of the depression. With boundless energy, she traveled throughout the country, observing conditions firsthand and reporting back to her husband. One of the few New Dealers deeply committed to civil rights for African Americans, she championed both individuals and the civil rights movement. She hosted a weekly radio show in which she discussed the pressing issues of the day, and she wrote a daily column syndicated in seventy-five newspapers. Although her critics sometimes ridiculed her for her nontraditional behavior, to millions of Americans, Eleanor Roosevelt represented the heart of the New Deal. She embraced liberal activism and redefined the role of first lady—and, as a result, Americans loved her.

Among the many problems the Roosevelt administration tackled, the plight of farmers proved particularly challenging. To meet the unusual European demand for farm products during World War I, many American farmers had over-expanded. They mortgaged their farms and borrowed money to buy expensive new farm equipment, but few profited during the relatively prosperous decade of the 1920s.

Unfortunately, the New Deal's Agricultural Adjustment Act benefited mainly large, prosperous farmers. Intended to reduce farm production and thus improve the prices farmers received for their goods, the act unintentionally encouraged large farmers to accept payment for reducing their crops, use the money to buy machinery, and evict the sharecroppers and tenants who had been working their land. Explaining to Dorothea Lange, one of the FSA photographers, why his family was traveling to California, one farmer simply said they had been "tractored out." With no land of their own to farm, sharecroppers and tenants packed their few belongings and families into old trucks and cars and took to the road looking for seasonal agricultural work. In so doing, they joined thousands of other American farm families displaced by the Dust Bowl. These Dust Bowl refugees, along with former tenants and sharecroppers, competed for jobs with Mexican Americans working as migrant laborers on the West Coast. (The novel and film *The Grapes of Wrath* present a vivid and profoundly influential tale of one such family's heartbreaking move west.[4]) For those left behind, especially in the

4. Author John Steinbeck won the Pulitzer Prize in 1940, and John Ford won an Academy Award for best director that same year for his film adaptation of the novel.

poverty-stricken areas of the rural Midwest and South, conditions were almost as terrible as in the migrant camps.

To aid these impoverished farm families, President Roosevelt created the Resettlement Administration (RA). The RA bought barren land and put it to non-agricultural use, including for state and national parks, and moved small farmers to more fertile ground. In 1935, the RA became the Farm Security Administration (FSA). Rexford Tugwell, an economics professor from Columbia University, headed the RA/FSA. Tugwell hired his former graduate student, the economist Roy Stryker, to direct the Historical Section of the agency.

Stryker's charge was to "show the city people what it's like to live on the farm." To that end, he hired a group of photographers to travel around the country and visually document the difficulties faced by small farmers, tenants, and sharecroppers. Stryker's team included Dorothea Lange, Walker Evans, Arthur Rothstein, Marion Post Wolcott, Gordon Parks, Russell Lee, John Vachon, Ben Shahn, Carl Mydans, and Theodor Jung. For nine years these photographers crossed the United States, and they took over eighty thousand depression-era pictures.[5] Stryker made the photographs widely available to national middle-class magazines like *Look* and *Life* and to newspaper editors. The Historical Section also organized traveling exhibits and encouraged authors to use the photographs in their articles and books. Through Stryker's efforts, the FSA photographs shaped how Americans perceived the depression in rural America.

The FSA photographs represented one part of an innovative partnership between government and the arts during the 1930s. New Deal programs also supported the arts through the Works Project Administration (WPA) and by commissioning post office murals and sponsoring films. Collectively, these undertakings intended to both put Americans back to work and build support for New Deal legislation. In particular, FSA leaders wanted to mobilize public opinion in support of their projects, including model migrant camps, rural cooperatives, health clinics, and federal relief for the poorest families.

The photographers did not simply document the Great Depression. They chose and arranged their subjects, they carefully composed their photographs, and they sometimes cropped the images. But, as the prominent environmental historian T. H. Watkins explained, "the essential truth of the images remained undiminished by manipulation, and they became the icons that still speak to Americans of what the Great Depression was like with a heightened reality and incomparable immediacy."[6]

Like the young people who wrote to Eleanor Roosevelt, the FSA photographers had a particular perspective and agenda. Both the letter writers and the picture takers wanted to generate

5. After 1941, FSA photographers were increasingly assigned to chronicle Americans' mobilization for the war effort. The FSA was transferred to the Office of War Information in late 1942.

6. T. H. Watkins, *The Hungry Years: A Narrative History of the Great Depression in America* (New York: Henry Holt, 1999), p. 452.

a response, the former on a personal level, the latter nationally. What kind of subjects did the photographs portray? What kind of life did the letters describe? What did the depression mean for rural Americans? What do the letters and pictures tell you about the appeal of the New Deal?

◆

## The Method

By the turn of the twentieth century, technological advances had made using cameras and developing photographs easier, but both the equipment and the developing methods were still cumbersome and primitive by today's standards. Nevertheless, people were fascinated by photography. Many talented amateurs spent hours taking pictures of their relatives, friends, and homes. Professional photographers catalogued the milestones of family life: weddings, anniversaries, first communions, service in the military. These photographs are an important source of evidence for social historians trying to reconstruct how Americans lived in the past.

But documentary photography was different. It had a particular purpose in this era of reform. During the late nineteenth and early twentieth centuries, middle-class Americans, particularly Progressives, increasingly became concerned about the growing number of poor families who depended on the labor of their children to supplement their meager standard of living. First Jacob Riis, the author of *How the Other Half Lives* (1890), and then Lewis Hine, in his work for the National Child Labor Committee, photographed the living and working conditions of children and documented the ill effects of child labor. These photographs were used to persuade the public to support the strict regulation or abolition of child labor.

Roy Stryker understood the power of photography. Before he began working for the FSA, he and Rexford Tugwell had collaborated on an economics textbook that relied heavily on photographs. He brought that experience into his leadership of the Historical Section of the FSA. Stryker also made sure, before sending his photographers out, that they understood the economy and region they were documenting. The dozen or so talented photographers whom Stryker hired to work for the Historical Section of the FSA were relatively young (most were in their twenties or thirties) and came from a variety of backgrounds. Most of the photographers, including Dorothea Lange, Walker Evans, Jack Delano, Carl Mydans, John Collier, Marion Post Wolcott, and Theodor Jung, were either established professionals or serious amateurs. Others took their first professional photographs for the Historical Section: Ben Shahn and Russell Lee had been painters, and Arthur Rothstein and John Vachon were unemployed college students. All the photographers were white, except Gordon Parks, a twenty-nine-year-old African American fashion photographer who joined the Historical Section in 1941. Parks never photographed farmers while at the FSA; instead, he sensitively documented the lives of African Americans and racial discrimination in Washington, D.C.

Photography is a particularly interesting medium for historians. The images appear "real"—not subject to the artist's interpretation in the same way as a painting or a movie. But documentary photography is neither neutral nor objective. Complete objectivity would be impossible even if it were desirable. As soon as a photographer frames a picture, poses subjects, or develops the negative, elements of manipulation and interpretation enter the image-making process. Further personal interpretation may be introduced in the cropping and printing of a photograph as well as in the selection of one image over another of the same subject. In an effort to educate viewers about depression conditions in rural America, the FSA photographers sought to document the suffering and poverty of their subjects in images that also portrayed the dignity and will to survive of these rural Americans. For example, for the photograph in Source 12, an image of a man and his children running toward shelter, Arthur Rothstein darkened the sky to recreate what it looked like during a dust storm (since he obviously could not photograph the actual storm). In 1936, Dorothea Lange, who had been a successful portrait photographer before she joined the FSA, took six photos of one California migrant mother and several of her children. Lange posed the woman and her children and kept moving in closer and closer until she captured the image that she thought best conveyed both the suffering of the migrant and

the nobility of the mother. The resulting image (Source 20) is considered an archetypal work of art and hangs in the Museum of Modern Art.

Personal letters, while a very different sort of source from photographs, present some similar complications for historians. The young people who wrote to Eleanor Roosevelt about their individual experiences conveyed, on the surface, a greater truth about the Great Depression than can be found in statistics or government policy. These children offer a unique—and uniquely compelling—perspective on life in rural America. As with all written evidence, however, one must pay careful attention to both the author and the audience.

In the case of the letters in this chapter, First Lady Eleanor Roosevelt's position of power, wealth, and prominence meant that correspondents used great deference when writing to her. The public image she cultivated influenced their perception of her as approachable and sympathetic. The young people wanted immediate help with specific financial problems, which shaped both what and how they wrote. The dynamic between a humble, poor, rural child and a powerful, rich, benevolent woman likely encouraged these children to present their situation in a particular style. It might also lead them to exaggerate their faith in or misunderstand her ability to solve their problems. (Roosevelt's office sent a form letter reply to the thousands upon thousands of correspondents; occasionally the first lady would add a particular piece of advice or sympathy.)

When analyzing the evidence, then, remember that neither personal letters nor documentary photographs offered an unbiased view of the Great Depression. Instead, both the letters and the photographs were intended to appeal to their audiences' emotions. And that emotional response needed to be strong enough to inspire action. As you read these letters and study these photographs, you will need to be specific about *what* is portrayed, *what* you feel, and *why* you feel that way.

These sources, while not wholly objective, nonetheless tell us a great deal about rural life during the Great Depression. Pay attention to the objective pieces of information offered in the letters and photographs, the details within the larger story or picture. What do these specifics tell you about the depth of poverty and desperation confronting rural Americans?

◆

## The Evidence

### DEPRESSION-ERA LETTERS

Sources 1 through 6 from Robert Cohen, ed., *Dear Mrs. Roosevelt: Letters from Children of the Great Depression* (Chapel Hill: University of North Carolina Press, 2002), pp. 43–44, 48–49, 139, 202–203, 232. Copyright © 2002 by the University of North Carolina Press. Used by permission of the publisher. www.uncpress.unc.edu

### 1. Letter from Fifth Grader in Petroleum, West Virginia, to Eleanor Roosevelt, February 1934.

*[To keep these young people's voices authentic, spelling and grammar have not been corrected.]*

February 26, 1934
Petroleum, West Virginia
Dear Mrs. Roosevelt,

I just wondered If you ever received a letter from a little girl like me. I am eleven years old the 24 of March. This is my fifth year in school. I think I will soon be ready for sixth Grade. I have got five perfect certificates and one gold star of honor. I have ... a hard way of getting what edication I have. But I expect to keep on trying. I have to walk two mile and a half to school through the mud. My Father is almost blind. We have no income of any form. Father has never recieved one cent of the money that the unemployed is supposed to get. We sure could use it. We have been told by many people that you was very kind to the poor and neady. So I thought I would ask you if you would or could send me a few things to wear. I wear size 12 year old dresses and a 14 year old coat. I am four feet and six inches tall and weigh 80 pounds. I also would like to have a pair of shoes size 3½ wide weidth. I would be the happiest person in the world. If I would recieve a package from you for my birthday. You would never miss this small amount I have asked for.

My relation helped to put President Roosevelt where he is. I dont ask for anything fine just serviceable. I do hope you will fix me up a little package and mail to me at once. My friends will be surprised.

Mrs Roosevelt please dont have this printed or broadcasted, as some of my people have radios and all take papers and I dont want any of them to know I asked you to send me the things.[7] But God knows I will remember you. And you surely will be rewarded. I send you my love and best wishes.

### 2. Letter from a Sixteen-Year-Old in Royse City, Texas, to Eleanor Roosevelt, September 1934.

Royse City, Texas
Sept. 6, 1934
Dear Friend:

Well I don't suppose you know who I am but I'm a 16 year old motherless girl that has to work hard for all she gets. I have a brother & a sister & daddy We are working at day labor for a living and don't get much of that to do. In the winter I could piece quilts if I had any scraps. We are trying to keep off the relief this winter so we are keeping every penny we can to buy groceries this winter, Whether we have sufficient clothes or not. We haven't even enough furniture. We haven't any bedsteads, a stove, or cabinet. some of our Neighbors are letting us use their stove, cabinet, & one bedstead. I thought you might have some old clothes, coats, and shoes. or any kind of clothing you could send to us. I have read so much about your kindness I know if you have any you will send them. I would send some money for postage but haven't any. Address to your loving friend Miss D. H.

### 3. Letter from E. B., a Sixteen-Year-Old from Double Springs, Alabama, to Eleanor Roosevelt, December 1934.

Double Springs, Ala.
Dec 27, 1934
Dear Mrs. Roosevelt,

I know you get letters like this almost every day. But here is one I hope and pray will be answer. I live in Ala. on a farm, and it seem mighty hard for us. We have so much sickness in our home we have a farm. But it seems if there isn't something done we will lose it. We owe lots of Hospital Bills. Wasnt for that we would Be in a better shape. My father and one of my sister had a operation the same year. My mother and father is in very bad Health. I am the oldest child at home and I am only 16. Mrs. Roosevelt if you please will send us a few dollars not

7. Secrecy was a common theme in the youth letters; young people routinely asked Mrs. Roosevelt to keep their identity confidential.

to pay our debts. But to get us a few clothes to wear if you can't send us none, please answer my letter and tell me why you can't if you possible can just send us a little bit. don't never think it will be wasted for it won't. I am sure it would be put to good use. we want to thank your Husband Mr. Roosevelt for his good plan he has planned for us poor people. We know it is for the poor people good. But it seems it hasn't reached us yet much. Mrs. Roosevelt this is my first time to write any one for any money or any of the familie. But I know you are very very rich. And we have to work hard. I don't dread working if we could only get one thing much for what we raise. Now if you please will send us a few dollars and it will grately Be appirshed. And we never can and never will thank you enough for it. Please answer my letter.

Your friend that lives in Ala.

E. B.

## 4. Letter from Miss R. S. and Miss M. J. M. of Twila, Kentucky, to Eleanor Roosevelt, May 1934.

Twila, Kentucky
May 16, 1934
Dear President & Wife:

It is indeed a great pleasure to write to the most beloved President and First Lady that the United States has ever had.

We are two girls age 17 years and have just finished our Junior Course at Wallins High School, Wallins Creek, Ky.

We had our hearts set on going to Knoxville, Tenn. This summer to take a beauty course, but as our fathers are miners and the mines here in the Southeastern coal fields have closed down it now looks impossible to obtain the necessary finance.

As the closest Beauty training school is in Knoxville, Tennessee it will be necessary to pay board buy uniforms, books, and other necessities, we would also have to pay for our training. So wont you please help us? We are not begging for money, we are just asking for a small loan. You can judge for yourself how much it would take to finance both of us.

Mr. & Mrs. Roosevelt we are two 100% girls and if you care to find out what kind of girls we are we refer you to:

Mr. L. P. M.—Principal of Wallins High School
Wallins Creek, Ky.
also
Miss M. L. J., Teacher Wallins High School
Wallins Creek, Ky.

As soon as we have finished our training and recieved our first pay we will begin sending small payments to you.

Won't you please give this, careful consideration? As the Summer Session begins May 28th. Please let us know at once if you can Help us.

Thanking you,
Miss R. S., Miss M. J. M

## 5. Letter from a Young Woman in Wachapreague, Virginia, to Eleanor Roosevelt, June 1934.

Wachapreague, Va.
June 20, 1934
Dear Mrs. Roosevelt,

Please don't consider this a foolish idea but, I knew no other to call on for help than the one who has been a mother to the country, regardless of color or creed.[8]

Mrs. Roosevelt, I am eager for an education. I have worked out since I was 11 yrs. old. I missed four school terms out of school, and graduate from high school at the age of 19 yrs.

I want to enter college in September. I have'nt a dime, and I cannot find work. What shall I do? To whom shall I turn to for help if you fail me? Mrs. Roosevelt I feel that you can help me and I feel that you will.

I am willing to work for you night and day to pay you for all that you do for me. Help me if you can.

The school that I have made application for is West Virginia State Teachers College, Institute, W. Virginia.

I want to make a woman of my self. I want to be some body. Help me in any way that you can I'll do any kind of honest work and I have had lots of experience.

I have a good reccomendation. Please, Mrs. Roosevelt, may I count on you to help me? I am sick at heart.

I graduated in "33" and I have been out of school all this winter.

I hope to hear from you at once please.

Sincerely yours
B. A. G.

## 6. Letter from a Fifteen-Year-Old Polio Patient from Chicago, Illinois, to Eleanor Roosevelt, November 1935.

Chicago, Ill.
Nov. 6, 1935
My dear Mrs. Roosevelt,

I am a little girl, fifteen years old. I was stricken with infantile paralysis last August 15—My legs are paralyzed—I am heart broken. I was going into my second

8. B. A. G. was an African American woman. Eleanor Roosevelt's support for civil rights inspired African American youth to write her and to anticipate her empathy.

year in High School—I am enclosing my picture, also the clipping about you—I think you are the most wonderful woman, and also our dear President to help so much in this sad world of ours. I get so lonely and depressed some days—then I think of President Roosevelt & all the great things he has done and he also suffered from this dreadful disease—I only hope some day I may get to Warm Springs—I pray dear God will soon help me walk again—Mrs. Roosevelt please write me a little letter, it would make me so happy—My best wishes to you and yours.

Love
V. F.

## FARM SECURITY ADMINISTRATION PHOTOGRAPHS

Source 7 from the United States Farm Security Administration, Historical Section, Library of Congress, Washington, D.C.

## 7. Abandoned Farm Home, Ward County, North Dakota, 1940 (John Vachon).

Vachon, John/Library of Congress

Source 8 from F. Jack Hurley, *Portrait of a Decade: Roy Stryker and the Development of Documentary Photographs in the Thirties* (Baton Rouge: Louisiana State University Press, 1972), 8.

**8. Drought-Stricken Farm, Mills, New Mexico, 1935 (Dorothea Lange).**

Dorothea Lange/Library of Congress

Source 9 from the United States Farm Security Administration, Historical Section, Library of Congress, Washington, D.C.

**9. "Tractored-out" Farm, Hall County, Texas, 1938 (Dorothea Lange).**

Dorothea Lange/Library of Congress

Sources 10 and 11 from Robert K. Reid, ed., *Back Home Again: Indiana in the Farm Security Administration Photographs, 1935–1943* (Bloomington: Indiana University Press, 1987), pp. 10, 2.

## 10. Eroded Farm Land, Martin County, Indiana, 1938 (Arthur Rothstein).

## 11. Soil Erosion on an Indiana Farm, Brown County, Indiana, 1935 (Theodor Jung).

Sources 12 and 13 from the United States Farm Security Administration, Historical Section, Library of Congress, Washington, D.C.

## 12. Farm Family from Cimarron County, Oklahoma, 1936 (Arthur Rothstein).

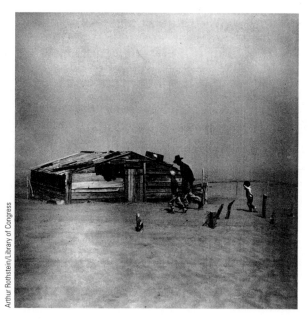

Arthur Rothstein/Library of Congress

## 13. Family on the Road in Oklahoma, 1939 (Dorothea Lange).

Dorothea Lange/Library of Congress

Sources 14 and 15 from F. Jack Hurley, *Portrait of a Decade: Roy Stryker and the Development of Documentary Photographs in the Thirties* (Baton Rouge: Louisiana State University Press, 1972), pp. 111, 135.

## 14. Plowing in the Shenandoah Valley of Virginia, Undated (Marion Post Wolcott).

Marion Post Wolcott/Library of Congress

**15. West Virginia Coal Miner's Child Carrying Home Kerosene for Lamps, Undated (Marion Post Wolcott).**

Marion Post Wolcott/Library of Congress

Sources 16 and 17 from the United States Farm Security Administration, Historical Section, Library of Congress, Washington, D.C.

## 16. Migrant Family Living in an Abandoned Truck Bed, Tennessee, 1936 (Carl Mydans).

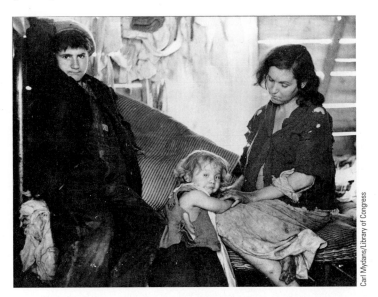

Carl Mydans/Library of Congress

## 17. Migrants from Oklahoma, Living in California, 1936 (Dorothea Lange).

Dorothea Lange/Library of Congress

Sources 18 and 19 from Robert K. Reid, ed., *Back Home Again: Indiana in the Farm Security Administration Photographs, 1935–1943* (Bloomington: Indiana University Press, 1987), pp. 11, 12.

### 18. Home of Ross Lundy Family, Martin County, Indiana, 1938 (Arthur Rothstein).

Arthur Rothstein/Library of Congress

19.  Mrs. Lundy and Daughter Inside Their Home, Martin County, Indiana, 1938 (Arthur Rothstein).

Arthur Rothstein/Library of Congress

Sources 20 through 25 from the United States Farm Security Administration, Historical Section, Library of Congress, Washington, D.C.

### 20. Migrant Mother, Nipoma, California, 1936 (Dorothea Lange).

Dorothea Lange/Library of Congress

### 21. Mexican Migrant Worker's Home, Imperial Valley, California, 1937 (Dorothea Lange).

Dorothea Lange/Library of Congress

**22.  Home of Fruit Packing-House Workers, Berrien, Michigan, 1940 (John Vachon).**

John Vachon/Library of Congress

**23.  Christmas Dinner, Iowa Tenant Farmer's Home, 1936 (Russell Lee).**

Russell Lee/Library of Congress

24. **Cotton Pickers, Pulaski County, Arkansas, 1935 (Ben Shahn).**

Ben Shahn/Library of Congress

25. **FSA Client Family, Beaufort, South Carolina, 1936 (Carl Mydans).**

Carl Mydans/Library of Congress

Source 26 from F. Jack Hurley, *Portrait of a Decade: Roy Stryker and the Development of Documentary Photographs in the Thirties* (Baton Rouge: Louisiana State University Press, 1972), p. 57.

## 26. Agricultural Workers and Children, Gee's Bend, Alabama, 1937 (Arthur Rothstein).

Arthur Rothstein/Library of Congress

Sources 27 through 29 from the United States Farm Security Administration, Historical Section, Library of Congress, Washington, D.C.

## 27. Plantation Owner and Workers, Clarksdale, Mississippi, 1936 (Dorothea Lange).

Dorothea Lange/Library of Congress

## 28. Owner of the General Store, Bank, and Cotton Gin, Wendell, North Carolina, 1939 (Marion Post Wolcott).

Marion Post Wolcott/Library of Congress

[ 230 ]

**29. Mule Dealer, Creedmoor, North Carolina, 1940 (Arthur Rothstein).**

Arthur Rothstein/Library of Congress

✦

## Questions to Consider

Begin your analysis with the letters written to Eleanor Roosevelt (Sources 1 through 6). What motivated these young people to write to the first lady? Think both about the economic circumstances within their homes *and* about the New Deal policies her husband, President Roosevelt, advanced.

What do these letters tell you about the effects of the Great Depression on family life? What particular economic and familial difficulties did these children confront? How did they and their families respond? What values and attitudes did these young people convey?

What can you learn from these letters about the United States in this era? What do the letters tell you about banks, health care, class tensions, environmental changes, educational institutions, and politics?

How did the letter writers perceive Eleanor Roosevelt and her husband? What did these young people imagine the president and first lady could do? Do you think the age of the writers shaped their perceptions? For example, did they reveal some youthful naiveté in their understanding of how government worked and what the New Deal would mean for their families? What does the absence of criticism in the letters to Eleanor Roosevelt tell you about these writers in particular and American political culture in general? (A contemporary corollary to these letters might be e-mails sent from citizens to their senators or representatives. Today we are much less deferential to and much more cynical about government officials.)

What emotional response do the letters evoke? What agenda did they seem to pursue?

Now turn to the visual sources. The photographs in Sources 7 through 11 depict what happened to the once-fertile farmlands of the plains and prairies. How would you describe these pictures to someone who had not seen them? What happened to the land and the people who lived there? What emotional response do these environmental pictures evoke?

Sources 12 through 27 show farm families, sharecroppers, and migrant workers caught in the financial crush of the depression. What story is told by these photographs? What message do they send about the need for a "new deal"? What values and attitudes did the subjects of these photographs seem to convey?

The great majority of the FSA photographs captured the lives of white Americans. What does this tell you about the program? Sources 24 through 27 depict African Americans. What do these images reveal about the living conditions of black southerners? What do they indicate about the economic and social relationships between poor black agricultural workers and white property owners (particularly Source 27)? Compare the images of black and white families and farmers. What similarities and what differences do you see in family life, economic circumstances, attitude of the subjects, and composition of the photographs?

Sources 27 through 29 depict relatively affluent white men. How are they portrayed? What emotional response do they evoke?

Use these photographs as a window into the Great Depression and New Deal policies. If a picture is worth a thousand words, what are some of the words these pictures suggest? What is happening to American children and families because of the Depression? The photographers intended to portray Americans both greatly in need of government aid and worthy of it. Did they succeed? Would these documentary photographs have been effective in creating sympathy and support for aid to these farm families?

Collectively, what do the FSA photographs tell you about the agenda of the Historical Section?

Finally, compare the letters to Eleanor Roosevelt with the FSA photographs. Do they tell a similar story? In what ways do the two types of sources diverge? Which do you think is generally more accurate and reliable in terms of depicting the experiences of rural Americans during the Great Depression: the FSA photographs or the children's letters? What are the strengths and weaknesses of the two types of evidence?

◆

# Epilogue

The images captured by FSA photographers brought shocking views of rural poverty to the attention of all Americans. Most of the photographers had never been in southern states, and the dire circumstances rural Americans endured, as well as the harsh effects of Jim Crow laws, appalled them—reactions they conveyed in their photography. (Stryker understood the political perils of displaying too much sympathy for blacks, however, so he carefully chose the images the FSA exhibited.) In the early 1940s, several of the photographers left the FSA. Walker Evans quit to collaborate with James Agee on a magazine assignment that evolved into their path-breaking book, *Let Us Now Praise Famous Men*. Dorothea Lange began to document the experiences of Japanese Americans interned during World War II. Many of her photographs of the internment camps were censored.[9] But long after the FSA photographers moved on to other projects, their pictures of the Great Depression continued to shape American public opinion and government policy.

Many middle-class white Americans had been unaware of the living and working conditions of families caught in the sharecropping or tenant farmer system. They found especially grievous the photographs of women and children. Homeless families living in cars, camping out or on the road looking for work particularly distressed middle-class Americans, who believed that home and family provided stability for the nation. The FSA images led some

9. *Let Us Now Praise Famous Men* was first published in 1941. For the censored Lange photographs, see Linda Gordon and Gary Y. Okihiro, eds., *Impounded: Dorothea Lange and the Censored Images of Japanese American Internments* (New York: W. W. Norton, 2006).

Americans to question their faith in unchecked capitalism.

President Roosevelt's New Deal sought to alleviate the financial crises facing Americans by recasting the relationship between government and economy. Through initiatives such as banking and securities regulation, funding of works projects, and Social Security, the federal government could promote financial stability for the nation and economic security for its citizens. Roosevelt believed that by protecting families from the gravest consequences of the Great Depression he was defending the American home and American democracy. Roosevelt's critics insisted that his programs undermined personal responsibility and individual freedom. The president responded to his opponents by challenging Americans to read the Bill of Rights and weigh whether they had lost any freedoms. In a fireside chat in June 1934, he confidently proclaimed, "The record is written in the experiences of your own personal lives." While this certainly did not convince his political opponents, Roosevelt easily won reelection. In fact, in 1936, he triumphed in the most lopsided presidential election in history, winning 523 electoral votes to his opponent's eight and carrying every state but Vermont and Maine. At the height of his presidency, Roosevelt enjoyed a popularity exceeded only by George Washington and, perhaps, Abraham Lincoln.

Yet the economic crisis continued into Roosevelt's second term of office. Indeed, in the fall of 1937 the "Roosevelt Recession" saw sharper declines in stock prices and industrial production and greater losses in jobs than in 1929. In 1939, nine million Americans remained unemployed, and the epidemic of rural poverty continued. On the other hand, banking and securities exchanges were regulated and stabilized; the Social Security Administration protected senior citizens and children; and programs such as the TVA brought electricity to rural America. (Historians have reason to celebrate at least one part of FDR's programs: the Writers Project Administration generated priceless oral histories to document southern slaves' lives.)[10]

In 1940, Franklin Roosevelt won an unprecedented third term. In his third inaugural address Roosevelt famously defined the "Four Freedoms": freedom of speech, freedom of religion, freedom from fear, and freedom from want. The government, he maintained, should be equally dedicated to defending all. In 1944, in his State of the Union Address, Roosevelt outlined an economic bill of rights, including:

> The right to a useful and remunerative job in the industries or shops or farms or mines of the nation;

> The right to earn enough to provide adequate food and clothing and recreation;

> The right of every farmer to raise and sell his products at a return which will give him and his family a decent living;

> The right of every businessman, large and small, to trade in an atmosphere of freedom from unfair competition and domination by monopolies at home or abroad;

10. These materials are used in *Discovering the American Past* Volume 1, Chapter 9.

The right of every family to a decent home;

The right to adequate medical care and the opportunity to achieve and enjoy good health;

The right to adequate protection from the economic fears of old age, sickness, accident, and unemployment;

The right to a good education.

But the last five years of Roosevelt's presidency would differ sharply from his first two terms, and the economic bill of rights never reached fruition. Throughout President Roosevelt's third term and into his fourth, international events towered over domestic concerns. The Japanese attack on Pearl Harbor on December 7, 1941, and the United States' subsequent entry into World War II marked a turning point in Roosevelt's presidency—and in the nation's history. Ironically, the war that overshadowed his domestic agenda also solved it. America's participation in World War II, not FDR's New Deal, finally brought an end to the Great Depression. Farmers and their sons went off to war, while wives and daughters headed to factories as the nation's economy was mobilized to defeat the Axis powers. Victory in 1945 shepherded in a period of unprecedented prosperity and power for the United States.

Americans continue to struggle with the philosophical, economic, and political questions raised by the New Deal. We contest the proper relationship between citizens and the federal government. We disagree over the roles government should play in the economy. And we continue to fiercely debate whether the welfare state (Social Security, health care, unemployment programs, Aid to Families with Dependent Children) protects our society or compromises our individual liberties.

# The American Judicial System and Japanese American Internment During World War II: *Korematsu v. United States* (323 U.S. 214)

## The Problem

On May 30, 1942, a young man who identified himself as Clyde Sarah was apprehended by police in San Leandro, California, as he was smoking a cigarette outside a drugstore. The man told police that he had been born in Las Vegas, was of Spanish-Hawaiian descent, that his parents were deceased, and that he was waiting for his girl-friend.[1]

Under further interrogation, however, "Clyde Sarah" confessed that he actually was Fred Toyosabuto Korematsu, a Nisei[2] who had been born in Oakland, California, in 1919; that his Issei parents were still very much alive; and that he had forged his Selective Service (draft) card and undergone a crude facial surgery procedure in an effort to conceal his Japanese identity. Apparently his plan had been to leave California, where anti-Japanese feeling after Pearl Harbor was particularly

1. The best treatment of Korematsu's background, arrest, and trials is in Peter Irons, *Justice at War* (New York: Oxford University Press, 1983), esp. pp. 93–96. See also Roger Daniels, *"Korematsu v. United States* Revisited," in Annette Gordon-Reed, ed., *Race on Trial: Law and Justice in American History* (New York: Oxford University Press, 2002), pp. 139–159.

2. An *Issei* is a person of Japanese extraction who was living in the United States but who was born in Japan. The Immigration Act of 1924 made Issei ineligible to become American citizens. A *Nisei* is a person of Japanese extraction who was born in the United States to Issei parents, and therefore is an American citizen. *Sansei* are those of the third generation, children of Nisei.

high, and relocate with his girlfriend Ida Boitano (an Italian American) to somewhere in the Midwest.

Before Fred Korematsu could put his plan into operation, however, the United States government began moving against all Japanese, citizens and aliens alike, living on the West Coast. Citing "military necessity," General John DeWitt, commander of the recently established Western Defense Command, issued a military order prohibiting all Japanese persons, both Issei and Nisei, from leaving Military Area Number 1 (the entire Pacific Coast). Three days later, however, DeWitt announced that a total evacuation "was in prospect for all Japanese" and that all Japanese would be required to report to one of sixteen "assembly centers" for relocation to one of the ten "relocation centers" for the duration of the war.[3] Korematsu, therefore, was caught in a trap: one order prohibited him from leaving San Leandro, whereas the following announcement predicted that all Japanese would be evacuated. While his parents and three brothers had reported to their designated assembly centers at Tanforan (south of San Francisco), Fred Korematsu instead decided to stay where

he was, hoping that his forged draft card and plastic surgery would prevent his arrest and forced evacuation. The police, however, acting on a tip from either the druggist who sold him the pack of cigarettes or from his girlfriend, seized Korematsu and turned him over to the military for either imprisonment or internment.

West Coast attorneys for the American Civil Liberties Union[4] began searching for Japanese American citizens who were willing to be represented by the ACLU in cases testing the constitutionality of the mass imprisonment of approximately 112,000 people, even though no charges ever were filed against the vast majority of detainees, roughly 62.5 percent of whom were American citizens supposedly protected by the Bill of Rights. Fearing even harsher treatment than they already had received, however, the vast majority of Japanese Americans refused. Ultimately only four individuals allowed the ACLU to represent them, and Fred Korematsu did so only hesitantly.[5] Found guilty in September 1942 of violating the military's exclusion order, he was sentenced to five years' probation.

3. The Western Defense Command consisted of the states of Arizona, California, Idaho, Montana, Nevada, Oregon, and Utah. Eighty pertcent of all Issei and Nisei living in the WDC resided in California. See Gen. J. L. DeWitt, *Final Report: Japanese Evacuation from the West Coast, 1942* (Washington: Government Printing Office, 1943), pp. 80–81. For assembly and relocation centers, see *ibid.*, pp. 151–289. For photographs, see *ibid.*, pp. 433–509; and Linda Gordon and Gary Y. Okihiro, eds., *Impounded: Dorothea Lange and the Censored Images of Japanese American Internment* (New York: W. W. Norton, 2006).

4. The ACLU was established in 1917 and was originally called the National Civil Liberties Bureau. It provided legal advice and services for conscientious objectors and those prosecuted under the 1917 Espionage Act and the 1918 Sedition Act.

5. Besides Korematsu, the other three were Min Yasui (Portland, Oregon; violation of curfew order), Gordon Hirabayashi (senior at the University of Washington; refused to register for evacuation or to obey the curfew order), and Mitsuye Endo (former clerical worker in the California Department of Motor Vehicles; dismissed for being a Japanese American and then refused to obey the evacuation order).

◆ CHAPTER 8

The American
Judicial System
and Japanese
American
Internment During
World War II:
*Korematsu v.*
*United States*
(323 U.S. 214)

Korematsu's appeal reached the United States Supreme Court in October 1944, by which time any danger of a Japanese invasion of the West Coast was highly unlikely. The decision in *Korematsu v. United States* was handed down on December 18, 1944, with Justice Hugo Black selected by Chief Justice Harlan Stone to write the majority opinion.

Your task in this chapter is to read carefully the Supreme Court's majority opinion in *Korematsu v. United States* (323 U.S. 214) together with one concurring opinion and the three dissenting opinions.[6] Some footnotes have been added by the authors to clarify certain points made and occasionally to provide important facts and background. Having read the opinions, together with the Background section of this chapter and relevant material

in your textbook, answer the following questions:

1. What constitutional issues were involved in *Korematsu v. United States*?
2. How did the majority and concurring opinions deal with the facts of the case as well as with the constitutional issues? How did the wartime situation affect these opinions, if at all?
3. How did the three dissenting opinions deal with the facts and the constitutional issues?
4. In your opinion, did the facts presented support the claim that the military situation justified the temporary suspension of parts of the Constitution? Defend your position.

A chart will help you to remember the main points as well as to keep the facts and constitutional issues straight.

◆

# Background

The story of Fred Korematsu begins several decades before he was born. In the late nineteenth and twentieth centuries, the comparatively small nation of Japan experienced rapid population growth, especially in the mushrooming industrial cities. As a result, an increasing number of Japanese sought opportunities outside of Japan, especially in Korea, Southeast Asia, and the United States, where at first they were welcomed as substitutes for Chinese

laborers who had become unpopular due to their efforts to organize for higher wages. Mostly young males, these Japanese immigrants to the West Coast of the United States were agricultural workers who intended to make money and return to Japan. Therefore, most had little interest in learning English, adopting American ways, or assimilating into the general population. In their minds, their home was Japan, not America. Their allegiance was to *Yamato Damashii*, the "Japanese Spirit."[7]

---

6. The case had been argued previously in the Federal District Court for Northern California and the Ninth District Court of Appeals.

7. For early Japanese immigrants' desires, see Page Smith, *Democracy on Trial: The*

Yet the rapid increase in Japanese immigration (from roughly 3,000 in 1890 to 127,000 from 1901 to 1908), combined with a desire of a growing number of people to remain in the United States, caused a dramatic upturn in anti-Japanese feelings.[8] Even as President Theodore Roosevelt was negotiating with the Japanese government to end the Russo-Japanese War, the city of San Francisco passed a school law that segregated all Asian children, an act that officials in Japan viewed as a slap in the face. "The infernal fools in California . . . insult the Japanese recklessly," Roosevelt wrote to his son Kermit, "and in the event of war it will be the Nation as a whole which will pay the consequences." To cool tempers, Roosevelt negotiated a "Gentleman's Agreement" in which Japan would stop issuing passports to Japanese to immigrate to the United States if the federal government promised not to pass a Japanese exclusion law similar to the Chinese Exclusion Act of 1882.[9]

The increase in the Japanese population in California, combined with a growing number of Japanese agricultural workers who were buying their own farms rather than continuing to work on white-owned land, led to a significant rise in efforts to stop further immigration. In 1909, one California state senator warned that within ten years Japanese in the state would outnumber whites ten to one. A few years later, Governor William Stephens of California asserted that "the fecundity of the Japanese race far exceeds that of any other people that we have in our midst." Throughout the western states (but especially in California), anti-Asian groups such as the Oriental Exclusion League of California, the Native Sons of the Golden West, and the California Joint Immigration Committee together with associations such as the American Legion, the Grange, and the Federation of Labor, began pressuring their congressmen, who in turn lobbied energetically in Washington, for anti-Japanese legislation.[10]

Not waiting for the federal government to act, in 1913 California passed a law denying Japanese immigrants the right to own property. Then, in 1922, the Supreme Court ruled (in *Ozawa v. United States*, 260 U.S. 178) that a person of Japanese extraction who was living in the United States was ineligible to apply for citizenship. Finally, in 1924, in response to a wave of anti-immigrant sentiment throughout the country but to anti-Japanese feelings on the West Coast especially, Congress passed the

*Japanese American Evacuation and Relocation in World War II* (New York: Simon & Schuster, 1995), p. 53.

8. For immigration statistics, see Roger Daniels, *Prisoners Without Trial: Japanese Americans in World War II* (New York: Hill and Wang, rev. ed., 2004), p. 8. Partially responsible for the change in attitude about returning to Japan was the fact that the "Gentlemen's Agreement" allowed Japanese women to come to America to join their husbands. Not a few of these women were "picture brides," who joined husbands they had never seen. *Ibid.*, p. 13.

9. For Roosevelt's typically intemperate remark, see Roosevelt to Kermit Roosevelt, October 27, 1906, quoted in Morton Grodzins, *Americans Betrayed: Politics and the Japanese Evacuation* (Chicago: University of Chicago Press, 1949), p. 6.

10. The senator's and governor's statements are quoted in *ibid.*, p.7. For the anti-Japanese organizations, see *ibid.*, pp. 4–11.

✦ CHAPTER 8

The American
Judicial System
and Japanese
American
Internment During
World War II:
*Korematsu v.*
*United States*
(323 U.S. 214)

National Origins Act of 1924, which established quotas for immigrants from all nations except those from Asia, who were entirely excluded. In Washington the Japanese ambassador resigned, while in Tokyo a protester committed suicide (*harikari*) in front of the American embassy. In the Japanese capital, July 1 was named "Humiliation Day" and was marked by "Hate America" demonstrations. A few years later, in a roundtable discussion at a Tokyo elementary school, students were asked whether they thought there would be a war between Japan and the United States. "Yes," said one discussant, "I think so. Americans are so arrogant. I'd like to show them a thing or two."[11]

The *Ozawa* decision and the National Origins Act of 1924 did not cause anti-Japanese feelings in the United States to subside. Japan's economic expansion and population increases made it increasingly difficult to produce enough food or secure critical raw materials, especially oil and iron. An increasing number of Japanese came to believe that most of the nation's problems had military solutions. And if those "solutions" would be bloody, the gains would more than offset the sacrifices.

On September 18, 1931, Japan began its conquest of Manchuria, a 585,000-square-mile region in northernmost China. Southern Manchuria fell to Japanese troops within 48 hours, and the remainder of the area was subdued weeks afterward. Soon the Japanese military established the puppet government of Manchukuo (their new name for Manchuria) and began relocating approximately five hundred thousand people (including twenty five thousand farmers and fifty thousand teenagers) from Japan to the new Japanese province. Ultimately, the plan called for the resettlement of one million Japanese households (five million people), which would relieve population pressures in Japan as well as provide for the growth of food and the extraction of natural resources in Manchukuo. Other nations were outraged, and the League of Nations protested vigorously. But the protest was toothless, and Japan responded by withdrawing from the League. The United States, not a member of the League, also protested, but mired in its own depression, with up to 25 percent of the work force unemployed and with isolationist feeling running high, the nation similarly did nothing.[12]

Convinced by international inaction that it could move with impunity in the Pacific, Japan was determined to fashion an empire that would include Manchukuo, parts of China, Southeast Asia, and the western Pacific, an empire that Japan called the Greater East Asia Co-Prosperity Sphere. Using a minor incident at the Marco Polo Bridge just

11. For the 1913 California Alien Land Law and the 1922 *Ozawa v. United States,* decision see Smith, *Democracy on Trial*, pp. 49–50. Ozawa challenged the 1906 Naturalization Act by claiming that Japanese were white. For "Humiliation Day" protests and elementary school discussion, see Sabuto Ienaga, *The Pacific War: World War II and the Japanese* (New York: Pantheon Books, 1978), p. 29.

12. On increased Japanese militarism, see Ienaga, *The Pacific War,* pp. 6, 28. On the conquest of Manchuria, see Henry L. Stimson, *The Far Eastern Crisis: Recollections and Observations* (New York: Harper and Row, 1936), Appendix 2, pp. 267–270. On the Japanese resettlement plans, see Akira Iriye, *Power and Culture: The Japanese American War, 1941–1945* (Cambridge: Harvard University Press, 1981), p. 3.

south of Beijing, Japan initiated a full-scale invasion of China. As the war in China deteriorated into a bloody stalemate, Japan began indiscriminately bombing civilians in order to terrorize them into surrendering.[13] In response, President Franklin Roosevelt delivered an angry speech in Chicago on October 5, 1937:

> It seems to be unfortunately true that the epidemic of world lawlessness is spreading. When an epidemic of physical disease starts to spread, the community approves and joins in a quarantine of the patients in order to protect the health of the community. . . . War is a contagion. . . .[14]

The American public thought the president's message was too belligerent. In Japan, however, diplomat Yosuke Matsuoka announced

> Japan is expanding. And what country in its expansion era has ever failed to be trying to its neighbors? Ask the American Indian or the Mexican how excruciatingly trying the young United States used to be once upon a time.[15]

Clearly the United States and Japan appeared to be on a collision course toward what many historians now believe was "a war that neither nation desired, but one that neither could avoid." As the United States put increasing economic pressure on Japan in an effort to arrest its expansion, Japan became convinced that only a quick war with America could achieve its demographic and economic goals. The result was Japan's surprise attack on Pearl Harbor in Hawaii, the home of the U.S. Navy's Pacific Fleet, which in 1940 had been moved from San Francisco to Pearl Harbor as a warning to Japanese expansionists.[16]

The days immediately following Pearl Harbor were extremely anxious ones for all Americans. Japanese Americans rushed to proclaim their loyalty to the United States, as one Nisei probably spoke for the vast majority when he said, "It sounds bad, but we live here and our loyalty is here." At the same time the Federal Bureau of Investigation, with previously signed warrants but often with no warrants at all, began rounding up approximately fifteen hundred Japanese (both Issei and Nisei) that the FBI had already identified as enemy aliens. By the afternoon of December 8, when President Roosevelt signed the proclamation authorizing these arrests, almost everyone on the FBI list already was in custody.[17]

13. It is generally thought that Japanese naval officer Nakajima Chikuhei was the first to advocate bombing civilians to terrorize them to surrender. See Haruo Tohmatsu and H. P. Willmott, *A Gathering Darkness: The Coming of War to the Far East and the Pacific, 1921–1942* (Lanham, MD: Rowman & Littlefield, 2004), p. 75.
14. Samuel I. Rosenman, ed., *The Public Papers and Addresses of Franklin D. Roosevelt* (New York: Harper & Brothers, 1950), Vol. 6, pp. 407–408.
15. John Toland, *The Rising Sun: The Decline and Fall of the Japanese Empire, 1936–1945* (New York: Random House, 1970), p. 48. See also Hashimoto Kingoro, "Address to Young Men," in Ryusaka Tsunoda, et. al., *Sources of Japanese Tradition* (New York: Columbia University Press, 1958), Vol. 2, pp. 289–290.

16. Jonathan G. Utley, *Going to War with Japan, 1937–1941* (Knoxville: University of Tennessee Press, 1985), p. xii; and Michael A. Barnhart, *Japan Prepares for Total War: The Search for Economic Security, 1919–1941* (Ithaca, NY: Cornell University Press, 1987), p. 21.
17. For Japanese proclamations of loyalty, see *Los Angeles Times*, December 8, 9, 10, 1941;

◆ CHAPTER 8

The American
Judicial System
and Japanese
American
Internment During
World War II:
*Korematsu v.*
*United States*
(323 U.S. 214)

Even as the FBI sweeps became known, however, federal government officials called for calm. In an address to the United States Conference of Mayors, Attorney General Francis Biddle pleaded for "precautions against the undemocratic treatment of innocent, loyal aliens by the amateur detective, the super-patriot, [and] the self-appointed sentinel. The Department of Justice is determined to prevent the injustices of the World War in this respect." Biddle and others urged that employers refrain from discharging their employees "merely because they are aliens." In California, Attorney General Earl Warren blocked the State Personnel Board from removing the names of job applicants who were of Japanese, German, or Italian descent.[18]

And yet a toxic combination of the press, West Coast politicians, and interest groups saw an opportunity to be rid of Japanese immigrants and citizens once and for all. Even as the *Los Angeles Times* reported that the

president of the city's Chamber of Commerce urged its ten thousand members to "discourage in every way possible the tendency to pass on and enlarge upon rumor and unfounded scare stories," between December 8, 1941, and February 23, 1942, that same newspaper ran the headlines "Jap Boat Flashes Message Ashore," "Japanese Here Sent Vital Data to Tokyo," "Japs Plan Attack in April," "Caps on Japanese Tomato Plants Point to Air Base," and several others, while one editorial warned "We Shall Not Forget This, Yellow Men." Stories of two Japanese youths who "hissed at Winston Churchill" during a movie newsreel, of Japanese language schools preaching pro-Tokyo propaganda, of a Japanese college student who predicted that "we SHALL take California" with high birth rates, and editorials urging white Californians not to "underestimate the cunning of these little brown men" helped to create a climate of fear, suspicion, and nearly mass hysteria. Even as Attorney General Biddle was calling for calm, he received a letter from Los Angeles that stated, "No Jap should be permitted to remain in America. . . . and no such opportunity as now exists may ever again be presented to us . . . to ship them back to Japan." Even the normally judicious Walter Lippmann, at the time probably America's most influential columnist, got carried away when he wrote, ". . . the Pacific Coast is in imminent danger of a combined attack from within and without. Some parts of it may at any moment be a battlefield. And nobody ought to be on a battlefield who has no good reason for being there. There is plenty

---

for alien arrests and Roosevelt's proclamation, see Francis Biddle, *In Brief Authority* (Garden City, N.Y.: Doubleday & Co., 1962), pp. 206–207; *New York Times*, December 8, 1941; and *Los Angeles Times*, December 11, 1941. When Germany and Italy declared war on the United States on December 11, 1941, mass internment of aliens was never considered. Of Italians, Roosevelt said, "They are a lot of opera singers." Of the Germans, however, he said, "The Germans are different, they may be dangerous." Biddle, *In Brief Authority*, p. 207.
18. *New York Times*, January 13, 1942. In his autobiography, Biddle claimed that there "was little hysteria for the first few months after Pearl Harbor." Biddle, *In Brief Authority*, p. 209. For Warren, see *New York Times*, February 8, 1942; and *Los Angeles Times*, February 8, 1942.

of room elsewhere for him to exercise his rights."[19]

In addition to the press's efforts to frighten Americans into calling for the removal of Issei and Nisei from Military Area Number 1 and, in some cases, all of the United States, an almost endless number of interest groups and civic associations also lobbied Congress and the Roosevelt administration for Japanese removal. Agricultural lobbies, such as the Western Growers Protective Association and the Grower-Shipper Vegetable Association, sought economic gain by the removal of competition from Japanese farmers. But other groups, such as the Lions, Elks, American Legion, Veterans of Foreign Wars, North Hollywood Home Owners, and others clearly thought they were offering their patriotic services by rooting out and removing what they feared were Japanese spies, fifth columnists, and saboteurs intent on undermining West Coast military defenses and war plants. Convinced that some Issei and Nisei were loyal to the United States but others were not *and* that it was impossible to tell one from the other, to these mistaken patriots the only solution was to remove them all. As Supreme Court Justice Hugo Black said years afterward in an attempt to justify his majority opinion in *Korematsu v. United States*, "They all look alike to a person not a Jap. Had they attacked our shores you'd have a large number fighting with the Japanese troops. And a lot of innocent Japanese Americans would have been shot in the panic."[20] As the war in the Pacific went badly for the United States in the early months of 1942, the pressure on Congress and President Roosevelt to remove all Issei and Nisei from the West Coast to internment camps was overwhelming. Almost all the mayors of West Coast cities urged immediate removal. Especially bellicose was Los Angeles Mayor Fletcher Bowron, who urged that all Japanese be relocated to various inland Indian reservations, and warned of the possibility of "a repetition of Pearl Harbor on the West Coast." Although the mayor's assertion (in a radio address) was both undocumented and extreme, virtually no elected officials rose to contest it. Finally, on February 13, the combined congressional delegation of congressmen and senators from California, Oregon, and Washington adopted a report recommending "the immediate evacuation of all persons, alien and citizen, from all strategic areas and . . . that such areas shall be enlarged . . . until they shall encompass the entire area of the States of California, Oregon, Washington, and the Territory of Alaska." After a sharp debate on February 18, the House of Representatives approved the delegation's recommendation.[21]

---

19. *Los Angeles Times*, December 23, 28, 1941; January 6,7,15, 23,1942; and Daniels, *Prisoners Without Trial*, p. 29. For the belief that Japanese language schools were "sources of Japanese nationalistic propaganda, cultivating allegiance to Japan," see *Hirabayashi v. United States* (320 U.S. 81), 1943 opinion of Chief Justice Harlan Stone. For the letter to Biddle, see J. R. Carter to Biddle, December 13, 1941, quoted in Grodzins, *Americans Betrayed*, p. 21. On Lippmann's February 12 article, see Daniels, *Prisoners Without Trial*, p. 45.

20. Grodzins, *Americans Betrayed*, chapter 2, esp. p. 21; and Biddle, *In Brief Authority*, p. 217. For Black's statement, see *New York Times*, September 25, 1971.

21. For Bowron, see *Congressional Record*, 77th Cong. 2nd Sess., Vol. 88, pt.8, pp. A653–654;

✦ CHAPTER 8

The American
Judicial System
and Japanese
American
Internment During
World War II:
*Korematsu v.
United States*
(323 U.S. 214)

The next day, on February 19, 1942, President Roosevelt issued Executive Order Number 9066, which authorized Secretary of War Henry Stimson and military commanders under him "to prescribe military areas in such places . . . as he or the appropriate military commander may determine, from which any and all persons may be excluded. . . . The Secretary of War is hereby authorized to provide for residents of any such area who are excluded therefrom, such transportation, food, shelter, and any other accommodations as may be necessary. . . ." According to Attorney General Francis Biddle, "I do not think he [Roosevelt] was much concerned with the gravity or implications of this step. He was never theoretical about things. What must be done to defend the country must be done."[22]

The removal of Issei and Nisei fell to Lt. General John DeWitt. DeWitt was willing to round up and incarcerate Japanese noncitizens but hesitated to remove United States citizens of Japanese extraction. On December 26, 1941, he told his superior, Major General Allen Gullion, "An American citizen, after all, is an American citizen. And while they may not be loyal, I think we can weed the disloyal out and lock them up if necessary."[23]

But DeWitt was not strong willed, and would be relieved and retired before the war was over. He was aware that Lieutenant General Walter Short and Rear Admiral Husband Kimmel, the military commanders at Pearl Harbor on December 7, had been charged by a presidential commission of inquiry with dereliction of duty and were attempting to retire before their trials commenced. DeWitt was terribly afraid that he would face Short's and Kimmel's fate if any Japanese invasion or act of treachery occurred on his watch. Even before Roosevelt's Executive Order, DeWitt made plans for mass removals. Yet in his 600-plus-page *Final Report: Japanese Evacuation from the West Coast, 1942*, DeWitt attempted to justify removal and internment as "impelled by military necessity." But in that same report he purposely withheld crucial evidence that cast doubt on his claim, evidence that years later would prove extremely embarrassing. By that time DeWitt was dead.[24]

To oversee the evacuation as well as to establish the assembly and relocation centers, Roosevelt's Executive

*Los Angeles Times*, February 6, 1942; and Grodzins, *Americans Betrayed*, pp. 100–106. For congressional delegation, see Grodzins, *Americans Betrayed*, pp. 76–90; and *Los Angeles Times*, January 31, February 14, 1942.

22. For Executive Order 9066, see *Congressional Record*, 77th Cong. 2nd Sess., House Report 2124; and *Los Angeles Times*, February 21, 1942. For Biddle's opinion, see Biddle, *In Brief Authority*, p. 219.

23. Transcript of telephone conversation between DeWitt and Gullion, December 26, 1941, quoted in Roger Daniels, *The Decision to*

*Relocate the Japanese Americans* (Philadelphia: J. B. Lippincott, 1975), p. 18. In January 1942, DeWitt told a Justice Department official that any proposal for mass evacuation was "damned nonsense." Biddle, *In Brief Authority*, p. 215.

24. On Short and Kimmel, see *Los Angeles Times*, February 8, 1942. On DeWitt shifting his position, see Daniels, *The Decision to Relocate*, pp. 18–20. On DeWitt's 1943 attempt at justification, see *Final Report: Japanese Evacuation from the West Coast, 1942* (Washington: Government Printing Office, 1943), esp. pp. vii, 3–24. DeWitt's tampering with the historical record was not unique. In 1942, Supreme Court Justice Owen Roberts reported that "a Japanese fifth column had aided the attackers" at Pearl Harbor, a patently false assertion. Daniels, *Prisoners Without Trial*, p. 37.

Order Number 9102 created the War Relocation Authority and selected as its head the Agriculture Department's Director of Information Milton Eisenhower, the youngest brother of General Dwight Eisenhower. Eisenhower's original plan was for all the evacuees to go to an assembly center, after which they would be settled individually in houses near their jobs, which Eisenhower thought would be on farms. But his comparatively gentle plan was greeted by a firestorm of opposition and he was forced to retreat. Governors in the western states almost unanimously wanted a concentration camp-style relocation for Japanese Americans. And while he tried to make the evacuation process and the relocation centers as humane as possible, Eisenhower wrote to his former boss at the Agriculture Department, "I feel most deeply that when the war is over and we consider calmly this unprecedented migration of 120,000 people, we as Americans are going to regret the avoidable injustices that may have been done." In that sense Eisenhower was prophetic.[25]

Fred Korematsu sought to evade the evacuation process through forged identification and plastic surgery, but he was apprehended almost immediately. While awaiting trial, however, he was allowed to work outside the relocation center as a welder and, because of that skill, he was never without employment. His case reached the Federal District Court for the Northern District of California on September 8, 1942, less than four months after his arrest.[26]

---

## The Method

It has been said that the wheels of justice grind exceedingly slowly. Surely this was true in the case of Fred Korematsu. Arrested on May 30, 1942, he appeared before Judge Adolphus St. Sure in the Federal District Court for the Northern District of California in September 1942 and was found guilty of having violated the Civilian Exclusion Order Number 34. But as St. Sure later put it, "I did not wish to send that man to jail," and therefore sentenced Korematsu to a five-year term of probation. In a surprising move, however, the judge never actually imposed the sentence, thus leaving Fred Korematsu in a state of legal limbo: He had been found guilty and yet no sentence had been ordered.[27]

Korematsu's attorneys filed an appeal to the Ninth Circuit Court of

25. Irons, *Justice at War*, pp. 69–74. On Eisenhower's misgivings, see his letter to Secretary of Agriculture Claude Wilkins, April 1, 1942, quoted in Roger Daniels, *Concentration Camps USA: Japanese Americans and World War II* (New York: Holt, Rinehart & Winston, 1972), p. 91.
26. Korematsu's trial would have taken place earlier than that except the original judge, Martin Welsh, went on vacation.
27. Irons, *Justice at War*, pp. 152–154. Although St. Sure set Korematsu's bail at $2,500, which was quickly posted, a military policeman refused to release him and Korematsu was escorted under armed guard back to the Tanforan Assembly Center. *Ibid.*, p. 154.

◆ CHAPTER 8

The American
Judicial System
and Japanese
American
Internment During
World War II:
*Korematsu v.
United States*
(323 U.S. 214)

Appeals on March 27, 1943. But since no sentence ever had been imposed, the Court of Appeals was unsure whether or not it had any jurisdiction to review the case and begged the United States Supreme Court to rule on that issue, which it did on June 1, 1943, ruling that the Court of Appeals did indeed have jurisdiction to hear Korematsu's appeal. Finally *Korematsu v. United States* was back in the hands of the Court of Appeals, which in December 1943 confirmed the District Court's initial judgment.

Predictably the case at last arrived in the United States Supreme Court once again, which, on December 18, 1944, issued its majority and dissenting opinions. It had taken over two and a half years for Fred Korematsu's case to reach the Supreme Court for what everyone assumed would be a final judgment—which in fact it wasn't. Ironically, the day before the Court announced its decision, the federal government announced that loyal Japanese Americans would no longer be interned and would be released.

Review the central questions you are required to answer:

1. What constitutional issues were involved in *Korematsu v. United States*?
2. How did the majority and concurring opinions deal with the facts of the case as well as with the constitutional issues? How did the wartime situation affect these opinions, if at all?
3. How did the three dissenting opinions deal with the facts and the constitutional issues?
4. In your opinion, did the facts presented support the claim that the

military situation justified the temporary suspension of parts of the Constitution? Prove your points.

Keep in mind that the business of the Supreme Court is not conducted in the same way that other judicial hearings are held. No witnesses, examination, or cross-examinations take place. Instead, the attorneys for each side are given a predetermined amount of time to present their statements, to be followed by questions from the Justices. The Court then retires and some days (or weeks) later the Justices assemble for a conference in which there is a good deal of give and take, a vote is taken, and the Chief Justice assigns one of the Justices to write the majority opinion. Other justices are free to write concurring or dissenting opinions, which become a part of the Court's record. Needless to say, between the hearing of the case and the conference, a good deal of lobbying and private conversations may take place. Of the several thousand cases the Supreme Court is asked to review each year, it can only hear a small fraction of them, usually cases which the Court believes deal with important constitutional issues. Therefore, although the Court did not have to hear the appeal of Fred Korematsu, it chose to do so based on the above criterion.

Read each of the opinions very carefully, making an outline of the general argument in each opinion. Due to space limitations, only portions of the opinions are reproduced in the Evidence section. For the complete opinions, note that *Korematsu v. United States* has been assigned the numbers 323 U.S. 214. A law school library or a law firm's office would have the Court cases. *Korematsu v. United States* is in volume 323, the U.S. standing for Supreme Court, beginning on page 214. District Court rulings also have volume and page numbers, with F. Supp. in the middle denoting a District Court. For the Circuit Court of Appeals, in the middle of the citation is F. 2nd. Armed with those codes, you will be able to find any federal case in American history.[28]

◆

## The Evidence

Sources 1 through 5 from *Korematsu v. United States* (323 U.S. 214–248).

### 1. Mr. Justice Black Delivered the Opinion of the Court. Vote 6–3.

The petitioner, an American citizen of Japanese descent, was convicted in a federal district court for remaining in San Leandro, California, a "Military Area," contrary to Civilian Exclusion Order No. 34 of the Commanding General of the Western Command, U.S. Army, which directed that after May 9, 1942, all persons of Japanese ancestry should be excluded from that area. No question was raised as to petitioner's loyalty to the United States. The Circuit Court of Appeals affirmed, and the importance of the constitutional question involved caused us to grant certiorari [that is, to hear a case from a lower court].

It should be noted, to begin with, that all legal restrictions which curtail the civil rights of a single racial group are immediately suspect. That is not to say that all such restrictions are unconstitutional. It is to say that courts must subject them to the most rigid scrutiny. Pressing public necessity may sometimes justify the existence of such restrictions; racial antagonism never can.

Exclusion Order No. 34, which the petitioner knowingly and admittedly violated, was one of a number of military orders and proclamations, all of which were substantially based upon Executive Order No. 9066, 7 Fed. Reg. 1407. That order, issued after we were at war with Japan, declared that "the successful prosecution of the war requires every possible protection against espionage and against sabotage to national-defense material, national-defense premises, and national-defense utilities . . ."

One of the series of orders and proclamations, a curfew order, which like the exclusion order here was promulgated pursuant to Executive Order 9066, subjected all persons of Japanese ancestry in prescribed West Coast military areas

28. For example, *Brown v. Board of Education* is located at 347 U.S. 483; *Miranda v. Arizona* is at 384 U.S. 436; *Bush v. Gore* is at 531 U.S. 98; *Roe v. Wade* is at 410 U. S. 113. In pre-Civil War Supreme Court cases, the name in the middle is the Court reporter. Therefore *Marbury v. Madison* is 1 Cranch 137 and *Dred Scott v. Sandford* is 19 How 393.

◆ CHAPTER 8

The American
Judicial System
and Japanese
American
Internment During
World War II:
*Korematsu v.
United States*
(323 U.S. 214)

to remain in their residences from 8 P. M. to 6 A. M. As is the case with the exclusion order here, that prior curfew order was designed as a "protection against espionage and against sabotage." In *Hirabayashi v. United States*, 320 U.S. 81, we sustained a conviction obtained for violation of the curfew order. . . .

[Hirabayashi v. United States *was the first case that tested the constitutionality of Executive Order 9066 and a supporting Act of Congress. The Court found Hirabayashi guilty of violating the curfew order, which the Court ruled was a legitimate exercise of the government's war powers.*]

We upheld the curfew order as an exercise of the power of the government to take steps necessary to prevent espionage and sabotage in an area threatened by Japanese attack.

In the light of the principles we announced in the *Hirabayashi* case, we are unable to conclude that it was beyond the war power of Congress and the Executive to exclude those of Japanese ancestry from the West Coast war area at the time they did. True, exclusion from the area in which one's home is located is a far greater deprivation than constant confinement to the home from 8 p.m. to 6 a.m. Nothing short of apprehension by the proper military authorities of the gravest imminent danger to the public safety can constitutionally justify either. But exclusion from a threatened area, no less than curfew, has a definite and close relationship to the prevention of espionage and sabotage. The military authorities, charged with the primary responsibility of defending our shores, concluded that curfew provided inadequate protection and ordered exclusion. They did so, as pointed out in our *Hirabayashi* opinion, in accordance with Congressional authority to the military to say who should, and who should not, remain in the threatened areas.

In this case the petitioner challenges the assumptions upon which we rested our conclusions in the *Hirabayashi* case. He also urges that by May 1942, when Order No. 34 was promulgated, all danger of Japanese invasion of the West Coast had disappeared. After careful consideration of these contentions we are compelled to reject them. . . .

We cannot say that the war-making branches of the Government did not have ground for believing that in a critical hour such persons could not readily be isolated and separately dealt with, and constituted a menace to the national defense and safety, which demanded that prompt and adequate measures be taken to guard against it.

Like curfew, exclusion of those of Japanese origin was deemed necessary because of the presence of an unascertained number of disloyal members of the group, most of whom we have no doubt were loyal to this country. It was because we could not reject the finding of the military authorities that it was impossible to bring about an immediate segregation of the disloyal from the loyal that we sustained the validity of the curfew order as applying to the whole group. In the instant case, temporary exclusion of the entire group was rested by the military on the same ground. The judgment that exclusion of the whole group was for the same reason a military imperative answers the contention that the exclusion was in the nature of group punishment based on antagonism to those of Japanese origin. That there were members of the group who retained loyalties to Japan has been confirmed by investigations made subsequent to the exclusion. Approximately five thousand American citizens of Japanese ancestry refused to swear unqualified allegiance to the United States and to renounce allegiance to the Japanese Emperor, and several thousand evacuees requested repatriation to Japan.

We uphold the exclusion order as of a time it was made and when the petitioner violated it . . . .

In doing so, we are not unmindful of the hardships imposed by it upon a large group of American citizens. But hardships are part of war, and war is an aggregation of hardships. All citizens alike, both in and out of uniform, feel the impact of war in greater or lesser measure. Citizenship has its responsibilities as well as its privileges, and in time of war the burden is always heavier. Compulsory exclusion of large groups of citizens from their homes, except under circumstances of direst emergency and peril, is inconsistent with our basic governmental institutions. But when under conditions of modern warfare our shores are threatened by hostile forces, the power to protect must be commensurate with the threatened danger . . . .

*[Here Justice Black addressed Korematsu's claim that he was caught in a trap—forbidden by one order to leave and by another to stay in San Leandro, which was within Military Area Number 1. But Black ruled that the Exclusion Order automatically voided the "freeze order."]*

It is said that we are dealing here with the case of imprisonment of a citizen in a concentration camp solely because of his ancestry, without evidence or inquiry concerning his loyalty and good disposition towards the United States. Our task would be simple, our duty clear, were this a case involving the imprisonment of a loyal citizen in a concentration camp because of racial prejudice. Regardless of the true nature of the assembly and relocation centers—and we deem it unjustifiable to call them concentration camps with all the ugly connotations that term implies—we are dealing specifically with nothing but an exclusion order. To cast this case into outlines of racial prejudice, without reference to the real military dangers which were presented, merely confuses the issue. Korematsu was not excluded from the Military Area because of hostility to him or his race. He *was* excluded because we are at war with the Japanese Empire, because the properly constituted military authorities feared an invasion of our West coast and felt constrained to take proper security measures, because they decided that the military urgency of the situation demanded that all citizens of Japanese ancestry be segregated from the West coast temporarily, and finally, because Congress, reposing its confidence in this time of war in our military leaders—as inevitably it must—determined that they should have the power to do just this. There was evidence of disloyalty on the part of some, the military authorities considered

✦ CHAPTER 8

The American
Judicial System
and Japanese
American
Internment During
World War II:
*Korematsu v.
United States*
(323 U.S. 214)

that the need for action was great, and time was short. We cannot—by availing ourselves of the calm perspective of hindsight—now say that at that time these actions were unjustified.

*Affirmed*

## 2. Mr. Justice Frankfurter, Concurring.

According to my reading of Civilian Exclusion Order No. 34, it was an offense for Korematsu to be found in Military Area No. 1, the territory wherein he was previously living, except within the bounds of the established Assembly Center of that area. Even though the various orders issued by General DeWitt be deemed a comprehensive code of instructions, their tenor is clear and not contradictory. They put upon Korematsu the obligation to leave Military Area No. 1, but only by the method prescribed in the instructions, i.e., by reporting to the Assembly Center. I am unable to see how the legal considerations that led to the decision in *Hirabayashi v. United States*, 320 U.S. 81, fail to sustain the military order which made the conduct now in controversy a crime. And so I join in the opinion of the Court, but should like to add a few words of my own.

The provisions of the Constitution which confer on the Congress and the President powers to enable this country to wage war are as much part of the Constitution as provisions looking to a nation at peace. And we have had recent occasion to quote approvingly the statement of former Chief Justice Hughes that the war power of the Government is "the power to wage war successfully."

Therefore, the validity of action under the war power must be judged wholly in the context of war. That action is not to be stigmatized as lawless because like action in times of peace would be lawless. To talk about a military order that expresses an allowable judgment of war needs by those entrusted with the duty of conducting war as "an unconstitutional order" is to suffuse a part of the Constitution with an atmosphere of unconstitutionality. . . .

## 3. Mr. Justice Roberts, Dissenting.

I dissent, because I think the indisputable facts exhibit a clear violation of Constitutional rights.

This is not a case of keeping people off the streets at night as was *Hirabayashi v. United States*, 320 U.S. 81, nor a case of temporary exclusion of a citizen from an area for his own safety or that of the community, nor a case of offering him an opportunity to go temporarily out of an area where his presence might cause danger to himself or to his fellows. On the contrary, it is the case of convicting a citizen as a punishment for not submitting to imprisonment in a concentration camp, based on his ancestry, and solely because of his ancestry, without evidence or inquiry concerning his loyalty and good disposition towards the United States. If this be a correct statement of the facts disclosed by this record, and facts of which we take judicial notice, I need hardly labor the conclusion that Constitutional rights have been violated. . . .

*[Here Roberts recited a chronology of all the Executive Orders, military orders, and Acts of Congress, some of which were in conflict with others, thus making it impossible for Korematsu to obey them all.]*

As I have said above, the petitioner, prior to his arrest, was faced with two diametrically contradictory orders given sanction by the Act of Congress of March 21, 1942. The earlier of those orders made him a criminal if he left the zone in which he resided; the later made him a criminal if he did not leave.

I had supposed that if a citizen was constrained by two laws, or two orders having the force of law, and obedience to one would violate the other, to punish him for violation of either would deny him due process of law. And I had supposed that under these circumstances a conviction for violating one of the orders could not stand.

We cannot shut our eyes to the fact that had the petitioner attempted to violate Proclamation No. 4 and leave the military area in which he lived he would have been arrested and tried and convicted for violation of Proclamation No. 4. The two conflicting orders, one which commanded him to stay and the other which commanded him to go, were nothing but a cleverly devised trap to accomplish the real purpose of the military authority, which was to lock him up in a concentration camp. The only course by which the petitioner could avoid arrest and prosecution was to go to that camp according to instructions to be given him when he reported at a Civil Control Center. We know that is the fact. Why should we set up a figmentary and artificial situation instead of addressing ourselves to the actualities of the case?. . .

Again it is a new doctrine of constitutional law that one indicted for disobedience to an unconstitutional statute may not defend on the ground of the invalidity of the statute but must obey it though he knows it is no law and, after he has suffered the disgrace of conviction and lost his liberty by sentence, then, and not before, seek, from within prison walls, to test the validity of the law.

Moreover, it is beside the point to rest decision in part on the fact that the petitioner, for his own reasons, wished to remain in his home. If, as is the fact, he was constrained so to do, it is indeed a narrow application of constitutional rights to ignore the order which constrained him, in order to sustain his conviction for violation of another contradictory order.

I would reverse the judgment of conviction.

## 4. Mr. Justice Murphy, Dissenting.

This exclusion of "all persons of Japanese ancestry, both alien and non-alien," from the Pacific Coast area on a plea of military necessity in the absence of martial law ought not to be approved. Such exclusion goes over "the very brink of constitutional power" and falls into the ugly abyss of racism.

In dealing with matters relating to the prosecution and progress of a war, we must accord great respect and consideration to the judgments of the military

✦ CHAPTER 8

The American
Judicial System
and Japanese
American
Internment During
World War II:
*Korematsu v.
United States*
(323 U.S. 214)

authorities who are on the scene and who have full knowledge of the military facts. The scope of their discretion must, as a matter of necessity and common sense, be wide. And their judgments ought not to be overruled lightly by those whose training and duties ill-equip them to deal intelligently with matters so vital to the physical security of the nation.

At the same time, however, it is essential that there be definite limits to military discretion, especially where martial law has not been declared. Individuals must not be left impoverished of their constitutional rights on a plea of military necessity that has neither substance nor support. Thus, like other claims conflicting with the asserted constitutional rights of the individual, the military claim must subject itself to the judicial process of having its reasonableness determined and its conflicts with other interests reconciled. "What are the allowable limits of military discretion, and whether or not they have been overstepped in a particular case, are judicial questions."

The judicial test of whether the Government, on a plea of military necessity, can validly deprive an individual of any of his constitutional rights is whether the deprivation is reasonably related to a public danger that is so "immediate, imminent, and impending" as not to admit of delay and not to permit the intervention of ordinary constitutional process to alleviate the danger. Civilian Exclusion Order No. 34, banishing from a prescribed area of the Pacific Coast "all persons of Japanese ancestry, both alien and non-alien," clearly does not meet that test. Being an obvious racial discrimination, the order deprives all those within its scope of the equal protection of the laws as guaranteed by the Fifth Amendment. It further deprives these individuals of their constitutional rights to live and work where they will, to establish a home where they choose and to move about freely. In excommunicating them without benefit of hearings, this order also deprives them of all their constitutional rights to procedural due process. Yet no reasonable relation to an "immediate, imminent, and impending" public danger is evident to support this racial restriction which is one of the most sweeping and complete deprivations of constitutional rights in the history of this nation in the absence of martial law. . .

That this forced exclusion was the result in good measure of this erroneous assumption of racial guilt rather than bona fide military necessity is evidenced by the Commanding General's Final Report on the evacuation from the Pacific Coast area.[29] In it he refers to all individuals of Japanese descent as "subversive," as belonging to "an enemy race" whose "racial strains are undiluted," and as constituting "over 112,000 potential enemies . . . at large today" along the Pacific Coast. In support of this blanket condemnation of all persons of Japanese descent, however, no reliable evidence is cited to show that such individuals were generally disloyal, or had generally so conducted themselves in this area as to constitute a special menace to defense installations or war industries, or had otherwise by their behavior furnished reasonable ground for their exclusion as a group.

29. Here Justice Murphy is referring to General DeWitt's *Final Report: Japanese Evacuation from the West Coast.* Written by DeWitt in 1943, the report was not released to the public until early 1944.

Justification for the exclusion is sought, instead, mainly upon questionable racial and sociological grounds not ordinarily within the realm of expert military judgment, supplemented by certain semi-military conclusions drawn from an unwarranted use of circumstantial evidence. Individuals of Japanese ancestry are condemned because they are said to be "a large, unassimilated, tightly knit racial group, bound to an enemy nation by strong ties of race, culture, custom and religion." They are claimed to be given to "emperor worshipping ceremonies" and to "dual citizenship." Japanese language schools and allegedly pro-Japanese organizations are cited as evidence of possible group disloyalty, together with facts as to certain persons being educated and residing at length in Japan. It is intimated that many of these individuals deliberately resided "adjacent to strategic points," thus enabling them "to carry into execution a tremendous program of sabotage on a mass scale should any considerable number of them have been inclined to do so." The need for protective custody is also asserted. The report refers without identity to "numerous incidents of violence" as well as to other admittedly unverified or cumulative incidents. From this, plus certain other events not shown to have been connected with the Japanese Americans, it is concluded that the "situation was fraught with danger to the Japanese population itself" and that the general public "was ready to take matters into its own hand." Finally, it is intimated, though not directly charged or proved, that persons of Japanese ancestry were responsible for three minor isolated shellings and bombings of the Pacific Coast area, as well as for unidentified radio transmissions and night signalling.

. . . to infer that examples of individual disloyalty prove group disloyalty and justify discriminatory action against the entire group is to deny that under our system of law individual guilt is the sole basis for deprivation of rights. Moreover, this inference, which is at the very heart of the evacuation orders, has been used in support of the abhorrent and despicable treatment of minority groups by the dictatorial tyrannies which this nation is now pledged to destroy. . . .

I dissent, therefore, from this legalization of racism. Racial discrimination in any form and in any degree has no justifiable part whatever in our democratic way of life. It is unattractive in any setting but it is utterly revolting among a free people who have embraced the principles set forth in the Constitution of the United States. All residents of this nation are kin in some way by blood or culture to a foreign land. Yet they are primarily and necessarily a part of the new and distinct civilization of the United States. They must accordingly be treated at all times as the heirs of the American experiment and as entitled to all the rights and freedoms guaranteed by the Constitution.

## 5. Mr. Justice Jackson, Dissenting.

Korematsu was born on our soil, of parents born in Japan. The Constitution makes him a citizen of the United States by nativity and a citizen of California by residence. No claim is made that he is not loyal to this country. There is no

✦ CHAPTER 8

The American
Judicial System
and Japanese
American
Internment During
World War II:
*Korematsu v.
United States*
(323 U.S. 214)

suggestion that apart from the matter involved here he is not law-abiding and well disposed. Korematsu, however, has been convicted of an act not commonly a crime. It consists merely of being present in the state whereof he is a citizen, near the place where he was born, and where all his life he has lived.

Even more unusual is the series of military orders which made this conduct a crime. They forbid such a one to remain, and they also forbid him to leave. They were so drawn that the only way Korematsu could avoid violation was to give himself up to the military authority. This meant submission to custody, examination, and transportation out of the territory, to be followed by indeterminate confinement in detention camps.

A citizen's presence in the locality, however, was made a crime only if his parents were of Japanese birth. Had Korematsu been one of four—the others being, say, a German alien enemy, an Italian alien enemy, and a citizen of American-born ancestors, convicted of treason but out on parole—only Korematsu's presence would have violated the order. The difference between their innocence and his crime would result, not from anything he did, said, or thought, different than they, but only in that he was born of different racial stock.

Now, if any fundamental assumption underlies our system, it is that guilt is personal and not inheritable. Even if all of one's antecedents had been convicted of treason, the Constitution forbids its penalties to be visited upon him, for it provides that "no attainder of treason shall work corruption of blood, or forfeiture except during the life of the person attainted." But here is an attempt to make an otherwise innocent act a crime merely because this prisoner is the son of parents as to whom he had no choice, and belongs to a race from which there is no way to resign. If Congress in peace-time legislation should enact such a criminal law, I should suppose this Court would refuse to enforce it. . . .

*[Here Justice Jackson cast doubts on DeWitt's assertions that internment was an act of military necessity. Once the war is over, however, a military order will be repealed, whereas a Supreme Court decision, "like a loaded weapon," will lie about, waiting for some governmental official to pick it up and use it. Then Justice Jackson turned to a consideration of the earlier case of Hirabayashi v. United States.]*

It argues that we are bound to uphold the conviction of Korematsu because we upheld one in *Hirabayashi v. United States*, 320 U.S. 81, when we sustained these orders in so far as they applied a curfew requirement to a citizen of Japanese ancestry. I think we should learn something from that experience.

In that case we were urged to consider only the curfew feature, that being all that technically was involved, because it was the only count necessary to sustain Hirabayashi's conviction and sentence. We yielded, and the Chief Justice guarded the opinion as carefully as language will do. He said: "Our investigation here does not go beyond the inquiry whether, in the light of all the relevant circumstances preceding and attending their promulgation, the challenged orders and statute *afforded a reasonable basis for the action taken in imposing the curfew.*" 320 U.S.

at 101. "We decide only the issue as we have defined it—we decide only that the *curfew order* as applied, and at the time it was applied, was within the boundaries of the war power." 320 U.S. at 102. And again: "It is unnecessary to consider whether or to what extent *such findings would support orders differing from the curfew order.*" 320 U.S. at 105. (Italics supplied.) However, in spite of our limiting words we did validate a discrimination on the basis of ancestry for mild and temporary deprivation of liberty. Now the principle of racial discrimination is pushed from support of mild measures to very harsh ones, and from temporary deprivations to indeterminate ones. And the precedent which it is said requires us to do so is *Hirabayashi*. The Court is now saying that in *Hirabayashi* we did decide the very things we there said we were not deciding. Because we said that these citizens could be made to stay in their homes during the hours of dark, it is said we must require them to leave home entirely; and if that, we are told they may also be taken into custody for deportation; and if that, it is argued they may also be held for some undetermined time in detention camps. How far the principle of this case would be extended before plausible reasons would play out, I do not know.

I should hold that a civil court cannot be made to enforce an order which violates constitutional limitations even if it is a reasonable exercise of military authority. The courts can exercise only the judicial power, can apply only law, and must abide by the Constitution, or they cease to be civil courts and become instruments of military policy.

Of course the existence of a military power resting on force, so vagrant, so centralized, so necessarily heedless of the individual, is an inherent threat to liberty. But I would not lead people to rely on this Court for a review that seems to me wholly delusive. The military reasonableness of these orders can only be determined by military superiors. If the people ever let command of the war power fall into irresponsible and unscrupulous hands, the courts wield no power equal to its restraint. The chief restraint upon those who command the physical forces of the country, in the future as in the past, must be their responsibility to the political judgments of their contemporaries and to the moral judgments of history. . . .

◆ CHAPTER 8

The American
Judicial System
and Japanese
American
Internment During
World War II:
*Korematsu v.
United States*
(323 U.S. 214)

◆

# Questions to Consider

By the time *Korematsu v. United States* finally reached the United States Supreme Court in October 1944, it had been heard by a Federal District Court and the Ninth Circuit Court.[30] In all the hearings, the central issue was whether serious military danger allowed the federal government to violate some of Fred Korematsu's constitutional rights. Before you analyze the five opinions in the Evidence section of this chapter, you will want to consult the United States Constitution to determine which of Korematsu's rights had been violated.[31]

Writing the Court's majority opinion, Justice Hugo Black (1886–1971) spoke directly to the issue above. In Black's view, what was the "military necessity" (the phrase that General John DeWitt used to justify his military orders)? Who should have determined whether (or not) there was such a "military necessity"?

You already are familiar with *Hirabayashi v. United States* (320 U.S. 81). How did Justice Black use that earlier decision as a precedent?

Clearly there were Japanese and Japanese Americans living in the United States who were loyal to Japan. Recall the FBI roundups in December 1941. How did Justice Black justify Korematsu's arrest and evacuation, even though there was no proof that he was disloyal, as Black admitted in the first paragraph of his opinion? Following his reasoning, were there any limits to government powers in times of war or imminent danger?

In an earlier hearing of the case, Fred Korematsu's attorneys argued that he was caught between two military orders, and that if he obeyed one he would automatically violate the other. How did Justice Black address that issue?

Finally, Justice Black dealt with the accusation that, since the military orders and acts of Congress applied only to people of Japanese ancestry, they were by definition acts of racial discrimination. How did Justice Black address that issue?

In his concurring opinion, Justice Felix Frankfurter (1882–1965) agreed with the majority opinion that *Hirabayashi v. United States* was in fact a precedent for the case under consideration. What did Justice Frankfurter add? See the opinion of former Chief Justice Charles Evans Hughes (1862–1948).[32]

---

30. In addition there had been two additional judicial actions dealing with the case, the first one by the Circuit Court asking the Supreme Court whether it had jurisdiction, and the other when the Supreme Court ruled that it did (319 U.S. 432).

31. In the original trial in the Federal District Court, Korematsu's attorneys used what legal historian Peter Irons later referred to as the "shotgun approach," claiming that the government had violated three articles of and nine amendments to the Constitution, claims that clearly were absurd. See Irons, *Justice at War*, p. 151.

32. According to historian Roger Daniels, Justices Black, Frankfurter, Douglas, and Chief Justice Harlan Stone should have recused themselves in all cases affecting Japanese Americans, since Black and Douglas had social contacts with General DeWitt, and Frankfurter and Stone because they had advised the

The three dissenting Justices (Owen Roberts [1875–1955], Frank Murphy [1890–1949], and Robert Jackson [1892–1954]) all agreed that Fred Korematsu—as well as all people on the West Coast of Japanese ancestry—had been the victims of racial discrimination. Yet, each dissenting opinion went beyond that assertion to attack the majority opinion. How did each Justice argue that the decisions of the lower courts should be overturned? In other words, each of the dissenting Justices had his own reasons for disagreeing with the majority opinion of Justice Black. What were those individuals' points?

## Epilogue

After nearly a half-century of anti-Asian prejudice, a brutal war in the Pacific, and war hysteria on the home front, anti-Japanese feelings, especially on the West Coast, were slow to die. Soon after Hiroshima and Nagasaki, the *Chicago Defender*, a weekly newspaper with a national circulation of primarily African American readers, reported the results of a public opinion poll of mostly white Americans which revealed that a twelve-to-one margin favored "dropping more atomic bombs on Japan." In an angry reaction, the newspaper asked, "Would the people have voted 12 to 1 for the use of the bomb against Germany or any other white race?"[33]

Gradually, however, as Americans began to learn about the internment camps, more than a few were overcome by a wave of shame. Indeed, well before the end of the war, the Roosevelt administration secretly began conversations about closing the ten retention centers, but may have hesitated due to a combination of the fear of the negative reaction and perhaps also fear of anti-Japanese violence and race riots. By war's end, an undetermined number of internees had been "furloughed."

Attempts by the Japanese Americans after the war to recover their property proved only partially successful. In 1948, Congress passed and President Harry Truman signed the Japanese American Claims Act that appropriated $38 million to assist claimants to recover their property. But this was estimated to be only about one-third of what was necessary. Was the government afraid of stirring up anti-Japanese prejudice?

Then, in 1951, Hollywood released the commercial film *Go for Broke*, about the 442nd Regimental Combat Team, a unit of all-volunteer Nisei that distinguished itself during World War II in Italy, France, and Germany, receiving 18,000 decorations including

government about these cases. See Daniels, "*Korematsu v. United States* Revisited," p. 147 n. 29.

33. African Americans were the only significant ethnic group of Americans who opposed the treatment of people of Japanese ancestry. See Harry Paxton Howard, "Americans in Concentration Camps," in *Crisis* (September 1942), pp. 281–284, 301–302; and *Negro Digest* (September 1944), quoted in Gordon and Okihiro, *Impounded*, p. 82.

◆ CHAPTER 8

The American
Judicial System
and Japanese
American
Internment During
World War II:
*Korematsu v.
United States*
(323 U.S. 214)

21 Medals of Honor, 52 Distinguished Service Crosses, 560 Silver Stars, 4,000 Bronze Stars, and an astounding 9,486 Purple Hearts. Slowly Americans came to understand that the vast majority of Japanese Americans had been loyal men and women who supported their country in the war.[34]

In the latter half of the twentieth century, as Japan became the United States' strongest ally in the Pacific, opinions about Japanese Americans shifted markedly. In 1976, President Gerald Ford repealed President Roosevelt's Executive Order 9066, a symbolic gesture but one that was appreciated by the approximately seven hundred thousand Americans of Japanese ancestry. Then, in 1980, Congress and President Jimmy Carter created the Commission on Wartime Relocation and Internment of Civilians, an independent federal commission to study the events surrounding the internment of American citizens and to "recommend appropriate remedies."[35]

As the Commission's report was being compiled, legal historian and attorney Peter Irons at the University of California, San Diego, discovered in the Justice Department files that General DeWitt had falsified information about Issei and Nisei on the West Coast immediately following the attack on Pearl Harbor. DeWitt knew, from reports by the FBI, the Office of Naval Intelligence, and the Federal Communications Commission, that accusations of espionage, planned sabotage, and information sent to the Japanese military from the West Coast for the most part were false. Therefore, DeWitt's attempt in his *Final Report* to justify his military orders and proclamations on the grounds of "military necessity" simply was deceitful. Worse, by 1944, when *Korematsu v. United States* at last arrived at the Supreme Court, the government knew it was not true and purposely had withheld evidence from the Court, an action that both Justices Murphy and Jackson may have suspected.[36]

Before the Commission's report was completed, Professor Irons approached Fred Korematsu, who had not spoken of his tribulations for forty years, and asked him if he would be willing to have his case reopened. Korematsu agreed, and Irons and a team of Japanese American attorneys had the case retried in the Federal District Court on the grounds of *coram nobis* (that the earlier conviction should be vacated or overturned due to "errors of the most fundamental character").

The judge hearing the case was Marilyn Hall Patel, a recent Carter appointee. The government had responded by offering a full pardon, but accepting it would have meant that Fred Korematsu was guilty of the charges, and therefore he refused the offer. The Commission's report was available, stating that the internment was a "grave injustice"

34. On the 1948 Claims Act, in 1988, President Ronald Reagan signed the Civil Liberties Act, which provided for a $20,000 "redress payment" to each of the 60,000 surviving internees, including Fred Korematsu. For the 442nd and the 100th Battalion, see Commission on Wartime Relocation and Internment of Civilians, *Personal Justice Denied: The Report* (Washington: Government Printing Office, December 1982), pp. 256–260.

35. Daniels, *Prisoners Without Trial*, pp. 90–92.

36. See *New York Times*, April 1, 2005.

and there was no "military necessity" for the internment. Rather, it was the result of "race prejudice, war hysteria and a failure of political leadership."[37]

Fred Korematsu stood and made a brief statement to the court, immediately after which Judge Patel handed down her verdict, warning that *Korematsu v. United States* "stands as a constant caution that in times of war or declared military necessity our institutions must be vigilant in protecting constitutional guarantees."[38]

It was over. Not fully understanding, Fred Korematsu asked Irons, "What happened?" "You won," Irons replied.[39]

In his senior years Fred Korematsu became something of a folk hero. He met Rosa Parks, another famous protester, and other luminaries. In 1998, he was awarded the Presidential Medal of Freedom by President Clinton. After 9/11/01 he expressed concern about the civil liberties in time of war. He died in 2005, at age 86.[40]

---

37. For the offer of a pardon, see the film "Of Civil Wrongs and Rights: The Fred Korematsu Story" (2000). For the findings see Commission on Wartime Relocation and Internment of Civilians, *Personal Justice Denied: The Report* (Washington: Government Printing Office, December 1982), p. 18.
38. Daniels, *Prisoners Without Trial*, p. 100.

39. "Of Civil Wrongs and Rights."
40. *New York Times*, April 1, 2005.

# 9

# The 1960 Student Campaign for Civil Rights

◆

## The Problem

In 1954, the United States Supreme Court issued one of the most significant decisions in American judicial history. The case began with a father, World War II veteran Oliver Brown, who wanted his daughter, Linda, to attend the elementary school closest to the family home. The Browns lived in Topeka, Kansas—a state whose laws strictly mandated racial segregation, including in restaurants, movie theatres, and the public schools. Linda walked six blocks through a railroad yard to meet the bus that carried her to school; Sumner Elementary School stood just a few blocks in the other direction from her house, but Linda Brown could not attend there because she was African American. By 1952, Mr. Brown had been joined by other parents in Topeka, and their suit, in turn, was combined with cases in four other jurisdictions collectively challenging the constitutionality of racially segregated public schools. In 1952, the Supreme Court heard opening arguments and the justices issued their decision in May 1954.

*Brown v. Board of Education of Topeka* was, then, not solely one man's fight for his child's education. Indeed,

it included two hundred plaintiffs and represented the culmination of years of effort and scores of cases brought by the National Association for the Advancement of Colored People (NAACP) legal defense team. Thurgood Marshall served as chief counsel for the NAACP. Building on the intellectual and legal foundation laid by his predecessor and mentor, Charles Hamilton Houston, Marshall led the NAACP's strategy to upend legalized racial segregation in the United States. A dozen lawyers on the NAACP team meticulously planned the case: litigating in jurisdictions outside the Deep South, carefully choosing the particular school districts to challenge, selecting a veteran as the first named plaintiff, and commissioning psychological studies of the effects of segregation on children. Marshall successfully argued the *Brown* case before the Supreme Court.[1] He and his

1. Marshall won twenty-nine of thirty-two cases he argued before the Supreme Court and later became the first African American to serve on the nation's highest court. For a full explanation of the *Brown* case and its history, see Richard Kluger, *Simple Justice: The History of Brown v. Board of Education and Black America's Struggle for Equality* (New York: Knopf, 1975).

team had previously won cases centered on graduate and professional education in segregated public universities in Missouri, Oklahoma, and Texas. While powerful precedents, the scope of these cases, because they necessarily applied to a very small percentage of the population, could not compare with the consequences of *Brown v. Board of Education.*

In the wake of the *Brown* decision, African Americans, particularly in the South, where segregation was especially pervasive and grinding, rejoiced. But hopes for a transformed South were soon dashed. The 1955 U.S. Supreme Court decision known as *Brown II*, in which the Court declared that desegregation should proceed with "all deliberate speed," inadvertently opened the door to southern resistance. In 1956, 101 representatives in the U.S. Congress signed the "southern manifesto," including the entire congressional delegations from Alabama, Arkansas, Georgia, Louisiana, Mississippi, South Carolina, and Virginia. Initially drafted by South Carolinian Strom Thurmond, the document rebuked the "unwarranted exercise of power by the Court" and blamed the Supreme Court justices for undermining the "amicable relations" between black and white southerners. Southern politicians also responded to *Brown* with hundreds of state and municipal laws antithetical to the Supreme Court decision and a wave of violence intended to intimidate African Americans and their white sympathizers. The year after the *Brown* verdict, Emmett Till, a fourteen-year-old boy from Chicago visiting relatives in the rural community of Money, Mississippi, was kidnapped, tortured, and murdered. His alleged offense: whistling at a white woman. In 1957, President Dwight D. Eisenhower had to send one thousand soldiers from the 101st Airborne Division to protect nine black students desegregating Central High School in Little Rock, Arkansas.

Inspired by both the momentum of *Brown* and the backlash it spawned, the NAACP and the Southern Christian Leadership Conference (SCLC) worked with community groups to organize several campaigns, most famously the Montgomery Bus Boycott in 1955. But despite national attention on the *Brown* decision, the Emmett Till lynching, and the Little Rock Nine, to a large degree the burgeoning Civil Rights Movement had stalled by the end of the 1950s. Many conservative black and white leaders urged the gradual dismantling of Jim Crow and the pursuit of justice through the federal courts—both protracted processes.

In the early weeks of 1960, however, an unlikely cohort of eighteen-year-old college students in North Carolina revived the movement. Ezell Blair Jr., Franklin McCain, Joseph McNeil, and David Richmond were freshmen at North Carolina Agricultural and Technical College (A&T) when they launched the student sit-in movement at the segregated lunch counter at Woolworth's in Greensboro, North Carolina, on February 1, 1960. Within a week, three hundred students from A&T, Bennett College (an African American women's school), and Dudley High School joined in the campaign. Sit-ins spread like wildfire, to Winston-Salem, Raleigh, and Charlotte, North Carolina, to Nashville, Tennessee, and to Richmond, Virginia.

No individual or organization in particular led the students—they operated as spontaneous, local campaigns. Student activists founded the Student Nonviolent Coordinating Committee (SNCC) in April 1960, and members led community organizing efforts and conducted protests across the South. But unlike the SCLC and the NAACP, SNCC operated in a decentralized manner, in terms of meeting style (everyone spoke as long as he or she wanted), strategy (set at the local level), and decision making (through group consensus). While SNCC provided a forum for and advice to local protest organizers, the organization did not direct the student movement. African American college students typically led the efforts, and high schoolers, white classmates, and members of their communities joined them. By springtime, student sit-ins against segregation were sweeping the South and transforming the Civil Rights Movement. The students launched immediate, personal, and peaceful confrontations of segregation, which diverged from the approaches of longstanding organizations such as the NAACP and forced police and political leaders to decide whether or not they would defend the rights of the protestors. The student body president of Knoxville College captured the convictions of the student activists when he insisted: "We do not intend to wait placidly for those rights which are already legally and morally ours to be meted out to us one at a time."[2]

In this chapter you will investigate the student protest movement. What changes did these young men and women bring to the Civil Rights Movement? What can we learn about 1960s youth culture and American society by studying this part of the Civil Rights Movement?

◆

## Background

In the wake of the Civil War, when the federal government forbade the continuation of racial slavery, white southerners faced a potentially radically transformed world. For a few years after the war, the United States military occupied the former Confederate states, and martial law ensured that African American men exercised their civil rights. But this transformation of the South did not long stand.

By 1877, Reconstruction had collapsed. In the North, white Americans, including many who opposed slavery, balked at continuing this exercise in racial equality. The majority of Americans lost interest in militarily occupying the South, and other national events took center stage. In the South, a vicious campaign of intimidation backed up by murder waged by the paramilitary

2. Quoted in William B. Wheeler, *Knoxville, Tennessee: A Mountain City in the New South* (Knoxville, TN: University of Tennessee Press, 2005), p. 125.

wing of the Democratic Party, the Ku Klux Klan, undermined Reconstruction governments. "Redeemed" state governments—in which power was wrested from black and white Republican politicians—revised their constitutions and passed a host of laws aimed at revoking the civil rights of African American citizens and reducing black men and women to a status as close to slavery as possible.

From the 1880s, former slaveholders dominated the Democratic Party, and they used the "redeemed" state governments to revive the hierarchical society of the Old South. Laws restricted the occupations African Americans could undertake and where they lived. "Anti-miscegenation" laws prohibited interracial marriages.[3] Several southern states required African Americans to contract their labor on an annual basis. It was a crime to leave a job without permission. Parchman Farm Prison, in Mississippi, became a vehicle—a profitable one at that—for forcing black men into lifelong servitude.[4] Vagrancy laws criminalized the physical movement of black families.

The post-Reconstruction justice system worked in tandem with sharecropping to disfranchise poor black as well as white southerners. Republican politicians debated redistributing land during the Reconstruction era, but ultimately rejected the idea. Former slaveholders kept their property, which left

3. The United States Supreme Court ended race-based marriage prohibitions in the *Loving v. Virginia* case in 1967.
4. For more on Parchman, see David Oshinsky, *Worse Than Slavery: Parchman Farm and the Ordeal of Jim Crow Justice* (New York: Free Press, 1997).

former slaves with few work opportunities besides agriculture. Sharecropping, the dominant system for agricultural production from the 1880s to the 1930s, was supposed to allow black families a chance at eventual landownership and economic autonomy. In design, poor black (and white) families grew cotton while rich white landowners provided them cotton seed, tools, and shelter. At the end of the year, the landowner sold the crop, kept his due, and split the profit with his laborers. If sharecropping families worked hard and lived frugally, in time, they could buy their own land and be independent. That was the theory. In practice, landowners routinely and systematically manipulated the math; sharecropping families seldom, if ever, finished the year with a profit. Laws prohibited their moving so long as a debt remained. So, for decades, poor black and white southerners lived in abject poverty, beholden to wealthy planters who controlled the land, the economy, and the law. Sharecropping and Democrat-dominated state governments thereby recreated a social order not dissimilar from that of the Old South: large landholders held sway over government and the economy, which left most white and black southerners impoverished and disfranchised. As you saw in Chapter 2, this racial agenda thwarted the alternative vision of a progressive, industrialized "New South" that would move out of the shadow of plantation agriculture and slavery.

The most important legal innovation to emerge in the South after the 1870s was the legal system known as "Jim Crow." These laws (the term derives from a minstrel show) racially segregated the South. Because slavery had so starkly defined the lives of black and white southerners, there was little reason to compel physical separation in the antebellum era. But after the United States defeated the Confederacy and outlawed slavery, white political elites desperately sought to redefine the lines between black and white southerners. Racial divisions became particularly pressing after "redemption" because the economic and political status of black and white non-elites was so similar. Jim Crow became the elites' best tool.

Hundreds of state and municipal laws physically separated black southerners from their white neighbors. African Americans could not drink from the same water fountains as white people; they entered restaurants and businesses through separate doors; they sat in the balcony of movie theatres; if they appeared in court, they swore on a separate Bible; pools, libraries, even cemeteries were segregated. But for white southerners, perhaps the most important and meaningful locus for the Jim Crow system was the public school system.

Both black and white southerners had long understood the power of education. Frederick Douglass maintained that learning changed his life and set him on the path toward self-liberation and abolitionism. During the era of slavery, southern states outlawed literacy among slaves; whites who taught slaves to read were themselves guilty of a crime. Education was power, and it was rigidly protected in the early twentieth century, just as it had been before the Civil War.

In terms of race, public education in the American South changed little between the 1880s and the 1950s. During Reconstruction, former slaves worked with the Freedman's Bureau to build and subsidize schools for African American students. But southern state legislatures consistently fought against funding these schools. African American children attended poorly financed, rigidly segregated schools. Certainly teachers in African American schools were dedicated, but textbooks, transportation, physical spaces, and faculty salaries were all far inferior to those in all-white schools. Higher education was generally segregated as well. African Americans were barred from attending whites-only state universities, even though their taxes supported those institutions.

One consequence of this segregated educational system was the growth of black colleges and universities. To avoid integration, many states funded (albeit parsimoniously) institutions such as North Carolina A&T, which attracted middle-class African American students like the Greensboro Four. Other private institutions of higher education, such as Fisk University in Nashville, emerged out of the efforts of black and white community leaders. Some universities and colleges, such as Tuskegee Institute in Alabama, focused heavily on practical education, training African American men and women in education, agriculture, and other trades. Under the leadership of Booker T. Washington, Tuskegee emphasized economic uplift and self-reliance.[5] Other universities, including North Carolina A&T, focused on mathematics, business, and military science,

5. For more on Washington, see Robert J. Norrell, *Up From Slavery: The Life of Booker T. Washington* (Cambridge: Harvard University Press, 2009).

in addition to agriculture. (When North Carolina created A&T, the state simultaneously chartered North Carolina A&M—now North Carolina State University—for white students.) Alongside black-owned newspapers and, particularly, black churches, these colleges and universities became not only powerful symbols of African American culture but leading centers for black activism in the early twentieth century.

Strictly racialized education was not illegal—indeed, the U.S. Supreme Court sanctioned segregation in the *Plessy v. Ferguson* case of 1896. According to the court, racially divided accommodations did not violate constitutional law. State governments quickly interpreted the ruling to apply to all public accommodations, but the *Plessy* case centered specifically on railroad cars. Homer Plessy was a passenger on a Louisiana train in the 1890s. Told to move to the car reserved for African Americans, he refused. Fined twenty-five dollars, he refused to pay and was arrested. He sued over the arrest and his case eventually reached the Supreme Court. Seven of nine justices voted to uphold the Louisiana law segregating railroad cars, finding that since the train provided "separate but equal" accommodations, the Fourteenth Amendment to the Constitution, which guaranteed equal protection and rights to all citizens, had not been violated. Justice John Marshall Harlan issued the only dissenting opinion, proclaiming "Our Constitution is colorblind." None of his fellow justices concurred.

While codified in law, segregation was also policed by vigilante violence, often orchestrated by white supremacists, including those involved in reviving the KKK, and condoned by White Citizens' Councils. White and African American southerners who challenged Jim Crow faced swift retribution. While lynching was not solely a southern phenomenon, most lynchings occurred in the region, and the great majority of victims were African American men. The violence was intentionally gruesome and widely publicized. A few examples from the pervasive pattern will illustrate the vicious reaction generated by challenges to white supremacy. In Atlanta in 1899, Sam Hose, a young farmer, was accused of killing a white man (which he had unintentionally done during an argument) and raping the victim's wife (which he had not). As railroads ferried Atlantans to the community where he sat in jail, a lynch mob overwhelmed the authorities. They stripped Hose naked and chained him to a tree. While thousands of spectators cheered, white men took turns cutting off his ears, fingers, and genitals. Still alive, Hose was set on fire. The mob dismembered his burned corpse, and members of the crowd took body parts as souvenirs.[6] Emmett Till was lynched in 1955 by J. W. Milam and Roy Bryant, who, by their own admission, kidnapped him from his uncle's home, brutally beat him, shot him in the head, and threw his body in the Tallahatchie River. Milam and Bryant were tried for kidnapping and murder and exonerated by an all-white jury, which deliberated only 67 minutes. In June 1963, Byron De La Beckwith shot Medgar Evers, field secretary for the NAACP, in his driveway in Jackson, Mississippi. During the murder trial, as Evers' widow,

6. Norrell, *Up From Slavery,* pp. 160–61.

Myrlie Evers, testified, the governor of Mississippi, Ross Barnett, walked into court and shook De La Beckwith's hand. An all-white jury found De La Beckwith not guilty.[7] Such was the justice system under Jim Crow—and the risk to African Americans who crossed the color line.

The young people who started the sit-in protests knew the stakes. Ezell Blair, Jr., remembered watching the news coverage of the Emmett Till lynching. Pictures from his open casket funeral appeared in *Jet* magazine in 1955, and journalists reported the story around the world. As a young child, Blair watched the KKK parade through his neighborhood.[8]

Jim Crow consistently shaped southern life between the 1880s and the 1950s, but a number of changes occurred in the 1940s and 1950s that would trigger a broad-based, revolutionary challenge to racial segregation.[9] The NAACP legal defense team was only one part of the organization's advocacy for equality. During the first half of the twentieth century, the NAACP also waged a

decades-long anti-lynching campaign and organized lobbying operations and social protests in pursuit of equal rights. Over one million African American men served in the armed forces during World War II. The hypocrisy of fighting fascism abroad while over twelve million U.S. citizens did not enjoy basic human rights at home was not lost on the black community or on some American leaders. President Harry Truman ordered the United States military desegregated in 1948; within a few years, integration was accomplished, including at primary and secondary schools on military bases. On one level, the Cold War presented an ideological obstacle to challenging America's racial order. White southerners disparaged anyone who criticized segregation as a communist and routinely used red-baiting to discredit civil rights activists. Other Americans, however, saw that racial discrimination presented the Soviet Union with a powerful tool for anti-U.S. propaganda. In this view, segregation damaged America's integrity and therefore posed a risk to national security. International relations thus raised the stakes in the contest over civil rights. The international human rights movement likewise influenced American domestic politics. By midcentury, the movement for Indian liberation led by Mahatma Gandhi was exerting a profound effect on many African Americans, including Martin Luther King, Jr. Gandhi pioneered nonviolent civil disobedience; he believed that by directly, peacefully, and relentlessly confronting inequality, justice could be won. Finally, the power of television should not be overlooked. By 1960, television had emerged as a dominant cultural force

---

7. De La Beckwith was retried in Mississippi in 1994 and was convicted.

8. *February One* (film documentary), Video Dialog, 2003.

9. Scholars have also explored the many challenges to the South's—and the nation's—racial order in the decades before the Civil Rights Movement. See, for example, John Egerton, *Speak Now Against the Day: The Generation before the Civil Rights Movement in the South* (Chapel Hill: University of North Carolina Press, 1995); and Glenda Elizabeth Gilmore, *Defying Dixie: The Radical Roots of Civil Rights, 1919–1950* (New York: W. W. Norton, 2008). For a model study of student-led antisegregation activism outside the South, see Stefan M. Bradley, *Harlem vs. Columbia: Black Student Power in the Late 1960s* (Urbana: University of Illinois Press, 2009).

in American life. Viewership skyrocketed in the 1950s. In 1950, less than 10 percent of American households owned television sets; by 1960, over 85 percent did. Television was so influential that many political commentators attribute John Kennedy's victory over Richard Nixon in the 1960 campaign to Nixon's poor performance in the nation's first televised presidential debate. Network news cameras brought Rosa Parks, the Little Rock Nine at Central High School, Emmett Till's funeral, and the student sit-ins into American's living rooms.

Despite these changes and the *Brown* decision, in the 1950s most African American parents, hoping to protect their children, continued to teach them how to negotiate Jim Crow, not challenge it. Adults warned children never to approach whites, to drop their eyes when they met on the street. Where one went, what one said, even one's body language could cost one one's life. By 1960, though, young people were increasingly dubious of their parents' generation and values. Even the brilliant, systematic legal strategy of the NAACP struck many young people as too slow and too accommodating. Many in the rising generation viewed gradual challenges to segregation with skepticism. As Franklin McCain remembered, he and his friends "trusted no one over

eighteen." The older generation, he believed, had its chance to change the system and failed to take it. The rising generation would not make that choice.

Ezell Blair, Jr., grew up in Greensboro, the son of a teacher, and became friends with Franklin McCain at Dudley High School when McCain's family moved from Washington, D.C. David Richmond was a track star and the most popular student at Dudley. In the fall of 1959, Richmond, Blair, and McCain enrolled in A&T, where they met and became fast friends with Joseph McNeil, a quiet, deeply intellectual physics major from New York. When McNeil returned to Greensboro in January 1960 after spending Christmas break in New York, he was refused service at the bus station. It was a breaking point for McNeil and his friends. Over the course of the following weeks, the four men carefully planned their next move. On February 1, they dressed in their Sunday best—Joe McNeil in his Air Force uniform—met outside the library, and headed downtown.

Why did young people like the Greensboro Four challenge Jim Crow in the way that they did and when they did? What was different about their motives and strategies? How did the student sit-ins change the Civil Rights Movement and American civic life?

◆

## The Method

Certain moments in American history—the creation of the Constitution, the Allied victory in World War II—are rightly celebrated for their

vision and valor. Americans collectively take pride in marking those events in their nation's past. The Civil Rights Movement has become one of those justifiably honored eras. It required a great deal of courage, resolve, and talent to wage that fight for social justice, to push America toward "a more perfect union." Americans collectively remember it as a noble era, and the leaders of the movement are honored in public spaces, including roads, parks, and statues. While historians can—some might say should—share in celebrating the high points in the nation's past, our job also involves explaining the context, significance, and implications of these eras.

The young people who risked their lives to secure justice for their communities will likely appeal to you, perhaps even inspire you. When they started the sit-in movement, they were the same age as the average college student taking an American history survey course today. In this chapter you will move through celebration and toward understanding.

Use the evidence in this chapter to cultivate a deeper understanding of the student sit-in movement. Certainly the Jim Crow laws are self-evident explanations of why African Americans resented segregation. But why did resentment produce this kind of resistance on campuses such as North Carolina A&T and Fisk University in 1960? How—and why—was the student campaign different from the efforts by the NAACP and other civil rights organizations? Interviews with sit-in leaders provide one kind of evidence. The student leaders explain their actions and intentions, but they also tell us a great deal about the context of their movement. Read these accounts closely: what assumptions and values underlay their accounts? How important was

personal experience versus organizations in mobilizing these students? What new ideas did they bring to the Civil Rights Movement?

The photographs from early sit-ins, the materials circulated by student leaders, the songs of the movement, and the defense of the student movement offered by Dr. King all offer additional context. What image did the organizers project? Why did they project such an image? What image did the opposition project? What philosophy did the students embrace? What attitude did they convey in their songs and organizational literature? How did the student movement fit in—or fail to do so—with the mainstream Civil Rights Movement? What challenge did they pose to mainstream movement leaders? How did they benefit movement leaders?

Coverage in the *New York Times* and the *Washington Post* reveals how quickly the sit-ins and national awareness of the protests spread. Like the interviews, these journalistic accounts also provide evidence about the background, societal implications, and larger meaning of the student protests. Read these articles carefully, paying attention to clues about the changes forged by the student protesters. What was innovative and controversial about their actions?

A second important issue you should consider as you read this evidence is the role of historical memory. You will notice that the interviewees speak in the past tense; they were interviewed years after the passage of the Civil Rights Act and Voting Rights Act. As you consider those narratives, as well as the last two images of the Greensboro Four, think about historical memory. How might subsequent experiences have shaped the way the sit-in leaders remembered their roles in the Civil Rights Movement? Why do we as a society collectively remember and commemorate certain parts of our past and ignore others?

## The Evidence

### JIM CROW LAWS

Source 1 from American Public Media, "Remembering Jim Crow" documentary and website. Accessed at http://americanradioworks.publicradio.org/features/remembering/laws.html

### 1. Compilation of Jim Crow Statutes.

#### EDUCATION

**Florida**: The schools for white children and the schools for negro children shall be conducted separately.

**Kentucky**: The children of white and colored races committed to reform schools shall be kept entirely separate from each other.

**Mississippi**: Separate schools shall be maintained for the children of the white and colored races.

**Mississippi**: Separate free schools shall be established for the education of children of African descent; and it shall be unlawful for any colored child to attend any white school, or any white child to attend a colored school.

**New Mexico**: Separate rooms shall be provided for the teaching of pupils of African descent, and such pupils may not be admitted to the school rooms occupied and used by pupils of Caucasian or other descent.

**North Carolina**: School textbooks shall not be interchangeable between the white and colored schools, but shall continue to be used by the race first using them.

#### ENTERTAINMENT

**Alabama:** It shall be unlawful to conduct a restaurant or other place for the serving of food in the city, at which white and colored people are served in the same room, unless such white and colored persons are effectually separated by a solid partition extending from the floor upward to a distance of seven feet or higher, and unless a separate entrance from the street is provided.

**Alabama**: It shall be unlawful for a negro and white person to play together or in company with each other at any game of pool or billiards.

**Alabama**: Every employer of white or negro males shall provide for such white or negro males reasonably accessible and separate toilet facilities.

**Georgia**: All persons licensed to conduct a restaurant, shall serve either white people exclusively or colored people exclusively and shall not sell to the two races within the same room or under the same license.

**Georgia**: It shall be unlawful for any amateur white baseball team to play on any vacant lot or baseball diamond within two blocks of a playground devoted to the Negro race, and it shall be unlawful for any amateur colored baseball team to play baseball within two blocks of any playground devoted to the white race.

**Georgia**: All persons licensed to conduct the business of selling beer or wine . . . shall serve either white people exclusively or colored people exclusively and shall not sell to the two races within the same room at any time.

**Louisiana**: All circuses, shows, and tent exhibitions, to which the attendance of more than one race is invited shall provide not less than two ticket offices and not less than two entrances.

**Virginia**: Any public hall, theatre, opera house, motion picture show or place of public entertainment which is attended by both white and colored persons shall separate the white race and the colored race.

## HEALTH CARE

**Alabama:** No person or corporation shall require any white female nurse to nurse in wards or rooms in hospitals, either public or private, in which negro men are placed.

**Louisiana**: The board of trustees shall maintain a separate building, on separate grounds, for the admission, care, instruction, and support of all blind persons of the colored or black race.

**Mississippi**: There shall be maintained by the governing authorities of every hospital maintained by the state for treatment of white and colored patients separate entrances for white and colored patients and visitors, and such entrances shall be used by the race only for which they are prepared.

## LIBRARIES

**Texas:** Negroes are to be served through a separate branch or branches of the county free library, which shall be administered by a custodian of the negro race under the supervision of the county librarian.

**North Carolina**: The state librarian is directed to fit up and maintain a separate place for the use of the colored people who may come to the library for the purpose of reading books or periodicals.

## MARRIAGE

**Arizona:** The marriage of a person of Caucasian blood with a Negro shall be null and void.

**Florida**: All marriages between a white person and a negro, or between a white person and a person of negro descent to the fourth generation inclusive, are hereby forever prohibited.

**Florida**: Any negro man and white woman, or any white man and negro woman, who are not married to each other, who habitually live in and occupy in the nighttime the same room, shall each be punished by imprisonment not exceeding 12 months, or by fine not exceeding five hundred dollars.

**Maryland**: All marriages between a white person and a negro, or between a white person and a person of negro descent, to the third generation, inclusive . . . are forever prohibited, and shall be void.

**Mississippi**: The marriage of a white person with a negro or mulatto or person who shall have one-eighth or more of negro blood, shall be unlawful and void.

**Wyoming**: All marriages of white persons with Negroes, Mulattos, Mongolians, or Malaya hereafter contracted in the State of Wyoming are, and shall be, illegal and void.

## SERVICES

**Georgia:** No colored barber shall serve as a barber to white women or girls.

**Georgia**: The officer in charge shall not bury, or allow to be buried, any colored persons upon ground set apart or used for the burial of white persons.

Source 2 from Trenholm State Technical College, accessed through Alabama State Archives at http://www.alabamamoments.alabama.gov/sec59ps.html.

## 2. Alabama Voter Questionnaire and Literacy Test.

*[Southern states required African Americans to pass literacy tests in order to register to vote. As the source below demonstrates, the tests were both exacting and vague. To thwart potential voters, by 1964 Alabama had created a hundred different tests. Prospective voters chose at random from a binder. In many locales, the paperwork was timed, so that no one could complete the form. Whites bypassed these requirements through grandfather clauses (if your grandfather was a registered voter, you could vote) and voucher programs (if a registered voter vouched for you, you could vote).]*

## APPLICATION FOR REGISTRATION

I, _____, do hereby apply to the Board of Registrars of _____ County, State of Alabama, to register as an elector under the Constitution and laws of the State of Alabama, and do herewith submit answers to the interroratories propounded to me by said board.

_____

(Applicant's Full Name)

## QUESTIONNAIRE

1.  State your name, the date and place of your birth, and your present address
    _____

2.  Are you single or married? _____ (a) If married, give name, resident and
    place of birth of your husband or wife, as the case may be: _____

3.  Give the names of the places, respectively, where you have lived during the last
    five years; and the name or names by which you have been known during the
    last five years: _____

4.  If you are self-employed, state the nature of your business: _____

    A. If you have been employed, by another during the last five years, state the
       nature of your employment and the name or names of such employer or
       employers and his or their addresses: _____

5.  If you claim that you are a bona fide resident of the State of Alabama, give the
    date on which you claim to have become such bona fide resident: _____
    (a) When did you become a bona fide resident of _____ County: _____
    (b) When did you become a bona fide resident of _____ Ward or Precinct
    _____

6.  If you intend to change your place of residence prior to the next general elec-
    tion, state the facts: _____

7.  Have you previously applied for and been denied registration as a voter?
    _____ (a) If so, give the facts: _____

8.  Has your name been previously stricken from the list of persons registered?
    _____

9.  Are you now or have you ever been a dope addict or a habitual drunkard?
    _____

    (A) If you are or have been a dope addict or habitual drunkard, explain as fully
        as you can: _____

10. Have you ever been legally declared insane? _____ (a) If so, give details:
    _____

11. Give a brief statement of the extent of your education and business experience:
    _____

12. Have you ever been charged with or convicted of a felony or crime or offense
    involving moral turpitude? _____ (a) If so, give the facts: _____

13. Have you ever served in the Armed Forces of the United States Government?
    _____

    (a) If so, state when and for approximately how long: _____

14. Have you ever been expelled or dishonorable discharged from any school or college or from any branch of the Armed Forces of the United States, or of any other Country? _____ If so, state facts: _____

15. Will you support and defend the Constitution of the United States and the Constitution of the State of Alabama? _____

16. Are you now or have you ever been affiliated with any group or organization which advocates the overthrow of the United States Government or the government of any State of the United States by unlawful means? _____
(a) If so, state the facts: _____

17. Will you bear arms for your county when called upon by it to do so? _____
If the answer is no, give reasons: _____

18. Do you believe in free elections and rule by the majority? _____

19. Will you give aid and comfort to the enemies of the United States Government or the Government of the State of Alabama? _____

20. Name some of the duties and obligations of citizenship: _____

(A) Do you regard those duties and obligations as having priority over the duties and obligations you owe to any other secular organization when they are in conflict? _____

21. Give the names and post office addresses of two persons who have present knowledge of your bona fide residence at the place as stated by you: _____

## Insert Part III (5)

(The following questions shall be answered by the applicant without assistance.)

1. What is the chief executive of Alabama called?
2. Are post offices operated by the state or federal government?
3. What is the name of the president of the United States?
4. To what national lawmaking body does each state send senators and representatives?

## Instructions "A"

The applicant will complete the remainder of this questionnaire before a Board member and at his instructions. The Board member shall have the applicant read any one or more of the following excerpts from the U.S. Constitution using a duplicate form of this Insert Part III. The Board member shall keep in his possession the application with its inserted Part III and shall mark thereon the words missed in reading by the applicant.

## EXCERPTS FROM THE CONSTITUTION

1. "The right of the people to be secure in their persons, houses, papers, and effects, against unreasonable searches and seizures, shall not be violated, and no warrants shall issue, but upon probable cause supported by oath or affirmation, and particularly describing the place to be searched, and the person or things to be seized."
2. "Representatives shall be apportioned among the several states according to their respective numbers, counting the whole number of persons in each state, excluding Indians not taxed."
3. "Treason against the United States, shall consist only in levying war against them, or in adhering to their enemies, giving them aid and comfort."
4. "The senators and representatives before mentioned, and the members of the several legislatures, and all executive and judicial officers, both of the United States and of the several states, shall be bound by oath or affirmation, to support this constitution."

### Instructions "B"

The Board member shall then have the applicant write several words, or more if necessary to make a judicial determination of his ability to write. The writing shall be placed below so that it becomes a part of the application. If the writing is illegible, the Board member shall write in parentheses beneath the writing the words the applicant was asked to write.

HAVE APPLICANT WRITE HERE, DICTATING WORDS FROM THE CONSTITUTION

_____

Signature of Applicant _____

### STUDENT VOICES

Source 3 from "Franklin McCain", from *My Soul is Rested* by Howell Raines, copyright © 1977 Howell Raines. Used by permission of G.P. Putnam's Sons, a division of Penguin Group (USA) Inc.

### 3. Franklin McCain Discusses the Greensboro Sit-In.

The planning process was on a Sunday night, I remember it quite well. I think it was Joseph who said, "It's time that we take some action now. We've been getting together, and we've been, up to this point, still like most people we've talked about for the past few weeks or so—that is, people who talk a lot, in fact, make very little action." After selecting the technique, then we said, "Let's go down and just ask for service." It certainly wasn't titled a "sit-in" or "sit-down" at that time. "Let's just go down to Woolworth's tomorrow and ask for service, and the tactic is going to be simply this: we'll just stay there." We never anticipated being served, certainly, the first day anyway. "We'll stay until we get served." And I think Ezell said, "Well, you know that might be weeks, that might be months, that might be never." And I think it was the consensus of the group, we said, "Well, that's just the chance we'll have to take."

What's likely to happen? Now, I think that was a question that all of us asked ourselves. . . . What's going to happen once we sit down? Of course, nobody had the answers. Even your wildest imagination couldn't lead you to believe what would, in fact, happen.

*Why Woolworth's?*

They advertise in public media, newspapers, radios, television, that sort of thing. They tell you to come in: "Yes, buy the toothpaste; yes, come in and buy the notebook paper. . . . No, we don't separate your money in this cash register, but, no, please don't step down to the hot dog stand. . . ." The whole system, of course, was unjust, but that just seemed like insult added to injury. That was just like pouring salt into an open wound. That's inviting you to do something. . . .

. . . Once getting there . . . we did make purchases of school supplies and took the patience and time to get receipts for our purchases, and Joseph and myself went over to the counter and asked to be served coffee and doughnuts. As anticipated, the reply was, "I'm sorry, we don't serve you here." And of course we said, "We just beg to disagree with you. We've in fact already been served; you've served us already and that's just not quite true." The attendant or waitress was a little bit dumbfounded, just didn't know what to say under the circumstances like that. And we said, "We wonder why you'd invite us in to serve us at one counter and deny service at another. If this is a private club or private concern, then we believe you ought to sell membership cards and sell only to persons who have a membership card. If we don't have a card, then we'd know pretty well that we shouldn't come in or even attempt to come in." That didn't go over too well, simply because I don't really think she understood what we were talking about, and for the second reason, she had no logical response to a statement like that. And the only thing that an individual in her case or position could do is, of course, call the manager.

[Laughs] Well, at this time, I think we were joined by Dave Richmond and Ezell Blair at the counter with us, after that dialogue.

*Were you afraid at this point?*

Oh hell yes, no question about that. [Laughs] At that point there was a policeman who had walked in off the street, who was pacing the aisle. . . behind us, where we were seated, with his club in his hand, just sort of knocking it in his hand, and just looking mean and red and a little bit upset and a little bit disgusted. And you had the feeling that he didn't know what the hell to do. You had the feeling that this is the first time that this big bad man with the gun and the club has been pushed in a corner, and he's got absolutely no defense, and the thing that's killing him more than anything else—he doesn't know what he can or what he cannot do. He's defenseless. Usually his defense is offense, and we've provoked him, yes, but we haven't provoked him outwardly enough for him to resort to violence. And I think this is just killing him; you can see it all over him.

People in the store were—we got mixed reactions from people in the store. A couple of old ladies . . . came up to pat us on the back sort of and say, "Ah, you should have done it ten years ago. It's a good thing I think you're doing."

*These were black ladies.*

No, these are white ladies.

*Really?*

Yes, and by the same token, we had some white ladies and white men to come up and say to us, "Nasty, dirty niggers, you know you don't belong here at the lunch counter. There's a counter—" There was, in fact, a counter downstairs in the Woolworth store, a stand-up type counter where they sold hot dogs. . . .

*But at any rate, there were expressions of support from white people that first day?*

Absolutely right. Absolutely. And I think probably that was certainly some incentive for additional courage on the part of us. And the other thing that helped us psychologically quite a lot was seeing the policeman pace the aisle and not be able to do anything. I think that this probably gave us more strength, more encouragement, than anything else on that particular day, on day one.

*Unexpected as it was, the well-wishing from the elderly white women was hardly more surprising than the scorn of a middle-aged black dishwasher behind the counter. She said, "That's why we can't get anyplace today, because of people like you, rabble-rousers, troublemakers. . . . This counter is reserved for white people, it always has been, and you are well aware of that. So why don't you go on out and stop making trouble?" He has since seen the woman at, of all places, a reunion commemorating the event in which she played so unsupportive a role.*

[She said] "Yes, I did say it and I said it because, first of all, I was afraid for what would happen to you as young black boys. Secondly, I was afraid of what would happen to me as an individual who had a job at the Woolworth store. I might have been fired and that's my livelihood. . . ."

It took me a long time to really understand that statement . . . but I know why she said it. She said it out of fear more than anything else. I've come to understand that, and my elders say to me that it's maturity that makes me understand why she said that some fifteen years ago.

*But, moved by neither praise nor scorn, he and the others waited for the waitress to return with the manager, a career Woolworth's employee named C. L. Harris.*

That was real amusin' as well [laughing] because by then we had the confidence, my goodness, of a Mack truck. And there was virtually nothing that could move us, there was virtually nothing probably at that point that could really frighten us off. . . . If it's possible to know what it means to have your soul cleansed—I felt pretty clean at that time. I probably felt better on that day than I've ever felt in my life. Seems like a lot of feelings of guilt or what-have-you suddenly left me, and I felt as though I had gained my manhood, so to speak, and not only gained it, but had developed quite a lot of respect for it. Not Franklin McCain only as an individual, but I felt as though the manhood of a number of other black persons had been restored and had gotten some respect from just that one day.

But back to Mr. Harris, who was the store manager, he was a fairly nice guy to talk to on that day. I think what he wanted to do more than anything else was to—initially—was to kill us with kindness, to say, "Fellas, you know this is just not the way we do business. Why don't you go on back to your campus? If you're just hungry, go downstairs," and that sort of thing.

We listened to him, paid him the courtesy of listening to what he had to say. We repeated our demands to him, and he ended up by saying, "Well, you know, I don't really set policy for this store. The policy for serving you is set by corporate headquarters." And of course, we found out that that was just a cop out. Corporate headquarters said, "No, it's up to local communities to set standards and set practices and that sort of thing, and whatever they do is all right with us." You know, the usual sort of game of rubber checkers.

The only reason we did leave is the store was closing. We knew, of course, we had to leave when the store was closing. We said to him, "Well, we'll have plenty of time tomorrow, because we'll be back to see you." [Laughs] I don't think that went over too well. But by the time we were leaving, the store was just crowded with people from off the streets and on the streets. . . . As a matter of fact, there were so many people standin' in front of the store, and we had to leave from the side entrance.

But back at the campus, there was just a beehive of activity. Word had spread. As a matter of fact, word was back on campus before we ever got back. There were all sorts of phone calls to the administration and to people on the faculty and staff. The mayor's office was aware of it and the governor's office was aware of it. I think it was all over North Carolina within a matter of just an hour or so.

*That night they met with about fifty campus leaders to form the Student Executive Committee for Justice.*

The movement started out as a movement of nonviolence and as a Christian movement, and we wanted to make that very clear to everybody, that it was a movement that was seeking justice more than anything else and not a movement to start a war. . . . We knew that probably the most powerful and potent weapon that people have literally no defense for is love, kindness. That is, whip the enemy with something that he doesn't understand.

*How much was the example of Dr. King and the Montgomery Bus Boycott in your mind in that regard?*

Not very much. The individual who had probably most influence on us was Gandhi, more than any single individual. During the time that the Montgomery Bus Boycott was in effect, we were tots for the most part, and we barely heard of Martin Luther King. Yes, Martin Luther King's name was well-known when the sit-in movement was in effect, but to pick out Martin Luther King as a hero. . . . I don't want you to misunderstand what I'm about to say: Yes, Martin Luther King was a hero. . . . No, he was not the individual that we had upmost in mind when we started the sit-in movement. . . .

*Most journalists and historians have been quite wrong about the impetus for the first sit-in, he insists. Although all of the students had read extensively on the Montgomery movement, they were not, as has been widely reported, directly inspired by a Fellowship of Reconciliation "comic book" entitled "Martin Luther King and the Montgomery Story." They had not heard of CORE's Chicago sit-in twenty years earlier. Nor were he and the others persuaded, as one history of the sit-ins has it, to make their protest by Ralph Johns, an eccentric white NAACP member who ran a haberdashery near the campus. The subject irritates him. Dignified even in his lighthearted moments, he now becomes even more formal.*

Credit for the initiation of the sit-in movement has been granted to one or two ministers, the NAACP, Ralph Johns,[10] CORE, at least a dozen people, and it's rather amusing when you do read some of these articles. I think it's a game. The same type tactic that has been used over and over and over by the white news media and the white press to discredit blacks with particular types of achievement. You don't have to look at the sit-in movement to see that. You can think of things like, well, for instance, the surveying of the laying out of the city of Washington, D. C., or the invention of the traffic signal, or the concept of Labor Day, or even Perry's expedition to the North Pole. These are the kinds of things that come into my mind when I think about the attempt to discredit the people who actually started the sit-in movement.

*So what you're saying is . . . the most simple explanation applies?*

Four guys met, planned, and went into action. It's just that simple.

*On the second day, they were joined by over twenty other A&T students, and they kept most of the stools occupied all day. On the fourth day the first white students joined them from the University of North Carolina Women's College in Greensboro. By the second week sit-ins had spread to a half-dozen North Carolina towns.*

From the Greensboro area there must have been people from six or seven university campuses who wanted to participate, who wanted to help sit-in, who wanted to help picket. We actually got to the point where we had people going down in shifts. It got to the point wherein we took all the seats in the restaurants. We had people there in the mornings as soon as the doors were open to just take every seat in the restaurant or at the lunch counter. . . .

As a manager, you've got to do something. You just can't continue to have people come in and sit around. The cash registers have to ring. What happened is that after we started to take all of the seats in the restaurants, they started to pull the stools up in the restaurants. So we just started to stand around then and take all the standing room. . . . I think at the height of the sit-in movement in Greensboro, we must have had at least, oh, ten or fifteen thousand people downtown who wanted to sit-in, but obviously there weren't that many chairs in downtown Greensboro for people to sit in. . . .

It spread to places like the shopping centers, the drugstores in the shopping centers, the drive-ins. . . . No place was going to be left untouched. The only criteria was that if it did not serve blacks, it was certainly going to be hit. . . .

---

10. Joseph McNeil's memory of Ralph Jones differs somewhat from that of Franklin McCain's. See Source 4.

*With such success came attention.*

The Congress of Racial Equality offered a funny sort of help, and that kind of help was, in effect, "If you let us control the show, we'll show you how the thing is supposed to be done." And four seventeen-year-old guys were just not in the mood to let someone take their show. That was our position. Our position was, we are probably as much experts about this as anybody else. We were experts because we had had one experience already, and that's more than most people had had.

We got a lot of attention from the Communist party. [Laughs] The Communist party sent representatives down to Greensboro to assist us in any way that we deemed appropriate. If it meant actual participation, they offered to sit-in with us. If it meant you needed x number of dollars to do this, or if you needed air fare to go here or there, if you needed anything, they made it known that money was available, assistance was available. Just don't sit down here in Greensboro and want for things that you need. But you know, again, it was a Christian movement, and Christians and Communists just don't mix.

*Did you avail yourself of any of that?*

No, we didn't need it. Even if we had needed it, there was no reason to affiliate with the Communist party. We were in the driver's seat. . . . Remember, too, you have four guys who were pretty strong-willed, pretty bull-headed, and who were keenly aware that people would rush in and try to take over the Movement, so to speak. And we were quite aware of that, and we felt—not felt—were very independent. . . . As a matter of fact, we were criticized on several occasions for being too damned independent. But I still don't regret it.

*Did the success that you experienced cause strains among the four of you?*

Never. There was enough to go around. [Laughs] . . .

Sources 4–7 from *Voices of Freedom* by Henry Hampton and Steve Fayer, copyright © 1990 by Blackside, Inc. Used by permission of Bantam Books, a division of Random House, Inc. and the Random House Group Ltd.

## 4. Joseph McNeil Remembers Greensboro.

I don't think there's any specific reason why that particular day was chosen. I had talked to a local merchant [Ralph Johns] who was extremely helpful to us in getting things rolling, in giving us some ideas. We had played over in our minds possible scenarios, and to the best of our abilities we had determined how we were gonna conduct ourselves given those scenarios. But we did walk in that day—I guess it was about four-thirty—and we sat at a lunch counter where blacks never sat before. And people started to look at us. The help, many of whom were black, looked at us in disbelief too. They were concerned about our safety. We asked for service, and we were denied, and we expected to be denied. We asked why couldn't we be served, and obviously we weren't given a reasonable answer and it was our intent to sit there until they decided to serve us. We had planned to come back the following day and to repeat that scenario. Others found out what we had done, because the press became aware of what was happening. So the next day when we decided to go down again, I think we went down with fifteen, and the third day it was probably a hundred and fifty, and then it probably mushroomed up to a thousand or so, and then it spread to another city. All rather spontaneously, of course, and before long, I guess it was probably in fifteen or twenty cities, and that's when we had our thing going.

## 5. John Lewis Describes the Nashville Sit-Ins.

*[John Lewis, born into poverty in rural Alabama, became a national leader for civil rights during his college years. The Nashville campaign began two weeks before his twentieth birthday. He went on to organize the Freedom Rides in 1961 and serve as national chairman of the Student Non-Violent Coordinating Committee (SNCC), which he helped found. Lewis has represented Georgia's Fifth Congressional District in the United States House of Representatives since 1987. Congressman Lewis is the last surviving speaker from the 1963 March on Washington.]*

We had on that first day over five hundred students in front of Fisk University chapel, to be transported downtown to the First Baptist Church, to be organized into small groups to go down to sit in at the lunch counters.

We went into the five-and-tens—Woolworth's, Kresge's, McClellan's— because these stores were known all across the South and for the most part all across the country. We took our seats in a very orderly, peaceful fashion. The students were dressed like they were on the way to church or going to a big social affair. They had their books, and we stayed there at the lunch counter, studying and preparing our homework, because we were denied service. The managers ordered that the lunch counters be closed, that the restaurants be closed, and we'd just sit there, all day long. . . .

The first day nothing in terms of violence or disorder happened. This continued for a few more days and it continued day in and day out. Finally, on

Saturday, February twenty-seventh, when we had about a hundred students prepared to go down—it was a very beautiful day in Nashville—we got a call from a local white minister who had been a real supporter of the movement. He said that if we go down on this particular day, he understood that the police would stand to the side and let a group of white hoodlums and thugs come in and beat people up, and then we would be arrested. We made a decision to go, and we all went to the same store. It was a Woolworth in the heart of the downtown area, and we occupied every seat at the lunch counter, every seat in the restaurant, and it did happen. A group of young white men came in and they started pulling and beating primarily the young women. They put lighted cigarettes down their backs, in their hair, and they were really beating people. In a short time police officials came in and placed all of us under arrest, and not a single member of the white group, the people that were opposing our sit-in, was arrested.

That was the first time I was arrested. Growing up in the rural South, you learned it was not the thing to do. To go to jail was to bring shame and disgrace on the family. But for me it was like being involved in a holy crusade, it became a badge of honor. I think it was in keeping with what we had been taught in the workshops, so it felt very good, in the sense of righteous indignation, about being arrested, but at the same time I felt the commitment and education on the part of the students.

## 6. Diane Nash Remembers the Nashville Campaign.

*[Diane Nash, a Chicago native studying at Fisk University, was twenty-two when she ran the Nashville Student Movement. With John Lewis, she was a founder of SNCC. She became a leading figure in organizing the Freedom Rides of 1961, the demonstrations in Birmingham in 1963, and the voter registration drive in Selma in 1965.]*

The sit-ins were really highly charged, emotionally. In our non-violent workshops, we had decided to be respectful for the opposition, and try to keep issues geared towards desegregation, not get sidetracked. The first sit-in we had was really funny, because the waitresses were nervous. They must have dropped two thousand dollars' worth of dishes that day. It was almost a cartoon. One in particular, she was so nervous, she picked up dishes and she dropped one, and she'd pick up another one, and she'd drop it. It was really funny, and we were sitting there trying not to laugh, because we thought that laughing would be insulting and we didn't want to create that kind of atmosphere. At the same time we were scared to death. . . .

After we had started sitting in, we were surprised and delighted to hear reports of other cities joining in the sit-ins. And I think we started feeling the power of the idea whose time had come. Before we did the things that we did, we had no inkling that the movement would become as widespread as it did. I can remember being in the dorm any number of times and hearing the newscasts, that Orangeburg had demonstrations, or Knoxville, or other towns. And we were really excited. We'd applaud, and say yea. When you are that age, you don't feel powerful. I remember realizing that with what we were doing, trying to abolish segregation, we were coming up against governors, judges, politicians, businessmen, and I remember thinking, I'm only twenty-two years old, what do I know, what am I doing? And I felt very vulnerable. So when we heard these newscasts, that other cities had demonstrations, it really helped. Because there were more of us. And it was very important.

The movement had a way of reaching inside you and bringing out things that even you didn't know were there. Such as courage. When it was time to go to jail, I was much too busy to be afraid.

## 7. C. T. Vivian Explains the Reactions to the Nashville Sit-Ins.

*[Reverend C. T. Vivian had trained for the ministry in Nashville and he was an advisor to the students and active participant in the movement. He was thirty-five when the protests started. He went on to become a close ally of Martin Luther King, Jr., and a leading figure in the SCLC.]*

Now, many of the parents were afraid, thought that their children's lives would be destroyed forever because of what would be on their record. Many telephone calls were coming from everywhere. Pressure was on the college presidents and the vice presidents and staff. But students made up their minds what they were going to do. It was a great point of their own development.

The police knew that they represented the city, the merchants, the thugs, more than they represented us. Yet here is the importance of nonviolence, that they did not want to appear too demanding, too brutal. They wanted to stop us, but when we would not stop, then they had to begin to work on the thugs, because the thugs will bring out the worst of segregation in a racist society, so that it even shames the people who are themselves racists and who keep the system going. They were caught in that dilemma and they were waiting for their orders from the businessmen.

The city fathers themselves had to see their relationship to the businessmen. Businessmen saw their relationship to profits. And the black people were beginning to respond all over, "What to do?" So the boycotts start, to force the businessmen to deal with the issue. As one of the businessmen put it, nobody came downtown. Blacks wouldn't come downtown, whites were afraid to come downtown, so the only people downtown were green people and there weren't many of them, all right? As a result, the businessmen began to lose money and they began to ask for a change. Remember, though, we were meeting with them, we were talking with them, trying to get them to understand, think for themselves, or react without our presence. We were constantly negotiating with them.

## ORGANIZING THE MOVEMENT

Source 8 from the North Carolina A&T University Archives and reproduced at http://www.pbs.org/independentlens/februaryone/transparencies.pdf.

### 8. Greensboro Four Letter to Fellow Students.

Dear fellow students,

For every effective organization there is a level of leadership. As far as we're concerned, this was the purpose of the Students Executive Committee for Justice. This committee is composed of the original formulators of this passive resistance movement now taking place and several other students who are quite reliable in conducting adequate guidance. And, since this committee has already drafted "plans-of-actions" to accomplish this objective and possess a more detailed knowledge of what is taking place "behind the scene", we feel that the responsibility of leadership should fall upon this group of persons. We sincerely hope that you will fully agree and cooperate with us in this respect.

A movement has been made on Kress' to obtain similar results expected from Woolworth. We are requesting that the students will fully Support these movements. However, we also request that no students shall go over the heads of the committee and start another such movement in that we must concentrate our efforts toward breaking down these places and we're certain that with success, the others will eventually fall in line.

As much as we desire the full cooperation of all students, we must insist that we show <u>no violence</u> under any circumstances. The insults received cannot harm us in anyway and any assault on any student will be dealt with immediately by the police department who have promised that there will be protection for <u>ALL</u> persons with no partisanship. We are asking that you will take no weapons with you such as knives, etc., but a Bible in its place.

The agitators who are heckling our group now are organized primarily for the purpose of "picking a fight." But if this happens, all of our previous work and desire are lost. Therefore we beg that you shall completely ignore these persons and neglect the *freak* accidents. Keep a "cool" head and we're always sure of being in the right.

You are aware of the support received yesterday from the Women's College students and this is self-evidence that the Negroes <u>are not</u> alone. Let us be certain that we do not let these people down as well as ourselves by losing ground in anyway.

INSTRUCTIONS

(1) Students will wear dress attire or other pertinent clothing. (Young ladies are urged to look their best and gentlemen wear ties).
(2) All students going down will report to the Library dispatcher so as to make certain that we do not become so crowded until we hinder the stores businesses.
(3) If the persons who arrive later or after the first shift has come, they will seek to relieve those who desire to be; if not, they will quietly check with the spokes-man and then leave quietly.
(4) At no time will we fight back with words or physically, but will do so by our sitting.

We must remember that we are now well known in the eyes of the world and we must do nothing to hurt the chances of the minority races nor rob the people who sympathize with us of the loyal support they are giving us.

Again we may strongly advocate, NO VIOLENCE NOR DRINKING WHILE WE ARE DOWN TOWN OR IN THE EYES OF THE PUBLIC. We know that we will receive your loyal support in our drive for justice and we hope that you will weigh this letter carefully and cooperate fully.

**STUDENTS EXECUTIVE COMMITTEE**

Source 9 from March 1960: Leaflet, "Wanted: Picketers". Records of the Office of Chancellor – William B. Aycock Series (#40020), University Archives, Wilson Library, University of North Carolina at Chapel Hill.

## 9. Guidelines to Prospective Demonstrators, UNC-Chapel Hill.

PICKETING
WHY we picket—

WE DO NOT PICKET
....just because we want to eat. We can eat at home or walking down the street.
....just because students in many other cities are picketing.

....to express our anger or resentment at anyone.

....to humiliate or put anyone out of business.

## WE DO PICKET

....to protest the lack of dignity and respect shown us as human beings.

....to enlist the support of all (whatever their color) in getting services in business places that will grant us dignity and respect.

....to help the businessman make changes that will bring us closer to the Christian and Democratic practices.

## WHO can picket—

We welcome picketers of any race, high school age and beyond, ONLY if they agree THAT UNDER NO CIRCUMSTANCES will they resort to violence.

We will use picketers ONLY if they agree to go through a short course of instruction on picketing.

Picketing will be done at stated hours and days decided by the Executive Committee and under the direction of a Picket Captain, trained for this work. Picketers must promise to obey the captain at all times.

REMEMBER—the teachings of Jesus, who, "when reviled, reviled not again."

## SOME DOs AND DON'Ts FOR PICKETERS

DO. . . .

. . . .walk slowly and quietly—at least four feet apart.

. . . .be careful to let anyone who wishes to enter the place of business do so.

. . . .refer all incidents or jostling, abuse by word, or anything of this nature to the picket captain.

. . . .be on time at the place set by the picket captain.

. . . .leave the place of picketing promptly on being relieved.

DON'T. . . .

. . . .be boisterous, laugh or joke with other picketers or by-standers.

. . . .hold conversation with by-standers or business owner.

. . . .block the entrance or make it difficult for people to enter the business.

. . . .come to the picket line without being neatly dressed.

. . . .answer insult with insult, argument with argument, blow with blow, anger with anger.

REMEMBER—the example and teachings of Martin Luther King who refused to hate anyone, but stood in love and firmness for human dignity and respect.

## MOVEMENT SONGS

Source 10 from http://www.gilderlehrman.org/historynow/06_2006/popups/jukebox1.php

### 10. Ain't Gonna Let Nobody Turn Me Around (Song Lyrics).

Ain't gonna let nobody, turn me around
Turn me around, turn me around
Ain't gonna let nobody, turn me around
Keep on a walking, keep on a talking
Marching up to freedom land

Ain't gonna let segregation (Lordy), turn me around
Turn me around, turn me around
Ain't gonna let segregation (Lordy), turn me around
Keep on a walking, keep on a talking
Marching up to freedom land

Ain't gonna let no jailhouse (Lordy), turn me around
Turn me around, turn me around
Ain't gonna let no jailhouse, turn me around
Keep on a walking, keep on a talking
Marching up to freedom land

Ain't gonna let no nervous Nellie (Lordy), turn me around
Turn me around, turn me around
Ain't gonna let no nervous Nellie (Lordy), turn me around
Keep on a walking, keep on a talking
Marching up to freedom land

Ain't gonna let Chief Pritchett[11] (Lordy), turn me around
Turn me around, turn me around
Ain't gonna let Chief Pritchett (Lordy), turn me around
Keep on a walking, keep on a talking
Marching up to freedom land

11. Laurie Pritchett served as police chief in Albany, Georgia, and succeeded in thwarting the movement there in 1962.

Ain't gonna let Mayor Kelley[12] (Lordy), turn me around
Turn me around, turn me around
Ain't gonna let Mayor Kelley (Lordy), turn me around
Keep on a walking, keep on a talking
Marching up to freedom land

Ain't gonna let no Uncle Tom (Lordy), turn me around
Turn me around, turn me around
Ain't gonna let no Uncle Tom (Lordy), turn me around
Keep on a walking, keep on a talking
Marching up to freedom land

Ain't gonna let nobody, turn me around
Turn me around, turn me around
Ain't gonna let nobody, turn me around
Keep on a walking, keep on a talking
Marching up to freedom land

Source 11 from  http://www.gilderlehrman.org/historynow/06_2006/popups/jukebox4.php

## 11. Eyes on the Prize (Song Lyrics).

Hold on, hold on
Keep your eyes on the prize
Hold on, why don't you hold on

When __ was locked in jail,
Had no money for to go his bail,
Keep your eyes on the prize
Hold on, why don't you hold on

Hold on, hold on
Keep your eyes on the prize
Hold on, why don't you hold on

12.  Asa Kelley was Albany's mayor. Through his and Pritchett's efforts, civil rights leaders failed
to achieve desegregation in the city.

Barnett Barnetr[13], don't you know,
Mississippi is next to go
Keep your eyes on the prize
Hold on, why don't you hold on

Hold on, hold on
Keep your eyes on the prize
Hold on, why don't you hold on

## REACTION TO THE STUDENT SIT-INS

### 12. *The New York Times*, February 3 (initial report).

NEGROES IN SOUTH IN STORE SITDOWN

Carolina College Students Fight Woolworth Ban on Lunch Counter Service

GREENSBORO, N. C., Feb. 2 (UPI)—A group of well-dressed Negro college students staged a sitdown strike in a downtown Woolworth store today and vowed to continue it in relays until Negroes were served at the lunch counter.

"We believe since we buy books and papers in the other part of the store we should get served in this part," said the spokesman for the group.

The store manager, C. L. Harris, commented:

"They can just sit there. It's nothing to me."

He declined to say whether it was the policy of the store not to serve Negroes.

The Negroes, students at North Carolina Agricultural and Technical College here, arrived shortly after 10 A. M. and sat at two sections of the lunch counter.

At 12:30 P. M. the group filed out of the store and stood on the sidewalk in this city's busiest downtown street. They formed a tight circle, threw their hands into a pyramid in the center and recited the Lord's Prayer.

The spokesman said that "another shift" of students would carry forward the strike and it would continue "until we get served."

13. Ross Barnett was the stridently pro-segregation governor of Mississippi.

**School Suit Is Filed**

Meanwhile, a school integration suit sponsored by the National Association for the Advancement of Colored People was filed in Federal court here against the Chapel Hill School board.

The suit was brought on behalf of a minor Negro, Stanley Boya Vickers, by Thomas Lee Vickers and Lattice Vickers, his parents. They asked that the child be assigned to Carrboro Elementary School, which is said to be nearer his home than Northside Elementary School he now attends.

The suit says Northside Elementary is "a facility maintained and operated solely for Negroes."

White children living at distances are assigned to Carrboro, the suit states.

"These white children are plaintiff's natural playmates and, in fact, during nonschool hours he does play with them," the suit declares.

The plaintiffs describe the suit as a class action.

### 13. *The New York Times*, February 11, 1960.

**NEGROES EXTEND STORE PICKETING**

Raleigh is 6th Carolina City Affected—Student Action May Spread Here

RALEIGH, N. C., Feb. 10—Negro student demonstrations against segregated lunch counters spread today to variety stores in this state capital. It is the sixth North Carolina city to be affected.

There were no major incidents. But eggs were tossed at demonstrators at one store here. Another closed after a crowd of white onlookers had become unruly.

Officials expressed fear that the movement might build up to violence, which would mar the state's tradition of even racial relations. Some called for an end to the protest, while others urged legal action against the college students.

The chief targets of the movement appeared to be two national variety chains, S. H. Kress & Co. and F. W. Woolworth & Co.

Gordon R. Carey, field secretary for the Congress for Racial Equality, said his organization had been negotiating with the headquarters of the two concerns in New York in behalf of the students.

A New York store of each chain will likely be picketed Saturday unless satisfactory agreements are reached, he said.

Mr. Carey said the movement would spread to other North Carolina cities and also to Virginia and South Carolina. He said students planned to appear at stores in High Point, N. C., tomorrow.

Officials of the congress, an anti-segregation group founded in 1942 at the University of Chicago, and Negro student leaders of various colleges contended that the movement started spontaneously Feb. 2 in Greensboro.

The congress took part in a similar protest last year in Miami, Fla. The store on which it had concentrated finally removed its counter facilities.

The Greensboro protest was called off last Saturday night by students at the college after a bomb threat at the Woolworth store. Another bomb threat was reported at a Durham high school.

However students from other Negro schools continued "sit-in, stand-in" demonstrations at lunch counters in Fayetteville, Winston-Salem, Durham, Charlotte and Raleigh.

They were refused service at all the downtown variety stores and soda fountains in the six cities. Most stores immediately closed their lunch counters when the Negroes appeared, and a few closed their doors.

However, students continued to file in and out of the open stores in relays to sit or stand quietly at the counters. Shortly after the demonstrations developed here today, Mayor William G. Enloe issued a statement deploring the possible effects on the city's reputation.

"It is regrettable that some of our young Negro students would risk endangering Raleigh's friendly and cooperative race relations by seeking to change a long-standing custom in a manner that is all but destined to fail," he said.

Malcolm B. Seawell, State Attorney General, said the students' actions "pose a serious threat to the peace and good order in the communities in which they occur."

While there is no state law requiring segregation in eating establishments, he added, "the right of the owner of a private business to sell or to refuse to sell customers has been recognized by our [State] Supreme Court."

Negroes from Shaw University and St. Augustine's College trooped into Fayetteville Street at mid-morning. They fanned out into variety and drug stores, which shut their eating facilities.

While a group sat at a counter in a variety store, a sullen crowd of white youths gathered outside.

Some whites entered the store and began shoving the manager and his assistants. One struggled briefly with a newspaper photographer.

The store then closed and the whites and Negroes moved to another next door.

## Hands-Off Policy

Spokesmen for Woolworth and Kress said here yesterday it was company policy to leave decisions to service to local managers.

Thomas J. Mullen of Woolworth said:

"Local discretion is governing the question of closing the lunch counters. We cannot interfere with local customs."

Karl H. Helfrich, public relations director for Kress, commented:

"Our policy must abide by customs of the local community. We cannot be the leaders in a change of customs."

He said he had met "cordially" with representatives of the Committee for Racial Equality and explained the company's policy.

## 14. *The New York Times*, February 15, 1960.

Negro Sitdowns Stirs Fear Of Wider Unrest in South

CHARLOTTE, N. C., Feb. 14—Negro student demonstrations against segregated eating facilities have raised grave questions in the South over the future of the region's race relations. A sounding of opinion in the affected areas showed that much more might be involved than the matter of the Negro's right to sit at a lunch counter for a coffee break.

The demonstrations were generally dismissed at first as another college fad of the "panty-raid" variety. This opinion lost adherents, however, as the movement spread from North Carolina to Virginia, Florida, South Carolina and Tennessee and involved fifteen cities.

Some whites wrote off the episodes as the work of "outside agitators." But even they conceded that the seeds of dissent had fallen in fertile soil.

## Backed by Negro Leaders

Appeals from white leaders to leaders in the Negro community to halt the demonstrations bore little fruit. Instead of the hoped-for statements of disapproval, many Negro professionals expressed support for the demonstrators.

A handful of white students joined the protests. And several state organizations endorsed it. Among them were the North Carolina Council on Human Relations, an inter-racial group, and the Unitarian Fellowship for Social Justice, which currently has an all-white membership. Students of race relations in the area contended that the movement reflected the growing dissatisfaction over the slow pace of desegregation in schools and other public facilities.

It demonstrated, they said, a determination to wipe out the last vestiges of segregation.

Moreover, these persons saw a shift of leadership to younger, more militant Negroes. This, they said, is likely to bring increasing use of passive resistance. The technique was conceived by Mohandas K. Gandhi of India and popularized among Southern Negroes by the Rev. Dr. Martin Luther King Jr. He led the bus boycott in Montgomery, Ala. He now leads the Southern Christian Leadership Conference, a Negro minister's group, which seeks to end discrimination. . . .

There was general agreement on all sides that a sustained attempt to achieve desegregation now, particularly in the Deep South, might breed racial conflict that the region's expanding economy could ill afford.

The spark that touched off the protests was provided by four freshmen at North Carolina Agricultural and Technical College in Greensboro. Even Negroes class Greensboro as one of the most progressive cities in the South in terms of race relations.

On Sunday night, Jan. 31, one of the students sat thinking about discrimination.

"Segregation makes me feel that I'm unwanted," McNeil A. Joseph [sic] said later in an interview. "I don't want my children exposed to it."

The 17-year-old student from Wilmington, N. C., said that he approached three of his classmates the next morning and found them enthusiastic over a proposal that they demand service at the lunch counter of a downtown variety store.

About 4:45 P. M. they entered the F. W. Woolworth Company store on North Elm Street in the heart of Greensboro. Mr. Joseph [sic] said he bought a tube of toothpaste and the others made similar purchases. Then they sat down at the lunch counter.

**Rebuked by a Negro**
A Negro woman kitchen helper walked up, according to the students, and told them, "You know you're not supposed to be in here." She later called them "ignorant" and a "disgrace" to their race.

The students then asked a white waitress for coffee.

"I'm sorry but we don't serve colored here," they quoted her.

"I beg your pardon," said Franklin McCain, 18, of Washington, "you just served me at a counter two feet away. Why is it that you serve me at one counter and deny me at another. Why not stop serving me at all the counters."

The four students sat, coffee-less, until the store closed at 5:30 P.M. then, hearing that they might be prosecuted, they went to the executive committee of the Greensboro N. A. A. C. P. to ask advice.

"This was our first knowledge of the demonstration," said Dr. George C. Simkins, who is president of the organization. He said that he had then written to the New York headquarters of the Congress of Racial Equality, which is known as CORE. He requested assistance for the demonstrators, who numbered in the hundreds during the following days.

Dr. Simkins, a dentist, explained that he had heard of a successful attempt, led by CORE, to desegregate a Baltimore restaurant and had read one of the organization's pamphlets.

CORE's field secretary, Gordon R. Carey, arrived from New York on Feb. 7. He said that he had assisted Negro students in some North Carolina cities after they had initiated the protests. The Greensboro demonstrations and the others that it triggered were spontaneous, according to Mr. Carey. All of the Negroes questioned agreed on this.

The movement's chief targets were two national variety chains, S. H. Kress & Co. and the F. W. Woolworth Company. Other chains were affected. In some cities the students demonstrated at local stores. The protests generally followed similar patterns. Young men and women and, in one case, high school boys and girls, walked into the stores and requested food service. Met with refusals in all cases, they remained at the lunch counters in silent protest. . . . The demonstrations attracted crowds of whites. At first the hecklers were youths with duck-tailed haircuts. Some carried small Confederate battle flags. Later they were joined by older men in faded khakis and overalls.

The Negro youths were challenged to step outside and fight. Some of the remarks to the girls were jesting in nature, such as, "How about a date when we integrate?" other remarks were not.

**Negro Knocked Down**

In a few cases the Negroes were elbowed, jostled and shoved. Itching powder was sprinkled on them and they were spattered with eggs.

At Rock Hill, S. C., a Negro youth was knocked from a stool by a white beside whom he sat. A bottle of ammonia was hurled through the door of a drug store there. The fumes brought tears to the eyes of the demonstrators.

The only arrests reported involved forty-three of the demonstrators. They were seized on a sidewalk outside a Woolworth store at a Raleigh shopping center. Charged with trespassing, they posted $50 bonds and were released.

The management of the shopping center contended that the sidewalk was private property.

In most cases, the demonstrators sat or stood at store counters talking in low voice, studying or staring impassively at their tormenters. There was little joking or smiling, now and then a girl giggled nervously. Some carried bibles.

Those at Rock Hill were described by the local newspaper, The Evening Herald, as "orderly, polite, well-dressed and quiet."

### "Complicated Hospitality"

Questions to their leaders about the reasons for the demonstrations drew such replies as:

"We feel if we can spend our money on other goods we should be able to eat in the same establishments," "All I want is to come in and place my order and be served and leave a tip if I feel like it," and "This is definitely our purpose: integrated seating facilities with no isolated spots, no certain seats, but to sit wherever there is a vacancy."

Some newspapers noted the embarrassing position in which the variety chains found themselves. The News and Observer of Raleigh remarked editorially that in these stores the Negro was a guest, who was cordially invited to the house but definitely not to the table. "And to say the least, this was complicated hospitality."

The newspaper said that to serve the Negroes might offend Southern whites while to do otherwise might result in the loss of the Negro trade.

"This business," it went on, "is causing headaches in New York and irritations in North Carolina. And somehow it revolves around the old saying that you can't have your chocolate cake and eat it too."

The Greensboro Daily News advocated that the lunch counters be closed or else opened on a desegregated basis.

North Carolina's Attorney General, Malcolm B. Seawell, asserted that the students were causing "irreparable harm" to relations between whites and Negroes.

Mayor William G. Enloe of Raleigh termed it "regrettable that some of our young Negro students would risk endangering these relations by seeking to change a long-standing custom in a manner that is all but destined to fail."

Some North Carolinians found it incomprehensible that the demonstrations were taking place in their state. They pointed to the progress made here toward desegregation of public facilities. A number of the larger cities in the Piedmont region, among them Greensboro voluntarily accepted token desegregation of their schools after the Supreme Court's 1954 decisions.

But across the state there were indications that the Negro had weighed token desegregation and found it wanting.

When commenting on the subject, the Rev. F. L. Shuttlesworth of Birmingham, Ala., drew a chorus of "amens" from a packed N.A.A.C.P. meeting in a Greensboro church, "We don't want token freedom," he declared. "We want full freedom. What would a token dollar be worth?"

Warming to the subject, he shouted:

"You educated us. You taught us to look up, white man. And we're looking up!"

Praising the demonstrators, he urged his listeners to be ready "to go to jail with Jesus" if necessary to "remove the dead albatross of segregation that makes America stink in the eyes of the world."

John H. Wheeler, a Negro lawyer who heads a Durham bank, said that the only difference among Negroes concerned the "when" and "how" of the attack on segregation.

He contended that the question was whether the South would grant the minority race full citizenship status or commit economic suicide by refusing to do so. . . .

### 15. *The Washington Post*, February 29, 1960.

Southern Moderates Fearful Sitdowns Endanger Negro Gains

ATLANTA, Feb. 28—The spread of the sitdown movement to the Deep South was viewed with apprehension today by Southern moderates.

Spokesmen for the moderate point of view on race relations fear that the sitdown demonstrations in Montgomery, Ala., last week may jeopardize the progress being made toward school desegregation.

It also is feared that further demonstrations in the Deep South may lead to much more serious violence than the skirmishing between white and Negro youths that has erupted in some areas.

Some Alabama segregationists are reported, on the other hand, to be eager for a showdown with Negro college students who are seeking to be served at lunch counters where only whites are now allowed to sit down and eat.

Further demonstrations are expected today in Montgomery. There are reports, too, that a sitdown is being organized in Birmingham, Ala., which is a stronghold of segregationist sentiment.

Negro students in Atlanta have considered staging a sitdown, but so far have been dissuaded from taking action by leaders of the Negro community who believe that a demonstration here would be a severe setback to the efforts now under way to desegregate the Atlanta schools.

Harold Flemings, executive director of the Southern Regional Council, noted today that the sitdown demonstrations have become much more than an economic matter now that they have been staged in the Deep South.

Fleming and other Southern moderates look upon the demonstrations as a protest against the slow progress being made in the desegregation of schools, in the expansion of employment opportunities for Negroes and delay in the enactment of civil rights legislation.

The moderates believe that a Southern filibuster in the Senate against legislation protecting the right of Negroes to vote will only goad the student demonstrators into taking new action.

Although the sitdown movement is only a month old, demonstrations have already been held in 23 cities in North Carolina, Virginia, South Carolina, Tennessee, Florida and now Alabama. They began in Greensboro, N. C., on Feb. 1.

The movement has spread so quickly that none of the Negro organizations has even been able to coordinate the demonstrations, which have been directed against variety or dime stores operated by national chains.

As the Southern Regional Council noted in a report on the movement it made public Saturday, it has been "spontaneous and contagious."

Fleming said that the Negro students have resisted adult direction of the movement. This resistance is widely considered to be a manifestation of the impatience of Southern youths with the slow progress in the adjudication of civil rights questions.

The failure of the demonstrators to break down the segregation barriers to service at variety store lunch counters has not, however, deterred demonstrations.

In none of the 23 cities where Negro students have sat down at variety store counters has the system of serving whites only been breached.

But now, Fleming noted, a Negro school whose students have not participated in the movement would appear in the eyes of some of the demonstrators to be behind the times.

Such Southern cities as Knoxville, Memphis, New Orleans, and Columbia and Charleston, S. C., are considered to be likely places for demonstrations.

The Rev. Martin Luther King, the Negro minister who led the successful bus boycott in Montgomery four years ago, is looked upon as the spiritual American father of the sitdown demonstrations, which are traced further to the passive resistance philosophy of India's Gandhi.

Although the Rev. Mr. King has made speeches in North Carolina in support of the sitdown movement, neither he nor his Southern Christian Leadership Council has succeeded in taking over the leadership of the demonstrations.

Some Negro leaders are talking about organizing boycotts against the variety stores, and in Winston-Salem, N. C., 300 Negroes decided on Saturday to urge other members of their race not to patronize the stores where they are not allowed to sit down and eat.

Boycotts are difficult to conduct, it is pointed out, and many of the Negroes need the stores as much as the stores need trade from the Negro community.

Negro leaders are aware that even the highly publicized Montgomery bus boycott did not break down desegregation on the buses. It was a U. S. Supreme Court decision which finally ended segregation on Montgomery buses.

Source 16 from James Melvin Washington, ed., *A Testament of Hope: The Essential Writings and Speeches of Martin Luther King, Jr.* (New York: Harper One, 1990), pp. 43–52, excerpted. Reprinted by arrangement with the Estate of Martin Luther King, Jr., c/o Writer House as agent for the proprietor New York, NY. Copyright 1963 Dr. Martin Luther King, Jr., copyright renewed 1991 Coretta Scott King.

### 16. Excerpts from Martin Luther King, Jr.'s 1961 Address Defending the Student Sit-Ins.

*[Many supporters of civil rights, including members of liberal groups such as the Southern Regional Council, an interracial organization working toward challenging segregation, and some leaders within the NAACP did not approve of the student sit-ins. They found the tactic too confrontational, radical, and dangerous. In November 1961, King spoke before the annual meeting of a group, the Fellowship of the Concerned, affiliated with the SRC.]*

Members of the Fellowship of the Concerned, of the Southern Regional Council, I need not pause to say how very delighted I am to be here today, and to have the opportunity of being a little part of this very significant gathering. I certainly want to express my personal appreciation to Mrs. Tilly and the members of the Committee, for giving me this opportunity.[14] I would also like to express just a personal word of thanks and appreciation for your vital witness in this period of transition which we are facing in our Southland, and in the nation, and I am sure that as a result of this genuine concern, and your significant work in communities all across the South, we have a better South

---

14. Dorothy Rogers Tilly extended the invitation to Dr. King. She was married to Milton E. Tilly, an Atlanta businessman and former member of President Harry Truman's Committee on Civil Rights.

today and I am sure will have a better South tomorrow with your continued endeavor and I do want to express my personal gratitude and appreciation to you of the Fellowship of the Concerned for your significant work and for your forthright witness.

Now, I have been asked to talk about the philosophy behind the student movement. There can be no gainsaying of the fact that we confront a crisis in race relations in the United States. This crisis has been precipitated on the one hand by the determined resistance of reactionary forces in the South to the Supreme Court's decision in 1954 outlawing segregation in the public schools. And we know that at times this resistance has risen to ominous proportions. At times we find the legislative halls of the South ringing loud with such words as interposition and nullification. And all of these forces have developed into massive resistance, but we must also say that the crisis has been precipitated on the other hand by the determination of hundreds and thousands and millions of Negro people to achieve freedom and human dignity. If the Negro stayed in his place and accepted discrimination and segregation, there would be no crisis. But the Negro has a new sense of dignity, a new self-respect and new determination. He has reevaluated his own intrinsic worth. Now this new sense of dignity on the part of the Negro grows out of the same longing for freedom and human dignity on the part of the oppressed people all over the world; for we see it in Africa, we see it in Asia, and we see it all over the world. Now we must say that this struggle for freedom will not come to an automatic halt, for history reveals to us that once oppressed people rise up against that oppression, there is no stopping point short of full freedom. On the other hand, history reveals to us that those who oppose the movement for freedom are those who are in privileged positions who very seldom give up their privileges without strong resistance. And they very seldom do it voluntarily. So the sense of struggle will continue. The question is how will the struggle be waged.

Now there are three ways that oppressed people have generally dealt with their oppression. One way is the method of acquiescence, the method of surrender; that is, the individuals will somehow adjust themselves to oppression, they adjust themselves to discrimination or to segregation or colonialism or what have you. The other method that has been used in history is that of rising up against the oppressor with corroding hatred and physical violence. Now of course we know about this method in Western civilization because in a sense it has been the hallmark of its grandeur, and the inseparable twin of western materialism. But there is a weakness in this method because it ends up creating many more social problems than it solves.

And I am convinced that if the Negro succumbs to the temptation of using violence in his struggle for freedom and justice, unborm [sic] generations will be the recipients of a long and desolate night of bitterness. And our chief legacy to the future will be an endless reign of meaningless chaos.

But there is another way, namely the way of nonviolent resistance. This method was popularized in our generation by a little man from India, whose name was Mohandas K. Gandhi. He used this method in a magnificent way to free his people from the economic exploitation and the political domination inflicted upon them by a foreign power.

This has been the method used by the student movement in the South and all over the United States. And naturally whenever I talk about the student movement I cannot be totally objective. I have to be somewhat subjective because of my great admiration for what the students have done. For in a real sense they have taken our deep groans and passionate yearnings for freedom, and filtered them in their own tender souls, and fashioned them into a creative protest which is an epic known all over our nation. As a result of their disciplined, nonviolent, yet courageous struggle, they have been able to do wonders in the South, and in our nation. But this movement does have an underlying philosophy, it has certain ideas that are attached to it, it has certain philosophical precepts. These are the things that I would like to discuss for the few moments left.

I would say that the first point or the first principle in the movement is the idea that means must be as pure as the end. This movement is based on the philosophy that ends and means must cohere. Now this has been one of the long struggles in history, the whole idea of means and ends. Great philosophers have grappled with it, and sometimes they have emerged with the idea, from Machiavelli on down, that the end justifies the means. There is a great system of thought in our world today, known as communism. And I think that with all of the weakness and tragedies of communism, we find its greatest tragedy right here, that it goes under the philosophy that the end justifies the means that are used in the process. So we can read or we can hear the Lenins say that lying, deceit, or violence, that many of these things justify the ends of the classless society.

This is where the student movement and the nonviolent movement that is taking place in our nation would break with communism and any other system that would argue that the end justifies the means. For in the long run, we must see that the end represents the means in process and the ideal in the making. In other words, we cannot believe, or we cannot go with the idea that the end justifies the means because the end is preexistent in the means. So the idea of nonviolent resistance, the philosophy of nonviolent resistance, is the philosophy which says that the means must be as pure as the end, that in the long run of history, immoral destructive means cannot bring about moral and constructive ends.

There is another thing about this philosophy, this method of nonviolence which is followed by the student movement. It says that those who adhere to or follow this philosophy must follow a consistent principle of noninjury. They must consistently refuse to inflict injury upon another. Sometimes you will read the literature of the student movement and see that, as they are getting ready for the sit-in or stand-in, they will read something like this, "If you are hit do not hit back, if you are cursed do not curse back." This is the whole idea, that the individual who is engaged in a nonviolent struggle must never inflict injury upon another. Now this has an external aspect and it has an internal one. From the external point of view it means that the individuals involved must avoid external physical violence. So they don't have guns, they don't retaliate with physical violence. If they are hit in the process, they avoid external physical violence at every point. But it also means that they avoid internal violence of spirit. This is why the love ethic stands so high in the student movement. We have a great deal of talk about love and nonviolence in this whole thrust.

Now when the students talk about love, certainly they are not talking about emotional bosh, they are not talking about merely a sentimental outpouring; they're talking something much deeper, and I always have to stop and try to define the meaning of love in this context. . . .

. . . *Agape* is understanding, creative, redemptive, good will to all men. It is an overflowing love which seeks nothing in return. Theologians would say that it is the love of God operating in the human heart. So that when one rises to love on this level, he loves men not because he likes them, not because their ways appeal to him, but he loves every man because God loves him. And he rises to the point of loving the person who does an evil deed while hating the deed that the person does. I think this is what Jesus meant when he said "love your enemies." I'm very happy that he didn't say like your enemies, because it is pretty difficult to like some people. Like is sentimental, and it is pretty difficult to like someone bombing your home; it is pretty difficult to like somebody threatening your children; it is difficult to like congressmen who spend all of their time trying to defeat civil rights. But Jesus says love them, and love is greater than like. Love is understanding, redemptive, creative, good will for all men. And it is this idea, it is this whole ethic of love which is the idea standing at the basis of the student movement. . . .

Another thing in this movement is the idea that there is within human nature an amazing potential for goodness. There is within human nature something that can respond to goodness. I know somebody's liable to say that this is an unrealistic movement if it goes on believing that all people are good. Well, I didn't say that. I think the students are realistic enough to believe that there is a strange dichotomy of disturbing dualism within human nature. Many of the great philosophers and thinkers through the ages have seen this. It caused Ovid the Latin poet to say, "I see and approve the better things of life, but the evil things I do." It caused even Saint Augustine to say "Lord, make me pure, but not yet." So that is in human nature. Plato, centuries ago said that the human personality is like a charioteer with two headstrong horses, each wanting to go in different directions, so that within our own individual lives we see this conflict and certainly when we come to the collective life of man, we see a strange badness. But in spite of this there is something in human nature that can respond to goodness. So that man is neither innately good nor is he innately bad; he has potentialities for both. So in this sense, Carlyle was right when he said that, "there are depths in man which go down to the lowest hell, and heights which reach the highest heaven, for are not both heaven and hell made out of him, ever-lasting miracle and mystery that he is?" Man has the capacity to be good, man has the capacity to be evil.

And so the nonviolent resister never lets this idea go, that there is something within human nature than can respond to goodness. So that a Jesus of Nazareth or a Mohandas Gandhi, can appeal to human beings and appeal to that element of goodness within them, and a Hitler can appeal to the element of evil within them. But we must never forget that there is something within human nature that can respond to goodness, that man is not totally depraved; to put it in theological terms, the image of God is never totally gone. And so the individuals who believe in this movement and who believe in nonviolence and our struggle in the South, somehow believe that even the worst segregationist can become an integrationist. Now sometimes it is hard to believe that this is what this movement says, and it believes it firmly, that there is something within human nature that can be changed, and this stands at the top of the whole philosophy of the student movement and the philosophy of nonviolence.

It says something else. It says that it is as much a moral obligation to refuse to cooperate with evil as it is to cooperate with good. Noncooperation with evil is as much a moral obligation as the cooperation with good. So that the student movement is willing to stand up courageously on the idea of civil disobedience. Now I think this is the part of the student movement that is probably misunderstood more than anything else. And it is a difficult aspect, because on the one hand the students would say, and I would say, and all the people who believe in civil rights would say, obey the Supreme Court's decision of 1954 and at the same time, we would disobey certain laws that exist on the statutes of the South today.

This brings in the whole question of how can you be logically consistent when you advocate obeying some laws and disobeying other laws. Well, I think one would have to see the whole meaning of this movement at this point by seeing that the students recognize that there are two types of laws. There are just laws and there are unjust laws. And they would be the first to say obey the just laws, they would be the first to say that men and women have a moral obligation to obey just and right laws. And they would go on to say that we must see that there are unjust laws. Now the question comes into being, what is the difference, and who determines the difference, what is the difference between a just and an unjust law?

Well, a just law is a law that squares with a moral law. It is a law that squares with that which is right, so that any law that uplifts human personality is a just law. Whereas that law which is out of harmony with the moral is a law which does not square with the moral law of the universe. It does not square with the law of God, so for that reason it is unjust and any law that degrades the human personality is an unjust law. . . .

There is a final thing that I would like to say to you, this movement is a movement based on faith in the future. It is a movement based on a philosophy, the possibility of the future bringing into being something real and meaningful. It is a movement based on hope. I think this is very important. The students have developed a theme song for their movement, maybe you've heard it. It goes something like this, "We shall overcome, deep in my heart, I do believe, we shall overcome," and then they go on to say another verse, "We are not afraid, we are not afraid today, deep in my heart I do believe, we shall overcome." So it is out of this deep faith in the future that they are able to move out and adjourn the councils of despair, and to bring new light in the dark chambers of pessimism. . . .

There is something in this student movement which says to us, that we shall overcome. Before the victory is won some may have to get scarred up, but we shall overcome. Before the victory of brotherhood is achieved, some will maybe face physical death, but we shall overcome. Before the victory is won, some will lose jobs, some will be called communists and reds, merely because they believe in brotherhood, some will be dismissed as dangerous rabblerousers and agitators merely because they're standing up for what is right, but we shall overcome. . . .

Sources 17–21 are photographs taken during, after, or to commemorate the historic lunch counter sit-ins in Greensboro, North Carolina and Nashville, Tennessee, in 1960.

## PICTURING THE STUDENT SIT-INS

### 17. Left to Right, David Richmond, Franklin McCain, Ezell Blair, Jr., Joseph McNeil, Greensboro, February 1960.

Jack Moebes/CORBIS

**18. Students at the Greensboro Woolworth's Lunch Counter, including Joseph McNeil and Franklin McCain (first and second from left), February 1960.**

Jack Moebes/CORBIS

**19. Nashville Students at the Previously Segregated Greyhound Terminal Lunch Counter, Including Diane Nash (third from left), May 1960.**

Gerald Holly/The Tennessean

**20. Joseph McNeil, Jibreel Khazan (formerly Ezell Blair, Jr.), Franklin McCain, and David Richmond at the Woolworth's Lunch Counter, 1990.**

AP Images/Chuck Burton

**21. Monument to Greensboro Four, North Carolina A&T University, Unveiled February 1, 2001.**

Andre Jenny/Alamy

✦

## Questions to Consider

To gain a deeper understanding of this phase of the Civil Rights Movement and to assess the significance of the student sit-ins, you must appreciate the context in which the protests occurred. Review the documents for clues about the background to the student sit-ins.

- What laws were the students challenging? Why did they challenge those laws in this particular way? Why did they follow some laws and rules—restricting the number of protestors so as to not impede sales, for example—and ignore others? What was different about their challenge to segregation laws from that of national organizations such as the NAACP and southern moderates?
- How important was Christianity to the student-led sit-ins? In what ways did religious faith shape their campaign for desegregation?
- What impact did class and regionalism exert in the student campaign? What role did black students from outside the region, including Diane Nash and Joseph McNeil, play in shaping the campaigns? Does it matter that the protests occurred in cities with black colleges and universities, while the majority of African Americans lived in rural regions of the South? How did the students—mostly middle class and well educated—differ in perspective from working class and poor black southerners?

- How would you describe the students themselves? How did the students physically present themselves at the sit-ins? What did they reveal about themselves in their songs and organizational literature? What were they conveying with that presentation of self?
- What generational tensions do you observe in the evidence? Why would college students see segregation in a different light than their parents and other adults?

Now locate the 1960 student sit-ins in the context of the struggle against segregation and compare their campaign to other parts of the Civil Rights Movement.

- What events and ideas shaped the values and attitudes of the students? How important were Gandhi, King, the Cold War, Little Rock, Montgomery, and existing national organizations? How was the student movement different?
- What were the students' philosophical beliefs? Why and how did they adhere to nonviolence? What did nonviolence achieve? What were its limitations? Why and how did they practice direct action? What did they achieve by this approach? What were its limitations?
- What did the students think about the NAACP, Dr. King and the SCLC, and southern "moderates"? How did these groups react to the sit-ins? What does this tell you about the politics of civil rights activism in 1960?

- The student sit-ins caught national leaders in the Civil Rights Movement by surprise. How did supporters of civil rights respond to the student movement? Why? How did southern whites respond to the sit-ins? Why? How did the national news media depict the students? What did the reactions—from white liberals, civil rights leaders, both black and white locals, the national media—reveal about the student campaign?

- Overall, in what ways did the student campaign differ from other, earlier desegregation efforts? What parts of the earlier Civil Rights Movement did the students adopt? What did they reject? What did they innovate? How did the student sit-ins change the struggle for civil rights in America?

- What challenges did the student movement pose to established American institutions (police, mayors, governors, and the federal government)? How did the students' tactics challenge and expand government's role in guarding citizens' rights?

Finally, reflect on the issue of historical memory, both personal and collective.

- What did protesting mean to the participants? When they were interviewed, what did the student leaders stress as important to remember? Why did they say they participated in the movement? Do you think their opinions would have changed over time? If so, why and in what ways? Here it might be useful to compare the picture taken at Woolworth's in 1960 (Source 18) with the photograph of the Greensboro Four taken in 1990 (Source 20).

- Why do we as a society commemorate certain events and people and not others? What does the statue of the Greensboro Four (Source 21), which was based on a photograph of the men taken in 1960 (Source 17), convey about the collective memory of the Greensboro sit-ins? What important parts of the story does it *not* tell?

- What parts of the Civil Rights Movement do we as a nation honor? What parts do we ignore? Why?

◆

## Epilogue

None of the Greensboro Four, the young men who launched the student sit-in movement, moved into national leadership positions in the Civil Rights Movement. Ezell Blair, Jr. (now Jibreel Khazan) became an educator and lives in New Bedford, Massachusetts. Joseph McNeil is an officer in the Air Force Reserve, and he enjoyed a distinguished career in finance. Franklin

McCain worked as a chemist, and spent most of his career in Charlotte, North Carolina. Unlike his three friends, David Richmond did not graduate from A&T, and he alone stayed in Greensboro, where resentment for his activism cast a long shadow. He struggled to find employment, and died in Greensboro in 1990 at the age of 49—but not before the four friends commemorated the 30th anniversary of their campaign (Source 20). The portion of the Woolworth's counter where they sat is now housed at the Smithsonian in Washington, D.C.

Several of the Greensboro Four's peers did emerge as national figures, most notably John Lewis. Raised in poverty in Pike County, Alabama, Lewis was a scholarship student at American Baptist Theological Seminary in 1960 when he joined Diane Nash, C. T. Vivian, and others in leading the Nashville student protest movement. Lewis went on to organize the Freedom Rides that began in 1961 and to serve as Chairman of SNCC. At the age of twenty-three he was the youngest person to speak at the 1963 March on Washington, in which Martin Luther King, Jr., gave his famous "I Have a Dream" speech.

The student campaign launched in early 1960 redefined the Civil Rights Movement. Sit-ins, wade-ins (at public pools), kneel-ins (at segregated churches), and parallel protests spread across the South and the nation. The student movement laid the foundation for Freedom Summer, when, in 1964, over one thousand volunteers, mostly college students, both black and white, moved to Mississippi to create Freedom Schools and register black voters. They were joined by doctors, who provided poor children with medical care, and lawyers, who waged the fight for racial equality in the courts. Mississippi convulsed. Hundreds of young people were arrested, scores beaten, and at least three—James Chaney, Andrew Goodman, and Michael Schwerner—were murdered in Mississippi that summer. The networks carried it all on the nightly news.

The student movement against segregation also had a profound effect on this generation of Americans. Their tactics were adopted by opponents of the Vietnam War, feminists, leaders of the American Indian Movement (AIM), and waves of New Left groups. That young people designed and populated these movements gave that generation a distinct identity and a powerful voice in civic life.

It is a complicated matter to assess the success of the student campaign for civil rights. In many regards, the mid-1960s, when student protests were most pervasive and effective, marked the zenith of the Civil Rights Movement. In spite of all the violence, the 1963 March on Washington, the 1964 Civil Rights Act, and the 1965 Voting Rights Act seemed to fulfill a century-long quest for black equality. Exactly one hundred years after the end of slavery, the United States federal government finally, officially rejected the idea that African Americans were second-class citizens. And yet civil rights did not ensure equality. De facto segregation continued, as did economic disparities, educational inequities, and racial discrimination.

The mainstream movement, centered around Dr. King and the philosophy of nonviolent direct action, was met by brutal violence, and not just the fire hoses in Birmingham and the rocks and clubs in Selma. Murder became an all-too-frequently employed political tactic. Medgar Evers, the NAACP field secretary, was gunned down outside his Mississippi home on June 12, 1963, the same summer as the March on Washington. Two weeks after the March on Washington, on a Sunday morning, a bomb ripped through the 16th Street Baptist Church in Birmingham, Alabama, killing four girls and deeply wounding the appeal of the nonviolent movement. President Kennedy was assassinated that November in Dallas. Malcolm X was murdered in February 1965. Robert Kennedy was shot and killed in June 1968, while campaigning for the presidency.

By the mid-1960s, Black Power, with its focus on African American self-reliance and its encouragement of self-defense, increasingly resonated with young African Americans who were tired of acting passively while they were being brutalized and frustrated by the slow pace of social change. Huey Newton and Bobby Seale founded the Black Panthers in Oakland, California, in 1966. That same year Stokely Carmichael, the new leader of SNCC, promoted Black Power within the organization and broadened its focus to include anti-war activism. SNCC changed its name in 1969 to the Student National Coordinating Committee. Movement leaders also increasingly moved their campaigns north, to fight slums and ghettos and redress economic disparities. While King's SCLC also expanded its agenda, the organization remained resolute in its passive-resistance philosophy, even in the darkest days of the movement.

The assassination of Martin Luther King, Jr., on April 4, 1968, spawned riots in over one hundred American cities. The night before he died, Dr. King gave what, in retrospect, many considered a prophetic last public address to an audience in Memphis:

Well, I don't know what will happen now. We've got some difficult days ahead. But it doesn't matter with me now. Because I've been to the mountaintop. And I don't mind. Like anybody, I would like to live a long life. Longevity has its place. But I'm not concerned about that now. I just want to do God's will. And He's allowed me to go up to the mountain. And I've looked over. And I've seen the promised land. I may not get there with you. But I want you to know tonight, that we, as a people, will get to the promised land. And I'm happy, tonight. I'm not worried about anything. I'm not fearing any man. Mine eyes have seen the glory of the coming of the Lord.

King was shot just after 6:00 p.m. the next evening, as he stood on the balcony of the Lorraine Motel.[15] Though the SCLC continued its efforts under the leadership of Reverend Ralph Abernathy, the movement became increasingly fragmented. The election of Richard Nixon and escalation of the Vietnam War diverted national

15. The Lorraine Motel is now the site of the National Civil Rights Museum.

attention from civil rights, as did the expanding Black Power movement and student antiwar activism.

On August 28, 2008, on the 45th anniversary of Dr. King's address at the 1963 March on Washington, Barack Obama, an African American, accepted the Democratic Party nomination for president. On January 20, 2009, Obama was sworn in as the 44th President of the United States. John Lewis sat on the stage. Historians, including those who disagreed with the Democrat's policies and opposed his candidacy, generally agreed that President Obama's election held great historical meaning: It signified a turning point in the nation's long, fraught racial history and was an event in which all Americans could take pride.

# A Generation in War and Turmoil: The Agony of Vietnam

◆

## The Problem

When the middle-class readers of *Time* magazine went to their mailboxes in January 1967, they were eager to find out who the widely read newsmagazine had chosen as "Man of the Year." To their surprise, they discovered that the "inheritors"—the whole generation of young people under twenty-five years of age—had been selected as the major newsmakers of the previous year. *Time*'s publisher justified the selection of an entire generation by noting that, in contrast to the previous "silent generation," the young people of the late 1960s were dominating history with their distinctive lifestyles, music, and beliefs about the future of the United States.

Those who wrote to the editor about this issue ranged from a writer who thought the selection was a long-overdue honor to one who called it an "outrageous choice," from a correspondent who described contemporary young people as "one of our best generations" to one who believed the choice of a generation was "eloquent nonsense." Furthermore, many writers were frightened or

worried about their children, and some middle-aged correspondents insisted that they themselves belonged to the "put-upon" or "beaten" generation.

There is no doubt that there was a generation gap in the late 1960s, a kind of sharp break between the new generation of young people comprising nearly half the population and their parents. The first segment of the so-called baby-boom generation came to adulthood during the mid- to late 1960s,[1] a time marked by the high point of the civil rights movement, the rise of a spirit of rebellion on college campuses, and a serious division over the United States' participation in the Vietnam War. For most baby boomers, white and black alike, the war was the issue that concerned them most immediately, for this was the generation that would be called on to fight

1. Although the birthrate began to climb during World War II (from 19.4 births per 1,000 in 1940 to 24.5 per 1,000 in 1945), the term *baby boom* generally is used to describe the increase in the birthrate between 1946 and the early 1960s.

or to watch as friends, spouses, or lovers were called to military service.

Your tasks in this chapter include identifying and interviewing at least one member of the baby-boom generation (preferably born between 1946 and 1956)[2] about his or her experiences during the Vietnam War era. Then, using your interview, along with those of your classmates and those provided in the Evidence section of this chapter, determine the ways in which the baby-boom generation reacted to the Vietnam War. On what issues did baby boomers agree? On what issues did they disagree? Finally, how can a study of people of the same generation help historians understand a particular era in the past?

◆

# Background

The year 1945 was the beginning of one of the longest sustained economic booms in American history. Interrupted only a few times by brief recessions, the boom lasted from 1945 to 1973. And although there were still pockets of severe poverty in America's deteriorating inner cities and in some rural areas such as Appalachia, most Americans had good cause to be optimistic about their economic situations.

The pent-up demand of the Depression and war years broke like a tidal wave that swept nearly every economic indicator upward. Veterans returning from World War II rapidly made the transition to the civilian work force or used the GI Bill to become better educated and, as a result, secure better jobs than they had held before the war. Between 1950 and 1960, real wages increased by 20 percent, and

disposable family income rose by a staggering 49 percent. The number of registered automobiles more than doubled between 1945 and 1955, and the American automobile industry was virtually unchallenged by foreign competition. At the same time, new home construction soared, as thirteen million new homes were built in the 1950s alone—85 percent of them in the new and mushrooming suburbs.[3]

New homes were financed by new types of long-term mortgage loans that required only a small down payment (5 to 10 percent) and low monthly payments (averaging $56 per month for a tract house in the suburbs). And these new homes required furniture and appliances, which led to sharp upturns in these industries. Between 1945 and 1950, the amount spent on household furnishings and appliances increased 240 percent, and most of these items were

2. A person born during the late 1950s to early 1960s would technically be considered a baby boomer but would probably have been too young to remember enough to make an interview useful.

3. There were 114,000 housing starts in 1944. In 1950, housing starts had climbed to nearly 1.7 million.

bought "on time" (that is, on installment plans).[4] Perhaps the most coveted appliance was a television set, a product that had been almost nonexistent before the war. In 1950 alone, 7.4 million television sets were sold in the United States, and architects began designing homes with a "family room," a euphemism for a room where television was watched.

This new postwar lifestyle could best be seen in America's burgeoning suburbs. Populated to a large extent by new members of the nation's mushrooming middle class, suburbanites for the most part were better educated, wealthier, and more optimistic than their parents had been. Most men commuted by train, bus, or automobile back to the center city to work, while their wives remained in the suburbs, having children and raising them. It was in these suburbs that a large percentage of baby boomers were born.

Sociologist William H. Whyte called America's postwar suburbs the "new melting pot," a term that referred to the expectation that new middle-class suburbanites should leave their various class and ethnic characteristics behind in the cities they had abandoned and become homogeneous. Men were expected to work their way up the corporate ladder, tend their carefully manicured lawns, become accomplished barbecue chefs, and serve their suburban communities as Boy Scout leaders or Little League coaches. For their part, women were expected to make favorable impressions on their husband's bosses

(to aid their husbands in their climb up the corporate ladder), provide transportation for the children to accepted after-school activities (scouts, athletics, music and dance lessons), and make a happy home for the family's breadwinner. Above all, the goal was to fit in with their suburban neighbors. Thus suburbanites would applaud the 1956 musical *My Fair Lady,* which was based on the premise that working-class flower seller Eliza Doolittle would be accepted by "polite society" as soon as she learned to speak properly.

The desire for homogeneity or conformity would have a less beneficial side as well. The cold war and the McCarthy era meant that the demand for homogeneity could be enforced by the threat of job loss and ostracism. In addition, many suburban women had met their husbands in college and hence had had at least some college education.[5] But the expectation that they be primarily wives and mothers often meant that they were discouraged from using their education in other ways. As a result, one survey of suburban women revealed that 11 percent of them felt that they experienced a "great deal of emotional disturbance." At the same time, men were expected to be good corporate citizens and good team players at work. It was rumored that IBM employees began each day by gathering together, facing the home office, and singing the praises of IBM and

4. Between 1946 and 1956, short-term consumer credit rose from $8.4 billion to almost $45 billion, most of it to finance automobiles and home furnishings. The boom in credit card purchases ("plastic money") did not occur until the 1960s.

5. One midwestern women's college boasted that "a high proportion of our graduates marry successfully," as if that was the chief reason for women to go to college in the first place. Indeed, in many cases it was. See Elaine Tyler May, *Homeward Bound: American Families in the Cold War Era* (New York: Basic Books, 1988), p. 83.

its executive vice president C. A. Kirk (to the tune of "Carry Me Back to Old Virginny"):

> Ever we praise our able leaders,
> And our progressive C. A. Kirk is
>   one of them,
> He is endowed with the will to go
>   forward,
> He'll always work in the cause of
>   IBM.

Finally, homogeneity meant that suburbanites would have to purchase new cars, furniture, television sets, and so on to be like their neighbors (it was called "keeping up with the Joneses"), even though monthly payments already were stretching a family's income pretty thin.

There was an underside to the so-called affluent society. Indeed, many Americans did not share in its benefits at all. As middle-class whites fled to the suburbs, conditions in the cities deteriorated. Increasingly populated by the poor—African Americans, Latin American immigrants, the elderly, and unskilled white immigrants—urban areas struggled to finance essential city services such as police and fire protection. Poverty and its victims could also be found in rural areas, as Michael Harrington pointed out in his classic study *The Other America,* published in 1962. Small farmers, tenants, sharecroppers, and migrant workers not only were poor but often lacked any access to even basic educational opportunities and health care facilities.

Young people who lacked the money or who were not brought up with the expectation of earning a college degree tended to continue in more traditional life patterns. They completed their education with high school or before, although some attended a local vocationally oriented community college or trade school for a year or two. They often married younger than their college counterparts, sought stable jobs, and aspired to own their own homes. In other words, they rarely rejected the values of their parents' generation.

The baby boomers began leaving the suburbs for college in the early 1960s. Once away from home and in a college environment, many of these students began questioning their parents' values, especially those concerned with materialism, conformity, sexual mores and traditional sex roles, corporate structure and power, and the kind of patriotism that could support the growing conflict in Vietnam. In one sense, they were seeking the same thing that their parents had sought: fulfillment. Yet to the baby boomers, their parents had chased false gods and a false kind of fulfillment. Increasingly alienated by impersonal university policies and by the actions of authority figures such as college administrators, political leaders, and police officers, many students turned to new forms of religion, music, and dress and to the use of drugs to set themselves apart from the older generation. The term *generation gap* could be heard across the American landscape as bewildered, hurt, and angry parents confronted their children, who (in the parents' view) had "gotten everything." Nor could the children seem to communicate to their confused parents how bankrupt they believed their parents' lives and values actually were. In the midst of this generational crisis, the Vietnam War was becoming a major conflict.

The Japanese defeat of Western colonial powers, particularly Britain and France, in the early days of World War II had encouraged nationalist movements[6] in both Africa and Asia. The final surrender of Japan in 1945 left an almost total power vacuum in Southeast Asia. As Britain struggled with postwar economic dislocation and, within India, the independence movement, both the United States and the Soviet Union moved into this vacuum, hoping to influence the course of events in Asia.

Vietnam had long been a part of the French colonial empire in Southeast Asia and was known in the West as French Indochina. At the beginning of World War II, the Japanese had driven the French from the area. Under the leadership of Vietnamese nationalist and Communist Ho Chi Minh, the Vietnamese had cooperated with American intelligence agents and fought a guerrilla-style war against the Japanese. When the Japanese were finally driven from Vietnam in 1945, Ho Chi Minh declared Vietnam independent.

The Western nations, however, did not recognize this declaration. At the end of World War II, France wanted to reestablish Vietnam as a French colony. But, seriously weakened by war, France could not reassert itself in Vietnam without assistance. At this point, the United States, eager to gain France as a postwar ally and member of the North Atlantic Treaty Organization, and viewing European problems as being more immediate than problems in Asia, chose to help the French

reenter Vietnam as colonial masters. From 1945 to 1954, the United States gave more than $2 billion in financial aid to France so that it could regain its former colony. United States aid was contingent upon the eventual development of self-government in French Indochina.

Ho Chi Minh and other Vietnamese felt that they had been betrayed. They believed that, in return for fighting against the Japanese in World War II, they would earn their independence. Many Vietnamese viewed the reentry of France, with the United States' assistance, as a broken promise. Almost immediately, war broke out between the French and their westernized Vietnamese allies and the forces of Ho Chi Minh. In the cold war atmosphere of the late 1940s and early 1950s, the United States gave massive aid to the French, who, it was maintained, were fighting against monolithic communism.

The fall of Dien Bien Phu in 1954 spelled the end of French power in Vietnam. The U.S. secretary of state, John Foster Dulles, tried hard to convince Britain and other Western allies of the need for "united action" in Southeast Asia and to avoid any use of American ground troops (as President Truman had authorized earlier in Korea). The allies were not persuaded, however. Rather than let the area fall to the Communists, President Eisenhower and his secretary of state eventually allowed the temporary division of Vietnam into two sections: South Vietnam, ruled by westernized Vietnamese formerly loyal to the French, and North Vietnam, governed by the Communist Ho Chi Minh.

6. Those in nationalist movements seek independence for their countries.

Free and open elections to unify the country were to be held in 1956. However, the elections were never held because American policymakers feared that Ho Chi Minh would easily defeat the unpopular but pro–United States Ngo Dinh Diem, the United States' choice to lead South Vietnam. From 1955 to 1960, the United States supported Diem with more than $1 billion of aid as civil war between the South Vietnamese and the Northern Vietminh (later called the Vietcong) raged across the countryside and in the villages.

President Kennedy did little to improve the situation. Facing his own cold war problems, among them the building of the Berlin Wall and the Bay of Pigs invasion,[7] Kennedy simply poured more money and more "military advisers" (close to seventeen thousand by 1963) into the troubled country. Finally, in the face of tremendous Vietnamese pressure, the United States turned against Diem, and in 1963 South Vietnamese generals, encouraged by the Central Intelligence Agency, overthrew the corrupt and repressive Diem regime. Diem was assassinated in the fall of 1963, shortly before Kennedy's own death.

Lyndon Johnson, the Texas Democrat who succeeded Kennedy in 1963 and won election as president in 1964, was an old New Dealer[8] who wished to extend social and economic programs to needy Americans. The "tragedy" of Lyndon Johnson, as the official White House historian, Eric Goldman, saw it, was that the president was increasingly drawn into the Vietnam War. Actually, President Johnson and millions of other Americans still perceived Vietnam as a major test of the United States' willingness to resist the spread of communism.

Under Johnson, the war escalated rapidly. In 1964, the Vietcong controlled almost half of South Vietnam, and Johnson obtained sweeping powers from Congress[9] to conduct the war as he wished. Bombing of North Vietnam and Laos was increased, refugees were moved to "pacification" camps, entire villages believed to be unfriendly were destroyed, chemical defoliants were sprayed on forests to eliminate Vietcong hiding places, and the number of troops increased until by 1968 about 500,000 American men and women were serving in Vietnam.

As the war effort increased, so did the doubts about it. In the mid-1960s, the chair of the Senate Foreign Relations Committee, J. William Fulbright, raised important questions about whether the Vietnam War was serving our national interest. Several members of the administration and foreign policy experts (including George Kennan, author of the original containment policy) maintained that escalation of the war could not be justified. Television news coverage of the destruction and

7. The Berlin Wall was a barricade created to separate East Berlin (Communist) from West Berlin. The Bay of Pigs invasion was a United States–sponsored invasion of Cuba in April 1961 that failed. The American role was widely criticized.

8. Johnson had served in Congress during the 1930s and was a strong supporter of New Deal programs.

9. The Tonkin Gulf Resolution gave Johnson the power to "take all necessary measures to repel any armed attack against the forces of the United States and to prevent further aggression."

carnage, along with reports of atrocities such as the My Lai massacre,[10] disillusioned more and more Americans. Yet Johnson continued the bombing, called for more ground troops, and offered peace terms that were completely unacceptable to the North Vietnamese.

Not until the Tet offensive—a coordinated North Vietnamese strike across all of South Vietnam in January 1968, in which the Communists captured every provincial capital and even entered Saigon (the capital of South Vietnam)—did President Johnson change his mind. Two months later, Johnson appeared on national television and announced to a surprised nation that he had ordered an end to most of the bombing, asked North Vietnam to start real peace negotiations, and withdrawn his name from the 1968 presidential race. Although we now know that the Tet offensive was a setback for Ho Chi Minh, in the United States it was seen as a major defeat for the West, evidence that the optimistic press releases about our imminent victory simply were not true.

As the United States' role in the Vietnam War increased, the government turned increasingly to the conscription of men for military service (the draft). Early in the war, all college men up to age twenty-six could get automatic deferments, which allowed them to remain in school while noncollege men (disproportionately poor and black) were drafted and sent to Vietnam. As the demand for men increased, however, deferments became somewhat more difficult to obtain. College students had to maintain good grades, graduate student deferments were ended, and draft boards increasingly were unsympathetic to pleas for conscientious objector status.[11] Even so, the vast majority of college students who did not want to go to Vietnam were able to avoid doing so, principally by using one of the countless loopholes in the system such as opting for ROTC (Reserve Officers' Training Corps) duty, purposely failing physical examinations, getting family members to pull strings, obtaining conscientious objector status, and so on. Only 12 percent of the college graduates between 1964 and 1973 served in Vietnam. Twenty-one percent of high school graduates and an even higher percentage of high school dropouts served.

As the arbitrary and unfair nature of the draft became increasingly evident, President Richard Nixon finally replaced General Lewis Hershey, who had headed the Selective Service System since 1948, and instituted a new system of conscription: a lottery. In this system, draft-age men were assigned numbers and were drafted in order from lowest to highest number until the draft quota was filled. With this action, the very real threat of the draft spread to those who had previously felt relatively safe. Already divided, an entire generation had to come face to face with the Vietnam War.

10. The My Lai massacre occurred in March 1968, when American soldiers destroyed a Vietnamese village and killed many of the inhabitants, including women and children.

11. Conscientious objectors are those whose religious beliefs are opposed to military service, such as the Society of Friends (Quakers).

✦

# The Method

Historians often wish they could ask specific questions of the participants in a historical event—questions that are not answered in surviving diaries, letters, and other documents. Furthermore, many people, especially the poor, uneducated, and members of minority groups, did not leave written records and thus often are overlooked by historians.

When dealing with the comparatively recent past, however, historians do have an opportunity to ask questions by using a technique called *oral history*. Oral history—interviewing famous and not-so-famous people about their lives and the events they observed or participated in—can greatly enrich knowledge of the past. It can help capture the "spirit of an age" as seen through the eyes of average citizens, and it often bridges the gap between impersonal forces (wars, epidemics, depressions) and personal, individual responses to them. Furthermore, oral history allows the unique to emerge from the total picture: the conscientious objector who would not serve in the army, the woman who did not marry and devote herself to raising a family, and so forth.

Oral history is both fascinating and challenging. It seems easy to do, but it is really rather difficult to do well. There is always the danger that the student may "lead" the interview by imposing his or her ideas on the subject. It is equally possible that the student may be led away from the subject by the person being interviewed.

Still other problems sometimes arise. The student may miss the subtleties in what is being said or may assume that an exceptional person is representative of many people. Some older people like to tell only the "smiling side" of their personal history—that is, they prefer to talk about the good things that happened to them, not the bad things. Others actually forget what happened or are influenced by reading or television. Some older people cannot resist sending a message to younger people by recounting how hard it was in the past, how few luxuries they had when they were young, how far they had to walk to school, and so forth. Yet oral history, when used carefully and judiciously along with other sources, is an invaluable tool that helps historians recreate a sense of our past.

Recently, much attention has been paid—and rightly so—to protecting the rights and privacy of human subjects. For this reason, the federal government requires that an interviewee consent to the interview and be fully aware of how the interview is to be used. The interviewer must explain the purpose of the interview, and the person being interviewed must sign a release form (for samples, see Sources 1 through 3). Although these requirements are intended to apply mostly to psychologists and sociologists, historians who use oral history are included as well.

When you identify and interview an individual of the baby-boom generation, you will be speaking with a member of a *birth cohort*. A birth cohort comprises those people born within a few years of one another who form a historical generation. Members of a birth cohort experience the same events—wars, depressions, assassinations, as well as personal experiences such as marriage and childbearing—at approximately the same age and often have similar reactions to them. Sociologist Glen Elder showed that a group of people who were relatively deprived as young children during the Great Depression grew up and later made remarkably similar decisions about marriage, children, and jobs. Others have used this kind of analysis to provide insights into British writers of the post–World War I era and to explain why the Nazi party appealed to a great many young Germans.

Yet even within a birth cohort, people may respond quite differently to the same event or experience. *Frame of reference* refers to an individual's personal background, which may influence that person's beliefs, responses, and actions. For example, interviews conducted with Americans who lived during the Great Depression of the 1930s reveal that men and women often coped differently with unemployment, that blacks and whites differed in their perceptions of how hard the times were, and that those living in rural areas had remarkably different experiences from city dwellers.

In this chapter, all the interviewees belong to the generation that came of age during the Vietnam War. Thus, as you analyze their frames of reference, age will not give you any clues. However, other factors, such as gender, race, socioeconomic class, family background, values, region, and experiences, may be quite important in determining the interviewees' frames of reference and understanding their responses to the Vietnam War. When a group of people share the same general frame of reference, they are a generational subset who tend to respond similarly to events. In other words, it may be possible to form tentative generalizations from the interviewees about how others with the same general frames of reference thought about and responded to the Vietnam War. To assist you in conducting your own interview of a member of the baby-boom generation (or birth cohort), we have included some instructions for interviewers and a suggested interview plan.

## Instructions for Interviewers

1. Establish the date, time, and place of the interview well in advance. You may wish to call and remind the interviewee a few days before your appointment.

2. State clearly the purpose of the interview *at the beginning*. In other words, explain why the class is doing this project.

3. Prepare for the interview by carefully reading background information about the 1960s and by writing down and arranging the questions you will be asking to guide the interview.

4. Keep most of your major questions broad and general so that the interviewee will not simply answer with a word or two ("What was your job in the army?"). Specific questions such as "What did the people in your town think about the war?" are useful for obtaining more details.

5. Avoid "loaded" questions such as "Everyone hated President Lyndon Johnson, didn't they?" Instead, keep your questions neutral: "What did you think about President Lyndon Johnson and his Vietnam strategy?"

6. Save any questions involving controversial matters for last. It is better to ask them toward the end of the interview, when the interviewee is more comfortable with you.

7. Be courteous, and be sure to give the person enough time to think, remember, and answer. Never argue, even if he or she says something with which you strongly disagree. Remember that the purpose of the interview is to find out what *that person* thinks, not what you think.

8. Take notes, even if you are tape-recording the interview (with permission). Notes will help clarify unclear portions of the tape and will be essential if the recorder malfunctions or the tape is accidentally erased.

9. Obtain a signed release form. Many who use the oral history method believe that the release forms should be signed at the beginning of the interview; others insist that this often inhibits the person who is to be interviewed and therefore should not be done until the end of the session. Although students who are using the material only for a class exercise are not always held strictly to the federal requirements, it is still better to obtain a signed release. Without such a release, the tape cannot be heard and used by anyone else (or deposited in an oral history collec-

tion), and the information the tape contains cannot be published or made known outside the classroom.

10. Write up the results of your interview as soon as possible after completing it. Even in rough form, these notes will help you capture the sense of what was said as well as the actual information that was presented.

## A Suggested Interview Plan

Remember that your interviewee is a *person* with feelings, sensitivities, and emotions. If you intend to tape-record the interview, ask permission first. If you believe that a tape recorder will inhibit the person you have selected, leave it at home and rely on your ability to take notes.

The following suggestions may help you get started. People usually remember the personal aspects of their lives more vividly than they remember national or international events. That is a great advantage in this exercise because part of what you are attempting to find out is how this person lived during the 1960s. Begin by getting the following important data from the interviewee:

1. Name
2. Age in 1968
3. Race and sex
4. Where the person lived in the 1960s and what the area was like then
5. Family background (what the interviewee's parents did for a living; number of brothers and sisters; whether the interviewee considered

himself or herself rich, middle class, or poor)

6. Educational background

Then move on to the aspects of the person's life that will flesh out your picture of the 1960s and early 1970s:

1. Was the person in college at any time? What was college life like during the period?
2. If the person was not in college, what did he or she do for a living? Did he or she live at home or away from home?
3. How did the person spend his or her leisure time? If unmarried, did the person go out on dates? What was dating like? Did he or she go to the movies (and if so, which ones)? Did he or she watch much television (and if so, which shows)?

These questions should give you a fairly good idea of how the person lived during the period. Now move on to connect the interviewee with the Vietnam War:

1. Did the person know anyone who volunteered or was drafted and sent to Vietnam? How did the interviewee feel about that? Did the person lose any relatives or friends in Vietnam? What was his or her reaction to that?
2. *(Male):* Was the person himself eligible for the draft? Did he volunteer for service or was he drafted? Was he sent to Vietnam? If so, what were some memorable Vietnam experiences? What did the person's family think of his going to Vietnam? *(Female):* If you intend to interview a female who went to Vietnam as a nurse, alter the preceding questions as needed.
3. Was the person a Vietnam War protester? If so, what was that experience like? If not, did the person know any Vietnam War protesters? What did the person think of them?
4. Did the person know anyone who tried to avoid going to Vietnam? What did the person think of that?

Finally, review the national events and people of the Vietnam era and develop some questions to ask your interviewee about these events and people. As you can see in this plan, you want to guide the interview through three stages, from personal information and background to the interviewee's reactions to a widening sphere of experiences and events.

◆

## The Evidence

### 1. Sample Unconditional Release for an Oral Interview.

<u>Tri-County Historical Society</u>

For and in consideration of the participation by <u>Tri-County Historical Society</u> in any programs involving the dissemination of tape-recorded memories and oral history material for publication, copyright, and other uses, I hereby release all right, title, or interest in and to all of my tape-recorded memoirs to <u>Tri-County Historical Society</u> and declare that they may be used without any restriction whatsoever and may be copyrighted and published by the said <u>Society,</u> which may also assign said copyright and publication rights to serious research scholars.

In addition to the rights and authority given to you under the preceding paragraph, I hereby authorize you to edit, publish, sell and/or license the use of my oral history memoir in any other manner which the <u>Society</u> considers to be desirable and I waive any claim to any payments which may be received as a consequence thereof by the <u>Society.</u>

PLACE   <u>Indianapolis,</u>

<u>Indiana</u>

DATE   <u>July 14, 1975</u>

<u>Harold S. Johnson</u>
(Interviewee)

<u>Jane Rogers</u>
(for <u>Tri-County Historical Society</u> )

## 2. Sample Conditional Release for an Oral Interview.

<u>Tri-County Historical Society</u>

I hereby release all right, title, or interest in and to all or any part of my tape-recorded memoirs to <u>Tri-County Historical Society,</u> subject to the following stipulations:

That my memoirs are to be *closed* until five years following my death.

PLACE <u>Indianapolis,</u>
<u>Indiana</u>
DATE <u>July 14, 1975</u>

<u>Harold S. Johnson</u>
(Interviewee)

<u>Jane Rogers</u>
(for <u>Tri-County Historical Society</u> )

Source 3 from the University of Tennessee.

## 3. Release Form Developed by a Large U.S. History Survey Class at the University of Tennessee, Knoxville, 1984.

This form is to state that I have been interviewed by _____ on <sub>(Interviewer)</sub> _____ on my recollections of the Vietnam War era. I understand that <sub>(date)</sub> this interview will be used in a class project at the University of Tennessee, and that the results will be saved for future historians.

_____
Signature

_____
Date

Sources 4 through 10 are from interviews conducted by the authors. Photographs were supplied by the interviewees.

### 4. Photograph of John and His Family (*left to right:* John's father, John, John's mother, and John's brother).

Cengage Learning

## John

*[John was born in 1951. His father was a well-to-do and prominent physician, and John grew up in a midwestern town that had a major university. He graduated from high school in 1969 and enrolled in a four-year private college. John dropped out of college in 1971 and returned home to live with his parents. He found work in the community and associated with students at the nearby university.]*

My earliest memory of Vietnam must have been when I was in the seventh grade [1962–1963] and I saw things in print and in *Life* magazine. But I really don't remember much about Vietnam until my senior year in high school [1968–1969].

I came from a repressive private school to college. College was a fun place to hang out, a place where you went after high school. It was just expected of you to go.

At college there was a good deal of apprehension and fear about Vietnam—people were scared of the draft. To keep your college deferments, you had to keep your grades up. But coming from an admittedly well-to-do family, I somehow assumed I didn't have to worry about it too much. I suppose I was outraged to find out that it *could* happen to me.

No, I was outraged that it could happen to *anyone*. I knew who were going to get deferments and who weren't going to get them. And even today my feelings are still ambiguous. On one hand I felt, "You guys were so dumb to get caught in that machine." On the other, and more importantly, it was wrong that *anyone* had to go.

Why? Because Vietnam was a bad war. To me, we were protecting business interests. We were fighting on George III's side, on the wrong side of an anticolonial rebellion. The domino theory didn't impress me at all.[12]

I had decided that I would not go to Vietnam. But I wasn't really worried for myself until Nixon instituted the lottery. I was contemplating going to Canada when my older brother got a CO.[13] I tried the same thing, the old Methodist altar boy gambit, but I was turned down. I was really ticked when I was refused CO status. I thought, "Who are you to tell me who is a pacifist?"

My father was conservative and my mother liberal. Neither one intervened or tried to pressure me. I suppose they thought, "We've done the best we could." By this time I had long hair and a beard. My dad had a hard time.

The antiwar movement was an intellectual awakening of American youth. Young people were concentrated on college campuses, where their maturing intellects had sympathetic sounding boards. Vietnam was part of that awakening. So was drugs. It was part of the protest. You had to be a part of it. Young people were waking up as they got away from home and saw the world around them and were forced to think for themselves.

I remember an argument I had with my father. I told him Ho Chi Minh was a nationalist before he was a Communist, and that this war wasn't really against communism at all. It's true that the Russians were also the bad guys in Vietnam, what with their aid and support of the North Vietnamese, but they had no business there either. When people tried to compare Vietnam to World War II, I just said that no Vietnamese had ever bombed Pearl Harbor.

The draft lottery certainly put me potentially at risk. But I drew a high number, so I knew that it was unlikely that I'd ever be drafted. And yet, I wasn't concerned just for myself. For example, I was aware, at least intellectually, that blacks and poor people were the cannon fodder in Vietnam. But I insisted that *no one,* rich or poor, had to go to fight this war.

Actually I didn't think much about the Vietnamese people themselves. The image was of a kid who could take candy from you one day and hand you a grenade the next. What in hell were we doing in that kind of situation?

---

12. The domino theory, embraced by Presidents Eisenhower, Kennedy, and Johnson, held that if one nation fell to the Communists, the result would be a toppling of other nations, like dominoes.
13. A "CO" is a conscientious objector.

Nor did I ever actually know anyone who went to Vietnam. I suppose that, to some extent, I bought the "damn baby napalmers" image. But I never had a confrontation with a veteran of Vietnam. What would I think of him? I don't know. What would he think of me?

Kent State[14] was a real shock to me. I was in college at the time, and I thought, "They were students, just like me." It seemed as if fascism was growing in America.

I was part of the protest movement. After Kent State, we shut down the campus, then marched to a downtown park where we held a rally. In another demonstration, later, I got a good whiff of tear gas. I was dating a girl who collapsed because of the gas. I recall a state policeman coming at us with a club. I yelled at him, telling him what had happened. Suddenly he said, "Here, hold this!" and gave me his club while he helped my date to her feet.

But there were other cops who weren't so nice. I went to the counter-inaugural in Washington in June 1973. You could see the rage on the cops' faces when we were yelling, "One, two, three, four, we don't want your f——ing war!" It was an awakening for me to see that much emotion on the subject coming from the other side. I know that I wasn't very open to other opinions. But the other side *really* was closed.

By '72 their whole machine was falling apart. A guy who gave us a ride to the counter-inaugural was a Vietnam vet. He was going there too, to protest against the war. In fact, he was hiding a friend of his who was AWOL,[15] who simply hid rather than go to Vietnam.

Then Watergate made it all worthwhile—we really had those f——ers scared. I think Watergate showed the rest of the country exactly what kind of "law and order" Nixon and his cronies were after!

I have no regrets about what I did. I condemn them all—Kennedy, Johnson, Nixon—for Vietnam. They all had a hand in it. And the war was wrong, in every way imaginable. While I feel some guilt that others went and were killed, and I didn't, in retrospect I feel much guiltier that I wasn't a helluva lot more active. Other than that, I wouldn't change a thing. I can still get angry about it.

How will I explain all that to my sons? I have no guilt in terms of "duty towards country." The *real* duty was to fight *against* the whole thing. I'll tell my sons that, and tell them that I did what I did so that no one has to go.

*[John chose not to return to college. He learned a craft, which he practices today. He married a woman who shared his views ("I wouldn't have known anyone on the other side, the way the country was divided"), had two children, and shared the responsibilities of child care. John and his wife are now divorced.]*

14. Kent State: On May 4, 1970, in the midst of an antiwar rally on the campus of Kent State University in Ohio, panicked National Guard soldiers fired into a crowd of protesters. Four students, two of whom were on their way to class and were not demonstrators, were killed and eleven were wounded. The tragedy increased campus unrest throughout the nation.
15. "AWOL" is an acronym for absent without leave.

## 5. Photograph of Mike in Vietnam.

Cengage Learning

### Mike

*[Mike was born in 1948. His family owned a farm in western Tennessee, and Mike grew up in a rural environment. He graduated from high school in 1966 and enrolled in a community college not far from his home. After two quarters of poor grades, Mike left the community college and joined the United States Marine Corps in April 1967. He served two tours in Vietnam, the first in 1967 to 1969 and the second in 1970 to 1971.]*

I flunked out of college my first year. I was away from home and found out a lot about wine, women, and song but not about much else. In 1967 the old system of the draft was still in effect, so I knew that eventually I'd be rotated up and drafted—it was only a matter of time before they got me.

My father served with Stilwell in Burma and my uncle was career military. I grew up on a diet of John Wayne flicks. I thought serving in the military was what was expected of me. The Marines had some good options—you could go in for two years and take your chances on the *possibility* of not going to Vietnam. I chose the two-year option. I thought what we were doing in Vietnam was a noble cause. My mother was against the war and we argued a lot about it. I told her that if the French hadn't helped us in the American Revolution, then we wouldn't have won. I sincerely believed that.

I took my six weeks of basic training at Parris Island [South Carolina]. It was sheer hell—I've never been treated like that in my life. Our bus arrived at Parris Island around midnight, and we were processed and sent to our barracks. We had just gotten to sleep when a drill instructor threw a thirty-two gallon garbage can down the center of the barracks and started overturning the metal bunks. We were all over the floor and he was screaming at us. It was that way for six weeks— no one ever talked to us, they shouted. And all our drill instructors geared our basic training to Vietnam. They were always screaming at us, "You're going to go to Vietnam and you're gonna f—— up and you're gonna die."

Most of the people in basic training with me were draftees. My recruiter apologized to me for having to go through boot camp with draftees. But most of the guys I was with were pretty much like me. Oh, there were a few s—— birds, but not many. We never talked about Vietnam—there was no opportunity.

There were a lot of blacks in the Corps and I went through basic training with some. But I don't remember any racial tension until later. There were only two colors in the Marine Corps: light green and dark green. My parents drove down to Parris Island to watch me graduate from basic training, and they brought a black woman with them. She was from Memphis and was the wife of one of the men who graduated with me.

After basic training I spent thirteen weeks in basic infantry training at Camp Lejeune [North Carolina]. Lejeune is the armpit of the world. And the harassment didn't let up—we were still called "scumbag" and "hairbag" and "whale——." I made PFC [private first class] at Lejeune. I was an 03-11 [infantry rifleman].

From Lejeune [after twenty days' home leave] I went to Camp Pendleton [California] for four-week staging. It was at Pendleton where we adjusted our training at Parris Island and Lejeune to the situation in Vietnam. I got to Vietnam right after Christmas 1967.

It was about this time that I became aware of antiwar protests. But as far as I was concerned they were a small minority of malcontents. They were the *protected,* were deferred or had a daddy on the draft board. I thought, "These people are disloyal—they're selling us down the drain."

We were not prepared to deal with the Vietnamese people at all. The only two things we were told was don't give kids cigarettes and don't pat 'em on the heads. We had no cultural training, knew nothing of the social structure or anything. For instance, we were never told that the Catholic minority controlled Vietnam and they got out of the whole thing—we did their fighting for them, while they stayed out or went to Paris or something. We had a Catholic chaplain who told us that it was our *duty* to go out and kill the Cong,[16] that they stood against Christianity. Then he probably went and drank sherry with the top cats in Vietnam. As for the majority of Vietnamese, they were as different from us as night and day. To be honest, I still hate the Vietnamese SOBs.

The South Vietnamese Army was a mixed bag. There were some good units and some bad ones. Most of them were bad. If we were fighting alongside South Vietnam units, we had orders that if we were overrun by Charley[17] that we should shoot the South Vietnamese first—otherwise we were told they'd turn on us.

I can't tell you when I began to change my mind about the war. Maybe it was a kind of maturation process—you can only see so much death and suffering until you begin to wonder what in hell is going on. You can only live like a nonhuman so long.

I came out of country[18] in January of 1969 and was discharged not too long after that. I came home and found the country split over the war. I thought, "Maybe there *was* something to this antiwar business after all." Maybe these guys protesting in the streets weren't wrong.

But when I got back home, I was a stranger to my friends. They didn't want to get close to me. I could feel it. It was strange, like the only friends I had were in the Marine Corps. So I re-upped[19] in the Marines and went back to Vietnam with a helicopter squadron.

Kent State happened when I was back in Vietnam. They covered it in *Stars and Stripes*.[20] I guess that was a big turning point for me. Some of the other Marines said, "Hooray! Maybe we should kill more of them!" That was it for me. Those people at Kent State were killed for exercising the same rights we were fighting for for the Vietnamese. But I was in the minority—most of the Marines I knew approved of the shootings at Kent State.

Meanwhile I was flying helicopters into Cambodia every day. I used pot to keep all that stuff out of my mind. Pot grew wild in Vietnam, as wild as the hair on your ass. The Army units would pick it and send it back. The first time I was in Vietnam nobody I knew was using. The second time there was lots of pot. It had a red tinge, so it was easy to spot.

But I couldn't keep the doubts out of my mind. I guess I was terribly angry. I felt betrayed. I would have voted for Lyndon Johnson—when he said we should be there, I believed him. The man could walk on water as far as I was concerned. I would've voted for Nixon in '68, the only time I ever voted Republican in my life. I believed him when he said we'd come home with honor. So I'd been betrayed twice, and Kent State and all that was rattling around in my head.

16. "Cong" is short for *Vietcong,* also known as "the VC."
17. "Charley" is a euphemism for *Vietcong.*
18. "Country" means Vietnam.
19. "Re-upped" means reenlisted.
20. *Stars and Stripes* is a newspaper written and published by the armed forces for service personnel.

I couldn't work it out. I was an E5 [sergeant], but got busted for fighting and then again for telling off an officer. I was really angry.

It was worse when I got home. I came back into the Los Angeles airport and was spit on and called a baby killer and a mother raper. I really felt like I was torn between two worlds. I guess I was. I was smoking pot.

I went back to school. I hung around mostly with veterans. We spoke the same language, and there was no danger of being insulted or ridiculed. We'd been damn good, but nobody knew it. I voted for McGovern in '72—he said we'd get out no matter what. Some of us refused to stand up one time when the national anthem was played.

What should we have done? Either not gotten involved at all or go in with the whole machine. With a different attitude and tactics, we could have *won*. But really we were fighting for just a minority of the Vietnamese, the westernized Catholics who controlled the cities but never owned the backcountry. No, I take that back. There was no way in hell we could have won that damned war and won anything worth winning.

I went to Washington for the dedication of the Vietnam Veterans Memorial. We never got much of a welcome home or parades. The dedication was a homecoming for me. It was the first time I got the whole thing out of my system. I cried, and I'm not ashamed. And I wasn't alone.

I looked for the names of my friends. I couldn't look at a name without myself reflected back in it [the wall].

One of the reasons I went back to school was to understand that war and myself. I've read a lot about it and watched a lot of TV devoted to it. I was at Khe Sanh and nobody could tell about that who wasn't there. There were six thousand of us. Walter Cronkite said we were there for seventy-two days. I kept a diary—it was longer than that. I'm still reading and studying Vietnam, trying to figure it all out.

*[Mike returned to college, repeated the courses he had failed, and transferred to a four-year institution. By all accounts, he was a fine student. After earning both bachelor's and master's degrees, he became a park ranger and was considered a valuable, respected, and popular member of his community. Presently Mike is retired, divorced, and has returned to his family's farm, which he now runs. He rarely speaks of his time in the service.]*

## 6. Photograph of M. M., Boot Camp Graduation.

**M. M.**[21]

[*M. M. was born in 1947 and grew up in a midsize southern city. He graduated from high school in 1965. A standout in high school football, he could not get an athletic scholarship to college because of low grades. As a result, he joined the United States Army two months after graduating from high school to take advantage of the educational benefits he would get upon his discharge. He began his basic training in early September 1965.*]

I went into the service to be a soldier. I was really gung ho. I did my basic training at Fort Gordon [Georgia], my AIT [advanced infantry training] at Fort Ord [California], and ranger school and airborne at Fort Benning [Georgia].

---

21. Since M. M.'s first name is Mike, his initials are used here to avoid confusion with Mike in Source 5.

All of this was during the civil rights movement. I was told that, being black, I had a war to fight at home, not in Vietnam. That got me uptight, because that wasn't what I wanted to do—I'd done some of that in high school.[22] I had one mission accomplished, and was looking for another.

A lot of guys I went into the service with didn't want to go to Nam—they were afraid. Some went AWOL. One guy jumped off the ship between Honolulu and Nam and drowned. Another guy shot himself, trying to get a stateside wound. He accidentally hit an artery and died. Most of us thought they were cowards.

I arrived in Nam on January 12, 1966. I was three days shy of being eighteen years old. I was young, gung ho, and mean as a snake. I was with the Twenty-fifth Infantry as a machine gunner and rifleman. We went out on search and destroy missions.

I did two tours in Vietnam, at my own request. You could make rank[23] faster in Nam and the money was better. I won two silver stars and three bronze stars. For my first silver star, I knocked out two enemy machine guns that had two of our platoons pinned down. They were drawing heavy casualties. The event is still in my mind. Two of the bronze stars I put in my best friend's body bag. I told him I did it for him.

I had a friend who died in my arms, and I guess I freaked a little bit. I got busted[24] seven times. They [the army] didn't like the way I started taking enemy scalps and wearing them on my pistol belt. I kept remembering my friend.

I didn't notice much racial conflict in Nam. In combat, everybody seemed to be OK. I fought beside this [white] guy for eleven months; we drank out of the same canteen. When I got home, I called this guy's house. His mother said, "We don't allow our son to associate with niggers." In Vietnam, I didn't run into much of that.

The Vietnamese hated us. My first day in Vietnam, Westmoreland[25] told us that underneath every Vietnamese was an American. I thought, "What drug is he on?" But they hated us. When we weren't on the scene, the enemy would punish them for associating with us. They would call out to us, "G.I. Number Ten."[26] They were caught between a rock and a hard place.

We could have won the war several times. The Geneva Convention[27] wouldn't let us, and the enemy had the home court advantage. To win, it would have taken hard soldiering, but we could have done it. America is a weak country because we want to be everybody's friend. We went in there as friends. We gave food and stuff

---

22. M. M. participated in sit-ins to integrate the city's lunch counters and movie theaters.
23. "Make rank" means to earn promotions.
24. "Busted" means demoted.
25. General William Westmoreland was an American commander in Vietnam.
26. "Number Ten" means bad or no good.
27. "The Geneva Convention" refers to international agreements for the conduct of war and the treatment of prisoners. The agreements began to be drawn up in the 1860s.

to the Vietnamese and we found it in the hands of the enemy. We just weren't tough enough.

I got out of the Army in 1970. I was thinking about making the Army a career and was going to re-enlist. But when they wanted me to go back for a third tour in Vietnam, I got out. Hell, everybody told me I was crazy for doing two.

*[M. M. used his GI Bill benefits to obtain three years of higher education: two years at 2 four-year colleges and one year at a business school. According to him, however, jobs were "few and far between." He described himself as "restless" and reported that automobile backfires still frightened him. He was married and divorced twice. In 1999, M. M. died at the age of fifty-two.]*

## 7. Photograph of Eugene *(second from right)* Marching.

Cengage Learning

### Eugene

*[Eugene was born in 1948 in a large city on the West Coast. He graduated from high school in June 1967 and was drafted in August. Initially rejected because of a hernia, he had surgery to correct that problem and then enlisted in the Marine Corps.]*

It was pretty clear from basic training on, no ifs, ands, or buts, that we were going to Vietnam. The DIs[28] were all Vietnam vets, so we were told what to expect when we got there. They'd tell us what to do and all we had to do was do it.

I got to Vietnam in June of 1968. Over there, the majority of blacks stuck together because they had to. In the field was a different story, but in the rear you really caught it. Blacks would catch hell in the rear—fights and things like that. When we went to the movies with Navy guys, they put us in the worst seats. Sometimes they just wanted to start a fight. My whole time in Vietnam I knew only two black NCOs[29] and none above that.

We were overrun three times. You could tell when we were going to get hit when the Vietnamese in our camp (who cleaned up hooches) disappeared. Usually Charley had informants inside our base, and a lot of info slipped out. They were fully aware of our actions and weapons.

When we were in the rear, we cleaned our equipment, wrote letters home, went to movies, and thought a lot about what we'd do when we got out. I had

28. "DIs" are drill instructors.
29. "NCOs" are noncommissioned officers or sergeants.

training in high school as an auto mechanic, and I wanted to start my own business.

You had to watch out for the rookies until they got a feel for what was going on. We told one new LT,[30] "Don't polish your brass out here or you'll tip us off for sure." He paid us no mind and Charley knocked out him and our radio man one night.

You could get anything over there you wanted [drugs]. Marijuana grew wild in the bush. Vietnamese kids would come up to you with a plastic sandwich bag of twenty-five [marijuana] cigarettes for five dollars. It was dangerous, but we smoked in the bush as well as out. At the O.P.s,[31] everybody knew when the officer would come around and check. We'd pass the word: "Here comes the Man." That's why a lot of guys who came back were so strung out on drugs. And opium—the mamasans[32] had purple teeth because of it.

We could have won the war anytime we wanted to. We could have wiped that place off the map. There was a lot of talk that that's what we should have done. But we didn't because of American companies who had rubber and oil interests in Vietnam, and no telling what else. To them, Vietnam was a money-making thing. We were fighting over there to protect those businesses.

It was frustrating. The Army and Marines were ordered to take Hill 881 and we did, but it was costly. A couple of weeks later we just up and left and gave it back.

When I got out [in January 1970], I was an E5.[33] I couldn't find a job. So I talked to an Air Force recruiter. I got a release from the Marines[34] and joined the Air Force. I rigged parachutes and came out in 1975.

I stayed in LA[35] until 1977. Then I became a long-distance truck driver. I was doing pretty good when I got messed up in an accident. My truck jackknifed on ice in Pennsylvania and I hit the concrete barrier.

*[Eugene has not worked regularly since the accident and he sued the trucking company. He is divorced.]*

30. "LT" refers to a lieutenant.
31. "O.P.s" are outposts.
32. "Mamasans" refers to elderly Vietnamese women.
33. "E5" means sergeant.
34. Eugene had four years of reserve obligation.
35. Los Angeles, California.

8. **Photograph of Helen** *(left)* **at an Army Hospital in Phu Bai, South Vietnam.**

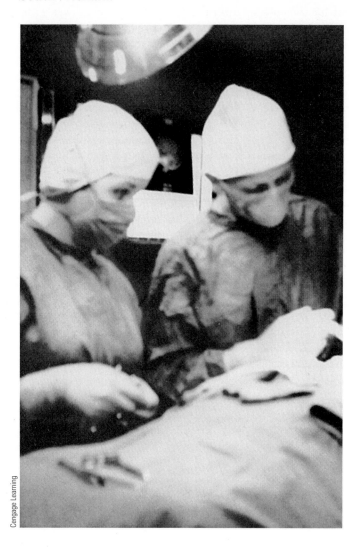

Cengage Learning

## Helen

*[Helen was born in 1942 in Cleveland, Ohio, and grew up there. Since grade school, she had wanted to be a nurse. After graduation from high school, she spent three years in nurses' training to become a registered nurse. She worked for three years in the operating rooms of a major medical facility in Cleveland. In 1966, she joined the United States Navy.]*

I joined the Navy in 1966 and reported to Newport, Rhode Island, for basic training. Our classes consisted of military protocol, military history, and physical education. There was only a passing reference made to our medical assignments and what was expected of us.

I was assigned to the Great Lakes Naval Hospital [outside Chicago]. Although I had been trained and had experience as an operating room surgical nurse, at first I was assigned to the orthopedic wards. It was there that I got my first exposure to mass casualties [from Vietnam]. Depending on the extent of their injuries, we would see patients at Great Lakes about seven to ten days after them being wounded in Vietnam.

I became attached to some of the boys—they were young, scared and badly injured. I remember a Negro who in tears asked for his leg to be taken off—he couldn't stand the smell of it anymore and had been to surgery once too often for the removal of dead tissue. He was in constant pain.

On the wards, we always kept nightlights on. If someone darkened a ward by accident, it produced a sense of terror in the patients. Many were disoriented, and a lot had nightmares.

When I made the decision to go to Vietnam, I volunteered in 1968 and requested duty aboard a hospital ship. It was necessary to extend my time on active duty in order to go. I felt I had a skill that was needed and it was something I felt I personally had to do. I didn't necessarily agree with our policy on being there, but that wasn't the point.

The median age of our troops in Vietnam was nineteen years old. It was like treating our kid brothers. I would have done as much for my own brothers. I know this sounds idealistic, but that's the way I felt then.

The troops got six weeks of staging, preparing them for duty in Vietnam. Most of the nurses were given no preparation, no orientation as to what to expect when you go into a war zone. No one said, "These are the things you'll see," or "These are the things you'll be expected to do."

I was assigned to the U.S.S. *Sanctuary,* which was stationed outside of Da Nang harbor. The *Sanctuary* was a front-line treatment facility. Casualties were picked up in the field combat areas and then brought by Medevac choppers to the ship. During our heaviest months, we logged over seven hundred patient admissions per month. That was at the height of the Tet offensive in January through March, 1968. I had just gotten to Vietnam.

It was terribly intense. There was nothing to shelter you, no one to hold your hand when mass casualties came in. If you had time to think, you'd have thought, "My God, how am I to get through this?" We dealt with multiple amputations, head injuries, and total body trauma. Sometimes injuries were received from our own people caught in crossfires. When all hell breaks loose at night in the jungle, a nineteen-year-old boy under ambush will fire at anything that moves.

How do you insulate yourself against all this? We relaxed when we could, and we put a lot of stock in friendships (the corpsmen were like our kid brothers). We played pranks and sometimes took the launch ashore to Da Nang. Occasionally we were invited to a party ashore and a helicopter came out for the nurses. The men wanted American women at their parties.

There were some people who had the idea that the only reason women were in the service was to be prostitutes or to get a man. Coming back from Vietnam, I was seated next to a male officer on the plane who said to me, "Boy, I bet you had a great time in Vietnam." I had my seat changed. When I got home and was still in uniform I was once mistaken for a police officer.

On the *Sanctuary,* we had Vietnamese patients too. But our guys were distrustful of them, especially children who had been observed planting mines (probably in exchange for a handful of rice). The Vietnamese were often placed under armed guard. I have friends who were nurses in country who harbor a real hatred for the Vietnamese.

I heard a story of a Vietnamese child running up to a chopper that was evacuating casualties and tossing a grenade into it. Everyone on board was killed in a split second; both crew and casualties, because they paused to help a child they thought needed them. A soldier I knew said, "If they're in the fire zone, they get killed." War really takes you to the lowest level of human dignity. It makes you barbaric.

After Vietnam, I was stationed at the Naval Academy in Annapolis to finish out my duty. There I dealt basically with college students—measles and sports injuries. It was a hard adjustment to make.

In Vietnam, nurses had a great deal of autonomy, and we often had to do things nurses normally aren't allowed to do. You couldn't do those things stateside. Doctors saw it as an encroachment on their areas of practice. I'd been a year under extreme surgical conditions in Vietnam, and then in Annapolis someone would ask me, "Are you sure you know how to start an IV?"[36] It was hard to tame yourself down. Also, in the civilian setting, mediocrity was tolerated. I heard people say, "That's not my job." Nobody would have said that in Vietnam. There, the rules were put aside and everybody did what they could. When we got back to the states, there was no one to wind us down, deprogram us, tell us that Vietnam was an abnormal situation. . . . It was as if no one cared, we were just expected to cope and go on with our lives. . . .

I guess the hardest thing about nursing in Vietnam was the different priorities. Back home, if we got multiple-trauma cases from, say, an automobile accident, we always treated the most seriously injured first. In Vietnam, it was often the reverse. I remember working on one soldier who was not badly wounded, and he kept screaming for us to help his buddy, who was seriously wounded. I couldn't tell him that his buddy didn't have a good chance to survive, and so we were passing him by. That was difficult for a lot of us, went against all we'd been trained to do. It's difficult to support someone in the act of dying when you're trained to do all you can to save a life. Even today, I have trouble with patients who need amputations or who have facial injuries.

36. An "IV" is an intravenous mechanism.

It is most important to realize that there is a great cost to waging war. Many men are living out their lives in veterans' hospitals as paraplegics or quadriplegics, who in World War II or Korea would not have survived. Most Americans will never see these people—they are hidden away from us. But they are alive.

Maybe the worst part of the war for many of these boys was coming home. The seriously wounded were sent to a military hospital closest to their own homes. Our orthopedic ward at Great Lakes Naval Hospital had forty beds, and it was like taking care of forty kid brothers. They joked around and were supportive of each other. But quite a few of them got "Dear John"[37] letters while they were there. Young wives and girlfriends sometimes couldn't deal with these injuries, and parents sometimes had trouble coping too. All these people were "casualties of war," but I believe that these men especially need our caring and concern today, just as much as they did twenty years ago.

*[On her discharge from the United States Navy in August 1969, Helen returned to nursing. She married in 1972. She and her husband, an engineering physicist, have two children. Helen returned to school and received her B.S. degree in nursing. She is now a coordinator of cardiac surgery and often speaks and writes of her Vietnam experience. She also actively participates in a local veterans' organization. When her daughter was in high school and offered her mother's services to speak on Vietnam to a history class, she was rebuffed by the teacher, who said, "Who wants to hear about that? We lost that war!" Both Helen and her daughter (who is proud of what her mother did in Vietnam) were offended.]*

37. A "Dear John" letter is one that breaks off a relationship.

**9. Photograph of Nick *(right)* with Some Buddies in Vietnam.**

Cengage Learning

### Nick

*[Nick was born in 1946 in a midsize southern city. Both his parents were skilled factory workers. Nick graduated from high school in 1964 and wanted to work for the fire department, but he was too young for the civil service. He got a job at the local utility company and married in 1966. Nick was drafted in 1967. He served in the · United States Army with the First Cavalry Division.]*

I suppose I could have gotten a deferment, but I didn't know they were available. My wife was pretty scared when I got drafted, but neither of us ever imagined that I would shirk my duty.

I did my boot camp at Fort Benning [Georgia]. About 80 percent of the people in boot camp with me were draftees. A number of the draftees were black. I had worked with blacks before the Army, had many black friends, and never saw any racial problems. We were then sent to Fort Polk, Louisiana, for advanced infantry training. They had built simulated Vietnamese villages that were very similar to what we later encountered in Vietnam. Overall, we were trained pretty well, but we were still pretty scared.

I arrived in Vietnam on December 12, 1967, and was assigned to go out on "search and destroy" missions. Even though I was prepared mentally, I was still very frightened. I was wounded once when we got ambushed while we were setting up an ambush of our own. Another time I got hit with some shrapnel from a 60 mm mortar. That was at 3:00 A.M. and the medics didn't arrive until 7:30.

I'm not proud of everything I did in Vietnam, but I won't run away from it either. You got so hard at seeing friends killed and things like that. We desecrated their dead, just as they did ours. We used to put our unit's shoulder patches on the VC dead (we nailed 'em on) to get credit for it.

I didn't like the Vietnamese themselves. Most of the civilians were VC sympathizers, and the South Vietnamese army just wouldn't fight. I was in some kind of culture shock. Here we were, trying to help these people, and some of them were living in grass huts. Once I asked myself, "What am I doing here?"

The highest rank I made was sergeant, but I was demoted when I caught a guy in my unit asleep on guard duty and busted him with a shotgun. I was demoted for damaging the shotgun, government property.

I got back to the States in December 1968. There were some protesters at the Seattle airport, but they just marched with signs and didn't harass us at all. Over time, I lost my hostility to the antiwar protesters, although at the time I despised them. Except for Jane Fonda[38] (who went too far), I have no bad feelings for them at all. I have a friend who threatened to run his daughter off because she had a Jane Fonda workout tape.

I'm no hero and didn't do anything special. But college students today need to know that the people who fought in that war are no less important than people who fought in World War I, World War II, or Korea.

*[Nick returned to his position with the utility company. He and his wife have two sons, born in 1969 and 1972. He never talked about Vietnam and wanted to throw his medals out, but his wife made him keep them. When his sons started asking questions, he told them about Vietnam. They convinced him to bring his medals out and display them. Since returning from Vietnam, he has never voted "and never will. . . . I have no use for politicians at all." He is now enjoying retirement.]*

38. Movie star and antiwar activist Jane Fonda organized shipments of food and medical supplies to North Vietnam and traveled to Vietnam during the war.

## 10. Photograph of Robyn as a College Student.

Cengage Learning

### Robyn

*[Robyn was born in 1955 and raised in a Wisconsin farming town of around fifteen
hundred people. Her father owned a small construction business and, like many other
men in town, had proudly served in World War II. Her mother was a high school
teacher. Robyn has three sisters and three brothers, none of whom served in Vietnam.]*

I remember starting to watch the war on television when I was about ten. I asked
my mother, "How come they're killing each other?" She said that America was
the land of freedom and that we were in Vietnam to help make the people free. As
a teacher, though, she always encouraged us to think for ourselves and find our
own answers.

The guys in town started going away [to Vietnam], and in a town that size,
everybody knows. When my ninth-grade algebra teacher suddenly disappeared,
no adults would talk about it. Later, we found out that he had received CO status.
In my town, that wasn't much different from being a Communist. The peer pressure was tremendous.

I have always believed the United States is the greatest country in the world,
but it's not perfect. The more I heard about the war, the more I realized something was wrong. Although only in high school, I felt obligated to let the government know that I thought it was in the wrong. And yet at no time while I was

protesting the war was I *ever* against the guys fighting it. My quarrel was with how the government was running the war.

I recall one of my first "protests." I was in the high school band and we were playing "The Star-Spangled Banner" at a basketball game. Although I stood and played with the rest of the band, I turned my back to the flag. When I came home that night, my father hit me for being disrespectful. So much for the right to free speech we were fighting to protect.

When I left for college in 1973, one brother had just gotten a medical deferral, and another would soon be registering for the draft. The war was becoming more and more personal. I skipped classes to attend rallies and antiwar events, and I wrote lots of letters to politicians. When the POW-MIA bracelets[39] came out, I helped sell them. There were quite a few heated discussions with some protesters who thought that wearing a bracelet (my guy is still MIA) was contrary to the cause. In those days, I tended to "discuss" things in decibels.

My second year of college ended with me skipping classes to watch the televised returns of our POWs. I would have loved to hug each one, so this was my way of saying "Welcome home" and to bear witness. I cried the whole time—for them, for their families, and for all the agony we'd all gone through during the war. Then I dropped out of school and just "vegetated" for a year. My idealistic perceptions of humanity had been severely challenged, and I was drained.

After Vietnam, I got involved in some projects that were targeted to help Vietnam vets. One of my best and proudest experiences will always be my work at the Vietnam Veterans Memorial in Washington, D.C. I worked at the wall as a volunteer every week for almost ten years. Unlike past memorials, this one doesn't honor the war. It's the Vietnam *Veterans* Memorial, not War Memorial, and it honors those who fought it.

I have seen firsthand its healing effects on vets and their families. And on me. At the wall, the former protester and the Vietnam veteran share something in common—our great sadness for those who were lost and those who haven't yet returned. Vietnam vets also don't seem to have the glorified view of war that older vets do.

The government's lack of support for Vietnam vets (during and after the war) might be part of the reason. If more people were aware of the other side of war, the side the vets saw, they'd have a lot more incentive to work things out. Instead of seeing war as an alternative solution, people would finally realize that war is simply the result of our failure to find a solution.

*[Robyn returned to college and eventually graduated from law school. She worked in Washington, D.C., for a nonprofit education organization and as a government relations consultant. Robyn now works at a public and government relations firm. She continues to work with Vietnam veterans and, in particular, on the POW-MIA issue.]*

39. Bracelets bearing the names of American POWs (prisoners of war) and MIAs (soldiers missing in action) were worn to remember those soldiers left behind in Vietnam and to urge the United States government to act on securing their return home.

✦

## Questions to Consider

The interviews in this chapter were conducted between 1985 and 1992. As you read through the seven interviews, try to get a sense of the tone and general meaning of each one. Then try to establish the respective frames of reference for the interviewees by comparing and contrasting their backgrounds. From which socioeconomic class does each person come? From what region of the country? What do you know about the interviewee's parents and friends? What did the person think was expected of him or her? Why?

After high school, the interviewees' experiences diverged greatly. Eventually, Mike, M. M., Eugene, and Helen enlisted in the armed services. What reason did each of them give (if any) for enlisting? How different were their reasons? For his part, Nick was drafted. What was his reaction to being drafted?

Both John and Robyn became involved in antiwar protests, but for very different reasons. Why did each become involved? Would John and Robyn have agreed on why the war should have been opposed?

Return to the five veterans. What were their feelings about the Vietnamese people? What did they believe were the reasons for American involvement in the war? What were their reactions to events of the time—the draft, antiwar protests, Kent State, and race relations in the armed services? What were their feelings about their respective roles in Vietnam? What did they think

about the situation of returning veterans? Some of the interviewees seem to have made the adjustment to civilian life better than others. Can you think of why that might have been so? Finally, what do you think each of the seven veterans or civilians learned from his or her personal experiences during the Vietnam War era?

Now look at the photographs closely. Are they posed or unposed? For whom might they have been intended? What image of each person is projected? How does each person help create that image?

Now consider carefully the interview that you conducted. You have done some important historical work by creating this piece of oral evidence. Now you must analyze it. What does your interview mean? In other words, how does it fit into or modify what you know about the Vietnam era? Begin by comparing and contrasting your interview with those in this chapter. Do the same with the interviews conducted by other students in your class. What major similarities and differences can you identify in the responses to the Vietnam War among members of this birth cohort? Do you see any patterns based on race, geographic region, socioeconomic class, or other factors? If so, describe and explain these patterns.

The majority of the people we interviewed had never met one another. Do you think they could meet and talk today about the Vietnam era? What might such a conversation be like?

# Epilogue

In the spring of 1971, fifteen thousand antiwar demonstrators disrupted daily activities in the nation's capital by blocking the streets with trash, automobiles, and their own bodies. Twelve thousand were arrested, but the protest movement across the country continued. In June, the Pentagon Papers, a secret 1967 government study of the Vietnam War, was published in installments by the *New York Times*. The Pentagon Papers revealed that government spokespersons had lied to the American public about several important events, particularly about the Gulf of Tonkin incident.

As part of his reelection campaign in 1972, President Nixon traveled first to China and then to the Soviet Union and accelerated the removal of American troops from Vietnam. "Peace," his adviser Henry Kissinger announced, "is at hand." Withdrawal was slow and painful and created a new group of refugees—those Vietnamese who had supported the Americans in South Vietnam. Nixon became mired in the Watergate scandal and resigned from office in 1974 under the threat of impeachment. The North Vietnamese entered Saigon in the spring of 1975 and began a "pacification" campaign of their own in neighboring Cambodia. Nixon's successors, Gerald Ford and Jimmy Carter, offered amnesty plans that a relatively small number of draft violators used. Many who were reported missing in action (MIA) in Vietnam were never found, either dead or alive. The draft was replaced by a new concept, the all-volunteer army.

The Vietnam veterans, who had no homecoming parades upon their return and who had been alternately ignored and maligned, finally got their memorial. A stark, simple, shiny black granite wall engraved with the names of 58,000 war dead, the monument is located on the mall near the Lincoln Memorial in Washington, D.C. The idea came from Jan Scruggs (the son of a milkman), a Vietnam veteran who was wounded and decorated for bravery when he was nineteen years old. The winning design was submitted by twenty-year-old Maya Lin, an undergraduate architecture student at Yale University. A representational statue designed by thirty-eight-year-old Frederick Hart, a former antiwar protester, stands near the wall of names, along with a statue dedicated to the nurses who served in Vietnam. All one hundred U.S. senators cosponsored the gift of public land, and the money to build the memorial was raised entirely through 650,000 individual public contributions. Not everyone was pleased by the memorial, and some old emotional wounds were reopened. Yet more than 150,000 people attended the dedication ceremonies on Veterans Day 1982, and the Vietnam veterans paraded down Constitution Avenue. Millions of Americans have viewed the monument, now one of Washington's most visited memorials.

As for the baby boomers, many have children old enough to have served in Operation Desert Storm, Somalia, Bosnia, Afghanistan, and the invasion and occupation of Iraq. A good number have put their Vietnam-era experiences behind them as they pursue careers, enjoy retirement, and await or play with grandchildren—a new birth cohort.

By the first decade of the twenty-first century, it became obvious that for the United States the Vietnam War was not a military aberration. Rather, it appeared to have been a *harbinger* of wars the nation would be forced to fight in the future: guerrilla-style conflicts in which the enemy, not unlike the Viet Cong, would strike suddenly and then melt away into the countryside or into the civilian population. In such military engagements, modern technology cannot be brought to bear so easily against what Americans increasingly refer to as "terrorists." Between 1991 and 2001, there were never fewer than 274 terrorist acts worldwide each year. Most shocking to Americans was the September 11, 2001, terrorist destruction of the World Trade Center towers in New York City and the damaging of the Pentagon in Washington. Even before those attacks, President George W. Bush had decided to oust the Taliban regime in Afghanistan that he was convinced was harboring terrorist

leader Osama bin Laden. United States-British bombing of Afghanistan began in early October 2001, and by late 2009 the United States had over sixty-five thousands troops in that country. On December 1, 2009, President Barack Obama ordered an additional 30,000 soldiers into Afghanistan, with no guarantee that the number would not continue to increase. Also believing that Iraqi leader Saddam Hussein was training and supplying terrorists, the United States once again invaded Iraq (an earlier invasion in 1991, Operation Desert Storm, drove the Iraqi army out of Kuwait but did not topple Saddam Hussein). Yet in both areas terrorist violence against U.S. troops continued and a military or a political victory seemed frustratingly far away. Still unanswered is the question of whether the American military or civilians possess the tactics or the patience to triumph in such a "new" kind of warfare.[40]

Thus, for many reasons, Vietnam is a chapter in American history that has not yet been closed. Does that era contain lessons that Americans—and historians—still need to learn?

40. In fact, Americans are hardly strangers to guerrilla warfare. Perhaps the most dramatic instance was the crushing of the Philippine insurrection after the United States acquired the Philippines from Spain in 1899—a particularly bloody affair.

# 11

# Who Owns History?
# The Texas Textbook
# Controversy

---

## The Problem

In addition to *Discovering the American Past*, your class may well be using a survey textbook on American history. The college-level text you purchased resulted from a lengthy, elaborate vetting process. Take, for example, Boyer, et al., *The Enduring Vision: A History of the American People*, now in its Seventh Edition. This text is published by Cengage Learning, the publisher that also publishes *Discovering the American Past*. A team of well respected historians collaborated to author that textbook. Each author on *The Enduring Vision* team is a leading figure in his or her respective field, and they write the chapters closest to their expertise. Neal Salisbury, for example, is a prominent colonial historian who writes about Native Americans, and Nancy Woloch has published widely in modern women's history. The team consults on particular themes to emphasize and subjects to cover so that the book coheres, and, with the publisher, the authors make decisions about everything from in-text images to special features within the book to web-based supplements. Once the historians have written their chapters, the publisher then asks other established scholars and experienced college teachers to anonymously evaluate the book, and it is revised accordingly. These anonymous readers' reports are foundational to scholarship: academic journals and university presses always employ this process to ensure the intellectual integrity of what they publish. In addition to this formal review process, the individual authors typically share their ideas with colleagues and seek extensive informal input: what works with students, what new books and articles should be consulted.

Finally, your professor decided which textbook to adopt. While some history departments opt to make a collective decision about which text they will all use in survey classes, in most cases, the individual professor reviews the range of available books and, based on academic interest or classroom experience, makes a choice. Because a lot of money is at stake, publishers seek out high-profile scholars to co-author textbooks, they employ savvy marketing campaigns, and their sales representatives compete for class-room adoptions. Leading companies, including Cengage, publish a number of different textbooks, which vary in emphasis and tone. No single textbook monopolizes the marketplace. Campus administrators do not force adoption, nor, in the case of public universities and colleges, do state legislatures. There are no mandated "standards" in college textbooks. Scholars and presses determine what to include, and their decisions are checked by teachers' preferences.

In creating university textbooks, then, scholarly excellence combines with market forces. Most high school textbooks, however, emerge out of an entirely different process. As with college textbooks, a lot of money is on the line. But after that, the similarities start to fade.

In 2009–2010, the controversy over history standards in the state of Texas threw into bold relief the extraordinarily complicated—and highly politicized—process of adopt-ing textbooks for public schools. Parents, political appointees, elected officials, teachers, journalists, and historians clashed over what exactly children should learn. These intense debates soon moved beyond Texas

schools and particular historical top-ics. The controversy transcended Texas in two ways. First, the buy-ing power of a state as large as Texas makes their decisions about textbook adoptions nationally significant. Sec-ond, the issues raised there have been replicated in many states and school districts across the country. Under mounting pressure from parents, school boards, and even the federal government to improve student per-formance, public schools increasingly turn to precise standards and objec-tive tests to measure educational effectiveness. Creating those stand-ards, as the Texas case shows, often sparks fierce debates—not just over content and method, but over ideol-ogy and politics as well. Questions about what children should learn lead inextricably to other, more vex-ing matters. Who should determine the content of American history text-books? What values should history teachers emphasize? What larger lessons should history reveal to stu-dents? Who decides? In short, who owns history?

In this chapter you will use evi-dence from the Texas textbook case to understand the difficulty and divi-siveness of defining what is impor-tant in history. You will consider two central questions: What should public school textbooks teach students about history? And who should make that decision?

# Background

How we teach American history and the kind of textbooks adopted in public schools are inextricably linked to the ongoing "culture wars" that have been carried on in the United States since the mid-twentieth century. In the 1960s and 1970s, the culture wars featured a generational conflict pitting, on the one hand, parents who belonged to the "greatest generation" and came of age during the Great Depression and fought valiantly in World War II against, on the other hand, their children who grew up with far more affluence and fewer restrictions. The materialism and conformity they perceived in their parents' generation led many young men and women in the 1960s and 1970s to experiment with different lifestyles and political values. Conflicts over the Civil Rights Movement, the Vietnam War, student protests, and feminism—which often fell along generational lines—shattered the calm that had prevailed in the 1950s, producing a divided and often angry nation.

During the Ronald Reagan presidency (1981–1989), which paralleled the rise to national prominence of a politicized evangelical and conservative Christian movement commonly referred to as the "religious right," the culture wars continued. But in the 1980s, Americans divided more along ideological rather than generational lines. Conservatives pursued what they considered to be moral issues, such as opposing abortion and gay rights, defending gun ownership and traditional gender roles in marriage, and generally seeking to integrate evangelical Christian values into civic life. Liberals emphasized just the opposite: pro-choice politics, stronger gun control laws, the expansion of gay rights, and policing what Thomas Jefferson called "the wall of separation" between religion and government.[1] To a degree, the line between conservative and liberal paralleled loyalties to the two national political parties, the Republicans and the Democrats. However, ideology transcended partisan identity, ethnicity, socio-economic class, generation, and region.

In 1991, James Davison Hunter's *Culture Wars: The Struggle to Define America* explored this deepening political divide, arguing that American politics and culture had become so polarized around contradictory worldviews—perspectives grounded in radically different attitudes toward religion, government, individual rights, and American history—that conservatives and liberals alike saw themselves as battling for the character of the country. In a speech before the 1992 Republican

---

1. Jefferson's often-quoted phrase appeared in a letter to a Baptist congregation in Danbury, Connecticut. The Danbury Baptists had written to compliment Jefferson on his election to the presidency (he had fought for religious freedom in Virginia, and the Baptists benefited from disestablishment) and to recommend he call for a national day of prayer. He declined, stating, "I contemplate with sovereign reverence that act of the whole American people which declared that their Legislature should 'make no law respecting an establishment of religion, or prohibiting the free exercise thereof,' thus building a wall of separation between Church and State."

National Convention, conservative commentator and presidential aspirant Pat Buchanan delivered a fiery address often referred to as the "culture war speech" that captured this conviction. Buchanan, who had challenged incumbent President George Bush during the primary season, asked his supporters to work to reelect President Bush. According to Buchanan, the other choice, Democrats Bill Clinton and Al Gore, represented environmental extremism, radical feminism, homosexual rights, gun restriction, and abortion on demand. Buchanan, a particularly skilled orator, proclaimed, "There is a religious war going on in our country for the soul of America." He closed his speech by calling on conservatives to "take back our cities, and take back our culture, and take back our country."

Over the last twenty years, Americans often viewed national politics through this ideological prism. In the late 1980s and 1990s, the growing influence of cable news with its 24-hour news cycle, created first by CNN and expanded by MSNBC and Fox News, served to heighten partisan attitudes and accentuate ideological differences. The often deliberately divisive and vitriolic rhetoric of talk radio also fanned the ideological flames, as did the Internet blogosphere. Some conservatives complained about the 1992 election of President Bill Clinton, maintaining that without the third-party candidate Ross Perot, Clinton never would have won the presidency. Some liberals responded in kind in 2000, charging that President George W. Bush "stole" Florida's electoral votes and that election. (Neither side succeeded in explaining away the re-election of these two men.) While the election in 2008 of President

Barack Obama was unambiguous both in terms of the Electoral College and the popular vote, the gulf separating conservatives and liberals over issues ranging from diversity to tax policy to the role of religion in civic life certainly did not close.

In the context of this persistent cultural divide, educating our young people has become increasingly politicized. Since at least the 1950s, public schools have born the imprint of America's culture wars. In the 1950s and 1960s, both northern and southern communities fought bitterly over desegregation, with some Americans convinced that integrated public schools could bridge the country's racial divide and others violently opposed to what they termed "race mixing." In the 1970s, busing schoolchildren to offset residential segregation, particularly in urban areas, became the source of fierce conflicts. In the mid-1970s, Boston, Massachusetts, erupted in mass protests and brutal violence. South Boston High School was the scene of dozens of racial incidents, including a near-fatal stabbing in 1974. After the community endured a flurry of violent assaults on buses, students, and citizens, the school temporarily closed. When South Boston reopened, school administrators had installed the first metal detectors in a public school in the country and five hundred police officers stood guard over the students.[2]

2. For more on the crisis in Boston, see Ronald P. Formisano, *Boston Against Busing: Race, Class, and Ethnicity in the 1960s and 1970s*, 2nd edition (Chapel Hill: University of North Carolina Press, 2003); and David Quigley, ed., *The Boston Busing Crisis: A Brief History with Documents* (New York: Bedford/St. Martin's, 2010).

Beginning in the 1980s, a different cultural debate began to take place within the public schools, fueled by the rise of the religious right. For many parents, public schools seemed since the 1960s and 1970s to move in a decidedly secular and liberal direction, both by their perceived disinterest in character instruction and in how particular subjects were taught. (In 1962, the United States Supreme Court, in the case *Engel v. Vitale*, began a series of rulings prohibiting organized prayer in public schools.) Indeed, some parents rejected entirely public education, opting to pay for their children to attend private or religious schools or, in a recent and growing trend, home-school their children. As of 2007, some 1.7 million U.S. children were being homeschooled. This represented nearly 3 percent of America's school-age children and an increase of nearly 75 percent from 1999. Many of the parents homeschooling their children emphasize religious and moral motivations, believing that the public school system offers a lax environment, excessive focus on diversity, and a secular approach to curriculum. Other parents and evangelical Christian activists, however, were determined to reform rather than reject public schools. Using school board elections and court cases, conservatives tried to integrate religious values into school curriculum. Liberals responded with their own agenda, including multicultural awareness, the separation of church and state, and progressive approaches to pedagogy, and the two sides clashed over issues ranging from the recognition of gay and lesbian student organizations to prayer at high school sporting events to library holdings.

In addition to the culture wars, a number of other factors have escalated tensions over public education. Schools are publicly financed. Taxpayers fund public schools, whether or not they have children and whether or not those children receive a public education. Education is compulsory: children start attending school at age five or six, and, on average, they remain under the care of teachers seven hours a day, ten months a year, for twelve years. School, therefore, exerts a tremendous influence in the lives of young people.

Because the stakes seem so high and the expense so great, parents, elected officials, and taxpayers want to get the most out of their public school investment. Creating standards, or benchmarks, to evaluate student learning offers a means of gauging one quantifiable definition of success. In universities, academic standards are determined by departments and colleges, disciplinary fields, and, in some cases, professional organizations. In the public schools, however, the federal government, individual states, municipalities, and boards of education set standards. In this model, school ratings (and sometimes teaching positions and funding) are connected to learning outcomes—that is, test scores. The federal program No Child Left Behind (NCLB) provides a recent example of government—in this case, the federal government—creating educational standards, administering evaluations, and apportioning funding. President George W. Bush proposed NCLB shortly after he took office in 2001, and the program, which seeks to raise standards and ensure accountability, won wide bipartisan support in Congress. The standards-based approach of NCLB is not without controversy and critics, including many experienced teachers who lament "teaching to the test." But the program has resulted in a number of successes, including improvements in reading and mathematics scores. States and individual school boards have likewise tried to create higher educational standards to boost student performance.

Setting content standards inadvertently plays into America's ideological divide, as the questions inevitably arise: What exactly should children learn? Who sets the standards?

With the exception of religion, few subjects lend themselves to the culture war divisions more than history. After all, how one understands the American past shapes how we view both our personal identity and sense of patriotism. Potentially divisive questions abound:

- How important was religion in America's history?
- Does the American past prize individual freedom or a shared commitment to community responsibility?
- Has the United States been an "exceptional" beacon of economic opportunity for all or a country where people and resources have been exploited by the few at the expense of the many?
- Who in our past should students learn about? Who should they idealize?

The lessons and values parents, students, teachers, and citizens find in the United States' past also reveal which side of the culture wars appears to be "winning" at any given time. As

a result, over the past 50 years, teaching history, which has always been politically important and often sharply debated, has become an increasingly politicized act.

One critical battleground in the ongoing ideological contest over the meaning of our past can be observed in the selection of history textbooks by public schools. That process differs thoroughly from how your college history textbook came to be adopted. For public elementary and secondary schools, textbook development involves more bureaucracy, politics, and, in recent years, controversy. Debates over public school textbooks reveal both the subjectivity of historical interpretation and the ways in which current political and religious concerns intrude into the classroom. The 2010 debate in Texas over that state's standards for adoptable history textbooks offers a powerful case in point.

By law, the Texas Educational Agency (TEA), the state's public school system, revises the curriculum for social studies every 10 years. The process begins with a panel of teachers proposing standards for the curriculum, involving courses in history, sociology, and economics, from elementary to high school. Fifteen elected representatives to the Texas State Board of Education (SBOE), serving four-year terms of office and representing various regions of the state, review those proposed standards. The SBOE makes the final decisions about curriculum standards. Once approved, those standards then become a template for publishers hoping to tap into the Texas textbook market. While individual school districts in

Texas choose which particular textbooks to adopt, they must select from a state-wide list of "conforming" books. In order to make that list, books must meet the standards set by the SBOE, which also reviews every history textbook submitted for potential adoption. Texas is one of twenty-two states that make textbook decisions on the state level.

The TEA buys books for over 4.7 million students. This creates a huge incentive for publishers and authors to comply with the standards set by the Texas SBOE. Given Texas' buying power, their decisions about interpretation and content in history textbooks exert a significant influence over the national market. And SBOE members exercise a critical shaping influence over what themes, individuals, and interpretations history teachers accentuate—and which ones they downplay.

The SBOE in Texas is an elected body, so personal, political, and religious perspectives on what is important in history can influence curricular decisions and textbook development. In response to the criticism that he seemed to be imposing his political and religious views on school children, SBOE member and dentist Don McLeroy, a self-identified fundamentalist Christian, replied: "We are a political body, we have to make political decisions."[3] McLeroy went on to note that every time he ran for the board, he spoke openly and consistently about his views. His constituents knew exactly where he stood on history and science education; McLeroy maintained that he was representing their collective will. (In March 2010, McLeroy narrowly lost his bid for reelection to the Texas State Board of Education in the Republican Party primary.)

Scholars, educators, and journalists across the United States quickly picked up on the curricular debates in Texas. They saw the larger issues at stake, and, in many instances, they noticed parallels to similar ideological struggles in their states and locales. As one editorial writer in Los Angeles cautioned, "Before Californians look down their noses, though, they should consider the rules governing this state's textbooks. The state regulates the portrayal of genders, minority groups, the elderly and the disabled by requiring proportional representation that also cannot show any group in a negative light."[4] Texas, then, certainly does not stand alone in entangling politics with academic lessons. Rather, the controversies in Texas over social studies standards and history textbooks have resonated across the country because they are simply the latest manifestation of a longstanding and troubling ideological divide in our nation. At play is not only the profound question, "Who owns history?" but also profoundly contentious disputes over who we have been as a nation and what we want the next generation to become.

---

3. The March 2010 interview with Don McLeroy on *Nightline* can be viewed at www.abcnews.com.

4. *Los Angeles Times*, March 28, 2010.

✦

# The Method

As you arrive near the end of your class, hopefully you have learned some important analytical lessons that transcend the study of American history. In particular, the chapters in this book have aimed to reveal to you the complexity of the past, the necessity of reasoned consideration of a wide range of issues, and the intellectual value of open-minded enquiry. By now, you have practiced being an historian, using a host of different sources and methodologies. As you have seen this academic term, the past gets a lot messier—and a lot more interesting—when you move beyond facts and dates. The skills you have cultivated in this course should give you richer insight into understanding contemporary debates. This chapter tests that skill set.

When you read this chapter's documents, do not focus on whether you agree or disagree with the specific points made by the authors. Concentrate instead on understanding the larger issues at stake and the values and conflicts revealed in the writings. In other words, analyze the context of the debate and the consequences of decisions. Avoid getting personally invested in the controversy. Be a historian, not an advocate.

Keep three interrelated sets of questions in mind:

1. What are the main articulated issues at stake in the Texas textbook debate? What are the major disagreements as regards content? Where do people disagree over process?

2. What are the larger, sometimes unarticulated issues at stake? What do these issues suggest to you about the perceived purpose of history education? Are proponents on both sides in fact arguing about the present rather than people and issues in the past?

3. Why do particular groups believe themselves best suited to determine history content for the public school system? Evaluate the merits and the limits of various perspectives: teachers, elected officials, educational experts, professional scholars, parents. What claims does each group make to determine what school children should learn about the American past?

Of course, the Texas case requires not only understanding, but also action. Only once you have thoughtfully considered all that is at stake will you be equipped to offer thoughtful answers to the central questions in this chapter. After *individually* considering the issues above, in conversation with your classmates, see if you can *collectively* decide: What should children learn about American history? Who should decide?

# The Evidence

## THE TEXAS PUBLIC EDUCATION SYSTEM

Source 1 from *Texas Education Agency Mission and Responsibilities*, Copyright © Texas Education Agency, 2002. Reproduced by permission.

## 1. Texas Education Agency Mission and Responsibilities.

### Mission
The mission of the Texas Education Agency is to provide leadership, guidance, and resources to help schools meet the educational needs of all students.

### Composition
The Texas Education Agency (TEA) is comprised of the commissioner of education and agency staff. The TEA and the State Board of Education (SBOE) guide and monitor activities and programs related to public education in Texas. The SBOE consists of 15 elected members representing different regions of the state. One member is appointed chair by the governor.

### Roles & Responsibilities
Located in Austin, Texas, at 1701 N. Congress Ave., the TEA is the administrative unit for primary and secondary public education. Under the leadership of the commissioner of education, the TEA:

- manages the textbook adoption process;
- oversees development of the statewide curriculum;
- administers the statewide assessment program;
- administers a data collection system on public school students, staff, and finances;
- rates school districts under the statewide accountability system;
- operates research and information programs;
- monitors for compliance with federal guidelines; and
- serves as a fiscal agent for the distribution of state and federal funds.

The TEA operational costs are supported by both state and federal funds.

Source 2 accessed at http://www.statutes.legis.state.tx.us/Docs/ED/htm/ED.31.htm.

## 2. Excerpts from the Texas State Education Code.

Sec. 31.001. FREE TEXTBOOKS. Textbooks selected for use in the public schools shall be furnished without cost to the students attending those schools.

Sec. 31.022. TEXTBOOK REVIEW AND ADOPTION.

(a) The State Board of Education shall adopt a review and adoption cycle for textbooks for elementary grade levels, including pre-kindergarten, and secondary grade levels, for each subject in the required curriculum under Section 28.002.

(b) The board shall organize the cycle for subjects in the foundation curriculum so that not more than one-sixth of the textbooks for subjects in the foundation curriculum are reviewed each year. The board shall adopt rules to provide for a full and complete investigation of textbooks for each subject in the foundation curriculum at least every six years. The adoption of textbooks for a subject in the foundation curriculum may be extended beyond the six-year period only if the content of textbooks for a subject is sufficiently current.

(c) The board shall adopt rules to provide for a full and complete investigation of textbooks for each subject in the enrichment curriculum on a cycle the board considers appropriate.

(d) At least 24 months before the beginning of the school year for which textbooks for a particular subject and grade level will be purchased under the review and adoption cycle adopted by the board, the board shall publish notice of the review and adoption cycle for those textbooks.

(e) The board shall designate a request for production of textbooks in a subject area and grade level by the school year in which the textbooks are intended to be made available in classrooms and not by the school year in which the board makes the request for production.

(f) The board shall amend any request for production issued for the purchase of textbooks to conform to the textbook funding levels provided by the General Appropriations Act for the year of implementation.

Sec. 31.023. TEXTBOOK LISTS.

(a) For each subject and grade level, the State Board of Education shall adopt two lists of textbooks. The conforming list includes each textbook submitted for the subject and grade level that meets applicable physical specifications adopted by the State Board of Education and contains material covering each element of the essential knowledge and skills of the subject and grade level in the student version of the textbook, as well as in the teacher version of the textbook, as determined by the State Board of Education under

Section 28.002 and adopted under Section 31.024. The nonconforming list includes each textbook submitted for the subject and grade level that:

(1) meets applicable physical specifications adopted by the State Board of Education;

(2) contains material covering at least half, but not all, of the elements of the essential knowledge and skills of the subject and grade level in the student version of the textbook, as well as in the teacher version of the textbook; and

(3) is adopted under Section 31.024.

(b) Each textbook on a conforming or nonconforming list must be free from factual errors.

Sec. 31.024. ADOPTION BY STATE BOARD OF EDUCATION.

(a) By majority vote, the State Board of Education shall:

(1) place each submitted textbook on a conforming or nonconforming list; or

(2) reject a textbook submitted for placement on a conforming or nonconforming list.

(b) Not later than December 1 of the year preceding the school year for which the textbooks for a particular subject and grade level will be purchased under the cycle adopted by the board under Section 31.022, the board shall provide the lists of adopted textbooks to each school district. Each nonconforming list must include the reasons an adopted textbook is not eligible for the conforming list.

## ASSESSING THE STANDARDS

Source 3 from Peter Marshall, President, Peter Marshall Ministries, *Review of Current Social Studies TEKS*, Copyright © 2010 by Peter Marshall. Reproduced by permission from the author.

### 3. An Evangelical Minister Evaluates TEKS (Texas Essential Knowledge and Skills).

*[In 2009, the Texas Board of Education sought outside evaluations of their existing social studies curriculum standards. Their website posts the evaluations of the six individuals consulted: two evangelical ministers and four scholars, the latter group representing the fields of history, government, and education. Reverend Peter Marshall's evaluation is excerpted below. Transcriptions of his entire assessment and those of the other evaluators are publicly available through the TEA Website.]*

Feedback on the current K -12 Social Studies TEKS

To: Monica Martinez

Division of Curriculum

Dear Ms. Martinez et al:

I have divided my comments into two sections, the first dealing with general concerns, and the second listing individual entries that seem deficient.

Section A

As I began my review of the current K-12 social studies TEKS I expected to find that the format of the TEKS was acceptable, and that I would only be recommending relatively minor changes in the content of the eight strands for the various grade levels. Unfortunately, that has not proven to be the case. . . .

Additionally, the trend in American education has been to study American culture in comparison to other cultures around the world, which leads to the rejection of the idea that there is anything unique or exceptional about American civilization. Yet, various Texas state laws concerning education correctly call for a teaching emphasis on patriotism, citizenship, and the free-enterprise system. Fulfilling these educational mandates in the State of Texas will require the students to learn why America is the greatest country in the world, and why they should be proud to be an American. . . .

Finally, the social studies skills strand affords no direction whatsoever for the textbook publishers or the teachers. Take, for example, the entries in Chapter I 13. 24.

Grade 8, (31). It says that "the student communicates in written, oral, and visual forms." [No kidding?]. "The student is expected to: (A) use social studies terminology correctly." [And just exactly, pray tell, what is "social studies terminology"?] (B) "use standard grammar, spelling, sentence structure, and punctuation." [That is usually covered under something called "English"]. (C) "transfer information from one medium to another . . . using computer software as appropriate" [these Jr. High students learned to do that 5 or 6 grades ago!]. (D) "create written, oral, and visual presentations of social studies information." [This is so vague as to be completely useless]. . . .

Besides the formatting of the TEKS there are other important general concerns. Nowhere to be found throughout the document is there any mention of the motivations of the discoverers, settlers, and founders of America. Reading through the TEKS as they are currently constituted could give the impression that history just "happens," that random impersonal forces control events. That is, of course, the false teaching of Marxism—i.e. that the "dictatorship of the proletariat" is inevitable. However, history is actually the results of decisions made by individual human beings—people make history. And their decisions and actions are a product of their belief systems, their worldview. Ideas shape history. There is always a context, a reason for the decisions made and the actions taken.

Studying history this way—telling the stories of real people and what motivated the decisions they made, and then what happened as a result of those decisions—gives the present-day student the exciting idea that he or she can influence the course of history. And that is one of the main things we are aiming at in the education of our children. We want them to reach young adulthood with the vision that they can be world changers!

Therefore, it is imperative that the textbooks and the teachers handle the teaching of history by considering the motivations of those who made American history. In our American situation it is indisputable that the motivational role of the Bible and the Christian faith was paramount in the settling of most of the original 13 colonies, notably Massachusetts, Connecticut, Rhode Island, New Hampshire, Pennsylvania, Delaware, Maryland, and Virginia. The settling of America was not "accidental" but purposeful. For example, the Pilgrims were motivated to risk their lives in coming to America because of their Christian faith, and their desire to propagate that faith in the American wilderness. Even small children need to understand that the Pilgrims were not just "people who liked to take long journeys in ships" (as one elementary history text puts it), but rather a group of people who believed in God and tried to live by the teachings of the Bible. Pilgrim Governor William Bradford made it clear that "they had a great hope and an inward zeal . . . of laying some good foundation . . . for the propagating and advancing of the Gospel of the Kingdom of Christ in those remote parts of the world." They were not refugees thrown up on the rocky shores of New England, but missionaries with a strong sense of call and purpose. They knew exactly what they were about.

When the New England Confederation was formed in 1643 between the Puritan colonies of New Haven, Connecticut, Plymouth, and Massachusetts Bay, they said "we all came into these parts with one and the same end and aim, namely, to advance the kingdom of our Lord Jesus Christ."

Additionally, William Penn noted that "The acquisition and government of the Colony (that bears his name today) was so to serve the truth and the people of the Lord, that an example may be set to the nations."

Similarly, the Founding Fathers were men who believed that government must be based on the God-given inalienable rights of life, liberty, and the pursuit of happiness that belong to all people. Without understanding their motivations, it is impossible to understand why they resisted the tyranny of Great Britain.

Countless other examples from colonial America may be adduced, but the point is that the discovery, settling, and founding of the colonies happened because of the Biblical worldviews of those involved. Only when this is taken into account can America's founding be properly understood. And, if the cause and effect relationship between people's worldview and their actions is made an integral element of the teaching of history, then the study of American history can become *inspirational* for our students in regard to the formation of their own lives, rather than simply *informational*. . . .

History should never be taught as a continuous progression of names, dates, and places, and events, but rather as a narrative. What students at all grade levels will remember best is stories, so the facts of history should be interwoven with narratives. For the lower grade levels, the story would be the main element of the history lesson. In the upper grade levels, history would be examined more analytically, but the stories would still play an important role in the teaching. At any grade level, a good history teacher is a good storyteller.

Second, it is a matter of great concern that there is no mention here of the foundational documents of American history —particularly the Mayflower Compact, the Massachusetts Body of Liberties, the Declaration of Independence, the Articles of Confederation, the Constitution, and the Northwest Ordinance. And there are others that should be included. While the TEKS (2) quoted above may not have been intended to be an exhaustive list of supplementary materials, and while some of the founding documents are mentioned briefly elsewhere, the centrality of these foundational documents in our history should be taught to all students, even those in elementary school. Further, since study of these documents is mandated by Texas State law during Freedom Week, the introduction to each major section of the TEKS should explicitly name them and underscore the importance of their use in the classroom. In this way, even young students will learn that Americans believe in a government of laws, and not one dictated by the whims and passions of men. This will, of course, begin to lay a proper foundation for their understanding of citizenship. . . .

At all levels of education, K-12, attention must be paid to the basic concepts that underlie the American tradition of constitutional law government. Further, it is impossible for students to understand American civilization if they do not learn the sources of those concepts. For example, the separation of powers in our Federal government is rooted in the Founding Fathers' clear understanding of the sinfulness of man. . . . . many other Founding Fathers believed that because of man's sinfulness, no one is to be entrusted with the absolute power of government. Hence, they rejected monarchy and gave us the separation of powers in our form of government.

Another foundational concept that reflects the Biblical influence on American government is the consent of the governed. To the last man, the Founding Fathers believed that no one has the right to govern another human being without that person's consent. As Lincoln said, that is "the sheet anchor of American government." Government by the consent of the governed found its earliest expression in our history in the Mayflower Compact of 1620, when the Pilgrim elders signed a one-page document that stated that they "freely covenanted together to form a civil body politic." But the roots of government by the consent of the governed can be traced all the way back to the Israelites in the Sinai wilderness under Moses. When he had read the laws of God to the people, they gave their consent to be governed by these laws (Exodus 24:3, 7).

In point of fact, American history cannot be understood without appreciating the importance of the word "covenant." From the earliest days of New England, the settlers were concerned to live up to the tenets of their Christian faith, which required them to "love their neighbors as themselves." Herein lay the only hope for a just society, for if we are not concerned for the welfare of our neighbors, justice is not possible. In fact, we make a mockery of the word justice if there is no civic concern, no commitment to care for others. Our second President, John Adams, in an address to the Massachusetts militia in 1798, said "Our Constitution was made only for a moral and religious people. It is wholly inadequate to the government of any other." In order for the Constitution to "work," then, we must be civic-minded—we must care for the rights and welfare of others. The Founding Fathers' Biblical worldview taught them that human beings were by nature self-centered, so they believed that the supernatural influence of the Spirit of God was needed to free us from ourselves so that we can care for our neighbors. That is what Adams means when he says that the Constitution can only work for a moral and religious people.

In light of the overwhelming historical evidence of the influence of the Christian faith in the founding of America, it is simply not up to acceptable academic standards that throughout the social studies TEKS I could find only one reference to the role of religion in America's past. . . .

Section B

I would also like to call attention to specific TEKS entries that seem deficient and should be rewritten. Unfortunately, many of the ones concerning history seem to be compiled by someone more concerned to be "politically correct" than to accurately portray American history. Out of many that could be listed, here is a sampling:

- 113.2 Kindergarten. (11) Culture. The student is expected to (B) "identify differences among people." This is precisely the kind of thing that can be better covered under geography.
- 113.3 Grade 1. (4) History. The student is expected to (A) "identify contributions of historical figures such as Henrietta King and Thurgood Marshall who have influenced," etc. These two selections are not strong enough examples in light of the multiplicity of persons who have impacted American history. Harriet Tubman and Sam Houston would be better choices, and there are hundreds of others.
- 113.3 Grade 2. (4) History. Again, in regard to (B) Amelia Earhart was an aviator, and not particularly an example of "inventiveness." People like Cyrus McCormick and Alexander Graham Bell would be better choices.
- 113.3 Grade 2. (11) Government. The student is expected to: "identify some governmental services in the community such as libraries, schools, and parks," etc., etc. These examples are not as good as: the fire and rescue department, the police, and school buses.
- 113.3 Grade 2. (14) Citizenship. (C) "Explain how selected customs, symbols, and celebrations reflect an American love of individualism, inventiveness, and freedom." It would be far better to have this read: "Explain how

selected customs, symbols, and celebrations reflect American beliefs and values such as freedom, love of country, and respect for the law."

- 113.3 Grade 3. (2) History. (A). "Identify reasons people have formed communities, including a need for security, law, and material well-being." This is not history—this is sociology, and should not be in a history unit.

- 113.7 Grade 5. (b) (1) History. (B) "describe the accomplishments of significant colonial leaders such as Anne Hutchinson, William Penn, John Smith, and Roger Williams." Anne Hutchinson does not belong in the company of these eminent gentlemen. She was certainly not a significant colonial leader, and didn't accomplish anything except getting herself exiled from the Massachusetts Bay Colony for making trouble.

- 113.7 Grade 5 (19) Citizenship (C). "Identify significant individuals such as Cesar Chavez and Benjamin Franklin who modeled active participation in the democratic process." To have Cesar Chavez listed next to Ben Franklin is ludicrous. Chavez is hardly the kind of role model that ought to be held up to our children as someone worthy of emulation.

- 113.7 Grade 5 (24) Science and technology and society. (A) Describe the contributions of famous inventors and scientists such as Neil Armstrong, John J. Audubon; Benjamin Banneker, Clarence Birdseye, George Washington Carver, Thomas Edison, and Carl Sagan." This is a rather pathetic list. The only ones worthy of inclusion are George Washington Carver and Thomas Edison. What about Thomas Watson, the Wright brothers, Henry Ford, Alexander Graham Bell?

- 113.24. Grade 8 (13) Economics. (A) "Identify economic differences among different regions of the United States." This belongs in geography. (B) "Explain reasons for the development of the plantation system, the growth of the slave trade, and the spread of slavery." This belongs in history. (C) "Analyze the causes and effects of economic differences among different regions of the United States at selected times in U.S. history." This belongs in geography. These are further examples of why a separate strand for economics is not really justified.

- 113.35. United States Government. (14) Citizenship. (C) "Analyze issues addressed in selected cases such as *Engel v. Vitale, Miranda v. Arizona,*" etc., etc. A glaring omission here is *Roe v. Wade,* which has arguably more impacted American life than any other Supreme Court decision in the twentieth century.

*[In early 2010, the SBOE revealed the proposed changes to the social studies curriculum. A flurry of debate ensued. A full rendering of the curriculum draft, with its extensive revisions, is too long to include here, but it can be viewed on the TEA Website (www .tea.state.tx.us).]*

## 4. A Texas Teacher Weighs in on the Curriculum Revision.

"The Texas State Board of Education and History Standards: A Teacher's Perspective"

By Ron Briley
Mr. Briley is Assistant Headmaster, Sandia Preparatory School.

As a young boy growing up in the Texas Panhandle in the 1950s and 1960s, I was indoctrinated into the myths of the Alamo and Texas exceptionalism, although I do not recall learning much about the right of Texas to secede from the Union.[5] Despite learning more about Texas high school football than the contributions of blacks and Hispanics to the making of the state, the conservative orientation of the curriculum did not prevent me from questioning the Vietnam War and embracing the Civil Rights Movement as a first generation college student. And I have confidence that the teachers and students of the Texas public school system will be able to rise above and see through the narrow and partisan history standards adopted by the Texas State Board of Education which have drawn the ire of many historians throughout the nation.

Unfortunately, this debate over standards often rages with little input from history teachers who are expected to implement mandated curriculum. This attitude derives from a fundamental lack of respect in our culture for teachers. Thus, it is assumed that dentists and real estate agents are better equipped to make curricular decisions than are history educators.

Of course, I must confess that I was not too impressed with my high school history teachers, who were primarily football coaches. Class activities were limited to outlining the textbook and preparing reports from *Encyclopedia Britannica*. One could either take a test on Friday or choose the Southwest Conference trivia option. But in defense of these coaches, it should be pointed out that their employment was dependent not upon their history knowledge, but rather their won/loss record on the football field. Fortunately, even Texas has moved somewhat beyond the stereotypical high school football coach as history teacher.

There are also some credential issues with history educators as often a teacher with a social studies degree may be teaching American history with as few as six college hours of history. Nevertheless, there is a strong movement to enhance history education around the nation, led by organizations such as the National Council for History Education, Society for History Education, World History Association, American Historical Association, and Organization of American Historians. The federally-financed Teaching American History grants provide excellent models of

5. This is a reference to Texas Governor Rick Perry's 2009 suggestion that his state might leave the United States.

collaboration between university professors and teachers in the schools. Opportunities for summer history education are also available through the National Endowment for the Humanities and the Gilder Lehrman Institute.

Perhaps the biggest problem for organizations such as the Texas State Board of Education, however, is a fundamental lack of understanding regarding history as an academic discipline. There is a popular assumption that history must be easy to teach, as it is an unchanging body of knowledge which does not require the analytical rigor of science and mathematics. Yet history is an exercise in interpretation in which we filter the past through the lens of the evolving present. Thus, the Civil Rights Movement and feminism have encouraged a more inclusive history that considers the contribution of women, Latino/as, Native Americans, African Americans, Asian Americans, and Muslim Americans to the building of America. The question is not simply which facts, but whose facts. It is a matter of perspective. The history of Western settlement may differ depending upon whether the story is told from the point of view of a pioneer or Native American. In fact, it seems to be the concept of multiple perspectives that most frightens those seeking to impose absolute standards upon the schools.

For example, it is not unreasonable that consideration be given to the role played by groups such as the National Rifle Association and "moral majority" in the 1980s resurgence of conservatism, but it would be difficult to tell the whole story of American politics in the late twentieth century without also including Ted Kennedy. Likewise, it would be a serious omission to discuss the rise of industry in the late nineteenth and early twentieth centuries without taking into account the countervailing power of Eugene Debs and the Socialist Party, which enjoyed strong support in Texas and Oklahoma before the First World War. The discipline offers an excellent opportunity for teachers to instill critical thinking by encouraging students to reach their own conclusions based upon research and analysis of primary documents and sources.

It is the fostering of critical thinking to which the Texas State Board seems most opposed. Rather than encouraging students to investigate the role of religion in the forging of the American nation, students are instructed to accept that the founders envisioned a Christian nation. According to the Texas standards, the Second Amendment is to be treated as an absolute, rather than presenting alternative interpretations and letting students reach their own conclusions. After all, the First Amendment freedom of speech is not recognized by the courts as absolute. It is important to examine the role of Ronald Reagan in ending the Cold War, but it is equally essential to appreciate the emergence of Mikhail Gorbachev in the Soviet Union, for American history must be placed within the global context in which students will be living during the twenty-first century.

Perhaps the issue boils down to the traditional nostrum that the purpose of history is to instill patriotism in the youth. Yet to assume their duties as citizens in a democracy, our students must learn to think critically and question the conventional wisdom. It is this type of engaged citizenry, rather than rote patriotism, which will propel the United States forward in the next century.

And this is the type of teaching which I attempt to offer my students. I tend to align myself more with the Howard Zinn[6] school of historiography and an emphasis upon history from the bottom up. It is, however, a perspective which I share with my students, urging them to challenge me with differing points of analysis. I view it as my charge to present students with multiple perspectives. Thus, when we study the New Deal, it is crucial for them to understand the concept of a social safety net program such as Social Security. It is equally important to recognize that the liberalism of the New Deal was questioned by conservatives who believed that the welfare state was undermining American individualism, while critics on the left insist that Roosevelt missed an opportunity to fundamentally alter the face of American capitalism.

If a teacher is going to foster multiple perspectives, one must be tolerant of opposing interpretations. One young man in my class took exception to the caricature of John D. Rockefeller as a robber baron. He wrote an outstanding research paper of approximately twenty-five pages defending the oil tycoon. I composed a five page rebuttal of my own, but he certainly deserved an A for his scholarship. In fact, some of my most memorable teaching moments arise from classroom debate in which students, with whom I disagree, raise challenging questions. This dialogue keeps me on my toes and makes me a better teacher. I hope that my classroom models a civil discourse which is all too often missing in the halls of Congress.

Yet, it is this type of vibrant democracy which the Texas State Board of Education seeks to stifle. For over thirty years, I have taught American history in an independent school, and I recognize that many of my public school colleagues are under greater pressure than I to adhere to state standards. Nevertheless, I have faith that dedicated teachers and inquiring young minds will find ways to subvert the antidemocratic directives of the Texas board. After all, the real teaching and learning begins when the classroom door closes.

## NEWSPAPER COVERAGE OF THE TEXAS CURRICULUM DEBATE

Source 5 from the *Austin American-Statesman*, March 11, 2010, "Politics, sex, religion are all fair game at education board meeting," by Kate Alexander. Copyright © 2010 *The Austin American-Statesman*. All rights reserved. Reproduced by permission.

## 5. The *Austin American-Statesman* Reports on SBOE Deliberations.

### Sex, money, religion and race.

State Board of Education members discussed it all Thursday, delivering a riveting drama as they trudged through another day of debate about social studies curriculum standards.

---

6. Zinn was a distinguished historian and committed civil rights activist who authored *A People's History of the United States*, an extraordinarily popular book that looked at history from the bottom up, emphasizing the experiences of Indians, slaves, laboring classes, and women.

The ideological divide on the 15-member [board] broke into a wide chasm by early evening, prompting board member Mary Helen Berlanga, D-Corpus Christi, to storm out of the meeting.

"I've had it. This is it. I'm leaving for the evening," Berlanga said. The board, she said, is pretending this is "white America, Hispanics don't exist."

Berlanga has focused almost exclusively on adding the names of minority historical figures to the standards. Not all of her suggestions have been embraced, and she said the board was preparing to undo many of her efforts.

"I've never seen a rewrite like this," said Berlanga, a board member since 1982. "This is a step backwards."

Board member David Bradley, R-Beaumont, characterized Berlanga's outburst as "poor boardmanship."

"Losing is hell," Bradley said.

The standards under consideration will serve as the framework for history, government and economics textbooks and lessons for the 4.7 million Texas public school students. And there are controversies on seemingly every page.

Board member Barbara Cargill, R-The Woodlands, objected to a standard for a high school sociology course that addressed the difference between sex and gender. It was eliminated in a 9-to-6 vote.

She worried that a discussion of that issue would lead students into the world of "transvestites, transsexuals and who knows what else."

"This is very, very inappropriate for high school students," Cargill said.

But board member Mavis Knight, D-Dallas, countered that it was naïve to think high school students would not know that some of their classmates were gay, bisexual or transgender.

"It is no secret to them, so you might as well bring it out into the open and discuss it," Knight said.

In a wide-ranging debate, the board members grappled with the right to bear arms, the gold standard, hip-hop and genocide in the Darfur region of Sudan.

They also polished up references to the American "free enterprise" economic system and removed most mentions of "capitalism," a word that board member Ken Mercer, R-San Antonio, said has a negative connotation.

The ideological tensions on the board came into sharp focus when Knight introduced a proposal that would emphasize the U.S. founders' yearning for a separation between church and state.

"We know that religion was one of the major influences but not the only influence as to the founding of our country," Knight said, defending her proposal to change the standards for a high school U.S. government course.

Board member Cynthia Dunbar, R-Richmond, shot back, saying that she and other conservatives on the board have been unfairly criticized for trying to inject their religious views into the standards.

"No we're not, but nor do we want our religious history to be tainted and to be drawn from a viewpoint that is not historically accurate," said Dunbar, a constitutional law professor at Regent University, which was founded by the Rev. Pat Robertson.

Knight's proposal failed.

Kathy Miller, president of the Texas Freedom Network, said the board's 10 Republicans had voted to "reject the most fundamental constitutional protection for religious freedom in America today: the principle that government may not disfavor or promote any religion over all others."

The Texas Freedom Network bills itself as a watchdog of the religious right.

The vote also drew a heated objection from the Anti-Defamation League, an organization that fights against anti-Semitism.

"The leaders who created our system of government were all too familiar with religious oppression and its consequences, and that influenced the principles on which they founded this nation," said Karen Gross, the Austin community director for the organization. "We believe that's a critical part of American history which Texas school children should learn and understand."

Jonathan Saenz, director of legislative affairs for the conservative Liberty Institute, heralded the victories of the board's conservative bloc.

"Thus far, the liberal efforts to infiltrate, indoctrinate and saturate our social studies with narrow ideology have failed," Saenz said.

A preliminary vote on the standards is scheduled for today, with a final decision in May.

## THE NATIONAL MEDIA COVERS THE TEXAS CONTROVERSY

Source 6 From *The New York Times*, March 13, 2010, "Conservatives on Texas Panel Carry the Day on Curriculum Change," by James C. McKinley, Jr., A10, copyright © 3/13/2010 *The New York Times*. All rights served. Used by permission and protected by the Copyright Laws of the United States. The printing, copying, redistribution, or retransmission of the material without express written permission is prohibited.

## 6. *The New York Times*.

AUSTIN, Tex. — After three days of turbulent meetings, the Texas Board of Education on Friday approved a social studies curriculum that will put a conservative stamp on history and economics textbooks, stressing the superiority of American capitalism, questioning the Founding Fathers' commitment to a purely secular government and presenting Republican political philosophies in a more positive light.

The vote was 10 to 5 along party lines, with all the Republicans on the board voting for it.

The board, whose members are elected, has influence beyond Texas because the state is one of the largest buyers of textbooks. In the digital age, however, that influence has diminished as technological advances have made it possible for publishers to tailor books to individual states.

In recent years, board members have been locked in an ideological battle between a bloc of conservatives who question Darwin's theory of evolution and believe the Founding Fathers were guided by Christian principles, and a handful of Democrats and moderate Republicans who have fought to preserve the teaching of Darwinism and the separation of church and state.

Since January, Republicans on the board have passed more than 100 amendments to the 120-page curriculum standards affecting history, sociology and economics courses from elementary to high school. The standards were proposed by a panel of teachers.

"We are adding balance," said Dr. Don McLeroy, the leader of the conservative faction on the board, after the vote. "History has already been skewed. Academia is skewed too far to the left."

Battles over what to put in science and history books have taken place for years in the 20 states where state boards must adopt textbooks, most notably in California and Texas. But rarely in recent history has a group of conservative board members left such a mark on a social studies curriculum.

Efforts by Hispanic board members to include more Latino figures as role models for the state's large Hispanic population were consistently defeated, prompting one member, Mary Helen Berlanga, to storm out of a meeting late Thursday night, saying, "They can just pretend this is a white America and Hispanics don't exist."

"They are going overboard, they are not experts, they are not historians," she said. "They are rewriting history, not only of Texas but of the United States and the world."

The curriculum standards will now be published in a state register, opening them up for 30 days of public comment. A final vote will be taken in May, but given the Republican dominance of the board, it is unlikely that many changes will be made.

The standards, reviewed every decade, serve as a template for textbook publishers, who must come before the board next year with drafts of their books. The board's makeup will have changed by then because Dr. McLeroy lost in a primary this month to a more moderate Republican, and two others—one Democrat and one conservative Republican—announced they were not seeking re-election.

There are seven members of the conservative bloc on the board, but they are often joined by one of the other three Republicans on crucial votes. There were no historians, sociologists or economists consulted at the meetings, though some members of the conservative bloc held themselves out as experts on certain topics.

The conservative members maintain that they are trying to correct what they see as a liberal bias among the teachers who proposed the curriculum. To that end, they made dozens of minor changes aimed at calling into question, among other things, concepts like the separation of church and state and the secular nature of the American Revolution.

"I reject the notion by the left of a constitutional separation of church and state," said David Bradley, a conservative from Beaumont who works in real estate. "I have $1,000 for the charity of your choice if you can find it in the Constitution."

They also included a plank to ensure that students learn about "the conservative resurgence of the 1980s and 1990s, including Phyllis Schlafly, the Contract With America, the Heritage Foundation, the Moral Majority and the National Rifle Association."

Dr. McLeroy, a dentist by training, pushed through a change to the teaching of the civil rights movement to ensure that students study the violent philosophy of the Black Panthers in addition to the nonviolent approach of the Rev. Dr. Martin Luther King Jr. He also made sure that textbooks would mention the votes in Congress on civil rights legislation, which Republicans supported.

"Republicans need a little credit for that," he said. "I think it's going to surprise some students."

Mr. Bradley won approval for an amendment saying students should study "the unintended consequences" of the Great Society legislation, affirmative action and Title IX legislation. He also won approval for an amendment stressing that Germans and Italians as well as Japanese were interned in the United States during World War II, to counter the idea that the internment of Japanese was motivated by racism.

Other changes seem aimed at tamping down criticism of the right. Conservatives passed one amendment, for instance, requiring that the history of McCarthyism include "how the later release of the Venona papers confirmed suspicions of communist infiltration in U.S. government." The Venona papers were transcripts of some 3,000 communications between the Soviet Union and its agents in the United States.

Mavis B. Knight, a Democrat from Dallas, introduced an amendment requiring that students study the reasons "the founding fathers protected religious freedom in America by barring the government from promoting or disfavoring any particular religion above all others."

It was defeated on a party-line vote.

After the vote, Ms. Knight said, "The social conservatives have perverted accurate history to fulfill their own agenda."

In economics, the revisions add Milton Friedman and Friedrich von Hayek, two champions of free-market economic theory, among the usual list of economists to be studied, like Adam Smith, Karl Marx and John Maynard Keynes. They also replaced the word "capitalism" throughout their texts with the "free-enterprise system."

"Let's face it, capitalism does have a negative connotation," said one conservative member, Terri Leo. "You know, 'capitalist pig!' "

In the field of sociology, another conservative member, Barbara Cargill, won passage of an amendment requiring the teaching of "the importance of personal responsibility for life choices" in a section on teenage suicide, dating violence, sexuality, drug use and eating disorders.

"The topic of sociology tends to blame society for everything," Ms. Cargill said.

Even the course on world history did not escape the board's scalpel.

Cynthia Dunbar, a lawyer from Richmond who is a strict constitutionalist and thinks the nation was founded on Christian beliefs, managed to cut Thomas Jefferson from a list of figures whose writings inspired revolutions in the late 18th century and 19th century, replacing him with St. Thomas Aquinas, John Calvin and William Blackstone. (Jefferson is not well liked among conservatives on the board because he coined the term "separation between church and state.")

His reference was to a bloc of social conservative Republicans on the board, including chairwoman Gail Lowe, who have rejected many of the recommendations of teachers and academics who were appointed to write new curriculum standards for Texas schools—subject to board approval. Perry appointed Lowe as chairwoman in July.

The changes made by the board—many reflecting a more conservative and religious view of U.S. history—have aroused opposition from educators and lawmakers in Texas and other states.

Many states will wind up with those standards as publishers often market textbooks geared for Texas across the nation.

"Help me tell the rest of the nation that Texas is better than some of the actions taken by our State Board of Education," White said in urging teachers to support him at the annual convention of the Texas State Teachers Association. The association has endorsed White in the governor's race.

"We can't afford to go backwards in education."

Social conservatives on the board contend they are representing the majority of Texans in writing the standards.

White also blamed Perry for record college tuition increases during his tenure. Those increases occurred after Republican leaders decided to deregulate tuition to ease a state revenue crunch in 2003.

"We will never be as good as we can be if college tuition goes up by 82 percent as it has under Governor Perry over the last six years," he said, arguing that tuition rates are now beyond the reach of many families.

The Democrat also repeated his criticism of the Republican governor for not doing more to stem the student dropout rate.

"The way to deal with the dropout problem is not to mislead people about it," he said, questioning Perry's assertion that the dropout rate is 10 percent. White says about 30 percent of students are unaccounted for.

"It doesn't add up," White said. "The fact is a lot of students slip through the cracks, and they don't know if about 800,000 young people [in each graduating class] graduate or not."

The Perry campaign has criticized White for using "misleading" figures.

"One dropout is one too many, but Texas does not have a 30 percent dropout rate as White has suggested," a spokesman for Perry said.

## LETTERS, OPINIONS, AND NEW MEDIA

Source 9 from *The New York Times*, March 16, 2010, "The Battle Over Textbooks in Texas," to the Editor, by Daniel Czitrom. Reprinted by permission from the author.

### 9. *New York Times* Letters to the Editor.

*[Following the* New York Times *coverage of the Texas curriculum debates, individuals from across the country expressed their reaction. The* Times *chose to print the following letters to the editor on March 16, 2010.]*

To the Editor:

Re "Conservatives on Texas Panel Carry the Day on Curriculum Change" (news article, March 13):

As a co-author of an American history textbook that was effectively banned in Texas eight years ago, I had a strong feeling of déjà vu all over again while reading about the state's latest curricular wars.

Back in 2002 the school board, egged on by well-organized conservative groups with deep pockets, excluded *Out of Many: A History of the American People* (Pearson Prentice Hall), allegedly for an offensive passage discussing prostitution on the Western frontier. But the real reason became clear as that controversy played out, and I think that it helps explain what's happening today.

Many conservatives are simply unwilling to accept how much the writing and teaching of American history have changed over the last 40 years. They want an American history that ignores or marginalizes African-Americans, women, Latinos, immigrants and popular culture. They prefer a pseudo-patriotic history that denies the fundamental conflicts that have shaped our past.

Rather than acknowledge that genuine disagreements over interpretation and emphasis are the lifeblood of history, they reduce it all to a cartoonish process of balancing "bias." This sort of right-wing political correctness impoverishes our students and teachers.

Daniel Czitrom
South Hadley, Mass., March 14, 2010

*[The writer is a professor of history at Mount Holyoke College.]*

To the Editor:

In a country so bitterly divided by fundamental values and beliefs, it is not shocking that a small faction of people would target the most powerful outlet for creating change: our education system.

Attacking educational systems is a proven method of change. Conservative madrasas throughout the Middle East know that. There, young students are receiving deeply disturbing educations based on fundamental misinterpretations of Islamic values and norms. Will this be the path of America's education system?

In the 30 days allotted for public comment, this decision, and all of its permeations, must be fought for the sake of our students and the sake of our country's education future.

Sarah Peck
Somerville, Mass., March 14, 2010

To the Editor:

For years, the historical profession overlooked the role of conservatism and of Latinos in American history, and the scholarly record has been enriched tremendously by the excellent work done in this area in the last 20 years.

K-12 textbooks stand to benefit from this more expansive perspective, though both groups are mistaken that the solution to the problems of the current curriculum resides in a "correct" history, revised based on their specific political interests. Such important inclusions are not mutually exclusive, nor need they constitute the victory of one infallible narrative.

Rather, teaching how conservatism and liberalism have emerged as powerful social and political phenomena instead of merely adding isolated facts to curriculums would transform how students learn about their past and shed light on the historical processes that have given rise to both the liberal and conservative movements vying for their curriculum.

Natalia Mehlman-Petrzela
New York, March 14, 2010

*The writer, an assistant professor of education studies and history at Eugene Lang College, the New School for Liberal Arts, is writing a book about grass-roots activism on the political right and left regarding controversial educational questions in the 1960s and 1970s.*

To the Editor:

My wife, who has been a senior social-science textbook editor for a major publisher, long complained about the ideological requirements of the Texas Board of Education, especially since Texas, a major textbook buyer, has influenced the content of books for other states, too. The recent conservative revisions by the board should not surprise.

The worst part of these actions by elected officials is that while scorning academicians as liberals, the board has decided to rewrite standard American history to suit its partisan values, to teach history as it thinks it should have been.

Conservatives who are scorning Big Government might well turn attention to Texas, which is about to require that a Republican fictional history be taught to children throughout the state. This is government mind-control of young students who do not know to contest it.

David Eggenschwiler
Los Angeles, March 13, 2010

*The writer is emeritus professor of English, University of Southern California.*

To the Editor:

As a former teacher in both elementary and high school, I find the actions of the Texans depressing. It would be just as depressing to slant history to emphasize or omit other points of view. The ultimate solution is to encourage teachers to know more and to present primary sources that reflect a variety of points of view.

The purpose of education is not to indoctrinate but to inform. The citizenry needs to learn how to understand, think critically, ask questions and make judgments.

Any textbook is limited by its very nature. My science texts are now very much out-dated, for example. Let's eliminate textbooks and emphasize core topics.

Joan L. Staples
Chicago, March 13, 2010

## 10. The Texas State Board of Education Chair Defends the Board's Actions.

*[Gail Lowe, a Republican from Lampasas, in central Texas, chairs the Texas State Board of Education. In late March, facing spreading national criticism of the SBOE, she responded to the* New York Times *and leading Texas newspapers. Her essay was posted to the Website texasinsider.org on March 25, 2010.]*

It did not take long for reverberations from the Texas State Board of Education's preliminary vote on Social Studies requirements to spread across the country. And predictably, the media coverage was woefully inaccurate and blatantly distorted.

The *New York Times* probably was not the first to report on the board's deliberations, but it joined a host of prominent Texas news outlets that incorrectly claimed Thomas Jefferson had been dropped from the curriculum framework used in Texas public schools.

Apart from Thomas Jefferson, the only historical figure with more emphasis in the Texas Essential Knowledge & Skills standards is George Washington.

The State Board of Education expects students at the elementary-grade level, in middle school and again in high school to study these Founding Fathers and to be well-versed in their contributions to American history and government.

Thomas Jefferson is included along with John Adams, Samuel Adams, Benjamin Franklin, Nathan Hale, the Sons of Liberty and George Washington as Founding Fathers and patriot heroes that Texas fifth-graders should study for their notable contributions during the Revolutionary period.

During Grade 8, in which the history of the United States from the early colonial period through Reconstruction is presented, the Social Studies TEKS framework requires students to explain the roles played by the following significant individuals:

- Abigail Adams
- John Adams
- Wentworth Cheswell
- Samuel Adams

- Mercy Otis Warren
- James Armistead
- Benjamin Franklin
- Crispus Attucks
- King George III
- Haym Salomon
- Patrick Henry
- Thomas Jefferson
- the Marquis de Lafayette
- Thomas Paine and
- George Washington

The U.S. Government course required for high school graduation mandates that students "identify the contributions of the political philosophies of the Founding Fathers, including:

- John Adams
- Alexander Hamilton
- Thomas Jefferson
- John Jay
- James Madison
- George Mason
- Roger Sherman and
- James Wilson on the development of the U.S. government."

In addition, high school students must "identify significant individuals in the field of government and politics, including George Washington, Thomas Jefferson, John Marshall, Andrew Jackson, Abraham Lincoln, Theodore Roosevelt, and Ronald Reagan."

To say the State Board of Education has excluded Thomas Jefferson from the curriculum framework is irresponsible and untruthful.

Jefferson not only penned the words of the Declaration of Independence, served as the third President of the United States and was father of the University of Virginia, but his promotion of the ideals of states' rights and a limited federal government have permeated our nation for centuries. No study of American history would be complete without his inclusion.

That is why Thomas Jefferson warrants such strong emphasis in the TEKS standards the State Board of Education has approved.

A critical skill Texas students should develop as part of their education is the ability to analyze information from primary source documents.

This should be a requirement for journalists, too. Many seem to have jumped to erroneous conclusions without even examining the actual curriculum standards.

One can disagree ideologically with the State Board of Education, but the TEKS standards themselves should be the point of reference for objective, thorough reporting.

Source 11 Emilio Zamora, Letter To the Texas State Board of Education, April 12, 2010, http://sensiblehistory.blogspot.com/p/letter.html, Reprinted by permission of Emilio Zamora.

## 11. Texas Historians' Open Letter to the SBOE.

*[In April 2010, a group of historians working at Texas universities responded to the curriculum proposal by crafting an open letter to the SBOE. The letter, printed below in its entirety, was circulated among historians, who were invited to sign to convey their support.]*

April 12, 2010
To the Texas State Board of Education:

Public schools must provide students with a sound elementary and high school education that prepares them to succeed in college and their future careers. Such a sound education must be fair, accurate and balanced and it must be based on rigorous, mainstream scholarship, not on ideological agendas.

Those of us who teach and conduct research in colleges and universities have grown concerned, however, that social studies curriculum standards in Texas do not meet student needs. We also believe that the Texas State Board of Education has been derelict in its duty to revise the public school curriculum. In short, recent proposals by Board members have undermined the study of the social sciences in our public schools by misrepresenting and even distorting the historical record and the functioning of American society.

Some of the problematic revisions that they have proposed include:

- Weakening the study of constitutional protections for religious liberty that keep government out of matters of faith;
- Minimizing the struggle of women and ethnic minorities for equal and civil rights;
- Striking Thomas Jefferson from a world history standard about the influence of Enlightenment thinkers on political changes since the 1700s; and
- Excluding an important historical figure from Latin America because some board members did not recognize him.

The integrity of the curriculum revision process has been compromised and we propose that the Board restore the trust of the public and the academic community by proceeding as follows:

- Delay the final adoption of social studies curriculum standards;
- Allow curriculum teams and a new panel of qualified, credentialed content experts from the state's colleges and universities to review changes that the Board has made and prepare a new draft of the standards that is fair, accurate and balanced;

- Permit the public to review and comment on the new draft of the standards before final adoption; and
- Make final changes to the draft of the standards only after public consultation with classroom teachers and scholars who are experts in the appropriate fields of study.

Like all members of the Texas State Board of Education, we have a vested interest in giving our schoolchildren the tools that they need to succeed in college and their future careers. For genuine college and work readiness to occur the Board must adhere to a more transparent, fair, and inclusive process of curriculum revisions, and it must make full and effective use of the faculty and researchers from our colleges and universities in Texas who can offer expert assistance and guidance.

Organizing Committee

Emilio Zamora (co-chair), University of Texas at Austin

Jeffrey P. Shepherd, University of Texas at El Paso

Anne M. Martínez, University of Texas at Austin

Laurie B. Green, University of Texas at Austin

Keith A. Erekson (co-chair), University of Texas at El Paso

Ernesto Chavez, University of Texas at El Paso

Sam Brunk, University of Texas at El Paso

## 12. A Libertarian Considers the Texas Debates.

*[Between 1995 and 2003, Bob Barr represented the 7th District of Georgia in the U.S. House of Representatives and was a leading figure in the Republican Party. In 2008, he ran for president of the United States on the Libertarian Party ticket. In addition to running a law practice and consulting firm in Atlanta, he writes a blog, "The Barr Code," for the* Atlanta Journal-Constitution. *On April 19, 2010, this Republican-turned-Libertarian weighed in on the Texas debates.]*

April 19, 2010, by Bob Barr

In her fascinating 2003 book, *The Language Police*, Diane Ravitch chronicles the dumbing down of our public education system through the pervasive and insidious censorship of textbooks. She lamented the homogenization of education brought about largely by the incessant quest to remove controversial topics, words and phrases from the educational process. Of particular concern to Ravitch was her conclusion that history texts are among the most profoundly infected with political correctness; leading her to note that "in no other subject do American seniors score as low as they do in U.S. history."

Oft times heated disputes between conservatives and liberals continue to surface when boards of education—especially in the larger states—consider changes to textbook language.

Most recently, this problem boiled over in Texas, the nation's second-largest consumer of textbooks for public school students. Last month, the Lone Star state's elected board of education met and agreed preliminarily to a number of changes to American history texts that will be acceptable for use in its public schools over the next decade. The changes are expected to be finalized when the board meets in May; but the fireworks have already started.

Among the more controversial decisions recommended by the Republican-dominated board:

- Downgrading the role Thomas Jefferson played in our nation's founding, apparently because his secular views conflicted with the more Christian-oriented views of a majority of the Texas board.
- Softening how textbooks treat former Wisconsin Senator Joseph McCarthy who berated and impugned those with whom he disagreed during the 1950s "Red Scare."
- Excluding reference to "hip-hop" music as a favorable example of modern American culture.
- Incorporating specific reference to "American exceptionalism."
- Including mention of recent, conservative-based political activities and personalities, such as 1994's "Contract With America," conservative icon Phyllis Schlafly, Jerry Falwell's "Moral Majority," and the National Rifle Association.
- Description of our nation's prevalent economic system as one based on "free enterprise."
- Changing references of our country's government structure as "democratic" to "constitutional republic."

In all, the school board has made more than 100 amendments to the state's history texts. Some of these, such as declining to elevate "hip-hop" to the status of being a cultural benefit, and properly describing our country as a "republic" rather than a "democracy," make a great deal of sense. Others, however (downplaying the importance of one of our great Founding Fathers, Thomas Jefferson, because he did not appear to be sufficiently religious), do not.

More troubling than is the process of crafting textbooks to reflect particular views or so as to highlight those individuals, political activities, or institutions one elected official prefers over others, is the fact that advocates on both sides of these proceedings appear to misunderstand what is the purpose of a history textbook in the first place.

American history textbooks are not intended to be, and should not be written or amended to serve as, laundry lists of favored cultural events or personalities. They are a tool, and not necessarily the most important tool, in a school system's "toolbox" of instruments with which to ensure that students understand what our nation was and is; and what is was intended to be. Whether we today like Thomas Jefferson or not (I happen to be among those who do), he was one of the most important figures of our formative era; and diminishing his role distorts history. And whether we like or disdain organizations such as the NRA (as a member of its board of directors, I am a strong supporter), its role in the modern political era probably is not among those critical to include in a history text.

Much more important than these fights over inclusion or exclusion, should be concerns over the education, training and teaching methods of those tasked with actually teaching from those textbooks—our teachers.

✦

## Questions to Consider

You will likely find the first set of questions—about the specific points of contention—the easiest to address. Those, in turn, will lead you to the larger issues at play. For example, when you see comments insisting on the inclusion of the Moral Majority, on the one hand, or Cesar Chavez, on the other, what is really behind such arguments? Why are the debates about content and process so intense? Why has the Texas case produced so much national interest?

As you turn to investigating the context of public school curricular debates, think broadly about the conflicting values that emerge in this chapter's documents.

- What does the evidence reveal about varying attitudes toward civics and differing definitions of patriotism? How is the Texas textbook controversy connected to America's ongoing culture wars? What does this case reveal about Americans' attitudes toward history education?
- What are the varying views on the role of religion in American civic life? Is there an appropriate place for political and religious ideology in shaping the themes and interpretations of history textbooks?
- How would you characterize the tone of the debates? Did the exchanges seem professional and thoughtful or personal and ideological?
- How would you characterize the tone, reliability, and effectiveness of the different forms of media you read—journalistic reporting, op-ed essays, and letters to editors?

- Is it possible that many people engaged in this textbook debate are missing the point—that a genuinely honest and fair appreciation of our nation's past requires the ability to think critically about *all* points of view? Is it, in fact, possible to achieve a truly "balanced" perspective in the writing of history? Is it desirable?

Next, begin to transition from analysis to evaluation.

- What are the differences in how teachers and politicians approach the textbook controversy? Is the perspective of teachers more or less persuasive than politicians' and journalists' opinions? What about citizens writing letters to newspaper editors? Professional historians? Where are the students' voices?

- Based on careful consideration of all points of view, who do you, individually, think should play the greatest part in deciding what is included in elementary and secondary school textbooks: elected officials, parents, professional historians, taxpayers, or teachers?
- What did your class as a whole decide? Were you able to reach a consensus? What are the implications of your class's outcome?

Finally, engage in a bit of self-reflection. How would you characterize the tone of your class discussion? Did your classmates with differing opinions approach the conversation with open minds? Did you and they listen to be persuaded? Or did you replicate the ideological divide and tone of the culture wars? What have you learned from this exercise?

## Epilogue

In March 2010, the Texas SBOE gave preliminary approval for the revised social studies curriculum. The vote occurred along strictly party lines: 10 Republicans voted in favor, while 5 Democrats opposed. Texas law requires the SBOE to disseminate the revisions and accept public feedback before conducting a final vote, and this occurred in the spring of 2010.

On May 21, 2010, after a lengthy and contentious public forum, the Texas SBOE formally adopted their new history standards. Teachers will begin training in the new standards in the fall of 2010, and they will be implemented in class rooms in 2011.

Meanwhile, the nation became embroiled in another historical controversy when Virginia's Republican Governor Robert McDonnell declared April "Confederate History Month" in his state. In 1997, Republican Governor George Allen, at the encouragement of the Sons of Confederate Veterans, had signed a similar proclamation. Allen's actions had similarly sparked a national debate, in part because he characterized the Civil War as a struggle for "independence and sovereign rights." In 2002, Democratic Governor Mark Warner (2002–2006), followed by his successor, Democrat Tim Kaine (2006–2010), abandoned the practice, rejecting such proclamations as divisive. The controversy surrounding Governor McDonnell's revival of Confederate History Month deepened when, after critics noted that he ignored slavery in the proclamation, he responded: "there were any number of aspects to that conflict between the states. Obviously, it involved slavery. It involved other issues. But I focused on the ones I thought were most significant for Virginia."[7] He later clarified his position on slavery, though Confederate History Month stood.

Contemporary Americans also stridently debate about perceived liberal bias in humanities higher education, the connections and disconnections between the emergent Tea Party movement and its revolutionary namesake, and the Founders' intentions regarding a seemingly endless number of issues, from gun ownership to privacy rights to the very nature of the United States Constitution.

History, then, remains hotly contested ground in twenty-first-century America. What we value in the past—which individuals and events we study, which themes we emphasize—discloses a great deal about our contemporary world. And the tenor of our debates over history is likewise revealing. As William Falkner wisely observed, "The past is never dead. It's not even past."

7. Quoted in the *Washington Post*, April 7, 2010.